THE EVERYTHING®
Family Christmas Book

Dear Reader,

When I think of Christmas, I think of family, and the traditions that I grew up with. When I was quite small, my Auntie Joy sent a gift of money for Christmas, and my mother and I found a lovely fairy doll—a beautiful, blonde girl dressed in white and silver, bearing a wand with a little star on top—in a local shop. She became the fairy that, each December, topped our Christmas tree. When I moved away from home, Mum asked me if I'd like to take the Christmas fairy with me.

I'm so glad that I said no, that she belonged on my parents' tree—our family tree. Today, my two amazing, energetic, and totally loved nephews open presents under the watchful eye of that very same fairy, a tradition that I'm so grateful to be a part of. And now my own tree bears a beautiful Christmas angel of its own, handmade by Mum.

It's memories like these that always make me smile when Christmas comes to mind. I hope that this book brings memories that will make you smile, too, at any time of the year—but especially at Christmas.

Yvonne Jeffery

Welcome to the EVERYTHING Series!

These handy, accessible books give you all you need to tackle a difficult project, gain a new hobby, comprehend a fascinating topic, prepare for an exam, or even brush up on something you learned back in school but have since forgotten.

You can choose to read an *Everything*® book from cover to cover or just pick out the information you want from our four useful boxes: e-questions, e-facts, e-alerts, e-ssentials. We give you everything you need to know on the subject, but throw in a lot of fun stuff along the way, too.

We now have more than 400 *Everything*® books in print, spanning such wide-ranging categories as weddings, pregnancy, cooking, music instruction, foreign language, crafts, pets, New Age, and so much more. When you're done reading them all, you can finally say you know *Everything*®!

Key Pieces of Christmas Information

Inspirational Ideas

Influential Christmas Icons

Holiday Lore

PUBLISHER Karen Cooper

DIRECTOR OF INNOVATION Paula Munier

MANAGING EDITOR, EVERYTHING SERIES Lisa Laing

COPY CHIEF Casey Ebert

ACQUISITIONS EDITOR Lisa Laing

SENIOR DEVELOPMENT EDITOR Brett Palana-Shanahan

MUSICAL NOTATION Ernie Jackson

EDITORIAL ASSISTANT Hillary Thompson

Visit the entire Everything® series at *www.everything.com*

THE
EVERYTHING®
FAMILY CHRISTMAS BOOK

Stories, songs, recipes, crafts, traditions, and more!

Yvonne Jeffery

Avon, Massachusetts

To my sister Lorraine, for being such
a wonderful and loving inspiration

An Everything® Series Book.
Everything® and everything.com® are registered trademarks of F+W Publications, Inc.

Published by Adams Media, an F+W Publications Company
57 Littlefield Street, Avon, MA 02322 U.S.A.
www.adamsmedia.com

Contains material adapted and abridged from *The Everything® Christmas Book*, by Michelle Bevilacqua and Brandon Toropov, copyright © 1996 by Adams Media Corporation, ISBN 10: 1-55850-697-7, ISBN 13: 978-1-55850-697-8.

ISBN 10: 1-59869-561-4
ISBN 13: 978-1-59869-561-8

Printed in the United States of America.

J   I   H   G   F   E   D   C   B   A

Library of Congress Cataloging-in-Publication Data
is available from the publisher.

This book is available at quantity discounts for bulk purchases.
For information, please call 1-800-289-0963.

Contents

Contents

Acknowledgments

As I worked on this guide to Christmas, I kept four people very much in mind: To William, Benjamin, Elizabeth, and Grace, thank you so much for helping me see the wonder and joy of Christmas through a child's eyes once again. As for the adults in the family: To Mum and Dad, your constant love and support means so much more than I can say—thank you. To Lorraine, I love our conversations so much—you always understand me, even when I don't, and I'm so grateful! And to the Jefferys in England—thank you for shrinking the Atlantic with your love.

I'm truly blessed to have people who make such a difference in my life: To my writer friends—Kerrie Etson, Katharine Fletcher, Judith Mulholland, Laura Byrne Paquet, Linda Poitevin, and Theresa Storm—you're simply wonderful. And to Susan and Stephen Yuzwak, thank you so much for always being in my corner.

I'm deeply grateful, too, to Barb Doyen, for her guidance, enthusiasm, and encouragement. And to the folks at Adams Media, it's always such a pleasure to work with you—thank you.

Top Ten Ways to Make Christmas Meaningful for Your Family

1. Find a favorite Christmas story and make it a tradition to read it aloud on Christmas Eve.

2. Share your good fortune with others at Christmas by volunteering as a family for a charity or nonprofit organization that's close to your hearts.

3. Decorate your home each year with a special item that you've chosen or made as a family.

4. Choose your favorite holiday baking recipes and share an afternoon with friends and family baking up a storm.

5. Create a calendar with a different family photo each month to send to family and friends who can't be with you during the year.

6. Plan an annual family activity for the Christmas season: It could be picking out the tree, tobogganing down a nearby hill, even heading to the local zoo—anything that captures the whole family's interest.

7. Light the candles of an Advent wreath in succession every Sunday during December, talking about their symbolic meanings, such as love, hope, peace, and joy.

8. Buy or make a special tree ornament each year for the children in your family, and present them with the whole set when they have their own tree for the first time.

9. Turn letters to Santa into an event, with hot chocolate, cookies, and plenty of colorful pens and stickers to help with the letter writing.

10. Make writing thank-you letters for gifts a much-loved tradition, too, with yummy treats and a fun reward when the letters are finished.

Introduction

There's so much to the Christmas holiday that this book could easily have been ten books. But really, when you distill the true meaning of the day—whether you celebrate on December 6, December 25, January 6, or a little bit on each of those days—it all comes down to a single word: wonder.

It was wonder that led the Magi to follow the Star to Bethlehem. It was wonder that filled the stable in Bethlehem the night that Jesus was born. It's wonder that you feel in church and carol services over Christmas, imagining the more than 2,000 years of tradition and history that have made Christmas what it is today. And it's wonder that fills the eyes of a five year old who starts down the stairs on Christmas morning to see the tree aglow and then shares the long tradition of exchanging gifts.

Christmas begins in the mists of long-distant history and extends along the future of the human family. It's informed by countless Christmases past and the knowledge that, as long as there are children and a sense of tradition, there are likely to be Christmases in the future. But the true event, the true day of days, is neither an account of old customs nor a prediction of the ways in which this holiday will continue to change and to grow. The true experience of Christmas is wonder.

And so, as you read about where and how Christmas began and how it has evolved through the years, across Europe to North America and around the world to the way that you celebrate it today, there's room not just for rituals, traditions, and customs, but also for Christmas your way. Using the past as a stepping stone, *The Everything® Family Christmas Book* looks at ways you can create a Christmas that fills you and your family with wonder, from favorite storytellers and songs to much-loved baking recipes. There are even some gift suggestions thrown in, along with ideas that can help reduce the stress that many people feel at this very busy time of year.

After all, the wonder of Christmas is tied inextricably to memory. For many, Christmases past are the standards by which they measure Christmases present and future. Like the Charles Dickens creation, Ebenezer Scrooge, in "A Christmas Carol," you can use your memories as a springboard to make each holiday better and more meaningful than the last.

Luckily, Christmas isn't about perfection. It's not about having the best-decorated house on the block, and it doesn't matter that the turkey took two extra hours to cook and the peas were left behind in the microwave (although hopefully not all on the same day). What matters is the creation of new memories, centered on a sense of family and being loved, whether you come with a ready-made family or one that you create yourself. Memory is, ultimately, the basis of tradition—and what is Christmas if not one of the fundamental traditions of our time? Warm and wonderful memories are certainly what this book wishes for you, just as it hopes to provide inspiration for the Christmases that are in your future.

Once a year, on December 25, Christmas reintroduces you to wonder on a scale that you should never forget. This book is intended as a celebration of that wonder. May you read it as part of the most precious gift that the holiday brings: the ability to see things, for a time, through the eyes you once had on Christmas morning.

1

The History of Christmas

The way in which people celebrate Christmas is a relatively recent development in the history of the holiday, which of course originates with the birth of Jesus, the Christ child, some 2,000 years ago. The festivities of December 25 have been shaped by many people and many cultures—from the early Romans to England's Queen Victoria—and they continue to change even today. Whether you celebrate the day as part of Christianity or simply as a time of family togetherness, the origins and evolution of Christmas span the globe.

The First Christmas

You might say that Christmas has been celebrated since the very night of Jesus' birth, when, the Bible says, the angels announced his arrival on the plains of Bethlehem (in what is now Israel) in an event that was later celebrated in a special Christes Masse, or Christ's Mass. The actual birth date is something that scholars still debate; however, a combination of Bible stories, historical records, and even astronomical events generally set the year between about 6 B.C. and A.D. 6

Most of the elements of our traditional Christmas story have their origin in the Bible, in the Gospels of St. Luke and St. Matthew. While the two gospels offer some historical contradictions, there's no doubt that together, they have created a picture of the birth of Jesus that is loved around the world.

From The Gospel According to St. Luke

Luke's gospel offers us not only a time and place for the birth of Jesus, but a real human and religious drama. Focusing on the trials of Joseph and Mary, Luke tells us a story of weary travelers forced to spend the night in a stable because there was "no room for them at the inn." With its focus on the humble manger birth, the gathering of shepherds and angels, and the enduring message of peace on earth, this passage has given us some of Christianity's best loved Christmas songs and traditions.

And it came to pass in those days, that there went out a decree from Caesar Augustus, that all the world should be taxed. (And this taxing was first made when Cyrenius was governor of Syria.)

And all went to be taxed, every one into his own city. And Joseph also went up from Galilee, out of the city of Nazareth, into Judea, unto the city of David, which is called Bethlehem; (because he was of the house and lineage of David) to be taxed with Mary his espoused wife, being great with child.

And so it was, that, while they were there, the days were accomplished that she should be delivered. And she brought forth her first-born son, and wrapped him in

swaddling clothes, and laid him in a manger; because there was no room for them in the inn.

And there were in the same country shepherds abiding in the field, keeping watch over their flock at night. And, lo, the angel of the Lord came upon them, and the glory of the Lord shone round about them; and they were sore afraid.

And the angel said unto them, "Fear not: for, behold, I bring you good tidings of great joy, which shall be to all people. For unto you is born this day in the city of David a Savior, which is Christ the Lord. And this shall be a sign unto you; Ye shall find the babe wrapped in swaddling clothes, lying in a manger."

And suddenly there was with the angel a multitude of the heavenly host praising God, and saying, "Glory to God in the highest, and on earth peace, good will toward men."

And it came to pass, as the angels were gone away from them into heaven, the shepherds said one to another, "Let us now go even unto Bethlehem, and see this thing which is come to pass, which the Lord hath made known unto us."

And they came with haste, and found Mary, and Joseph, and the babe lying in a manger. And when they had seen it they made known abroad the saying which was told them concerning this child. And all they that heard it wondered at those things which were told them by the shepherds.

But Mary kept all these things, and pondered them in her heart. And the shepherds returned, glorifying and praising God for all the things that they had heard and seen, as it was told unto them.

From The Gospel According to St. Matthew

The Gospel accounts of Christ's birth often surprise readers with the information that they don't contain, rather than what they do include. The Gospel of Matthew, for instance, is the undeniable source for the "Three Kings of Orient"—long celebrated in song—and yet it makes no mention of any king other than Herod, and it does not specify any particular number of men following the "star in the east." The reverence and devotion of these figures, however, certainly leaves an indelible impression on hearts and minds.

Now when Jesus was born in Bethlehem of Judea in the days of Herod the king, behold, there came Wise Men from the east to Jerusalem, saying, "Where is he that is born King of the Jews? For we have seen his star in the east, and are come to worship him."

When Herod the king had heard these things, he was troubled, and all Jerusalem with him. And when he had gathered all the chief priests and scribes of the people together, he demanded of them where Christ should be born. And they said unto him, "In Bethlehem of Judea: for thus it is written by the prophet, 'And thou Bethlehem, in the land of Judah, art not the least among the princes of Judah: for out of thee shall come a Governor, that shall rule my people Israel.'"

Then Herod, when he had privily called the Wise Men, inquired of them diligently what time the star appeared. And he sent them to Bethlehem, and said, "Go and search diligently for the young child; and when ye have found him, bring me word again, that I may come and worship him also."

When they had heard the king, they departed; and lo, the star, which they saw in the east, went before them, till it came and stood over where the young child was. When they saw the star, they rejoiced with exceeding great joy.

And when they were come into the house, they saw the young child with Mary his mother, and fell down, and worshiped him: and when they had opened their treasures, they presented unto him gifts: gold, and frankincense, and myrrh. And being warned of God in a dream that they should not return to Herod, they departed into their own country another way.

And when they were departed, behold, the angel of the Lord appeareth to Joseph in a dream, saying, "Arise, and take the young child and his mother, and flee into Egypt, and be thou there until I bring thee word: for Herod will seek the young child to destroy him." When he arose, he took the young child and his mother by night, and departed into Egypt.

Early Christianity

Christmas had to wait more than 300 years after the birth of Jesus before it began to be popularized in a meaningful way. Instead, the first Christians were focused on spreading the word about Christianity while avoiding official persecution, which began as early as A.D. 64 under the Roman emperor Nero. For the next two centuries and more, Christians endured prison and death at the hands of the Roman Empire, while Egyptian, Greek, and Persian gods continued to be worshiped freely.

In the first centuries A.D., the Roman Empire extended around the Mediterranean Sea, encompassing areas we now know as northern Africa (including Egypt), the Middle East (including present-day Israel, Jordan, and Syria), Europe (including France, England, Italy, and Greece), and the region where Europe borders Asia (Turkey).

Things began to change when Emperor Constantine, who came to power over the Roman Empire in 306, gradually converted to Christianity. As a result, Christianity became the state religion, and public funds were used to build churches. Constantine commissioned the building of the Church of the Nativity on a spot in Bethlehem that was believed to be the exact birthplace of Christ. By the end of the fourth century, the old forms of worship had been banned and Christianity began spreading.

Setting a Date

Scholars don't just disagree on the year of Jesus' birth, they also disagree on the time of year in which he was born. While there is one record of Christmas being celebrated in Antioch (Turkey) on December 25 in the middle of the second century, there is no record of its being observed on that date in Rome until the year 336. It wasn't until 350 that Pope Julius I declared December 25 the official date.

The Gospels don't provide specific details about the date, so historians have tried to use clues from them instead: for example, the fact that shepherds were watching their flocks by night. Some say that the sheep would not have been exposed during the winter; others say that the mild Mediterranean nights of December would have been fine for the animals.

In fact, various dates have been proposed for Jesus' birth—including March and September—based on a number of different theories. And for many of the early years of Christianity, it was January 6 that was celebrated to commemorate a number of events, including both the birth and the baptism of Jesus and the visit of the wise men to the holy infant.

The Winter Solstice

As Christianity established itself, church leaders wanted to move the general population away from their celebrations of other gods and religions, including the winter solstice festivals that were important to the cultures of pre-Christian Europe and Asia.

Ancient peoples believed that the days grew shorter in December because the sun was leaving them, perhaps even dying. Festivals held right before December 21, the winter solstice, featured rituals designed to appease the sun and make it return. After the solstice, the shortest day of the year, the days became longer again, and grand celebrations were held in honor of the sun's return. Along with the idea of the physical presence of the sun were underlying themes of harvest, rebirth, and light.

Festive Fact

Based on Mithra, the god of light and wisdom, the Mithraic religion was a major religion of the Roman era, with close similarities to Christianity. Mithra, born from a rock on December 25, symbolizes the sun. Naturally, his birth was celebrated as a major holiday by believers.

December 25 was, in the Roman calendar, the day after the solstice, which was why the solar feast, also known as *Natalis inviciti solis*, or "birth of the unconquered sun," was one of the celebrations associated with the winter solstice. In fact, in the third century (that is, in the century before Constantine began the Empire's conversion to Christianity), Emperor Aurelian declared December 25 *Dies Invicti Solis* (the Day of the Invincible Sun).

The Roman Saturnalia

Although the basic concept of the solstice festival was common to all lands, each area had its unique variations. But the tradition that left its mark most indelibly on Christmas was the Roman Saturnalia. The Saturnalia was observed in December and was a nominal celebration of a number of different events, among them Saturn's triumph over Jupiter. According to belief, Saturn's reign had heralded the Golden Age in Rome. Although the god later lost out to Jupiter, during the Saturnalia he was believed to return, allowing Rome to relive the Golden Age for a brief time. It is not surprising that the Romans, who associated Saturn closely with the sun, would celebrate this festival near the solstice.

During the festivities, no one worked except those who provided food, drink, or entertainment. Masters and slaves became equals and there was much feasting, dancing, gambling, and general revelry. Candles were used as decoration to scare away the darkness and celebrate the sun and light.

Another recognizable ritual was the giving of gifts, which was done in honor of the goddess of vegetation, Strenia. The people felt that in time of darkness and winter, it was important to honor someone who had a hand in the harvest. At first, produce and baked goods were exchanged, but as time went on, inedible gifts became fashionable.

The Saturnalia was followed by the calends of January (the calends marked the first day of the month). Observed on January 1–3, this period meant still more parties.

Recognizing Christmas

Many early Christian leaders, including Gregory of Nazainzus, spoke out against combining pagan and Christian ways. This isn't hard to understand: The celebrations, after all, could take on orgiastic proportions. After years of mostly futile attempts to abolish these pagan festivals and rituals, however, the church realized it would be better served by allowing them—revised so that their focus was to honor Christ.

Incorporating Mithraic or solstice rites into the celebration of Christmas was easy to justify: Christ represents life, triumph over death and darkness, and restored hope and light. Rather than celebrating the sun as before, people would be celebrating the Son of God. Simply put, the birth of Christ replaced the birth of the sun as a cause for celebration.

Both church and popular interests were thus satisfied: The people were able to keep their time of fun, while the church ensured that the birth of Christ would be celebrated with all due decorum and festivity. In this way, many parts of the old festivals remained, while others were reformed to honor Christ's birth. Some of the retained elements that have remained popular to this day are greenery, candles, singing, tree decorating, Yule logs, and feasting.

Christmas Spirit

Emperor Justinian declared Christmas a civic holiday in 529. Further legislation by the Council of Tours in 567 officially made the pre-Christmas Advent period a season of fasting and preparation. The time from Christmas to Epiphany (the twelve days of Christmas) was also declared part of the festive season.

Today, Christmas is celebrated on December 25 by Roman Catholics and Protestants, but not by many Orthodox churches, which continue to combine Epiphany and Nativity celebrations on January 6. A small portion of English believers also observed the January 6 tradition until about 1950—not because of any connection with the rites of Eastern churches, but because some of their own observances followed the old Julian calendar rather than the current Gregorian version.

The Yule Connection

The so-called "barbarian invasions" of the Roman Empire that began in the fifth century brought the Nordic and Germanic peoples into direct contact with Christianity, and therefore with Christmas. In northern and western Europe, the Germanic and Celtic peoples had their own solstice rituals, which were later incorporated into Christmas.

The December Julmond festival, for example (*Jul* later became *Yule*), was a celebration of harvest and rebirth, with wheat representing life triumphing over death. Anything made of wheat, such as bread or liquor, was consumed heartily, and also given as gifts. Evergreens were used as a symbol of life, and what we would later call the Yule log was lit to symbolize the eventual triumph of light over dark. The festive meal was boar's head. These traditions have been presented in centuries-old carols, including wassail songs, holly carols, and boar's-head carols still sung today.

The Dawn of Christmas in Europe

Christianity gradually made its way across Europe, bringing Christmas with it. The holiday came to England, for example, via St. Augustine, the first Archbishop of Canterbury, who reportedly baptized more than 10,000 English people on December 25, 598. Acting under the direction of Pope Gregory I, Augustine was also instrumental in bringing the celebration of Christmas to the area.

At the end of the sixth century, the pope instructed Augustine to make over the midwinter Yule festival into Christmas observances, emphasizing the importance of condoning any customs from the festival that could be found to contain Christian significance. It was a well-tested strategy, and it worked.

In ninth-century England, Alfred the Great declared that the twelve days between Christmas and Epiphany should be reserved for seasonal festivities, thus formalizing observation of the twelve days of Christmas in England.

Alfred was serious about celebrating: As part of his declaration, he made working during this period illegal. He followed his own rules, even at great cost. In 878, he refused to go to war during the twelve days of Christmas. His failure to do so is said to have caused England to lose the Battle of Chippenham to the Danes.

Christmas arrived in Germany in 813, via the Synod of Mainz, and was brought to Norway in the mid-900s by King Hakon the Good. By the end of the ninth century, Christmas was observed all over Europe with trees, lights, gifts, and feasts. The items that had held significance for the old religions were either tossed aside or altered to fit within a Christian context. Over the centuries, the holiday was increasingly reformed to contain fewer of the old pagan elements.

There are some who believe that King Arthur celebrated the first English Christmas in 521 with his Knights of the Round Table, without the input of either Augustine or Gregory. Given the legends surrounding King Arthur, however, this remains the territory of myth, rather than fact.

Medieval Celebrations

While Christmas today is thought of as a time of joy and peace, Christmas in medieval England after 1066 instead achieved heights of extravagance and rowdiness. Celebrating the season for the full twelve days was no problem: People would attend church in masks and costumes as on Halloween, and churchgoers would sing off-color songs and even roll dice on the altar.

Christmas during this period was a time for some good-natured ribbing of the church's solemnity. A touch of comedy was added to the sermons, which were so serious during the rest of the year. The festivities weren't entirely irreverent, however: There was also devout caroling and Nativity plays, although in the latter Herod was often portrayed in a comic vein.

The king and court had a grand time trying to outdo each other with outrageous abundance. Henry III had 600 oxen killed and prepared for a single feast—and that was just the main course. Merchants and other higher ups paid their respects to the king by giving him gifts and cash, and there were guidelines for gift giving based on one's social position. Henry once closed merchants until they paid their proper dues, although in 1248 he seemed to regain a bit of his Christmas spirit when he established a custom of giving food to the needy for the holiday.

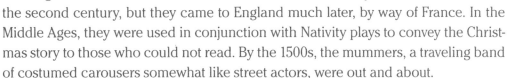

Gambling was also a big part of the festivities around the court; stories of royalty using loaded dice to insure against losing seem to capture the spirit of the age. But royal excess at Christmas surely reached its height in 1377. In that year, Richard II had a Christmas feast for more than 10,000 people. Records don't indicate whether the 2,000 employed at the feast enjoyed the holiday.

The fourteenth century also saw the beginning of widespread caroling. Carols had been used in Roman churches as early as the second century, but they came to England much later, by way of France. In the Middle Ages, they were used in conjunction with Nativity plays to convey the Christmas story to those who could not read. By the 1500s, the mummers, a traveling band of costumed carousers somewhat like street actors, were out and about.

Christmas Spirit

Fortunately, for historians and carol lovers alike, a young man named Richard Hill kept a written record of, among other things, the popular English carols of the time. Spanning the years 1500–1536, Hill's diary was extremely valuable in helping to keep alive such secular songs as "The Boar's Head Carol."

In 1533, Henry VIII made himself the Supreme Head of the Church of England, taking on the power of regulating religious holidays, including Christmas. He then proceeded to rival Henry III in yuletide extravagance.

Under his rule, Christmas became a very big deal indeed, both socially and ecclesiastically, and Christmas celebrations were filled with dancing, plays, general carousing, and, of course, food. This tradition was carried on by his daughter, Elizabeth I, and upon the accession of James I in 1603, by the Stuarts.

Outlawing Christmas

It's not surprising that some members of the clergy objected to the way in which Christ's birth was being commemorated: Aside from the gluttony and games, they worried about observing Jesus' birth as if he were a person rather than the Incarnate

God. They argued that celebrations of the Nativity should be more spiritual, or perhaps abolished outright.

The more Christmas became established in the customs and hearts of the people, the more worried the clergy became. Old worries about the pagan elements of the celebration began to surface again, and some church officials questioned the prudence of having allowed them to continue in the first place.

With the Protestant Reformation in Europe, these objections gained the backing of an organized power. Beginning in 1517 with the posting of Martin Luther's ninety-five theses, the Reformation attacked religious feasts and saint's days, among other things, as corrupt practices. Christmas was outlawed in Scotland in 1583.

The Protestants and Puritans of England also condemned the gluttony, drinking, and partying associated with Christmas celebrations and argued for all pagan customs to be done away with. Most Protestants observed Christmas as a day of quiet reflection; the Puritans, however, did not observe it at all. Strict interpreters of the Scriptures, the Puritans pointed to the commandment to devote six days for work and one to rest. Unless Christmas happened to fall on the Sabbath, it was considered a workday.

By the middle of the seventeenth century, the holiday was under fire. The feelings of previously small pockets of objectors began to have a bigger impact as the political situation in England became increasingly unstable. From 1642 to 1649, the country was engaged in civil war as a result of the power struggle between the Stuart kings and Parliament. During this time, England entered its Commonwealth period and was ruled by Oliver Cromwell and the Puritans. The government issued official policies outlawing all religious festivals.

The era of the Puritan government was filled with such laws, updated over the years to become even more strict. At first, such declarations caused a great deal of upheaval among the people, who were unprepared for such a step. In the initial days of these ordinances, the people tried to disobey and there was even some rioting. Gradually, however, the Puritans won out. Christmas was outlawed, and those who celebrated it in any way were outlaws. Carols were deemed illegal and churches were locked, even to the clergy.

Festive Fact

"Whereas some doubts have been raised whether the next Fast shall be celebrated because it falleth on the day which, heretofore, was usually called the Feast of the Nativity of our Saviour, the lords and commons do order and ordain that published notice be given, that the Fast appointed to be kept on the last Wednesday in every month, ought to be observed until it be otherwise ordered by both houses; and that this day particularly is to be kept with the same solemn humiliation because it may call to remembrance our sins and the sins of our forefathers, who have turned this Feast, pretending the memory of Christ, into an extreme forgetfulness of him, by giving liberty to carnal and sensual delights."—1644 English proclamation outlawing public Christmas revelries

Technically, the Puritans objected to Christmas not as a Christian event, but as an excessive festival with pagan roots. Apparently, they believed the only way to deal with such impious doings was to abolish the day and everything associated with it. They meant to banish this wrong not only from the country, but also from the hearts of its subjects. They came very close to succeeding—but then came the Restoration.

Christmas Returns to England

Christmas was legitimized when the English monarchy, led by Charles II, returned to power in 1660. The holiday could be observed freely, and people were happy. The popular sentiment of the time was expressed in this verse:

Now thanks to God for Charles' return,
Whose absence made old Christmas mourn;
For then we scarcely did it know,
Whether it Christmas were or no.

With the goodwill of the new leaders, and with the lifting of the formal bans instituted under the Puritans, Christmas seemed to be positioned for a comeback of titanic proportions in England. But it was not to be.

The holiday was, at the outset of the Restoration, a shadow of what it had been. The pagan excesses and riotous elements were not the only things lost to the Puritan purge; the Christmas spirit seemed to have left many hearts and minds.

Indeed, although the Puritans had been deposed, much of their philosophy still carried a lot of weight, and many carried on as if they were still in power. Christmas may have been legal, but it was still opposed by some powerful members of the clergy. This left a good many parishioners in a bind, and kept the holiday from making much of a public recovery. The middle of the eighteenth century brought still more obstacles.

In this time of the Industrial Revolution, all thoughts had seemingly turned toward work; everything took a back seat to the quest for money and progress. In this fast-paced atmosphere, it appeared, there was simply no room for holidays.

The numbing, inescapable want of most English workers and their families was one of the chief reasons that people had a hard time finding much to celebrate during this period.

Common people didn't have much to celebrate with and they didn't have much time, either. England had entered into an era of child labor, miserable working conditions, and endless workweeks.

In 1761, the Bank of England closed for forty-seven holidays over the course of a year; in 1834, it closed for only four. Employees of the mid-nineteenth century considered themselves lucky to get a half-day off for Christmas.

Throughout this period, there were small, quiet groups of people who kept the holiday alive in their hearts and homes. But mass enjoyment of the holiday would not take place again until the Victorian Era.

The Germans Keep the Flame Alive

While public celebration of Christmas faced both religious objections and adverse social conditions in England, the German people were enjoying a wonderful and expansive Christmas tradition that had been building up over the centuries. It is very likely that the American love affair with Christmas that began in the late nineteenth and early twentieth centuries, so influential in the way the whole world now views the holiday, would never have occurred if it had not been for the enthusiastic influence of Christmas-loving German immigrants.

The Germans had long espoused the idea of keeping the spirit of Christmas alive inside—in one's heart, mind, and spirit—and turning that feeling outward in mass celebration. The German Christmas is one filled with trees, gingerbread houses, cookies, feasts, and carols; but most of all, it is the Christmas of childhood wonder and joy.

The German people have had an enormous part to play in shaping Christmas into the form we know and love today. It has been said that the Germans had such an abundance of Christmas spirit that they gave some of it to the rest of the world.

The Christmas season in Germany is about the longest anywhere: a month and a half. Starting with St. Andrew's Night on November 30, the country throws itself into a festive abandon that doesn't wind down until January 13, the Octave of Epiphany. Between those days, sixteen holidays are observed, and life is filled with both strict devotion to the Christ Child and joyous merriment. The cities are brimming with Christkindlmarkts (Christ Child Markets), fairs, parades, and carolers. The smell of gingerbread and other delicious treats is in the air, and Christmas trees are everywhere. Other German contributions to the world's celebration of Christmas include the timeless carols "O Tannenbaum" ("Oh, Christmas Tree") and "Silent Night."

One of the beneficiaries of the German love of Christmas was Victorian England. Queen Victoria assumed the throne in 1837 at the age of eighteen; three years later, she married Prince Albert, who became Prince Consort. Albert, being of German descent, brought with him to England many of his homeland's wonderful Christmas traditions.

The Victorian Christmas

Christmas soon became a special occasion for the Royal Family. Their celebration of it emphasized the importance of family closeness and an appreciation of children, and revived the idea of the holiday meal and holiday decorations.

In 1841, for example, Prince Albert introduced the first Christmas tree to Windsor Castle, setting the stage for the subsequent popularity of Christmas trees in England. Since Victoria and her family enjoyed an astonishing popularity, much of what they did was widely emulated. Newspapers and magazines such as *The Illustrated London News* provided a hungry audience with chronicles of the royals' daily activities. Anything seen in the castle, it seemed, was soon copied in homes throughout the country.

As a result, the Victorian Christmas was quaint and warm, highlighted by family togetherness. It commanded a special spirit, full of kindness and charity. More prevalent than the excesses of the past, was the idea of giving and of concern for others, particularly those less fortunate. As Charles Dickens said, Christmas was "the only time I know of, in the long calendar of the year, when men and women seem by one consent to open their shut-up hearts freely."

Charles Dickens also played a large role in reviving the Christmas spirit in his countrymen. Along with a stinging indictment of the living conditions brought about by the Industrial Revolution, Dickens's publication of "A Christmas Carol" in 1843 reminded people what the holiday truly meant, and all that it could bring to their lives.

The Christmas card was created during the Victorian Era, and it enjoyed great popularity. So did carols, which got their biggest boost since they had become legal again under Charles II. There was now caroling in church, caroling in homes, and bands of carolers roaming the streets. Most of the images we have today of outdoor carolers are from these times.

After all that caroling and good cheer, there were bound to be some hungry mouths to feed. The Victorian Christmas menu is the one most people envision when thinking of a classic Christmas dinner: turkey, goose, or roast beef; mince pie; Yorkshire and plum pudding; wassail; and eggnog. To aid in digestion, there were games like Shadow Buff, the Memory Game, Poker and Tongs, and the Minister's Cat; there was also the ubiquitous sprig of mistletoe.

The custom of giving gifts on Christmas Day did not come about until the last few decades of the century; before that, England adhered to the old Roman tradition of waiting until New Year's Day. When Christmas eventually became the day for gifts, it was England's turn to borrow from America, whose Santa Claus became the model for the English Father Christmas.

By the beginning of the twentieth century, Christmas was fully re-established as a holiday, steeped again in tradition and spirit. The Victorians had helped to mold a Christmas tradition that would forever alter the way Christmas was celebrated in England and America.

Christmas in America

Columbus's 1492 voyage to the New World ended when he ran aground on Christmas Eve, and he and his men were rescued by native peoples. His was, of course, the first of many such expeditions to what would eventually be called the Americas. Later explorers found the inhabitants of these unfamiliar lands engaging in end-of-the-year festivals just as people did back in Europe. Peoples in the Pacific Northwest and Alaska had winter celebrations; a tribe in North Dakota hung gifts on cedar trees.

To understand modern Christmas traditions, however, you need to look toward Europe. The first wave of European settlers to the colonies came from English, Dutch, and Germanic backgrounds. These groups, representing a variety of churches and religious affiliations, organized communities according to the traditions and values of their heritage. Among other religious, cultural, and political differences during the colonial period, was the question of Christmas. In this case, there was scant middle ground: Some were completely for it, some completely opposed.

Outlawing Christmas in America

The celebration of Christmas in early America depended very much on where the settlers had come from in the Old World. Those with traditional English backgrounds tended to recognize the holiday, while the Separatist or Puritan pilgrims brought with them the sentiments of the Protestant Reformation in seventeenth-century England: They believed that the day didn't necessarily reflect Christ's true birth date, and they disapproved of the excesses involved in its celebration. Excerpts from the diary of Governor Bradford of Plymouth Colony, for example, give a dismal description of Christmas in 1621, describing only work and the discouragement of celebration.

Christmas was officially banned in Massachusetts between 1659 and 1681, rolled in together with such frowned-upon activities as gambling. Those who disobeyed the law, and were found celebrating the holiday by feasting or drinking, for example, could be fined five shillings.

Not surprisingly, the traditions of the English grew even more unpopular after the American Revolution. Christmas had a long way to go in the new United States of America.

Christmas Comes Back

The Puritans were not the only group of settlers in early America, however. In Virginia, the Cavaliers (seventeenth-century English royalists) observed Christmas by ringing bells, decorating evergreens, and feasting. Dutch immigrants also arrived in the seventeenth century, along with their Christmas traditions, which included Sinter Klaas. And, of course, settlers from Germany also brought their strong holiday traditions with them.

This steady influx of moderates from overseas brought about the repeal of the anti-Christmas law in 1681, and the first Christmas services were held in Boston Town Hall in 1686. Still, even when it was no longer illegal, Christmas remained a workday in Boston. Although Alabama declared Christmas a legal holiday in 1836, the first state to do so, the same was not done in Boston until 1856, and children there were attending school on Christmas Day until 1870.

Hessian troops at Trenton, unwilling to forsake their customary celebrations during the Christmas season of 1776, were taken by surprise by General Washington in one of the turning points of the Revolutionary War. As it happens, Hessians, who came from central Germany, are believed to have been the first to set up a Christmas tree on American soil.

In the nineteenth century, it seemed that wherever Germans settled in America, they brought Christmas cheer. In Pennsylvania, New York, Virginia, and elsewhere they kept their love of Christmas alive. In some places they were surrounded by some of the holidays' staunchest opponents, but they carried on anyway, and gradually gained converts to their merry ways. An infusion of Victorian Christmas spirit that began in the middle of the nineteenth century, coupled with the continued dedication to the holiday by German immigrants and their descendants, brought about the beginning of the Christmas that Americans recognize today.

Another important influence in bringing Christmas to America was author Washington Irving. He introduced St. Nicholas in his 1809 book *A History of New York*, and followed that up with *The Sketchbook of Geoffrey Crayon, Gent.* in 1819, in which his stories about an English manor house Christmas evoked traditional elements of the holiday, including a Lord of Misrule. In Irving's Christmas writings, peace and generosity ruled, rather than the raucous partying that had so dismayed Puritan leaders and led to the holiday's banning.

The American South led the way in returning Christmas, with Alabama, Louisiana, and Arkansas all declaring the day an official holiday in the 1830s. The federal government didn't follow until 1870. In 1890, Oklahoma—the last contiguous state or territory that did not officially recognize Christmas as a holiday—also changed its mind. The country was now celebrating from sea to shining sea, gradually incorporating customs and traditions from all over the world.

Creating an American Christmas

Today, when many people think of Christmas, some of their fondest images come directly from the popularity of the holiday that grew throughout the 1800s and into the 1900s. Clement Moore's "A Visit from St. Nicholas" (or "'Twas the Night Before Christmas") appeared in 1822, for example, while Francis P. Church's "Yes, Virginia, There Is a Santa Claus" was published in 1897. (These can be found in Chapters 6 and 7.)

Images of Santa Claus were also popping up with regularity, including Thomas Nast's interpretations in *Harper's* magazine from 1863 through the 1890s, and the famous Coca-Cola Santa images between 1930 and 1964. It's largely from these illustrations that we get our present-day image of Santa as either bearded and cloaked or bearded, red-suited, and jolly.

"Rudolph the Red-Nosed Reindeer" is one of the most popular songs of all time. The character was created by Robert L. May in 1939 in a free, giveaway poem for Montgomery Ward customers. The story was turned into music and lyrics in 1949 by Johnny Marks and was sung originally by Gene Autry.

Today, the Christmas season in the United States starts unofficially with Macy's Thanksgiving Day Parade, an event watched by millions of Americans both in person and on television. It began in New York City in 1924, welcoming Santa Claus onto Macy's balcony, although he's been ending his parades at Herald Square ever since. Balloons made their appearance in 1927, and continue to become more colorful and elaborate.

More officially, the White House leads the country in celebrating Christmas, with its annual lighting of the National Christmas Tree and the beginning of the Christmas Pageant of Peace in Washington, D.C. Both serve to brighten the nation's capital and, indeed, the nation.

The overwhelming sentiment of the American Christmas matched its Victorian English counterpart in its emphasis on family, peace, and goodwill. The excesses of medieval times were left behind, replaced instead by a sense of charity toward those less fortunate and a coming together of family and friends. Today, it can be argued that the American celebration of Christmas that grew gradually stronger through the nineteenth century has done much to influence celebrations around the world.

2

The Life and Times of Santa Claus

He's called Santa Claus, Sinter Klaas, Father Christmas, and Père Noël, among other names, but the title of St. Nicholas comes closest to the historical roots of this giver of gifts. Although modern Santa's appearance and traditions spring largely from the last two centuries of popular story and art, the legends associated with him begin with a real person on the shores of the fourth-century Mediterranean Sea. Over the years, he's evolved into an engaging combination of reality and myth whose hearty, "Ho, ho, ho!" proves impossible to resist each Christmas season.

Who Is Santa Claus?

Although his roots reach back into antiquity, the man we know as Santa Claus has been refined and popularized largely through the media of the nineteenth and twentieth centuries. In fact, two written accounts—Clement C. Moore's 1822 poem, "A Visit from St. Nicholas" (see Chapter 7) and the *New York Sun's* famous response to young Virginia O'Hanlon's 1897 query about him (see Chapter 6)—probably did the most to establish Santa as a figure in the popular imagination.

But, even though his most memorable features are relatively recent, Santa Claus evolved from many sources over many years—most notably from the life and deeds associated with St. Nicholas, an early Christian bishop in the land of Asia Minor, in what is now western Turkey.

These days, the Vatican has its doubts about St. Nicholas. A special report penned in 1969 by senior Church officials concluded that many of the recorded deeds of some of the early saints—including the forerunner of Santa—may well be those of legendary heroes rather than historical personages.

The records of Nicholas's life certainly appear to be a mixture of fact and fantastic myth, but there is no denying the impact that this revered figure had on the development of the Santa Claus tradition. As a saint, he remains immensely popular in Europe, where there are more churches named for him than for any apostle.

Where St. Nicholas Lived

Today, the town of Demre lies on the Mediterranean coast of Turkey, where an alluvial plain spreads out from the feet of the Taurus Mountains in the distance to the warm sapphire sea close by. Also known as Kale, Demre was once the location of the ancient city of Myra, and it's where you can still find the Church of St. Nicholas—a two-story stone-block building with a single bell tower.

The first church built here was destroyed by an earthquake shortly after Nicholas's death in the fourth century, but some of the existing building's walls date back as far as the fifth century. Reconstructed after Arab raids in the seventh and eighth centuries, and again by Byzantine Emperor Constantine XI in 1043, the building's current appearance owes much to a renovation in the mid-1800s that gave it a flat-roofed second story and bell tower.

Among the historic elements are arched windows and side-by-side, semicircular chapels within the main building. Worn frescoes show painted medallions of saints, hinting at the deep colors that once decorated the church's interior walls. On the floor, marble mosaics create starburst and knot-like effects. It's quiet and cool inside, an escape from the heat of the sun, remaining a fitting resting place for what is said to be the saint's sarcophagus, a stone casket carved with acanthus leaves.

While St. Nicholas is no longer laid to rest in this church, it remains a tangible link to the man who once preached in Myra and who remains such a well-loved figure around the world.

The Story of St. Nicholas

Before the legend began to take over, St. Nicholas was a figure of historic fact. He became the Bishop of Myra while still in his teens, earning the nickname of Boy Bishop. Through his courage and generosity, he is said to have touched the lives of many people, saving any number from famine and despair. He founded an orphanage and was known for his love of and wonderful relationship with children.

Christmas Spirit

Nicholas also spent some time in captivity, imprisoned by the Roman Empire during a time of religious persecution. He and others were finally reprieved by Emperor Constantine, whose attitude toward Christianity was softening (Constantine eventually adopted Christianity himself).

Nicholas died on December 6 in approximately A.D. 343, and—as was the church's custom—the date of his death became recognized as his official saint's day.

Inspiring tales about Nicholas made him extremely popular throughout Christendom; he was named the patron saint of children, sailors, merchants, bakers, brides, hobos, pawnbrokers, and bankers—as well as of New York, Russia, Greece, and Sicily. It is not surprising, then, that Nicholas was so revered even in death. In later years, his body was stolen from its crypt in Myra by sailors from Bari, Italy, who were seeking to protect his remains from invaders. The sailors brought the remains to Bari and buried them in a basilica there; to this day, St. Nicholas's Day is celebrated by the people of Bari on May 9, the date of the sailors' arrival. The theft brought Nicholas the distinction of patron saint of thieves, and added to his already sizeable legend.

The Legends Begin

Beyond evidence that Nicholas was a very good man, there are the rumors and legends that suggest he was nothing short of otherworldly. His birth is said to have been a miraculous one, as his parents, according to legend, had been married thirty years and had long since given up hope of ever conceiving a child. It is said that shortly after his birth, he was able to stand up in his crib, as if praying.

Nicholas appears to have had no doubt about his vocation; he prepared to enter the monastery at a young age. Before devoting his life to his faith, however, he was required to rid himself of all his worldly possessions. The way he accomplished this has helped to establish his reputation as a gift giver.

As the story goes, there was a family in town with three daughters of marriageable age, but they were so poor that they had no dowry—and no dowry meant no marriage. Nicholas, hearing of their plight, disguised himself and went at night to their house, where he threw three bags of gold coins down their chimney, saving the daughters from a life of prostitution. The gold is said to have landed in the girls' stockings, which were hanging in the fireplace to dry (thus giving us our "stockings by the chimney" tradition). As legend has it, the father of the family caught Nicholas in the act, and though Nicholas tried to swear him to secrecy, the story spread through the town quickly.

The Bishop of Myra

Soon after Nicholas entered the monastery, the church in Myra was having great difficulty replacing its former bishop and the people were at their wits' end as to a solution. One night, a church official dreamt that the first person to enter the church for Mass the next day should be the new bishop, and that his name would be Nicholas. About that time, Nicholas was traveling on a ship that had encountered rough weather. He prayed for safety, and when he arrived on land he headed immediately for the church, in Myra, to give thanks. The rest is history.

During his lifetime, St. Nicholas would undergo another rough voyage on a ship, a journey that would result in his being named patron saint of sailors. While returning from a pilgrimage to the Holy Land, the vessel that carried him ran into a terrible storm. Nicholas began to pray for help; witnesses said the sea calmed the instant Nicholas dropped to his knees. So important did he become to sailors, Greek and Russian seamen always sailed with an icon of St. Nicholas.

A Storied Life

There are many legends surrounding St. Nicholas. One of the more famous legends has Nicholas stopping for rest at an inn during his travels. The innkeeper offered him meat, which turned out to be the flesh of three little boys the innkeeper had killed. Though the stories differ concerning who the boys were, how they were killed, and whether they were stuck in salt or pickle barrels, the result remains the same: Nicholas figured out what the innkeeper was up to and brought the boys back to life. (This act is commemorated in current St. Nicholas's Day celebrations, particularly in Lorraine, France.)

Nicholas's status as the patron saint of sailors helped to make him known in other lands. Italian and Dutch sailors introduced St. Nicholas to the West, and by the Middle Ages he was as popular in Europe as he was in his homeland. Vladimir of Russia discovered Nicholas in Constantinople in 1003, and brought his legend home to Russia, where Nicholas later became the patron saint. Nicholas was soon an important part of the Christmas holiday season—and so, not coincidentally, was the idea of giving gifts to children.

Saint's Day

Beginning in the sixteenth century, the Protestant Reformation led many parts of Europe to reject the culture of saints and anything associated with them. The legend of St. Nicholas might have died then and there, but it seems his popularity was simply too great. Most countries did change his name slightly, while leaving his background and other characteristics fully intact.

The day of St. Nicholas's death (December 6) is still observed in many parts of Europe as St. Nicholas's Day—it marks the beginning of the Christmas season in many countries, where children receive gifts said to be from the kindly saint.

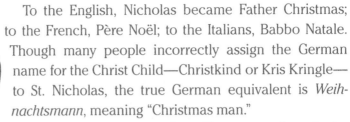

To the English, Nicholas became Father Christmas; to the French, Père Noël; to the Italians, Babbo Natale. Though many people incorrectly assign the German name for the Christ Child—Christkind or Kris Kringle—to St. Nicholas, the true German equivalent is *Weihnachtsmann*, meaning "Christmas man."

Though popular throughout Europe, nowhere is the saint more celebrated than in Holland, where his name was transformed to Sinter Klaas. The bearded saint in this version wears breeches and a broad-brimmed hat; he carries a long Dutch pipe; and he rides a white horse with a basket of treats for good children and birch rods for naughty ones.

According to the Dutch, Sinter Klaas spends the majority of the year in Spain with his servant Black Peter (a Moor), who keeps scrupulous records of the behavior of girls and boys. A few weeks before St. Nicholas's Eve, Sinter Klaas packs up for the Netherlands. Dressed in full bishop regalia, he arrives by steamer on the last Saturday in November; the whole city turns out to greet him and there is a ceremony featuring all the area officials.

St. Nicholas spends the time before St. Nicholas's Eve visiting hospitals, schools, and markets, giving little gifts to good children, while Black Peter gives switches to the bad ones. The biggest presents are left for St. Nicholas's Eve; children leave their shoes out at night filled with hay for Sinter Klaas's horse and are given gifts in return—not wrapped, but disguised or cleverly hidden. Each present comes with a note that must be read aloud and often contains a line or two that will embarrass the recipient.

Many of the Dutch customs that surround St. Nicholas are carryovers from old Norse mythology and ritual. The god Wodin (whom the American St. Nicholas often resembled in the late eighteenth century) was said to ride around on his horse checking up on little children.

In Germany, children were warned to behave by the prospect of an encounter with a dirty, rather sinister figure known as Pelznicken ("furred Nicholas"), who carried not only gifts for good boys and girls but also long switches for naughty children. Eventually, an ogre-like companion joined the saint, to mete out justice to errant little ones.

Interpreting St. Nicholas

Gift givers inspired by St. Nicholas—who differ from the saint only in name and in a few particulars—can be found elsewhere in Europe. Russia's Nikolai Chudovorits, for example, evolved into Father Frost, who lives beyond the Arctic Circle and comes to Russia on New Year's Day on a reindeer-pulled sleigh with his daughter, the Snow Maiden, to place presents under trees.

The Scandinavian gift givers are much more impish and mischievous. The Norwegian Julesvenn, the Danish Julenisse, and the Swedish Jultomten are left treats on St. Nicholas's Eve in an effort to get them to return the favor, to dissuade them from trickery, and, in the case of farmers, to ensure they'll protect the livestock.

Festive Fact

In some places, St. Nicholas is also celebrated as the youthful Boy Bishop who took over the church in Myra. In England, for instance, a Boy Bishop was chosen to preside over the solstice festival, along with St. Nick's older incarnation, Father Christmas.

In some parts of Europe, the legend of St. Nicholas was incorporated into the winter solstice festivals. St. Nicholas's Day had long opened the Christmas season, and as we have seen, the saint's selfless gift giving and love of children was in keeping with the themes of the Nativity. Because of the closeness in time, some places eventually merged the two days.

Germany and France, for example, transferred most of the activities surrounding St. Nicholas's Eve to Christmas Eve. The majority of European countries still keep the two separate, however; St. Nicholas brings goodies on his day, and the Christ Child or the Three Wise Men deliver on Christmas or Epiphany Eve.

Santa in the New World

St. Nicholas came to America by way of the Dutch in the 1600s. Sinter Klaas, as the name was rendered, was obviously an important figure to the Dutch settlers: They named their first church in the New World the St. Nicholas Collegiate Church. In the Dutch settlement of New Amsterdam—later New York City—St. Nicholas Day and Christmas were celebrated in a merry fashion unknown to the rest of the colonies, where the strictly Puritan background of most of the settlers precluded any celebration of saints or Christmas.

It was only in the years after the American Revolution that Christmas began to win slow acceptance in various regions of the United States, however, and only at the dawn of the nineteenth century that any meaningful references to Santa Claus began to appear. The change in the national attitude can be traced at least in part to the influx of German immigrants to the new country: German immigrants were perhaps the most enthusiastic celebrants of Christmas in northern cities during this period.

A Visit from St. Nicholas

Although Washington Irving's nostalgic turn-of-the century satires of New Amsterdam society feature some of the earliest American literary treatments of the St. Nicholas legend, the evolution from St. Nicholas to the American Santa recognized today appears to have begun in earnest at least two or three decades later.

Clement C. Moore's enormously influential poem "A Visit from St. Nicholas" was written in 1822, but it did not become widely popular until several years after that. Moore wrote the verses for his own children, reciting it before his family for the first time on Christmas Eve. The poem was published anonymously, and to increasingly enthusiastic public response, until 1837, when Moore finally acknowledged authorship.

Christmas Spirit

Much of what we now consider as essential to Santa—such as his plumpness—first appeared in Clement C. Moore's poem "A Visit from St. Nicholas." Moore apparently based his St. Nick on a rotund gardener who worked for him, but preferred to call the character St. Nicholas rather than Santa Claus.

Although Santa has grown over the years from the elflike stature Moore assigned to him, it is from Moore's lines that the first (and by far the most influential) concrete physical description of Santa comes:

He was dressed all in fur from his head to his foot,
And his clothes were all tarnished with ashes and soot;
A bundle of toys he had flung on his back,
And he looked like a peddler just opening his pack.

His eyes, how they twinkled! his dimples, how merry!
His cheeks were like roses, his nose like a cherry;
His droll little mouth was drawn up like a bow,
And the beard on his chin was as white as the snow.

The stump of a pipe he held tight in his teeth,
And the smoke it encircled his head like a wreath.
He had a broad face and a little round belly
That shook, when he laughed, like a bowl full of jelly.

Moore's portrayal of St. Nicholas as a generous gift giver and friend to children was, of course, an outgrowth of the legends surrounding St. Nicholas. The influence of Irving's (often imaginative) accounts of the Dutch legend is also apparent through-out Moore's poem.

Thomas Nast's 1863 illustrations for the poem "A Visit from St. Nicholas"—which itself went a long way toward standardizing the jolly one's physical appearance—were the turning point in Nast's career. Although his later political cartoons also won him national acclaim, he made a tradition of supplying fresh drawings of Santa for the Christmas issue of *Harper's Weekly* each year.

Moore was not the first to assign a reindeer to St. Nicholas, but he was the first to set the total at eight, and the first to popularize the names now associated with the animals. (They are, for the record: Dasher, Dancer, Prancer, Vixen, Comet, Cupid, Donner, and Blitzen.)

Santa Evolves

In 1842, a popular children's book featured illustrations of a stout, bearded, gift-giving character it referred to as Kriss Kringle. Although uniform depictions of this figure would not surface for another twenty years, the book's drawings were in fact the first modern representations of the St. Nicholas we think of today.

This concept of Santa flying in a sleigh pulled by a reindeer had long been popular in Russia, where Father Frost arrived in the villages in a reindeer-drawn sleigh. The Norse god, Wodin, was said to ride his horse, Sleipner, through the air to make sure people were behaving; in Holland, St. Nicholas still rides Sleipner.

The name by which we more commonly know him would not gain currency until the middle of the century, when the pronunciation of Sinter Klaas had either evolved or been corrupted, depending on your outlook, to Santa Claus.

Although it had far less influence on the vision of Santa than Moore's poem, the *New York Sun*'s editorial response to young Virginia O'Hanlon's query about his existence has probably had a greater effect on the way people think about him. The piece, which ran first in 1897 and has resurfaced seemingly every holiday season thereafter, captured for both adults and children the essential innocence and trust of the Santa Claus tradition.

The *Sun* piece also supplied the nation with a catchphrase that helped unify the previously disparate roles Santa had played in various ethnic traditions. It is probably no coincidence that the phrase "Yes, Virginia, there is a Santa Claus" entered the national lexicon at about the same time the mass media in general—and advertisers in particular—began in earnest to capitalize on the bearded one's popularity. The nation finally had a single perception of Santa to which publishers and marketers alike could appeal.

Although Thomas Nast's drawings had the greatest impact as far as standardizing the various images of St. Nicholas into a single chubby, smiling figure, the final touches were added (or at least formalized) in the 1920s by artist Haddon Sundblom in a series of Coca-Cola ads. Sundblom's Santa had red cheeks, wore a red gown with white-fur trim, and radiated a rotund good cheer. Not surprisingly, he also liked

Coca-Cola. The ad campaign ran for thirty-five years, and was even revived in the 1990s.

Francis Church, the writer for the *New York Sun* who penned the famous response to Virginia O'Hanlon's 1897 query about Santa Claus, never received credit for the work during his lifetime. That's not unusual for newspaper editorial writers, however; staff on newspaper editorial pages often write as the voice of the paper as a whole rather than as individuals.

And so St. Nicholas has made his way from Asia Minor to American department stores, undergoing a few alterations on the way. Indeed, it's doubtful whether St. Nicholas would recognize himself in the Santa Claus of today if the two were to come face to face. Still, perhaps somewhere, somehow, St. Nicholas is aware of the joy his existence has brought to children and the children at heart everywhere.

After all, if it were not for this quietly devout and generous man, there would be no Santa Claus. And who could imagine Christmas without Santa?

3

The Traditions of Christmas

Many of the best-loved Christmas traditions come from the original stories of the Bible. In fact, the gospels of Luke and Matthew hold the keys to explaining the ways in which many people celebrate the holiday today—from the Christmas star that led the Wise Men to the stable in Bethlehem where Jesus was born to the Nativity displays that recreate the scene inside the stable. While customs have changed over the centuries, many traditions still provide a direct link to the time of Jesus' birth.

Xmas

The *X* in *Xmas* stands for the Greek letter *Chi*, the first letter in the Greek word for Christ. Over time, the letter *X* came to stand for the name of Christ. The practice gained very wide usage in the mass media during the twentieth century—but not, as many believe, because of a reluctance to use the word *Christmas* or to make it easier to write. Often, *Xmas* simply fits better in a headline.

Christkind

Christkind, the German name for the Christ Child, originally referred directly to the Holy Infant Jesus himself, who was said to bring gifts to children in Germany, Austria, Switzerland, and the Pennsylvania Dutch region on Christmas Eve. (Other forms of the name are *Christkindl, Christkindli,* and *Chriskindlein.*)

Later, the name came to stand for the embodiment of the Child's spirit, in angelic form, that brought the gifts in his place. Veiled in white, with gold wings upon his shoulders, he arrives secretly, often through an open window. When he is through with his work, he rings a bell to notify all that the presents have arrived.

Over the years, the name has evolved to *Kris Kringle*, but contrary to popular belief, the Christkind is not another form of Santa Claus.

Special Days

For most of the churches that follow Christianity, Christmas is only one day—albeit a very important one—in an entire season that focuses on the birth of Jesus. The season begins approximately four weeks before Christmas Day, and carries on through January and even into February. Each of the special days within the season brings with it an opportunity to reflect on the message of peace, joy, and goodwill.

The Season of Advent

For most western Christian churches, Advent begins on the fourth Sunday before Christmas. The word *advent* originates with the Latin word for "coming," and indeed, this season of preparation is a solemn time to make ready for the coming of Christ and Christmas.

 In Eastern Orthodox churches, Advent can last for forty days, and may be referred to as the Nativity Fast, Winter Lent, or Christmas Lent. This goes back to a time in the Greek churches when the weeks before Christmas were marked by fasting.

As a way to mark the passage of time, churches often use an Advent Wreath or candle arrangement that contains five candles. On the first Sunday of Advent, one candle is lit; on the second, two candles are lit; and so on. These candles, which can be various colors depending on the church, often represent such ideas as hope, peace, love, and joy. Finally, on Christmas Eve, the fifth candle is lit, representing Christ, the light of the world.

Christmas Eve

The day before Christmas Day is one of great anticipation, and is marked in many countries and cultures. The most popular Christmas Mass for Roman Catholics is the midnight Mass, a tradition that began in the early 400s. Midnight Mass is traditionally held at midnight, as Christmas Eve becomes Christmas Day, because it's believed that Jesus was born at midnight. In today's churches, both Catholic and Protestant, services may be held at midnight or earlier, often incorporating carols and the Nativity.

 In Spanish and Latin countries, Midnight Mass is referred to as the Mass of the Rooster, after the legend that says the only time a rooster ever crowed at midnight was at the moment of Christ's birth. The Polish Midnight Mass is called *Mass Pasternak* (Mass of the Shepherds), in commemoration of the shepherds present in accounts of the first Christmas.

Of course, the night of Christmas Eve is also when Santa Claus and his many variants are believed to travel the world, leaving behind presents for the children on the well-behaved list. Although in many countries people open presents on Christmas morning, some open them on Christmas Eve—this includes Canada's Quebec province, as well as Denmark, Iceland, Norway, and Portugal.

Christmas Eve is a time when families begin to gather to celebrate Christmas Day, often traveling to be with each other, and enjoying a Christmas Eve supper together. Historically, it was also the day when Christmas trees and decorations were set up; however, the festive garlands are now often in place weeks beforehand.

Christmas Day

For many people, Christmas morning is a time when children bounce out of bed, eager to see what Santa has brought them in the night. Presents can be found under the tree, with wrapping eagerly discarded by tykes still in their pajamas, watched just as eagerly by parents remembering their own childhood Christmases. Then, they create new memories as a family, making time later in the day to gather with extended family and friends for a large meal, often of roast turkey, beef, or ham.

Christmas Day also finds many people attending church services as a centerpiece for the entire Christmas-season celebration. In keeping with the theme of charity and hope, many religious and secular organizations make time for those less fortunate, offering a Christmas meal or delivering Christmas hampers to those who may be homeless or struggling in some way.

Boxing Day

Despite the name, it has nothing to do with prizefighting. In England, it was customary for churches to open their alms boxes to the poor on the first workday after Christmas in an attempt to give some cheer to those who could not afford a very merry Christmas. Out of this custom grew Boxing Day, on which day service people and other workers would collect money or treats from their employers. It was popularized during Queen Victoria's reign in England, in the mid-nineteenth century, and remains a day off work in many countries.

Epiphany

The Wise Men's visit to Jesus is commemorated on Epiphany, also known in some places as Twelfth Night or Three Kings' Eve. Originally, Epiphany marked the manifestation of God to the world in the form of Jesus, so it included both the birth and the baptism of Jesus. Later, when the Romans began introducing Christianity to the West, they moved the birth of Jesus to December 25, and represented Epiphany as the day the Wise Men presented their gifts.

In the legend of La Befana, an elderly woman chose not to join the Wise Men in journeying to the Baby Jesus because she was too busy cleaning her house. When she regretted her decision and set out after the Wise Men, she became lost. She still wanders the world, leaving gifts with children in honor of the one child she missed—which is how gifts arrive for Italian children on Epiphany Eve. A similar legend exists in Russia, about a woman called the Babushka.

Tradition marks this event on January 6, which remains the date of the Eastern Orthodox Christmas in many countries. You'll note that there are twelve days between December 25 and January 6, which is where our celebration of the Twelve Days of Christmas comes from.

Candlemas Day

A passage from the Gospel of Luke describes an event that would later become a lesser-known religious holiday, one that in many places marks the true close of the Christmas season. According to Jewish law, a mother was to be taken to the temple to be purified forty days after the birth of her child. Mary was no exception to this rule, as Luke describes: "The days of her purification according to the law of Moses were accomplished."

If Jesus was born on December 25, then February 2 would have been the day Mary underwent this ritual, an event that was commemorated in the church as early as the fourth century (although it was often scheduled for the fortieth day after Epiphany, and still is for those churches that recognize Epiphany as the birth of Jesus). It became more formalized over successive centuries, by Emperor Justinian in the sixth century and Pope Sergius I in the seventh century.

The day is marked by a ceremony in which candles are blessed, thus giving it the name Candlemas Day. In some European countries, it is considered bad luck to keep Christmas greenery up after this day.

Stars and Wise Men

The Star of Bethlehem, often found at the top of a Christmas tree or on a plate of Christmas cookies, is strictly Christian in origin, from the Gospel of Matthew. The nature of the star mentioned in the gospel remains a mystery; however, the science of astronomy has provided some possible explanations for accounts of a magical star at the time of Jesus' birth.

Some have argued that it must have been a comet, but records of that time mark the only comets near this period at 17 B.C. (too early), and A.D. 66 (too late). Chinese astronomers, the best in history, observed a nova in 4 B.C., but there is no way to know whether this is the star mentioned in the story.

Another explanation comes from the fields of astronomy and astrology. In the year 6 or 7 B.C., there was an alignment of the planets Jupiter and Saturn in the constellation of Pisces, a fact confirmed by the School of Astronomy at Sippar in Babylon and by the world-renowned astronomer Johannes Kepler. Ancient astrological legend, moreover, asserts that the meeting of these planets would signify the Messiah's birth. The sign for Pisces is two fish joined by their tails; this is also the sign of the Messiah. However, it's possible that 6–7 B.C. is too early to be the year of Jesus' birth.

Careful reading of Matthew shows that it gives no specific number for the Wise Men who were following the star and never refers to them as kings. Over the years, popular culture settled on the number three, presumably because of the three gifts that Matthew mentions: gold, frankincense, and myrrh. Their status as kings is believed to come from a passage in Psalms that refers to kings bearing gifts, though they are also referred to as Magi.

Nativity Scenes

The first Nativity scene was created at the church of Santa Maria Maggiore in tenth-century Rome. The custom was soon popular at other churches, each one constructing ornate mangers with gold, silver, jewels, and precious stones. Though popular among high

The Everything Family Christmas Book

society, such opulence was far removed from the original circumstances of Christ's birth, as well as being inaccessible to the poorer masses.

The more accurate crèche scene is due to St. Francis of Assisi, who in 1224 sought to remedy these problems by creating the first manger scene that was true to the Biblical account of Christ's birth.

Called a crèche, the scene that St. Francis set up for the village of Greccio was made up of hay, carved figures, and live animals, capturing for the town's unlettered people more of the spirit and the story of Christ's birth than any splendid art treasure could convey.

The popularity of St. Francis's crèche spread throughout the world. In Italy it is called a *presepio*; in Germany, a *Krippe*. It is a *nacimiento* in Spain and Latin America, a *jeslicky* in the Czech Republic, a *pesebre* in Brazil, and a *portal* in Costa Rica.

Christmas Animals

Along with the comparatively recent addition of reindeer, a few other animals have commonly been linked to Christmas. Camels, goats, sheep, horses, and donkeys have all been associated with the Biblical story of the Nativity, although only sheep are mentioned explicitly, and most recreations of the Nativity include some, if not all, of these animals. In some countries, the Camel of Jesus brings gifts to the children.

In addition, there are abiding legends about animals having received the power to speak on the night Christ was born; some say that every year between Christmas Eve and Christmas morning this power returns and the animals speak. Another legend has the oxen kneeling every Christmas Eve at midnight. In *Hamlet*, Shakespeare cites a legend of the "bird of dawning," which was said to sing the whole night through at Christmastime.

The Boy Bishop

The Boy Bishop was a popular figure in medieval Christmas festivities, inspired by the life of St. Nicholas, who was appointed Bishop of Myra while still in his teens. In medieval times, the boy chosen to be Bishop would preside over certain portions of the Christmas festivities.

The Boy Bishop's "reign" usually began on December 6, St. Nicholas's Day, and would last until December 28, the Feast of the Holy Innocents. During this time, the Boy Bishop acted as a priest of sorts, blessing people, bringing up the offerings, and leading the choir. He always dressed the part, and in some countries Boy Bishop services were very elaborate.

In time, however, the innocence of this tradition was lost, as it became overshadowed by rowdiness; Boy Bishop services were often seen as an excuse to parody the church and have wild parties. The Boy Bishop had become too closely associated with the figure of the Lord of Misrule (described in Chapter 4) for many people's taste, and as a result was eventually outlawed by the church. The popular tradition did not die out completely, however, until Henry VIII banned it from England in 1542.

Candles

In the time of darkness surrounding the winter solstice, candles were important as a source of light and heat. During the Saturnalia, Romans lit candles to convince the sun to shine again and to ward off evil. From this pagan start, the candle has gone on to become an essential part of Christmas lighting, both in church ceremonies and at home.

For Christians it symbolizes Christ himself, the light of the world; candles are used during Advent to mark the days before the coming of Christmas. The Candlemas services that celebrate the purification of Mary forty days after Christ's birth take their name from the candles that are blessed during the ceremony.

In Victorian times, candles came to represent concern and goodwill for the poor and unfortunate during the holiday season. Candles were placed in windows during the twelve days of Christmas as a sign to needy passersby that shelter and warmth could be found within.

The first string of electric Christmas-tree lights was not sold until 1903. Only the wealthy could afford them, however, and only those with indoor electric outlets could use them. Most people continued to follow the earlier (and dangerous) tradition of affixing small lighted candles to the boughs of the tree. Larger trees bore hundreds of candles.

Candles were the preferred means of lighting Christmas trees for many years. Although replaced on trees and in windows by electric replicas for the most part, real candles are still used—with care—in many caroling ceremonies and church celebrations today.

Stockings

The idea of hanging stockings out on Christmas Eve is believed to have come from Amsterdam, where children leave out their shoes on St. Nicholas's Eve in hopes that he will fill them with goodies. But where did the people of Amsterdam get the idea? Perhaps from St. Nicholas himself.

One of the most popular stories surrounding the saint concerns his generosity to the three daughters of a poor family. It seems the daughters were of marriageable age, but could not marry because they had no dowry. Nicholas heard of their plight and set out to help them. In the middle of the night (he wanted his act to be a secret), Nicholas threw bags of gold coins down the girl's chimney. The bags landed in the girl's stockings, which they had hung up by the chimney to dry. (For a more detailed account of the life of St. Nicholas, see Chapter 2.)

Greenery

Pagan peoples long revered evergreens for their ability to stay alive during the cold, dark winters. Often considered magical for this reason, greenery in various forms adorned the inside and outside of houses during the winter solstice festivals.

Church officials at first attempted to banish greenery, then decided it would better serve their purpose to translate the beloved custom into Christian terms. Evergreens came to symbolize Christ, who in his triumph over death gave the gift of everlasting life to the world.

The legend of the Christmas Rose tells of a young girl who wanted to worship the baby Jesus, but felt she could not because she had no present. Saddened, the girl began to cry; as her tears fell to the ground, they created a bush bearing a beautiful white rose, which she gave to the Holy Infant.

Greenery generally refers to those trees and plants that remain green and flourishing all year round. Though cypress, box, yew, rosemary, and laurel are all considered greenery, they are not as common to Christmas as holly, ivy, mistletoe, and, of course, the Christmas tree.

4

All the Trimmings

As Christmas celebrations evolved over the centuries, these traditions echoed those of earlier times—some from before the time of Jesus, when pagan gods were honored (or appeased) with various customs, others from new cultural or even technological developments. Not as religious in nature as other traditions, these "trimmings" of holiday fun range from the customary colors of red and green (now joined by every color in the rainbow) to the ornaments that are placed on that happiest of decorations, the Christmas tree.

Red and Green

Why are red and green the colors of Christmas? No one really knows for sure, but there have been plenty of educated guesses. Green is the easier of the two to theorize about, because it's the color of the evergreens that symbolize so much that is important to the meaning of the holiday. The holly berry seems to be responsible for the color red, as it's the red berry that lives through winter, symbolizing life in the face of death, and thus representing Christ.

Bells and Other Joyous Noisemakers

A holdover from pagan times, bells and other noisemakers were believed to frighten away evil spirits. As part of the midwinter solstice festivals, bell-ringing activities were very rowdy, mixing some fun in with the serious intent. As late as the 1890s in the United States, children thought of Christmas and noisemakers as nearly synonymous.

The demise of the tiny, wildly popular Christmas firecracker may have as much to do with care for parental eardrums as with safety concerns. Bells, however—particularly church bells—have remained a staple of the holiday. Today, their peals serve as unmistakable heralds of the arrival of the Christmas season.

Feasts

Extravagant feasts played a large part in the winter solstice festivals of ages past. Apart from being a gathering where people exchanged goodwill and cheer, the mere existence of these feasts displayed faith in the prosperity of the upcoming year.

Holiday feasting hit its peak in medieval England, where the king and his court were constantly trying to outdo each other with outrageous quantities of food and drink. The guests at these festivities preferred their food to be presented looking as much like its animal of origin as possible—not that the work was admired for long once it made it to the table. Conspicuous consumption was, after all, the order of the day.

By Victorian times, the boar's head, roasted oxen, and other wild beasts had been replaced by turkey, goose, plum pudding, and Yorkshire pudding. Though there are still many traditional menu items, these days the food on the table is not as important as the idea of a gathering with family and friends, full of warmth and Christmas spirit.

The Boar's Head

According to an old English legend, there was once a philosophy student who fended off an attacking wild boar by choking the animal with a book on Aristotle. When the boar was dead, the student cut off his head to remove the book, then brought the head back to his college, where he and his friends had a grand feast. Soon, boar's head was a must for every English household at Christmas.

Perhaps a more likely explanation for the popularity of boar's head as part of the Christmas feast, however, is that the custom is another remnant of pagan times. In some places, the German god Frey was considered responsible for the well-being of livestock. As Frey was symbolized by the boar, a boar was often sacrificed in hopes of a prosperous spring herd.

Like many Christmas traditions popular in medieval England, the boar's-head custom eventually became impractical and died out. Boars became increasingly hard to track down and were dangerous to catch once they were found. Then, too, the week's worth of cooking and preparation required was more conducive to a well-staffed castle kitchen than that of a home. The boar's head was gradually replaced by the more familiar pork, roast beef, turkey, and goose.

Wassail

Wassail was a popular Christmas drink in England, particularly in Victorian times. The drink's name comes from the old toast expression *waes hael* (to your health), and was made of eggs, curdled cream, nuts, spices, roasted apples, and mulled ale.

In pagan times, wassail was thought to provide more than just good cheer. During the agricultural festivals, groups would visit apple trees and douse them with wassail to ensure that the next apple harvest would be plentiful. This ritual also involved a great deal of noise making to ward off evil, which helped to instill a festive atmosphere. From this ritual grew wassail's association with parties.

Now that its significance to the apple harvest has been more or less forgotten, wassail is considered no more than a tasty holiday drink—a rowdy eggnog. (The tradition of mulled wine—a warmed mixture of wine and spices such as cloves—also has associations with the tradition of wassail.)

The Lord of Misrule and the Mummers

The Lord of Misrule played a major part in the Christmas festivities in medieval England. Like the Boy Bishop, he was the leader of many holiday activities, but he also had real power, and his whims had to be obeyed by all, even the king. The Lord of Misrule was a strictly secular figure, appointed by the king and the nobility to reign over the twelve days of Christmas. The man chosen for this position, however, was generally wise enough not to abuse his power when dealing with the nobility.

Much of the custom surrounding the Lord of Misrule had parallels with the Roman Saturnalia, during which masters and slaves changed places, with general rowdiness abounding.

Out on the streets among the common people, the Lord of Misrule was head of the mummers, a traveling band of rowdy players who roamed the streets in costume performing plays, songs, and so on. Though they stuck to the streets for the most part, the mummers were sometimes known to barge into churches and disrupt the service, an act that did not sit well with church officials.

The mummers, roving street carousers all, offered just about anything that would win the attention of passersby. The classic mummer's play has a number of variations, but it always focuses on the death and revival of one of the principals. The ancestors of street actors, the mummers did it all: plays, songs, comedy routines, and nearly any other diversion that came to mind.

Like carolers, mummers would often perform in exchange for goodies, though their performances were often disruptive and sacrilegious. When the Puritans came to power, they did away with the Lord of Misrule and his companions. Though the restored monarchy reinstated most of the Christmas traditions outlawed by the Puritans, the Lord of Misrule remained an outlaw. He and the mummers never again enjoyed the freedom and popularity they had had in medieval England; however, Christmas mummers can still be found in some parts of the world, including Ireland and Canada's Newfoundland.

The Christmas Tree

The Christmas tree is by far the most popular form of holiday greenery in the United States. Indeed, it has become such an integral part of the Christmas celebration that most people cannot imagine celebrating the holiday without one in their living room. Yet the tree is a relatively recent innovation.

No one seems to be able to explain the reasons behind the popularity of the Christmas tree, but, along with Santa, it is now a Christmas icon. The beauty, the smell, the fun of decorating, the spirit, the memories of holidays past—whether of pine, fir, or cedar—there's simply nothing like a good Christmas tree.

Combining Legends and History

As early as the Roman Saturnalia, trees were hung with decorations, but this custom did not become part of Christmas until the Middle Ages. Like all greenery with pagan origins, the tree has long been assigned Christian significance, but how it came to be so important to Christmas is the subject of much debate. The earliest record of a decorated tree is from an English book printed in 1441, which describes a tree set up in the middle of a village, decorated with ivy. The popular consensus, however, is that the Christmas tree originated in Germany.

According to one legend, St. Boniface, who helped organize the Christian church in France and Germany during the mid-700s, was responsible for the first Christmas tree. One Christmas Eve, St. Boniface was traveling through the forest and happened upon a group of people gathered around an oak tree preparing to sacrifice a child to the god Thor. In protest of this act, St. Boniface destroyed the oak, either with an ax or a single blow from his fist. When the oak was felled, a fir tree appeared in its place. St. Boniface informed the people that this was the Tree of Life, representing Christ.

One of the most popular Christmas-tree legends concerns Martin Luther. One Christmas Eve, as Luther was ambling through the forest, he became enraptured by the beauty of the starlight playing off the evergreen branches. Luther chopped down a tree and brought it home, where he lit it with candles in an effort to duplicate the scene for his family. Though Luther himself never mentioned this event, the legend spread throughout the land.

Another familiar legend holds that when Christ was born, all the animals received the power to speak, and the trees bloomed and brought forth fruit, despite the harsh winter. All the grand trees came forth to pay homage to the Lord, except one tiny fir tree, embarrassed by her stature. But then the Lord came down and lighted the fir tree's branches, making her sparkle, and she was no longer ashamed.

In yet another legend, a poor man gave shelter and food to a needy child one Christmas Eve; the child turned out to be the Christ Child. In return for the man's generosity, the Child created a small, lighted fir tree that grew outside the house.

Because of Martin Luther's supposed association with the Christmas tree, strictly Roman Catholic inhabitants of southern Germany would not have trees in their homes until the nineteenth century, when news of the custom's popularity in America traveled overseas.

The Paradise Tree

Though these legends are entertaining, most experts believe that the truth behind the Christmas tree is much less spectacular. In the fourteenth and fifteenth centuries, pine trees were used in Europe as part of the miracle plays performed in front of cathedrals at Christmas time. The plays detailed the birth and fall of humanity, its salvation through the death and resurrection of Christ, and Christ's promise of redemption. The pine trees, decorated with apples, symbolized the Tree of Life in the Garden of Eden.

Though such plays were later banned by the church, the tradition of this Paradise Tree, or Paradeisbaum, was kept alive in individual homes. People began decorating the trees with wafers to represent the Eucharist; later, these wafers evolved into cookies, cakes, fruit, and other goodies. At first, these foods were shaped to represent some aspect of the Nativity, but in time they came to depict anything the decorator's heart desired.

To this day, the Christmas tree enjoys incredible popularity in Germany. The decorating of the tree is one of the most anticipated events of the holiday, and in some homes each family member has his or her own tree. So beloved is the Christmas tree there that the most popular carol in Germany after "Silent Night" is "O Tannenbaum" ("Oh, Christmas Tree").

By the 1800s, the Christmas tree had spread to Norway, Finland, Sweden, Denmark, and Austria. In Scandinavia, fishermen trimmed trees with fish nets and flags. Today, it is more common in those countries to decorate with cookies, candy, fruit, and flags.

The most famous tree in Great Britain is a gift each year from Norway, in appreciation for Britain's help during World War II. When Norway was occupied by the Nazis, King Haakan set up a free Norwegian government in London. Since 1947, each year Norway has presented the people of Britain with an enormous tree at least seventy feet high, which is set up in Trafalgar Square for all to enjoy.

Christmas Trees in America

The tradition of the decorated Christmas tree, which German immigrants followed for years, did not spread to other parts of colonial American society until the 1830s. After it caught on, however, it became almost as beloved as it is in Germany. At the end of the nineteenth century, combination tree stands and music boxes that rotated the tree and played soothing music were popular with wealthy Americans. Today, most homes have some type of Christmas tree during the holidays; trees can be found everywhere from department stores to offices to churches. Even trees growing outside are decorated.

It is said that the Hessians (who came from an area of Germany) defeated by George Washington in the Battle of Trenton in 1776 may have been observing the holiday in the custom of their homeland by setting lighted candles upon the boughs of a tree.

The United States has its own famous Christmas trees. The ninety-foot-high tree in New York's Rockefeller Center has been a tradition since 1933, with its annual lighting now an event that's televised throughout North America. In Washington, a tree near the White House in Sherman Square, known as the National Living Christmas Tree, is lit every year by a member of the First Family. And the Nation's Christmas Tree is located in General Grant National Park in Sanger, California. The huge Sequoia was given this honor on Christmas Day, 1925. It measures 267 feet high and 107 feet around and is 3,500 years old. And for more than thirty years, the Canadian province of Nova Scotia has donated a giant Christmas tree to the people of Boston, as a thank you for the city's help after a harbor explosion in 1917 devastated the province's capital, Halifax.

The first church in this country to display a decorated tree was that of pastor Henry Schwan in Cleveland, Ohio, in 1851. President and Mrs. Franklin Pierce were the first to popularize the Christmas tree in the White House, beginning in 1856.

Christmas Ornaments

Originally, Christmas trees were the means by which presents were displayed on Christmas morning before their owners claimed them. Small toys, candies, and other treats were hung on the boughs; children would awaken and strip the tree. The earliest Christmas ornaments thus consisted of edible goodies, typically fruits and nuts; eventually, these made way for cookies, candy, and cakes. Flowers and paper decorations provided nonedible beauty.

Candy canes appear to have originated in seventeenth-century Germany, when the choirmaster at Cologne's cathedral gave candy sticks shaped like a shepherd's crook to children attending Christmas ceremonies. They debuted in America in the mid-1850s, but didn't gain their red stripe until the early 1900s.

The first commercial ornaments for Christmas trees were actually hollow, brightly colored containers that held good things to eat. The most popular of these was probably the cornucopia. When the goodies got too heavy for the tree, German glassblowers began manufacturing the first glass ornaments. But these, and other purely decorative elements, would not be the main attraction of the Christmas tree for some years.

Bringing Nature Inside

While the Christmas tree forms the focal point of holiday greenery, it's not the only piece of nature that people bring inside. At a time of the year when winter brings darker, colder days to much of the northern hemisphere, it's a treat to bring color into your home in the form of natural beauty.

Of course, those who celebrate Christmas in warm weather don't depend so much on greenery to decorate their holiday as Europeans and those living in colder climates. The Christmas bell (bell-shaped flowers) and the Christmas bush (little red flowers) are common Christmas sights in Australia, while the poinsettia abounds in Mexico during the holiday season.

The Legend of the Poinsettia

The legend of the plant now associated so strongly with Christmas arose years ago in Mexico, where it was traditional to leave gifts on the altar for Jesus on Christmas Eve. As the story goes, among a group of worshipers one night was a poor boy that had no present. Upset by his inability to provide a gift, the boy knelt outside the church window and prayed. In the spot where he knelt sprang a beautiful plant with vibrant red leaves. In Mexico, this plant is called the Flower of the Holy Night.

Christmas Spirit

The first American Ambassador to Mexico (1825–1829), Dr. Joel Roberts Poinsett, was so impressed by the vibrant plant that Mexicans called the Flower of the Holy Night that he brought it to America, where it was subsequently renamed in his honor.

With 80 percent of flowering poinsettias grown in Encinitas, California, this city just north of San Diego is known as the poinsettia capital of the world. Although traditionally red, the flower now comes in paler varieties as well, including pink and white.

The Yule Log

The tradition of the Yule log has very deep pagan roots. Celts, Teutons, and Druids burned the massive logs in winter ceremonies in celebration of the sun. The selection of each season's Yule log was of the highest importance and surrounded by ceremony, as the log was to start the celebration fires and last for the duration of the winter festival.

In the Christian era, the log was often cut on February 2 (Candlemas Day), then set outside to dry during the late spring and summer; sometimes it was soaked in spices and decorated with greenery. Often a piece of the previous year's log was used to light the new log. In Scandinavia, this saved piece had the additional significance of representing goodwill from Thor. Scandinavians believed that Thor's lighting bolt would not strike burned wood and that their houses were safe from lightning as long as they had this Yule brand.

When Christianity emerged in Europe, the Yule log remained popular in England and Scandinavia. In order to justify this pagan ritual, church officials gave it a new significance, that of the light that came from Heaven when Christ was born. The log was lit on Christmas Eve and left burning throughout the twelve days of Christmas.

In some parts of France, the Yule log was presented as the source of children's gifts. The log was covered with cloth and brought into the house, where the children whacked it with sticks, beseeching it to bring forth presents. When no presents came, the children were sent outside to confess the sins they had committed that year; when they returned, the log was uncovered, surrounded by gifts.

In the American South, plantation slaves always tried to select the biggest possible Yule log. As long as the log burned, the slaves had to be paid for any work they did.

Changes brought by the Industrial Revolution finally made the Yule Log impractical. Few had the time or space for the preparations it required, and the small fireplaces of the city could not accommodate such a massive thing. Like the boar's head, the huge Yule log became, for most people, an emblem of the past.

It does, however, live on in the tradition of a delicious Christmas dessert: a cake rolled into the shape of a log, covered with chocolate icing, and decorated with greenery and icing sugar. You can find it in many countries, particularly England and France.

The Bird's Christmas Tree

Also known as the Sheaf of Grain, the Bird's Christmas Tree is a Scandinavian custom. A sheaf of grain is hung on a pole on Christmas Eve or Christmas Day as a way of sharing the Christmas spirit with the animals. Including the animals in Christmas is very important in Scandinavia, as it is believed that kindness to animals will help to ensure a prosperous new year.

Boughs of Holly

In ancient times, holly was thought to be magical because of its shiny leaves and its ability to bear fruit in winter. Some believed it contained a syrup that cured coughs; others hung it over their beds to produce good dreams. The plant was a popular Saturnalia gift among the Romans, who later brought holly to England, where it was also considered sacred.

In medieval times, holly, along with ivy, became the subject of many Christmas songs. Some of these songs gave the holly and ivy genders (holly is male, ivy female), while other, more religious, songs and poems portray the holly berry as a symbol of Christ.

Eternal Ivy

In pagan times, ivy was closely associated with Bacchus, the god of wine, and played a big part in all festivals in which he figured. English tavern keepers eventually adopted ivy as a symbol and featured it on their signs. Its festive past has not kept ivy from being incorporated into modern Christian celebrations, however: It represents the promise of eternal life.

Mistletoe

To this day, mistletoe—a parasitic plant that grows on oak and other nonevergreen trees—is the only form of greenery not allowed inside many Christian churches during the holiday season. That's because although other greenery was also used in pagan festivals, mistletoe was actually worshiped.

Both Druids and Romans considered the plant sacred, as a healing plant and a charm against evil. Mistletoe was thought to be the connection between earth and the heavens, because it grew without roots, as if by magic. It was also considered a symbol of peace; warring soldiers who found themselves under mistletoe quickly put down their weapons and made a temporary truce. In a related custom, ancient Britons hung mistletoe in their doorways to keep evil away. Those who entered the house safely were given a welcome kiss.

While the custom of kissing under the mistletoe lost popularity in most other countries, it remained popular in England and the United States. Today, most consider mistletoe an excuse for kissing and nothing more, but some people in France still brew it as a cure for stomachaches.

The Kissing Bough

The kissing bough was very popular, particularly in England, before the heyday of the Christmas tree. Though its name might suggest otherwise, it wasn't made just out of mistletoe, but included holly, ivy, and other evergreens. Shaped in a double hoop with streamers flowing from the top, the kissing bough was decorated with apples, pears, ribbon, and lighted candles. As with plain mistletoe, anyone found under the bough was to be kissed right away!

Sending Christmas Wishes

Although the electronic age is beginning to replace the signing, addressing, and sending of paper Christmas cards, many people hold onto this custom with fervor. They'll carefully choose a design that represents their favorite interpretation of the holiday, and add greetings for the friends and family that will receive it as a welcome connection to loved ones both near and far.

Christmas Cards

The distinction of having created the first Christmas card is usually given to John Calcott Horsley of England. Horsley printed his card in 1843 for Sir Henry Cole, the friend who had given him the idea. The card looked much like a postcard and consisted of three panels. The central panel pictured the typical English family of the day enjoying the holiday (this panel caused some controversy, as it showed a child drinking wine). The other panels depicted acts of charity, so important to the Victorian Christmas spirit. The card's inscription read "Merry Christmas and a Happy New Year to You." A thousand copies of the card were printed, selling for one shilling apiece.

But around the same time, two other men, W. A. Dobson and Reverend Edward Bradley, were designing cards and sending them to their friends. These cards, however, were handmade instead of printed, which is why the credit generally goes to Horsley.

Christmas cards, which tended not to be particularly religious, soon became the popular means of sending holiday greetings among the Victorians. The launch of the penny post in 1840 made it affordable for people to send greetings by mail, and the invention of the steam press made mass production of these cards possible.

At one time in Britain, the Post Office (also known as the Royal Mail) delivered on Christmas Day, which is when most people received their cards. As could be expected, this process soon became too much for postal workers, who eventually got the day off.

Across the water in America, the Christmas card was popularized by the firm of Marcus Ward & Co., and later by Louis Prang, a German-born printer and lithographer. Prang first turned his talents toward Christmas cards in 1875, designing and printing them from his Roxbury, Massachusetts, shop. Prang created chromos, as he called the colored lithographs, in eight colors. His cards depicted Nativity scenes, family Christmas gatherings, nature scenes, and later, Santa.

The beauty of Prang's cards did much to ensure their popularity, but so did his marketing technique. He would hold contests all across the country, offering prizes for the best card designs, which spurred public interest. Prang's cards went strong until 1890, when the states began importing cheaper cards from German manufacturers. Americans reclaimed the market twenty years later.

Christmas Seals

Like Easter, Christmas has a special seal dedicated to helping those in need. The Christmas Seal, which changes in design each year, was originated in Denmark in 1903 by postal worker Einar Holboell, who felt there should be a special stamp to benefit tuberculosis sufferers. The first seal was printed in 1904, with a picture of Queen Louise of Denmark; more than four million were sold. Sweden followed suit that same year, and Norway had its own seals by 1905.

The original American Seal, designed in 1907 by Emily Bissell, pictured holly, a cross, and the words "Merry Christmas and Happy New Year." By 1908, the Christmas Seal was circulating nationwide for the benefit of various charities. In 1919, the National Tuberculosis Association (later the American Lung Association) became the seal's sole beneficiary. That same year, the double-barred Cross of Lorraine became the seal's signature element.

The Christmas Seal is popular in America largely due to the efforts of Emily Bissell, state secretary of the Red Cross in Wilmington, Delaware. Word of the success of the seal in Scandinavia had spread to America, and Bissell sought to use such a seal to keep a local tuberculosis treatment center open.

Christmas Stamps

Christmas stamps, not to be confused with Christmas Seals, are issued seasonally by the post offices of various countries to give the mail some holiday spirit. The stamps generally feature different religious or secular Christmas scenes each year, and are often eagerly awaited by stamp collectors.

The very first Christmas stamps were printed in Canada in 1898; the United States did not have its own until 1962. For some years, the most popular stamp in U.S. history—until the Elvis stamp came along in the 1990s—was a Christmas stamp picturing a reproduction of the Renaissance painting *The Adoration of the Shepherds*, by the Italian painter Giorgione; more than one billion were printed.

The Christmas Bonus and Other Economic Niceties

The Christmas bonus was first instituted by department store owner F. W. Woolworth in 1899. Woolworth, savvy to the ever-growing fiscal importance of the Christmas shopping season, decided to take steps to ensure that his stores ran smoothly through the frenzied buying time. Working under the assumption that happy workers are reliable and productive workers, Woolworth gave a bonus of $5 to each employee for every year of service, bonuses not to exceed $25—quite a sum of money in those days.

In 1876, publishing magnate James Gordon Bennett, Jr., left his breakfast waiter a Christmas tip of $6,000—perhaps $200,000 in today's funds. Initially, the flabbergasted waiter gave the money to his supervisor to return, but Bennett later insisted that he had meant to leave the sum. The end result was that Bennett's tip was—and is—among the most generous on record.

The holiday bonus has a cousin, the Christmas tip, extended to letter carriers, newspaper deliverers, apartment-complex employees, and other workers. Both are outgrowths of the English tradition of giving to the needy on Boxing Day.

The custom of giving employees the day off for Christmas was apparently not observed in the United States until about 1875. Up until that time, nearly all workers were expected to report as usual—unless the holiday fell on a Sunday, of course. (No matter the time of year, merchants were forbidden to sell their wares on the Sabbath, although some were arrested for trying to do so during the holiday season.) Store clerks of the era were paid by the day, and worked thousands of unpaid overtime hours during the holiday rush each year. Woolworth's later generosity toward his workers was the culmination of a long series of concessions by the owners of retail establishments to harried store workers.

5

Gift Giving

The giving and receiving of gifts has become one of the central themes of the modern American Christmas. Indeed, a strong holiday selling season often means the difference between a good and a bad year for retailers. There was, however—not so long ago—a time when Christmas involved no gift exchange whatever, and in some countries that remains the case. The union of Christmas and gift giving was a gradual one, and, in fact, the full story of the bright packages beneath the tree begins in the days before the birth of Christ.

Gifts and Celebrations, Old and New

In ancient Rome, gifts were exchanged during the Saturnalia and New Year's celebrations. At first these gifts were very simple—a few twigs from a sacred grove, statues of gods, food, and the like. Many gifts were in the form of vegetation in honor of the fertility goddess Strenia. During the Northern European Yule, fertility was celebrated with gifts made from wheat products, such as bread and alcohol. As time went on, gifts became more elaborate and less edible.

Like many old customs, gift exchange was difficult to get rid of, even as Christianity spread and gained official status. Early church leaders tried to outlaw it, but the people cherished it too much to let it go. So instead, as with other customs, church leaders sought a Christian justification for the practice. They found it in the Magi's act of bearing gifts to the infant Jesus, and in the concept that Christ was a gift from God to the world, bringing in turn the gift of redemption and everlasting life.

Festive Fact

While most giving was done on a voluntary basis, some leaders did their best to ensure a plentiful season for themselves. One year, Emperor Caligula of Rome declared that he would be receiving presents on New Year's Day; he then ridiculed gifts he deemed inadequate or inappropriate. And Henry III closed down the merchants of England one December because he was not impressed with the amount of their monetary gifts.

After Christianity had established itself throughout Europe, Christmas celebrations were quite common; gift giving as a component of Christmas Day, however, was not. The concept of a gift exchange on the holiday itself remained more the exception than the rule, and much of the gift giving at that time was confined to New Year's, as in the days of the ancient Romans. Some countries, particularly those under Spanish cultural influence, saved gift giving for Epiphany (January 6), the day marking the visit of the Magi to Jesus.

England Leads the Way

Even though the roots of the Christmas present extend to ancient times, the gift-giving tradition of today owes perhaps the most to Victorian England. The Victorians, who brought a renewed warmth and spirit to Christmas after it had experienced a long period of decline, made the idea of family (and particularly children) an integral part of the celebration. Also important to them was the act of helping the less fortunate in society. Friendliness and charity filled many hearts during their Christmas season, so giving gifts was a natural.

No one personifies "It's the thought that counts" more than the Victorians. To them, the act of giving was far more important than the present, and the ultimate reason for giving a gift was as an expression of kindness, a sentiment that tied in nicely with the historical tradition of the holiday.

Accordingly, Victorians surrounded the act of gift giving with a great deal of ingenuity and merriment; simply tearing into a cache of wrapped boxes would have been to miss the point. Far more thought and preparation were in order during the holiday season.

Cobweb parties, for instance, were lots of messy fun. Each family member was assigned a color, then shown to a room crisscrossed with yarn of various colors. They then had to follow their assigned color through the web of yarn until they reached the present tied to the end. Yarn was also used to wrap small gifts: The ball was unwound, then rewound to conceal the present.

The Christmas pie was another favorite diversion, although it was not exactly edible. Small gifts were concealed in a large bowl of grain. After Christmas dinner, everyone gathered around the pie and took turns taking a spoonful. Whatever treat was in your spoonful was yours to keep.

Though Victorian gift giving was filled with the spirit of Christmas, much of the actual exchange was still done on New Year's Day. It was only in the late 1800s that the custom was finally transferred to Christmas.

Across the pond, Christmas was taking a similar shape in America, where the Victorians greatly influenced the American Christmas, including gift giving. America expanded on the concept with the addition of Santa Claus, however, whose forerunner, St. Nicholas, was legendary for his generosity. The association with gifts was a natural one, and soon, Santa or one of his earlier incarnations became responsible for the presents left in an ever-increasing number of stockings.

The Economics of Christmas

By the late nineteenth century, the simple and essentially nonmaterialistic gift-giving tradition had begun to fade. Christmas had come face to face with commercialism, and the new message was: Buy. It wasn't long before shopping and the idea of gifts had woven itself into the fabric of the holiday. This transition was encouraged by merchants (and everyone else in the developing economies of Europe and America) who stood to benefit from a year-end buying binge.

It was—and is—an open question whether this development did more harm than good to the holiday. Skeptics wonder whether the emphasis on buying, shopping, and getting ultimately brings more happiness or disappointment—especially to those who can afford little.

Others have found a new and robust variation on the holiday spirit in the shopping-related hustle and bustle around Christmastime. Perhaps, they argue, it is too much to expect that Christmas, having adapted itself to so many civilizations over the years, wouldn't be affected by the modern consumer culture in which we live. In the end, it's likely that the best way to approach Christmas gift giving is with both viewpoints in mind.

What Was Given?

Back in the days of Ancient Rome, a citizen might have received the makings of a nice salad for Saturnalia; a Victorian chap might have had the pleasure of a new pipe or a snuff box. But what about here in North America?

Twentieth-Century Toys

In the first part of the twentieth century, gifts were a great deal simpler than they are today. Clothing was a staple for adults and children, with the latter getting a toy or two for enjoyment. The first decade of the past century, however, gave us two childhood classics: the Crayola crayon, which was first produced in 1903; and the teddy bear, which came along four years later.

The teddy bear was created by Morris and Rosie Michtom, after they saw a cartoon of the day that detailed a hunting trip taken by President Teddy Roosevelt. The president had refused to shoot a bear that had been tied up for him; in the cartoon, the bear was portrayed as tiny and helpless.

After Rosie Michtom made a stuffed bear cub in 1907, her husband displayed it in the window of his store, along with a cartoon of Roosevelt saving a bear cub, which had inspired her. The bear was very popular, and eventually the Michtoms received permission from the president himself to mass market the stuffed cubs as Teddy Bears.

For youngsters who liked to tinker, Tinker Toys came along in 1914. Raggedy Ann dolls were mass produced in 1918, becoming one of the more popular dolls of that time. In general, dolls and games were favorites during this period, as they still are today. Other highlights of this time were rideable toys: sleds, rocking horses, and red wagons.

Toys of the Great Depression

Despite the Depression of the 1930s, toy manufacturers continued to come up with occasional classics that people somehow managed to scrape enough money together to buy. Yo-yos were quite popular, and the Red Ryder BB gun was a big seller. Introduced in 1938, the gun got its name from a comic-book character, one of the first of a very long (and ever-growing) list of toys based on comic, television, or movie characters.

Guns as a whole were popular at this time, along with other cowboy and cops-and-robbers paraphernalia. War toys were also big sellers, especially toy soldiers. A fascination with science and science fiction also seems to have begun in this period, as witnessed by the popularity of chemistry sets and fantasy stories.

After America made it through the Depression and World War II, the country began to prosper as never before. Industry and technology were in high gear, and more and better jobs meant Americans had more discretionary income to spend on things like Christmas gifts. It was the beginning of a glorious time for toys.

The Postwar Toy Boom

The number of American children exploded in the years after the war, and so, not surprisingly, did the national appetite for toys. Some of the most enduring playthings of today—such as the Etch-A-Sketch, Play Doh modeling clay, and the Barbie doll—were introduced in the decade and a half following the end of World War II.

In the late 1940s and early 1950s, science-fiction toys remained popular, while toys connected with comic characters and other media-driven figures began to loom large in the market. Television left its mark on the gift-giving tradition in the 1950s, as toys associated with characters benefited by being seen by a steadily larger audience. For a time, Howdy Doody presents were all the rage. Dolls of Howdy, Clarabell, Princess Summer-Fall-Winter-Spring, puzzles, sewing kits, stuffed animals, comic books, paint sets, and more made their way under a lot of Christmas trees in the early 1950s.

Not all the big gifts were connected to Howdy and his gang, of course. A Jackie Robinson doll was quite popular in 1950. This may have been the first mainstream doll portraying an African American that did not parody racial characteristics.

The bestselling toy of 1953 was an update of that 1930s classic, the Red Ryder No. 960 Noisemaker BB gun. It did everything a real BB gun did—except shoot. Perhaps the most popular toy for boys in the early 1950s was the electric train. These were times to remember for Lionel, American Flyer, and Marx.

Buck Rogers had a very big year in 1954, but the adventurer was outdone the following year, when Davy Crockett coonskin hats and guns topped many a boy's Christmas list. Crockett merchandise was incredibly popular. One story has it that a tent manufacturer, stuck with thousands of unsold units, stenciled the words "Davy Crockett" on each—and got rid of them all in a matter of days. Total 1955 retail sales of Crockett-related items was estimated at a cool $100 million.

What else did the initial wave of Baby Boomers want for Christmas? The list from the decade of the 1950s includes: Silly Putty; Frisbees (originally called Pluto Platters); hula hoops; Mr. Potato Head sets; slot cars; Betsy Wetsy dolls; Lego blocks; the Game of Life; pogo sticks; matchbox cars; and, for the younger set, the classic Chatter telephone from Fisher-Price.

Barbie Takes Over

Although she made her debut in the 1950s, it was in the following decade that Barbie hit the big time. It's hard to fix a single event that marks Barbie's emergence as a perennial favorite, but she appeared in the Sears Christmas catalog for the first time in 1961. From that day to this, Barbie, Skipper, Ken, and their many companions and accessories (sold, as ever, separately) have brightened many a young girl's Christmas morning.

Barbie's male counterpart, G.I. Joe, enjoyed a similar robust popularity during the 1960s. Although he was put to rest in 1978, he later made a major comeback in the 1980s.

Other popular 1960s Christmas gifts included: Beatles records, coloring books, toy guitars, lunchboxes, and related merchandise; Hot Wheels miniature cars; the Super Ball; Instant Insanity, a colored cube game akin to the later Rubik's cube; Tonka trucks; and the Twister game (Right foot, green!).

Board games were also a very popular gift category in the 1960s. Strong sellers included: Clue, Risk, Candyland, Go to the Head of the Class, Cooties, Scrabble, Yahtzee, Operation!, Parcheesi, and Jeopardy (the Art Fleming, rather than Alex Trebek, incarnation). The Mousetrap game sold 1.2 million copies in 1963.

After about 1966, spy-related toys and dolls (or, to use the preferred terminology, action figures) were brisk-selling Christmas gifts. Products based on the James Bond movies and the television series *The Man from U.N.C.L.E.* were the hits in this category. Kids could go undercover with briefcases, cigarette cases, and fake lighters that concealed toy cameras and the like. Also available were lunch boxes, cars, puzzles, bubblegum cards, costumes, books, and records, all specially designed for the preteen espionage crowd.

By the middle 1960s, against the background of a supercharged economy and a generation that was beginning to rebel against the "establishment," the American middle class was buying for Christmas at a fevered pitch—and children weren't the only ones on the receiving end. Adults were indulging in some "toys" of their own, and not all of them were cheap. There were home steam baths and saunas, jewelry, and, for quiet (or not-so-quiet) evenings at home, newfangled color television sets. As one Chicago retailer put it, Americans were loaded.

And it seems that some retailers priced their merchandise based on that belief. For one Christmas buying season, Tiffany's in New York offered their upscale patrons the opportunity to purchase a $550 sterling-silver watering can. Neiman-Marcus's offerings included $300 lace hankies, $10,000 wristwatches, $20,000 teapots, and $125,000 diamond rings. Not to be outdone, San Francisco's Joseph Magnin sold three-liter flacons of Shalimar perfume for $2,500, to be delivered to the lucky recipient via Rolls-Royce.

Into the 1970s

The unparalleled prosperity of the middle 1960s yielded to social division, inflation, and an energy crisis in the 1970s. Despite all that, America still found the stamina to purchase Big Wheels, Inchworms, Huffy bikes, Mrs. Beasely Dolls, and Pitchback baseball. For adults, Christmas 1973 brought novelty "I Am Not a Crook" watches bearing an image of President Nixon, his eyes shifting back and forth with each movement of the second hand. Other memorable Christmas gifts of the era included eight-track cartridges and players, trolls with tufts of incandescent hair, and Super Spirographs.

The merchandising/mass-entertainment link reached new heights of commercial success as George Lucas's *Star Wars* movies launched scores of lucrative toys, books, and related paraphernalia. In a foreshadowing of the video boom to come, the first basic home arcade games appeared at the end of the decade. A television-friendly version of the arcade hit Pong (which seems quaint and simple by today's gaming standards) was a huge hit.

Christmas giving in the 1970s was also affected by fads (CB radios and pet rocks) and fashion diversions (puka-shell necklaces and mood rings), about which the less said, the better.

From the Cabbage Patch to Bart Simpson

In the 1980s, America entered the consumer-electronics age in earnest. Along with the usual stereo, photographic, and appliance electronics, there were now compact disc players, video cassette recorders, and sophisticated video games. It was during this decade, after a brief incursion by the ubiquitous Cabbage Patch Kids, that the word *video* began to figure prominently in just about anything that found its way to the top of the average kid's Christmas list.

In one year, the Nintendo company was responsible for three of the top-ten toys sold at retail, including the number-one item, the Nintendo Action Set. Coming years would bring Nintendo NES, Nintendo Super Mario Bros., Nintendo Game Boy, and Nintendo Game Genie, among countless other offerings. For a time, blinking, beeping video games of one brand or another (but usually Nintendo) were poised to take over every living room and young, unoccupied palm in the country. And then, it seemed, they did.

The 1980s marked the debut of the Teenage Mutant Ninja Turtles, whose reign would extend well into the next decade (and who are even now making a comeback attempt). Radioactive turtles may have seemed an implausible idea for a toy, game, film, and video juggernaut, but young boys had an insatiable appetite for the heroes.

Other popular toys from the 1980s included the talking Pee-Wee Herman doll, assorted Smurf paraphernalia, the Li'l Miss Makeup doll, and, for younger kids, the Fisher-Price tape recorder. For adults, top gifts of the era included exercise bikes, ice cream makers, Trivial Pursuit and Pictionary games, camcorders, VCRs, and, toward the end of the decade, laptop computers.

As the 1990s began, yet another television-spawned merchandising bonanza enjoyed remarkable popularity, but this time the innocence of Howdy Doody was nowhere to be found. Bart Simpson, who would probably do something quite rude to Howdy if he could get within a yard of him, became one of the biggest television stars in the country. Bart and his antiutopian world, complete with odd relatives, served as a weekly vehicle for biting social satire and remarks likely to embarrass teachers when repeated in class. Kids couldn't get enough of him, and cash registers rang up huge sales for his books, clothes, and other products during the holidays.

The 1980s success of high-tech toys carried over into the 1990s. Yet ironically, and despite white-hot sales of things like Power Rangers sets, the toys that have remained popular through decades of trends are the ones that don't require batteries, plugs, head-phones, or TV tie-ins—just imagination, the desire for fun, and maybe a few friends.

A New Century Dawns

The close of the twentieth century saw Beanie Babies and Tickle Me Elmo enjoying their time in the spotlight, but technology also remained strong: The transition was made from videos to DVDs and from portable CD players to digital audio players such as the Apple iPod and the MP3 player. For younger children, computer games often sported an educational factor, such as the LeapPad series of educational handheld games. For older children, computer simulation games have become ever-more sophisticated.

Toys based on movie and cartoon characters remain very popular, from Buzz Lightyear to Spiderman; however, the chances are good that children will, for the foreseeable future, wake up Christmas morning and find that Santa has left them one or two things that he left for their parents many years ago. As the twenty-first century unfolds, dolls, board games, building blocks, stuffed animals, Play Doh, Legos, cray-ons, and bicycles are sure to make that journey, too.

Great Gift Ideas

As Christmas draws near each year, it can be a challenge to come up with gift ideas for the hard-to-buy-for people on your list. Careful listening can provide hints: Keeping track of people's interests and wishes in a small notebook or com-puter file will automatically create a list of choices. You can even note items such as their favorite colors or the décor scheme in their home to help you when you're out shopping.

Shopping catalogs and, increasingly, the Internet are great sources for gift ideas. A few minutes spent browsing from the comfort of your own home can often save hours in the mall. Here are a few additional suggestions to kick start your gift list.

You say you're in trouble? It's Christmas Eve and you've forgotten someone? Don't panic. Buy a beautiful Christmas card and tuck a gift card inside for the recipient's favorite store. Many drugstores and supermarkets now have "gift-card malls," where you can select from a variety of gift cards loaded with a preset spending limit for other retail outlets.

Awesome Autos

If you have a gearhead that you're buying for, find out what their top auto picks are—limited-edition small-scale models of those vehicles may be a welcome gift at Christmas. For do-it-yourself types, check whether there are new tools that they need or whether they have a rolling platform that makes it so much easier to slide under vehicles when working on them. Even high-end seat covers or floor mats might be just the ticket.

For the Book Lover

There's no end to gift ideas for those who love books. A subscription to the *New York Times Literary Supplement* will help them keep up with all of the latest reviews. A beautiful blank-page notebook can be a place to write up their own book reviews or even jot down bon mots from the books they're currently reading. Gorgeous bookmarks don't cost very much, but will prove a lovely reminder of you each time a book is opened. And making a gift of the latest bestseller while it's still in hardcover can be a real treat.

Fashionista File

While it's definitely a challenge to buy clothes, jewelry, or accessories for those who are into fashion (unless you're a fashionista, too), there are other options. Try a beautiful, illustration-filled book that describes the history of fashion or focuses on a particular designer's work. And gift certificates or gift cards to a favorite store, especially if it's usually out of the recipient's budget range, will always be a worthy option. Booking a wardrobe or makeup makeover—if it's something that the recipient really wants—can leave a lasting (and positive) legacy.

In the Garden

Even when many parts of the country are covered in snow, gardeners don't forget that blooms will appear with spring's milder weather. Reward their time outside with pretty and practical gardening gloves to protect their hands and soap and moisturizer sets designed to soothe and rejuvenate. Kneeling mats, ergonomically designed garden tools, and gift certificates for local nurseries (to be used as soon as planting can be carried out) are also good ideas, as are blank journals in which to chart the growth of the garden each year.

Kitchen Helpers

More people are spending quality time in the kitchen these days, experimenting with recipes that span the globe. As a result, there are kitchen gadgets galore to thrill the budding chef on your list, from stainless steel garlic presses to silicone heat- and stain-resistant utensils. Consider giving a blank book, in which your recipient can enter favorite recipes, or even gather some family favorites to give to them. Cooking lessons or tickets for local wine tastings might also be very welcome under the tree.

Movie Magic

Try the DVD of *Citizen Kane* (considered one of the greatest American films of all time), perhaps even packaged with *Plan Nine from Outer Space* (considered one of the worst American films of all time). Gift certificates for movie-rental outlets or local movie theaters can give a gift that lasts all year long: Try packaging the gift with bags of microwave popcorn or movie-star-style sunglasses, just for fun!

The Great Outdoors

If you're shopping for someone who loves the outdoors, just head to the nearest store (online or in person) that specializes in their activity of choice, whether it's camping, hiking, or fishing. You'll find plenty of items, large and small, to fill their stockings: Stuff bags are great for holding all kinds of gear; hiking poles (that look like ski poles) make walking on uneven surfaces easier; and specialized clothing (such as padded socks that wick moisture away from the foot) can make their time outdoors more enjoyable.

Sports Nuts

Tickets to see a favorite sports team play will score you big points, especially if they're packaged with sports memorabilia or merchandise from that team. A program from a particularly important game, perhaps framed and signed, might be a big win, too. Also try books about particular teams or sports, or items that will make time in stadiums or arenas more comfortable, such as seat cushions and binoculars.

The Traveler

You won't go wrong with travel books—guidebooks for their next trip, coffee-table books about a favorite destination, or literary travel accounts (Bill Bryson is a great author for humorous approaches to travel). Blank journals for recipients to keep track of their own vacations are also fun, as are travel gadgets such as phrase books, electronic translators, digital audio players, electrical converters and adapters, luggage straps, neck pillows, and map/passport holders.

Gifts That Keep On Giving

For the person who has everything, or the gift giver who wants a gift that keeps on giving, there are any number of charitable or nonprofit organizations to choose from. You can adopt an animal from a zoo or a wildlife association, for example, or contribute to building funds, homeless shelters, health research, arts foundations, and so much more in the gift recipient's name. Such gifts often include tickets to fundraising events or discounts on museum gift-shop merchandise, which serve as ways to extend the gift even further. And they're a wonderful way to recognize the spirit of the Christmas season.

6

The Stories of Christmas

The classic Christmas tales that you'll find in this chapter highlight the season's most wonderful qualities: faith, hope, generosity, and the warmth of the human spirit. Some are short, others are longer, but all of them would make ideal read-aloud stories to share with your family, whether you tackle a few pages a day, or an entire story. Make some hot chocolate, tuck yourselves into the sofa, and choose your favorite story to begin.

The Little Women's Christmas

Louisa May Alcott

Published in 1868 and set in New England during the Civil War, Little Women *was an instant success, particularly with female readers. "The Little Women's Christmas" provides excerpts from the book's first two chapters: "Playing Pilgrims" and "A Merry Christmas," in which the little women remind us that even a penniless Christmas can be cause for celebration—if it is filled with selfless generosity, love, and faith.*

"Christmas won't be Christmas without any presents," grumbled Jo, lying on the rug.

"It's so dreadful to be poor!" sighed Meg, looking down at her old dress.

"I don't think it's fair for some girls to have lots of pretty things, and other girls nothing at all," added little Amy, with an injured sniff.

"We've got father, and mother, and each other, anyhow," said Beth, contentedly, from her corner.

The four young faces on which the firelight shone brightened at the cheerful words, but darkened again as Jo said sadly, "We haven't got father, and shall not have him for a long time." She didn't say "perhaps never," but each silently added it, thinking of father far away, where the fighting was.

Nobody spoke for a minute; then Meg said in an altered tone, "You know the reason mother proposed not having any presents this Christmas was because it's going to be a hard winter for every one; and she thinks we ought not to spend money for pleasure, when our men are suffering so in the army. We can't do much, but we can make our little sacrifices, and ought to do it gladly. But I am afraid

I don't," and Meg shook her head, as she thought regretfully of all the pretty things she wanted.

"But I don't think the little we should spend would do any good. We've each got a dollar, and the army wouldn't be much helped by our giving that. I agree not to expect anything from mother or you, but I do want to buy *Undine and Sintram* for myself; I've wanted it *so* long," said Jo, who was a bookworm.

"I planned to spend mine in new music," said Beth, with a little sigh, which no one heard but the hearth brush and kettleholder.

"I shall get a nice box of Faber's drawing pencils; I really need them," said Amy, decidedly.

"Mother didn't say anything about our money, and she won't wish us to give up everything. Let's each buy what we want, and have a little fun; I'm sure we grub hard enough to earn it," cried Jo, examining the heels of her boots in a gentlemanly manner.

"I know *I* do—teaching those dreadful children nearly all day, when I'm longing to enjoy myself at home," began Meg, in the complaining tone again.

"You don't have half such a hard time as I do," said Jo. "How would you like to be shut up for hours with a nervous, fussy old lady, who keeps you trotting, is never satisfied, and worries you till you're ready to fly out of the window or box her ears?"

"It's naughty to fret, but I do think washing dishes and keeping things tidy is the worst work in the world. It makes me cross; and my hands get so stiff, I can't practice good a bit." And Beth looked at her rough hands with a sigh that any one could hear that time.

"I don't believe any of you suffer as I do," cried Amy; "for you don't have to go to school with impertinent girls, who plague you if you don't know your lessons, and laugh at your dresses, and label your father if he isn't rich, and insult you when your nose isn't nice."

"If you mean *libel* I'd say so, and not talk about *labels*, as if Pa was a pickle-bottle," advised Jo, laughing.

"I know what I mean, and you needn't be 'statirical' about it. It's proper to use good words, and improve your *vocabilary*," returned Amy, with dignity.

"Don't peck at one another, children," said Meg.

It was a comfortable old room, though the carpet was faded and the furniture was plain, for a good picture or two hung on the walls, books filled the recesses, chrysanthemums and Christmas roses bloomed in the windows, and a pleasant atmosphere of home peace pervaded it.

Margaret, the eldest of the four, was sixteen, and very pretty. Fifteen-year-old Jo was tall, thin and brown, and reminded one of a colt; for she never seemed to know what to do with her long limbs, which were very much in her way. Elizabeth—or Beth, as every one called her—was a rosy, smooth-haired, bright-eyed girl of thirteen. Amy, though the youngest, was a most important person, in her own opinion at least.

The clock struck six; and, having swept up the hearth, Beth put a pair of slippers down to warm. Somehow the sight of the old shoes had a good effect upon the girls, for Mother was coming, and every one brightened to welcome her.

"They are quite worn out; Marmee must have a new pair."

"I thought I'd get her some with my dollar," said Beth.

"No, I shall!" cried Amy.

"I'm the oldest," began Meg, but Jo cut in with a decided—"I'm the man of the family, now Papa is away, and *I* shall provide the slippers, for he told me to take special care of Mother while he was gone."

"I'll tell you what we'll do," said Beth; "let's each get her something for Christmas, and not get anything for ourselves."

"That's like you, dear! What will we get?" exclaimed Jo.

Every one thought soberly for a minute; then Meg announced, as if the idea was suggested by the sight of her own pretty hands, "I shall give her a nice pair of gloves."

"Army shoes, best to be had," cried Jo.

"Some handkerchiefs, all hemmed," said Beth.

"I'll get a little bottle of Cologne; she likes it, and it won't cost much, so I'll have some left to buy something for me," added Amy.

"How will we give the things?" asked Meg.

"Put 'em on the table, and bring her in and see her open the bundles," answered Jo.

"Well, dearies, how have you got on today?" said a cheery voice at the door. "There was so much to do, getting the boxes ready to go tomorrow, that I didn't come home to dinner. Has any one called, Beth? How is your cold, Meg? Jo, you look tired to death. Come and kiss me, baby."

While making these maternal inquiries Mrs. March got her wet things off, her hot slippers on, and sitting down in the easy chair, drew Amy to her lap, preparing to enjoy the happiest hour of her busy day. The girls flew about, trying to make things comfortable, each in her own way. Meg arranged the tea table; Jo brought wood and set chairs, dropping, overturning, and clattering everything she touched; Beth trotted to and fro between parlor and kitchen, quiet and busy; while Amy gave directions to every one, as she sat with her hands folded.

As they gathered about the table, Mrs. March said, with a particularly happy face, "I've got a treat for you after supper."

A quick, bright smile went round like a streak of sunshine. Beth clapped her hands, regardless of the hot biscuit she held and Jo tossed up her napkin, crying, "A letter! A letter! Three cheers for Father!"

"Yes, a nice long letter. He is well, and thinks he shall get through the cold season better than we feared. He sends all sorts of loving wishes for Christmas, and an especial message to our girls," said Mrs. March, patting her pocket as if she had got a treasure there.

"Hurry up, and get done. Don't stop to quirk your little finger, and prink over your plate, Amy," cried Jo, choking in her tea, and dropping her bread, butter side down, on the carpet, in her haste to get at the treat.

Beth ate no more, but crept away, to sit in her shadowy corner and brood over the delight to come, till the others were ready.

"I think it was so splendid in Father to go as a chaplain when he was too old to be drafted, and not strong enough for a soldier," said Meg warmly.

"When will he come home, Marmee?" asked Beth, with a little quiver in her voice.

"Not for many months, dear, unless he is sick. He will stay and do his work faithfully as long as he can, and we won't ask for him back a minute sooner than he can be spared. Now come and hear the letter."

They all drew to the fire, Mother in the big chair with Beth at her feet, Meg and Amy perched on either arm of the chair, and Jo leaning on the back, where no one would see any sign of emotion if the letter should happen to be touching.

Very few letters were written in those hard times that were not touching, especially those which fathers sent home. In this one little was said of the hardships endured, the dangers faced, or the homesickness conquered; it was a cheerful, hopeful letter, full of lively descriptions of camp life, marches, and military news; and only at the end did the writer's heart overflow with fatherly love and longing for the little girls at home.

"Give them all my dear love and a kiss. Tell them I think of them by day, pray for them by night, and find my best comfort in their affection at all times. A year seems very long to wait before I see them, but remind them that while we wait we may all work, so that these hard days need not be wasted. I know they will remember all I said to them, that they will be loving children to you, will do their duty faithfully, fight their bosom enemies bravely, and conquer themselves so beautifully, that when I come back to them I may be fonder and prouder than ever of my little women."

Everybody sniffed when they came to that part; Jo wasn't ashamed of the great tear that dropped off the end of her nose, and Amy never minded the rumpling of her curls as she hid her face on her mother's shoulder and sobbed out, "I *am* a selfish pig! But I'll truly try to be better, so he mayn't be disappointed in me by and by."

"We all will!" cried Meg. "I think too much of my looks, and hate to work, but won't any more, if I can help it."

"I'll try and be what he loves to call me, 'a little woman,' and not be rough and wild; but do my duty here instead of wanting to be somewhere else," said Jo, thinking that keeping her temper at home was a much harder task than facing a rebel or two down South.

Beth said nothing, but wiped away her tears with the blue army-sock, and began to knit with all her might, losing no time in doing the duty that lay nearest her, while she resolved in her quiet little soul to be all that Father hoped to find her when the year brought round the happy coming home.

Jo was the first to wake in the gray dawn of Christmas morning. No stockings hung at the fireplace, and for a moment she felt as much disappointed as she did long ago, when her little sock fell down because it was so crammed with goodies. Then she remembered her mother's promise, and slipping her hand under her pillow, drew out a little crimson-covered book. She knew it very well, for it was that beautiful old story of the best life ever lived, and Jo felt that it was a true guidebook for any pilgrim going the long journey. She woke Meg with a "Merry Christmas," and bade her see what was under her pillow. A green-covered book appeared, with the same picture inside, and a few words written by their mother, which made their one present very precious in their eyes. Presently Beth and Amy woke, to rummage and find their little books also—one dove-colored, the other blue; and all sat looking at and talking about them, while the East grew rosy with the coming day.

"Girls," said Meg, seriously, looking from the tumbled head beside her to the two little night-capped ones in the room beyond, "mother wants us to read and love and mind these books, and we must begin at once. We used to be faithful about it; but since Father went away, and all this war trouble unsettled us, we have neglected many things. You can do as you please; but I shall keep my book on the table here, and read a little every morning as soon as I wake, for I know it will do me good, and help me through the day."

Then she opened her new book and began to read. Jo put her arm around her, and, leaning cheek to cheek, read also, with the quiet expression so seldom seen on her restless face.

"How good Meg is! Come, Amy, let's do as they do. I'll help you with the hard words, and they'll explain things if we don't understand," whispered Beth, very impressed by the pretty books and her sister's example.

"I'm glad mine is blue," said Amy; and then the rooms were very still while the pages were softly turned, and the winter sunshine crept in to touch the bright heads and serious faces with a Christmas greeting.

"Where is Mother?" asked Meg as she and Jo ran down to thank her for their gifts, half an hour later.

"Goodness only knows. Some poor creeter come a-beggin', and your ma went straight off to see what was needed. There never *was* such a woman for givin' away vittles and drink, clothes, and firin'," replied Hannah, who had lived with the family since Meg was born, and was considered by them all more as a friend than a servant.

"She will be back soon, I guess; so do your cakes, and have everything ready," said Meg, looking over the presents which were collected in a basket and kept under the sofa, ready to be produced at the proper time. "Why, where is Amy's bottle of Cologne?" she added, as the little flask did not appear.

"She took it out a minute ago, and went off with it to put a ribbon on it, or some such notion," replied Jo, dancing about the room to take the first stiffness off the new army-slippers.

"How nice my handkerchiefs look, don't they? Hannah washed and ironed them for me, and I marked them all myself," said Beth, looking proudly at the somewhat uneven letters which had cost her such labor.

"Bless the child, she's gone and put 'Mother' on them instead of 'M. March'; how funny!" cried Jo, taking up one.

"Isn't it right? I thought it was better to do it so because Meg's initials are 'M. M.' and I don't want any one to use these but Marmee," said Beth, looking troubled.

"It's all right, dear, and a very pretty idea; quite sensible, too, for no one can ever mistake them now. It will please her very much, I know," said Meg, with a frown for Jo, and a smile for Beth.

'There's Mother; hide the basket, quick!' cried Jo, as a door slammed, and steps sounded in the hall.

Amy came in hastily, and looked rather abashed when she saw her sisters all waiting for her.

"Where have you been, and what are you hiding behind you?" asked Meg, surprised to see, by her hood and cloak, that lazy Amy had been out so early.

"Don't laugh at me, Jo. I didn't mean any one should know till the time came. I only meant to change the little bottle for a big one, and I gave *all* my money to get it, and I'm truly trying not to be selfish any more."

As she spoke, Amy showed the handsome flask which replaced the cheap one; and looked so earnest and humble in her little effort to forget herself, that Meg hugged her on the spot, and Jo pronounced her "a trump," while Beth ran to the window, and picked her finest rose to ornament the stately bottle.

"You see, I felt ashamed of my present, after reading and talking about being good this morning, so I ran round the corner and changed it the minute I was up; and I'm glad, for mine is the handsomest now."

Another bang of the street-door sent the basket under the sofa, and the girls to the table eager for breakfast.

"Merry Christmas, Marmee! Lots of them! Thank you for our books; we read some, and mean to every day," they cried in chorus.

"Merry Christmas, little daughters! I'm glad you began at once, and hope you will keep on. But I want to say one word before we sit down. Not far away from here lies a poor woman with a little new-born baby. Six children are huddled into one bed to keep from freezing, for they have no fire. There is nothing to eat over there; and the oldest boy came to tell me they were suffering hunger and cold. My girls, will you give them your breakfast as a Christmas present?"

They were all unusually hungry, having waited nearly an hour, and for a minute no one spoke; only a minute, for Jo exclaimed impetuously, "I'm so glad you came before we began!"

"May I go and help carry the things to the poor little children?" asked Beth, eagerly.

"*I* shall take the cream and the muffins," added Amy, heroically giving up the articles she most liked.

Meg was already covering the buckwheats, and piling the bread into one big plate.

"I thought you'd do it," said Mrs. March, smiling as if satisfied. "You shall all go and help me, and when we come back we will have bread and milk for breakfast, and make it up at dinner-time."

They were soon ready, and the procession set out. Fortunately it was early, and they went through back streets, so few people saw them, and no one laughed at the funny party.

A poor, bare, miserable room it was, with broken windows, no fire, ragged bed-clothes, a sick mother, wailing baby, and a group of pale, hungry children cuddled under one old quilt, trying to keep warm. How the big eyes stared, and the blue lips smiled, as the girls went in!

"*Ach, mein Gott!* It is good angels come to us!" cried the poor woman, crying for joy.

"Funny angels in hoods and mittens," said Jo, and set them laughing.

In a few minutes it really did seem as if kind spirits had been at work there. Hannah, who had carried wood, made a fire, and stopped up the broken panes with old hats, and her own shawl. Mrs. March gave the mother tea and gruel, and comforted her with promises of help, while she dressed the little baby as tenderly as if it had been her own. The girls, meantime, spread the table, set the children round the fire, and fed them like so many hungry birds; laughing, talking, and trying to understand the funny broken English.

"*Das ist gut!*" "*Die angel-kinder!*" cried the poor things, as they ate, and warmed their purple hands at the comfortable blaze. The girls had never been called angel children before, and thought it very agreeable. That was a very happy breakfast, though they didn't get any of it; and when they went away, leaving comfort behind, I think there was not in all the city four merrier people than the hungry little girls who gave away their breakfasts, and contented themselves with bread and milk on Christmas morning.

"That's loving our neighbor better than ourselves, and I like it," said Meg, as they set out their presents, while their mother was upstairs collecting clothes for the poor Hummels.

Not a very splendid show, but there was a great deal of love done up in the few little bundles; and the tall vase of red roses, white chrysanthemums, and trailing vines, which stood in the middle, gave quite an elegant air to the table.

"She's coming! Strike up, Beth. Open the door, Amy. Three cheers for Marmee!" cried Jo, prancing about, while Meg went to conduct Mother to the seat of honor.

Beth played her gayest march, Amy threw open the door, and Meg enacted escort with great dignity. Mrs. March was both surprised and touched; and smiled with her eyes full as she examined her presents, and read the little notes which accompanied them. The slippers went on at once, a new handkerchief was slipped into her pocket, well scented with Amy's cologne, the rose was fastened in her bosom, and the nice gloves were pronounced "a perfect fit."

There was a good deal of laughing, and kissing, and explaining, in the simple, loving fashion which makes these home festivals so pleasant at the time and so sweet to remember long afterward.

Beth nestled up to her mother, and whispered softly, "I'm afraid Father isn't having such a merry Christmas as we are."

Born in Pennsylvania, Louisa May Alcott (1832–1888) lived much of her life in Concord, Massachusetts, a center of literary talent that included Ralph Waldo Emerson and Henry David Thoreau. She based the four sisters of Little Women on herself and her three sisters, breathing life and imagination into her characters' stories of growing up.

The Little Match Girl

Hans Christian Andersen

Reflecting the poverty from which Andersen himself came, "The Little Match Girl"

offers us a heroine who shows how faith makes it possible to transcend the hardships

of everyday life. The story has become one of the timeless classics of the holidays.

It was terribly cold and nearly dark on the last evening of the old year, and the snow was falling fast. In the cold and the darkness, a poor little girl, with bare head and naked feet, roamed through the streets. It is true she had on a pair of slippers when she left home, but they were not of much use. They were very large, so large, indeed, that they had belonged to her mother, and the poor little creature had lost them in running across the street to avoid two carriages that were rolling along at a terrible rate. One of the slippers she could not find, and a boy seized upon the other and ran away with it, saying that he could use it as a cradle, when he had children of his own.

So the little girl went on with her little naked feet, which were quite red and blue with the cold. In an old apron she carried a number of matches, and had a bundle of them in her hands. No one had bought anything of her the whole day, nor had anyone given her even a penny. Shivering with cold and hunger, she crept along; poor little child, she looked the picture of misery. The snowflakes fell on her long, fair hair, which hung in curls on her shoulders, but she regarded them not.

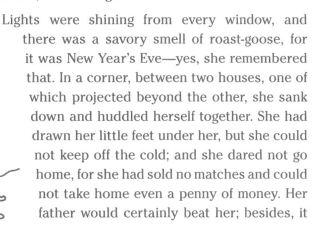

Lights were shining from every window, and there was a savory smell of roast-goose, for it was New Year's Eve—yes, she remembered that. In a corner, between two houses, one of which projected beyond the other, she sank down and huddled herself together. She had drawn her little feet under her, but she could not keep off the cold; and she dared not go home, for she had sold no matches and could not take home even a penny of money. Her father would certainly beat her; besides, it was almost as cold at home as here, for they had only the roof to cover them, through which the wind howled, although the largest holes had been stopped up with straw and rags.

Her little hands were almost frozen with the cold. Ah! Perhaps a burning match might be some good, if she could draw it from the bundle and strike it against the wall, just to warm her fingers. She drew one out—scratch!—how it sputtered as it burnt! It gave a warm, bright light, like a little candle, as she held her hand over it.

It really was a wonderful light. It seemed to the little girl that she was sitting by a large iron stove, with polished brass feet and a brass ornament. How the fire burned! And it seemed so beautifully warm that the child stretched out her feet as if to warm them, when, lo, the flame of the match went out, the stove vanished, and she had only the remains of the half-burnt match in her hand.

She rubbed another match on the wall. It burst into flame, and where its light fell upon the wall it became as transparent as a veil, and she could see into the room. The table was covered with a snowy white tablecloth, on which stood a splendid dinner service and a steaming roast goose, stuffed with apples and dried plums. And what was still more wonderful, the goose jumped down from the dish and waddled across the floor, with a knife and fork in its breast, to the little girl. Then the match went out, and there remained nothing but the thick, damp, cold wall before her.

She lighted another match, and then she found herself sitting under a beautiful Christmas tree. It was larger and more beautifully decorated than the one which she had seen through the glass door at the rich merchant's. Thousands of tapers were burning upon the green branches, and colored pictures, like those she had seen in the show-windows, looked down upon it all. The little one stretched out her hand toward them, and the match went out.

The Christmas lights rose higher and higher, till they looked to her like the stars in the sky. Then she saw a star fall, leaving behind it a bright streak of fire. "Someone is dying," thought the little girl, for her old grandmother, the only one who had ever loved her, and who was now dead, had told her that when a star falls, a soul was going up to God.

She again rubbed a match on the wall, and the light shone round her; in the brightness stood her old grandmother, clear and shining, yet mild and loving in her appearance. "Grandmother," cried the little one, "oh, take me with you: I know you will go away when the match burns out; you will vanish like the warm stove, the roast goose, and the large, glorious Christmas tree." And she made haste to light the whole bundle of matches, for she wished to keep her grandmother there. And the matches glowed with a light that was brighter than the noon-day.

Her grandmother had never appeared so large or beautiful. She took the little girl in her arms, and they both flew upwards in brightness and joy far above the earth, where there was neither cold nor hunger nor pain, for they were with God.

* * * * *

In the dawn of the morning, there lay the little one, with pale cheeks and smiling mouth, leaning against the wall; she had been frozen to death on the last evening of the year, and the New Year's sun rose and shone upon a little corpse. The child still sat, in the stiffness of death, holding the matches in her hand, one bundle of which was burnt. "She tried to warm herself," said some. No one imagined what beautiful things she had seen, nor into what glory she had entered with her grandmother, on New Year's Day.

Hans Christian Andersen (1805–1875) wrote more than 155 fairy tales during his lifetime, many of them inspired by folk stories that he heard growing up as a child in his native Denmark. His stories often contain lessons within them, especially about the value of every individual, no matter how they might appear to other people.

Yes, Virginia, There Is a Santa Claus

Francis P. Church

Editor Francis P. Church's letter to Virginia O'Hanlon is one of the most touching written demonstrations of the importance in believing in what cannot be seen, touched, or proven. The letter originally appeared in the September 21, 1897 edition of the New York Sun. *More than a century later, it remains a classic.*

We take pleasure in answering at once and thus prominently the communication below, expressing at the same time our great gratification that its faithful author is numbered among the friends of the *Sun*:

DEAR EDITOR—I am 8 years old.

Some of my little friends say there is no SANTA CLAUS. Papa says 'If you see it in the Sun it's so.' Please tell me the truth, is there a SANTA CLAUS?

VIRGINIA O'HANLON, 115 West Ninety-fifth street.

Virginia, your little friends are wrong. They have been affected by the skepticism of a skeptical age. They do not believe except they see. They think that nothing can be which is not comprehensible by their little minds. All minds, Virginia, whether they be men's or children's are little. In this great universe of ours man is a mere insect, an ant, in his intellect, as compared with the boundless world about him, as measured by the intelligence capable of grasping the whole of truth and knowledge.

Yes, Virginia, there is a Santa Claus. He exists as certainly as love and generosity and devotion exist, and you know that they abound and give to your life its highest beauty and joy. Alas! How dreary would be the world if there were no Santa Claus! It would be as dreary as if there were no Virginias. There would be no childlike faith then, no poetry, no romance to make tolerable this existence. We should have no enjoyment, except in sense and sight. The eternal light with which childhood fills the world would be extinguished.

Not believe in Santa Claus! You might as well not believe in fairies! You might get your papa to hire men to watch in all the chimneys on Christmas Eve to catch

Santa Claus, but even if they did not see Santa Claus coming down, what would that prove? Nobody sees Santa Claus, but that is no sign that there is no Santa Claus. The most real things in the world are those that neither children nor men can see. Did you ever see fairies dancing on the lawn? Of course not, but that's no proof that they are not there.

Nobody can conceive or imagine all the wonders there are unseen and unseeable in the world.

You tear apart the baby's rattle and see what makes the noise inside, but there is a veil covering the unseen world which not the strongest man, nor even the united strength of all the strongest men that ever lived, could tear apart. Only faith, fancy, poetry, love, romance, can push aside that curtain and view and picture the supernal beauty and glory beyond. Is it all real? Ah, Virginia, in all this world there is nothing else real and abiding.

No Santa Claus! Thank God! He lives, and he lives forever. A thousand years from now, Virginia, nay, ten times ten thousand years from now, he will continue to make glad the heart of childhood.

Francis Pharcellus Church (1839–1906) was one of the editorial writers at the New York Sun *when he wrote this letter. He was a veteran writer and editor, having covered the Civil War for the* New York Times. *He also came from a publishing family: Both his father and his brother founded newspapers and magazines.*

A Christmas Carol

Charles Dickens

With the publication in 1843 of "A Christmas Carol in Prose" (as the full title originally read), Charles Dickens bestowed a timeless message of repentance and hope to generations of readers. The 6,000-copy first printing sold out in a single day; second and third editions went almost as quickly, no doubt to be read aloud, as Dickens's stories were always meant to be.

Marley was dead, to begin with. There is no doubt whatever about that. The register of his burial was signed by the clergyman, the clerk, the undertaker, and the chief mourner. Scrooge signed it. And Scrooge's name was good upon 'Change for anything he chose to put his hand to. Old Marley was dead as a doornail.

Mind! I don't mean to say that I know, of my own knowledge, what there is particularly dead about a doornail. I might have been inclined, myself, to regard a coffin nail as the deadest piece of ironmongery in the trade. But the wisdom of our ancestors is in the simile; and my unhallowed hands shall not disturb it, or the Country's done for. You will therefore permit me to repeat, emphatically, that Marley was as dead as a doornail.

Scrooge knew he was dead? Of course he did. How could it be otherwise? Scrooge and he were partners for I don't know how many years. Scrooge was his sole executor, his sole administrator, his sole assign, his sole residuary legatee, his sole friend, and sole mourner. And even Scrooge was not so dreadfully cut up by the sad event but that he was an excellent man of business on the very day of the funeral, and solemnized it with an undoubted bargain.

The mention of Marley's funeral brings me back to the point I started from. There is no doubt that Marley was dead. This must be distinctly understood, or nothing wonderful can come of the story I am going to relate. If we were not perfectly convinced that Hamlet's

Father died before the play began, there would be nothing more remarkable in his taking a stroll at night, in an easterly wind, upon his own ramparts, than there would be in any other middle-aged gentleman rashly turning out after dark in a breezy spot—say Saint Paul's Churchyard, for instance—literally to astonish his son's weak mind.

Scrooge never painted out Old Marley's name. There it stood, years afterward, above the warehouse door: *Scrooge and Marley.* The firm was known as Scrooge and Marley. Sometimes people new to the business called Scrooge Scrooge, and sometimes Marley, but he answered to both names. It was all the same to him.

Once upon a time—of all the good days in the year, on Christmas Eve—old Scrooge sat busy in his countinghouse. It was cold, bleak, biting weather: foggy withal: and he could hear the people in the court outside go wheezing up and down, beating their hands upon their breasts, and stamping their feet upon the pavement stones to warm them. The city clocks had only just gone three, but it was quite dark already—it had not been light all day—and candles were flaring in the windows of the neighboring offices, like ruddy smears upon the palpable brown air. The fog came pouring in at every chink and keyhole, and was so dense without, that although the court was of the narrowest, the houses opposite were mere phantoms. To see the dingy cloud come drooping down, obscuring everything, one might have thought that Nature lived hard by, and was brewing on a large scale.

The door of Scrooge's countinghouse was open, that he might keep his eye upon his clerk, who, in a dismal little cell beyond, a sort of tank, was copying letters. Scrooge had a very small fire, but the clerk's fire was so very much smaller that it looked like one coal. But he couldn't replenish it, for Scrooge kept the coalbox in his own room; and so surely as the clerk came in with the shovel the master predicted that it would be necessary for them to part. Wherefore the clerk put on his white comforter and tried to warm himself at the candle, in which effort, not being a man of imagination, he failed.

"A merry Christmas, Uncle! God save you!" cried a cheerful voice. It was the voice of Scrooge's nephew, who came upon him so quickly that this was the first intimation he had of his approach.

"Bah!" said Scrooge. "Humbug!"

He had so heated himself with rapid walking in the fog and frost, this nephew of Scrooge's, that he was all in a glow; his face was ruddy and handsome; his eyes sparkled, and his breath smoked again.

"Christmas a humbug, Uncle!" said Scrooge's nephew. "You don't mean that, I am sure."

"I do," said Scrooge. "Merry Christmas! What right have you to be merry? What reason have you to be merry? You're poor enough."

"Come, then," returned his nephew gaily. "What right have you to be dismal? What reason have you to be morose? You're rich enough."

Scrooge having no better answer ready on the spur of the moment, said, "Bah!" again; and followed it up with, "Humbug!"

"Don't be cross, Uncle!" said the nephew.

"What else can I be?" returned the uncle, "when I live in such a world of fools as this? Merry Christmas! Out upon merry Christmas! What's Christmas time to you but a time for paying bills without money, a time for finding yourself a year older and not an hour richer, a time for balancing your books and having every item in 'em through a round dozen of months presented dead against you? If I could work my will," said Scrooge indignantly, "every idiot who goes about with 'Merry Christmas,' on his lips should be boiled with his own pudding, and buried with a stake of holly through his heart. He should!"

"Uncle!" pleaded the nephew.

"Nephew!" returned the uncle sternly. "Keep Christmas in your own way, and let me keep it in mine."

"Keep it!" repeated Scrooge's nephew. "But you don't keep it."

"Let me leave it alone, then," said Scrooge. "Much good may it do you! Much good it has ever done you!"

"There are many things from which I might have derived good, by which I have not profited, I dare say," returned the nephew. "Christmas among the rest. But I am sure I have always thought of Christmas time, when it has come round—apart from the veneration due to its sacred name and origin, if any thing belonging to it can be apart from that—as a good time; a kind, forgiving, charitable, pleasant time; the only time I know of the long calendar of the year, when men and women seem by one consent to open their shut-up hearts freely, and to think of people below them as if they really were fellow passengers to the grave, and not another race of creatures bound on other journeys. And therefore, Uncle, though it has never put a scrap of gold or silver in my pocket, I believe that it has done me good and will do me good; and I say God bless it!"

The clerk in the tank involuntarily applauded. Becoming immediately sensible of the impropriety, he poked the fire and extinguished the last grail spark forever.

"Let me hear another sound from you," said Scrooge, "and you'll keep your Christmas by losing your situation. You're quite a powerful speaker, sir," he added, turning to his nephew. "I wonder you don't go into Parliament."

"Don't be angry, Uncle. Come! Dine with us tomorrow."

Scrooge said that he would see him—yes, indeed he did. He went the whole length of the expression, and said that he would see him in that extremity first.

"But why?" cried Scrooge's nephew. "Why?"

"Why did you get married?" said Scrooge.

"Because I fell in love."

"Because you fell in love!" growled Scrooge, as if that were the only one thing in the world more ridiculous than a merry Christmas. "Good afternoon!"

"Nay, Uncle, but you never came to see me before that happened. Why give it as a reason for not coming now?"

"Good afternoon," said Scrooge.

"I want nothing from you; I ask nothing of you; why cannot we be friends?"

"Good afternoon," said Scrooge.

"I am sorry, with all my heart, to find you so resolute. We have never had any quarrel to which I have been a party. But I have made the trial in homage to Christmas, and I'll keep my Christmas humor to the last. So, a Merry Christmas, Uncle!"

"Good afternoon!" said Scrooge.

"And a Happy New Year!"

"Good afternoon!" said Scrooge.

His nephew left the room without an angry word, notwithstanding. He stopped at the outer door to bestow the greetings of the season on the clerk, who, cold as he was, was warmer than Scrooge; for he returned them cordially.

"There's another fellow," muttered Scrooge, who overheard him. "My clerk, with fifteen shillings a week and a wife and family, talking about a merry Christmas. I'll return to Bedlam."

This lunatic, in letting Scrooge's nephew out, had let two other people in. They were portly gentlemen, pleasant to behold, and now stood, with their hats off, in Scrooge's office. They had books and papers in their hands, and bowed to him.

"Scrooge and Marley's I believe," said one of the gentlemen, referring to his list. "Have I the pleasure of addressing Mr. Scrooge or Mr. Marley?"

"Mr. Marley has been dead these seven years," Scrooge replied. "He died seven years ago, this very night."

"We have no doubt his liberality is well represented by his surviving partner," said the gentlemen, presenting his credentials.

It certainly was; for they had been two kindred spirits. At the ominous word "liberality" Scrooge frowned and shook his head and handed the credentials back.

"At this festive season of the year, Mr. Scrooge," said the gentleman, taking up a pen, "it is more than usually desirable that we should make some slight provision for the poor and destitute, who suffer greatly at the present time. Many thousands are in want of common necessaries, hundreds of thousands are in want of common comforts, sir."

"Are there no prisons?" asked Scrooge.

"Plenty of prisons," said the gentleman, laying down the pen again.

"And the Union workhouses?" demanded Scrooge. "Are they still in operation?"

"They are. Still," returned the gentleman. "I wish I could say they were not."

"The Treadmill and the Poor Law are in full vigor, then?" said Scrooge.

"Both very busy, sir."

"Oh! I was afraid, from what you said at first, that something had occurred to stop them in their useful course," said Scrooge. "I am very glad to hear it."

"Under the impression that they scarcely furnish Christian cheer of mind or body to the multitude," returned the gentleman, "a few of us are endeavoring to raise a fund to buy the Poor some meat and drink and means of warmth. We choose this time, because it is a time of all others, when Want is keenly felt, and Abundance rejoices. What shall I put you down for?"

"Nothing!" Scrooge replied.

"You wish to be anonymous?"

"I wish to be left alone," said Scrooge. "Since you ask me what I wish, Gentlemen, that is my answer. I don't make merry myself at Christmas, and I can't afford to make idle people merry. I help to support the establishments I have mentioned—they cost enough, and those who are badly off must go there."

"Many can't go there; many would rather die."

"If they would rather die," said Scrooge, "they had better do it, and decrease the surplus population. Besides—excuse me—I don't know that."

"But you might know it," observed the gentleman.

"It's not my business," Scrooge returned. "It's enough for a man to understand his own business, and not to interfere with other people's. Mine occupies me constantly. Good afternoon, Gentlemen!"

Seeing clearly that it would be useless to pursue their point, the gentlemen withdrew. Scrooge resumed his labor with an improved opinion of himself, and in a more facetious temper than was usual with him.

At length the hour of shutting up the countinghouse arrived. With an ill will Scrooge dismounted from his stool and tacitly admitted the fact to the expectant clerk in the tank, who instantly snuffed his candle out and put on his hat.

"You'll want all day tomorrow, I suppose?" said Scrooge.

"If quite convenient, sir."

"It's not convenient," said Scrooge, "and it's not fair. If I was to stop half-a-crown for it, you'd think yourself ill-used, I'll be bound?"

The clerk smiled faintly.

"And yet," said Scrooge, "you don't think *me* ill-used, when I pay a day's wages for no work."

The clerk observed it was only once a year.

"A poor excuse for picking a man's pocket every twenty-fifth of December!" said Scrooge, buttoning his greatcoat to the chin. "But I suppose you must have the whole day. Be here all the earlier the next morning."

The clerk promised that he would; and Scrooge walked out with a growl. The office was closed in a twinkling, and the clerk, with the long ends of his white comforter dangling below his waist (for he boasted no greatcoat), went down a slide on Cornhill, at the end of a lane of boys, twenty times, in honor of its being

Christmas Eve, and then ran home to Camden Town as hard as he could pelt, to play at blindman's buff.

Scrooge took his melancholy dinner in his usual melancholy tavern; and having read all the newspapers, and beguiled the rest of the evening with his banker's book, went home to bed. He lived in chambers which had once belonged to his deceased partner. They were a gloomy suite of rooms, in a lowering pile of building up a yard, where it had so little business to be, that one could scarcely help fancying it must have run there when it was a young house, playing at hide-and-seek with other houses, and have forgotten the way out again. It was old enough now, and dreary enough; for nobody lived in it but Scrooge, the other rooms being all let out as offices. The yard was so dark that even Scrooge, who knew its every stone, was faint to grope with his hands. The fog and frost so hung about the black old gateway of the house that it seemed as if the Genius of the Weather sat in mournful meditation on the threshold.

Now it is a fact that there was nothing at all particular about the knocker on the door, except that it was very large. It is also a fact that Scrooge had seen it, night and morning, during his whole residence in that place; also that Scrooge had as little of what is called fancy about him as any man in the City of London, even including—which is a bold word—the corporation, aldermen, and livery. Let it also be borne in mind that Scrooge had not bestowed one thought on Marley since his last mention of his seven-years dead partner that afternoon. And then let any man explain to me, if he can, how it happened that Scrooge, having his key in the lock of the door, saw in the knocker, without its undergoing any intermediate process of change—not a knocker, but Marley's face.

Marley's face. It was not in impenetrable shadow, as the other objects in the yard were, but had a dismal light about it, like a bad lobster in a dark cellar. It was not angry or ferocious, but looked at Scrooge as Marley used to look, with ghostly spectacles turned up on its ghostly forehead. The hair was curiously stirred, as if by breath of hot air; and, though the eyes were wide open, they were perfectly motionless. That, and its livid color, made it horrible; but its horror seemed to be in spite of the face, and beyond its control, rather than a part of its own expression.

As Scrooge looked fixedly at this phenomenon, it was a knocker again.

To say that he was not startled, or that his blood was not conscious of a terrible sensation to which it had been a stranger from infancy, would be untrue. But he put his hand upon the key he had relinquished, turned it sturdily, walked in, and lighted his candle.

He *did* pause, with a moment's irresolution, before he shut the door; and he *did* look cautiously behind it first, as if he half expected to be terrified with the sight of Marley's pigtail sticking out into the hall. But there was nothing on the back of the door except the screws and nuts that held the knocker on, so he said, "Pooh, pooh!" and closed it with a bang.

The sound resounded through the house like thunder. Every room above and every cask in the wine merchant's cellar below appeared to have a separate peal of echoes of its own. Scrooge was not a man to be frightened by echoes. He fastened the door and walked across the hall and up the stairs, slowly, too, trimming the candle as he went.

Up Scrooge went, not caring a button for that. Darkness is cheap, and Scrooge liked it. But before he shut his heavy door, he walked through his rooms to see that all was right. He had just enough recollection of the fact to desire to do that.

Sitting-room, bedroom, lumber room. All as they should be. Nobody under the table, nobody under the sofa; a small fire in the grate; spoon and basin ready; and the little saucepan of gruel (Scrooge had a cold in his head) upon the hob. Nobody under the bed; nobody in the closet; nobody in his dressing gown, which was hanging up in a suspicious attitude against the wall. Lumber room as usual. Old fireguard, old shoes, two fish baskets, washing stand on three legs, and a poker.

"Humbug!" said Scrooge, and walked across the room.

After several turns, he sat down again. As he threw his head back in the chair, his glance happened to rest upon a bell, a disused bell that hung in the room and communicated for some purpose now forgotten with a chamber in the highest story of the building. It was with great astonishment, and with a strange, inexplicable dread, that as he looked, he saw this bell begin to swing. It swung so softly in the outset that it scarcely made a sound; but soon it rang out loudly, and so did every bell in the house.

This might have lasted half a minute, or a minute, but it seemed an hour. The bells ceased as they had begun, together. They were succeeded by a clanking noise, deep down below, as if some persons were dragging a heavy chain over the casks in the wine merchant's cellar.

Scrooge then remembered to have heard that ghosts in haunted houses were described as dragging chains.

The cellar door flew open with a booming sound, and then he heard the noise much louder, on the floors below; then coming up the stairs; then coming straight toward his door.

"It's humbug still!" said Scrooge. "I won't believe it."

His color changed, though, when, without a pause, it came on through the heavy door and passed into the room before his eyes. Upon its coming in, the dying flame leaped up, as though it cried, "I know him! Marley's ghost!" and then fell again.

The same face; the very same. Marley in his pigtail, usual waistcoat, tights, and boots; and tassels on the latter bristling like his pigtail, and his coat skirts, and the hair upon his head. The chain he drew was clasped about his middle. It was long and wound about him like a tail; and it was made (for Scrooge observed it closely) of cashboxes, keys, padlocks, ledgers, deeds, and heavy purses wrought in steel. His body was transparent, so that Scrooge, observing him and looking through his waistcoat, could see the two buttons on his coat behind.

Scrooge had often heard it said that Marley had no bowels, but he had never believed it until now.

"How now!" said Scrooge, caustic and cold as ever. "What do you want with me?"

"Much!" Marley's voice, no doubt about it.

"Who are you?"

"Ask me who I *was*."

"Who *were* you, then?" said Scrooge, raising his voice. "You're particular, for a shade." He was going to say "to a shade," but substituted this, as more appropriate.

"In life I was your partner, Jacob Marley."

"Can you—can you sit down?" asked Scrooge, looking at him.

"I can."

Scrooge asked the question because he didn't know whether a ghost so transparent might find himself in a condition to take a chair; and felt that in the event of its being impossible, it might involve the necessity of an embarrassing explanation. But the ghost sat down on the opposite side of the fireplace, as if he were quite used to it.

"You don't believe in me," observed the Ghost.

"I don't," said Scrooge.

"What evidence would you have of my reality beyond that of your own senses?"

"I don't know," said Scrooge.

"Why do you doubt your senses?"

"Because," said Scrooge, "a little thing affects them. A slight disorder of the stomach makes them cheats. You may be an undigested bit of beef, a blot of mustard, a crumb of cheese, a fragment of an underdone potato. There's more of gravy than of grave about you, whatever you are!"

Scrooge was not much in the habit of cracking jokes, nor did he feel in his heart by any means waggish then. The truth is that he tried to be smart, as a means of distracting his own attention, and keeping down his terror, for the specter's voice disturbed the very marrow of his bones.

To sit staring at those fixed glazed eyes, in silence for a moment, would play, Scrooge, felt, the very deuce with him. There was something very awful, too, in the specter's being provided with an infernal atmosphere of his own. Scrooge could not feel it himself, but this was clearly the case; for though the Ghost sat perfectly motionless, its hair and skirts and tassels were still agitated as by the hot vapor from an oven.

"You see this toothpick?" said Scrooge, returning quickly to the charge for the reason just assigned, and wishing, though it were only for a second, to divert the vision's stony gaze from himself.

"I do," replied the Ghost.

"You are not looking at it," said Scrooge.

"But I see it," said the Ghost, "notwithstanding."

"Well!" returned Scrooge, "I have but to swallow this, and be for the rest of my days persecuted by a legion of goblins, all of my own creation. Humbug, I tell you; humbug!"

At this the spirit raised a frightful cry, and shook its chain with such a dismal and appalling noise that Scrooge held on tight to his chair to save himself from falling in a swoon. But how much greater was his horror when, the phantom taking off the bandage round its head, as if it were too warm to wear indoors, its lower jaw dropped down upon its breast!

Scrooge fell upon his knees, and clasped his hands before his face.

"Mercy!" he said. "Dreadful apparition, why do you trouble me?"

"Man of the worldly mind!" replied the Ghost. "Do you believe in me or not?"

"I do," said Scrooge. "I must. But why do spirits walk the earth and why do they come to me?"

"It is required of every man," the Ghost returned, "that the spirit within him should walk abroad among his fellow men, and travel far and wide; and if that spirit goes not forth in life, it is condemned to do so after death. It is doomed to wander through the world—oh, woe is me!—and witness what it cannot share, but might have shared on earth, and turned to happiness!"

Again the specter raised a cry, and shook its chain and wrung its shadowy hands.

"You are fettered," said Scrooge, trembling. "Tell me why?"

"I wear the chain I forged in life," replied the Ghost. "I made it link by link, and yard by yard; I girded it on of my own free will, and of my own free will I wore it. Is its pattern strange to you?"

Scrooge trembled more and more.

"Or would you know," pursued the Ghost, "the weight and length of the strong coil you bear yourself? It was full as heavy and as long as this seven Christmas Eves ago. You have labored on it since. It is a ponderous chain!"

Scrooge glanced about him on the floor, in the expectation of finding himself surrounded by some fifty or sixty fathoms of iron cable; but he could see nothing.

"Jacob," he said imploringly. "Old Jacob Marley, tell me more. Speak comfort to me, Jacob!"

"I have none to give," the Ghost replied. "It comes from other regions, Ebenezer Scrooge, and is conveyed by other ministers, to other kinds of men. Nor can I tell you what I would. A very little more is all that is permitted to me. I cannot rest, I cannot stay, I cannot linger anywhere. My spirit never walked beyond our countinghouse—mark me!—in life my spirit never roved beyond the narrow limits of our money-changing hole; and weary journeys lie before me!"

It was a habit with Scrooge, whenever he became thoughtful, to put his hands in his breeches' pockets. Pondering on what the Ghost had said, he did so now, but without lifting up his eyes, or getting off his knees.

"You must have been very slow about it, Jacob," Scrooge observed in a business-like manner, though with humility and deference.

"Slow!" the Ghost repeated.

"Seven years dead," mused Scrooge. "And traveling all the time?"

"The whole time," said the Ghost. "No rest, no peace. Incessant torture of remorse."

"You travel fast?" said Scrooge.

"On the wings of the wind," replied the Ghost.

"You might have got over a great quantity of ground in seven years," said Scrooge.

The Ghost, on hearing this, set up another cry and clanked its chain so hideously in the dead silence of the night, that the Ward would have been justified in indicting it for a nuisance.

"Oh! Captive, bound and double-ironed," cried the phantom, "not to know that ages of incessant labor, by immortal creatures, for this earth must pass into eternity before the good of which it is susceptible is all developed. Not to know that any Christian spirit working kindly in its little sphere, whatever it may be, will find its mortal life too short for its vast means of usefulness. Not to know that no space of regret can make amends for one life's opportunities misused! Yet such was I! Oh! Such was I!"

"But you were always a good man of business, Jacob," faltered Scrooge, who now began to apply this to himself.

"Business!" cried the Ghost, wringing its hands again. "Mankind was my business. The common welfare was my business; charity, mercy, forbearance, and benevolence were all my business. The dealings of my trade were but a drop of water in the comprehensive ocean of my business!"

It held up its chain at arm's length, as if that were the cause of all its unavailing grief, and flung it heavily upon the ground again.

"At this time of the rolling year," the specter said, "I suffer most. Why did I walk through crowds of fellow beings with my eyes turned down, and never raise them to that blessed Star which led the Wise Men to a poor abode? Were there no poor homes to which its light would have conducted me?"

Scrooge was very much dismayed to hear the specter going on at this rate, and began to quake exceedingly.

"Hear me!" cried the Ghost. "My time is nearly gone."

"I will," said Scrooge. "But don't be hard upon me! Don't be flowery, Jacob! Pray!"

"How it is that I appear before you in a shape that you can see, I may not tell. I have sat invisible beside you many and many a day."

It was not an agreeable idea. Scrooge shivered and wiped the perspiration from his brow.

"That is no light part of my penance," pursued the Ghost. "I am here tonight to warn you that you have yet a chance and hope of escaping my fate. A chance and hope of my procuring, Ebenezer."

"You were always a good friend to me," said Scrooge. "Thank'ee!"

"You will be haunted," resumed the Ghost, "by Three Spirits."

Scrooge's countenance fell almost as low as the Ghost's had done.

"Is that the chance and hope you mentioned, Jacob?" he demanded, in a faltering voice.

"It is."

"I—I think I'd rather not," said Scrooge.

"Without their visits," said the Ghost, "you cannot hope to shun the path I tread. Expect the first tomorrow, when the bell tolls one."

"Couldn't I take 'em all at once, and have it over?" hinted Scrooge.

"Expect the second on the next night at the same hour. The third, upon the next night when the last stroke of twelve has ceased to vibrate. Look to see me no more; and look that, for your own sake, you remember what has passed between us!"

When it had said these words, the specter took its wrapper from the table and bound it round its head, as before. Scrooge knew this by the smart sound its teeth made, when the jaws were brought together by the bandage. He ventured to raise his eyes again, and found his supernatural visitor confronting him in an erect attitude, with its chain wound over and about its arm.

The apparition walked backward from him; and at every step it took, the window raised itself a little, so that when the specter reached it, it was wide open. It beckoned Scrooge to approach, which he did. When they were within two paces of each other, Marley's Ghost held up its hand, warning him to come no nearer. Scrooge stopped.

Not so much in obedience, as in surprise and fear; for on the raising of the hand, he became sensible of confused noises in the air; incoherent sounds of lamentation and regret; wailings inexpressibly sorrowful and self-accusatory. The specter, after listening for a moment, joined in the mournful dirge; and floated out upon the bleak, dark night.

Scrooge followed to the window, desperate in his curiosity. He looked out.

The air was filled with phantoms, wandering hither and thither in restless haste, and moaning as they went. Every one of them wore chains like Marley's Ghost; some few (they might be guilty governments) were linked together; none were free. Many had been personally known to Scrooge in their lives. He had been quite familiar with one old ghost, in a white waistcoat, with a monstrous iron safe attached to its ankle, who cried piteously at being unable to assist a wretched woman with an infant, whom it saw below, upon a doorstep. The misery with them all was, clearly, that they sought to interfere, for good, in human matters, and had lost the power forever.

Whether these creatures faded into mist, or mist enshrouded them, he could not tell. But they and their spirit voices faded together; and the night became as it had been when he walked home.

Scrooge closed the window and examined the door by which the Ghost had entered. It was doubled-locked, as he had locked it with his own hands, and the bolts were undisturbed. He tried to say, "Humbug!" but stopped at the first syllable. And being, from the motion he had undergone, or the fatigues of the day, or his glimpse of the Invisible World, or the dull conversation of the Ghost, or the lateness of the hour, much in need of repose, went straight to bed without undressing, and fell asleep upon the instant.

* * * * *

When Scrooge awoke it was so dark that, looking out of bed, he could scarcely distinguish the transparent window from the opaque walls of his chamber. He was endeavoring to pierce the darkness with his ferret eyes, when the chimes of a neighboring church struck the four quarters. So he listened for the hour.

To his great astonishment, the heavy bell went on from six to seven, and from seven to eight, and regularly up to twelve; then stopped. Twelve! It was past two when he went to bed. The clock was wrong. An icicle must have got into the works. Twelve!

He touched the spring of his repeater, to correct this most preposterous clock. Its rapid little pulse beat twelve and stopped.

"Why, it isn't possible," said Scrooge, "that I can have slept through a whole day and far into another night. It isn't possible that anything has happened to the sun, and this is twelve at noon!"

This idea being an alarming one, he scrambled out of bed and groped his way to the window. He was obliged to rub the frost off with the sleeve of his dressing gown before he could see anything; and could see very little then. All he could make out was that it was still very foggy and extremely cold, and that there was no noise of people running to and fro and making a great stir, as there unquestionably would have been if night had beaten off bright day and taken possession of the world. This was a great relief, because *Three days after sight of this First of Exchange pay to Mr. Ebenezer Scrooge on this order,* and so forth, would have become a mere United States security if there were no days to count by.

Scrooge went to bed again and thought and thought, and thought it over and over, and could make nothing of it. The more he thought the more perplexed he was; and the more he endeavored not to think the more he thought.

Marley's ghost bothered him exceedingly. Every time he resolved within himself, after mature inquiry, that it was all a dream, his mind flew back again, like a strong spring released, to its first position, and presented the same problem to be worked all through: Was it a dream or not?

Scrooge lay in this state until the chime had gone three quarters more, when he remembered, on a sudden, that the Ghost had warned him of a visitation when the bell tolled one.

He resolved to lie awake until the hour was passed; and, considering that he could no more go to sleep than go to heaven, this was perhaps the wisest resolution in his power.

The quarter was so long, that he was more than once convinced that he must have sunk into a doze unconsciously and missed the clock. At length it broke upon his listening ear.

Ding, dong!

"A quarter past," said Scrooge, counting.

Ding, dong!

"Half past," said Scrooge.

Ding, dong!

"A quarter to it," said Scrooge.

Ding dong!

"The hour itself," said Scrooge triumphantly, "and nothing else!"

He spoke before the hour bell sounded, which it now did with a deep, dull, hollow, melancholy one. Light flashed up in the room upon the instant, and the curtains of his bed were drawn.

The curtains of his bed were drawn aside, I tell you, by a hand. Not the curtains at his feet, nor the curtains at his back, but those to which his face was addressed. The curtains of his bed were drawn aside; and Scrooge, starting up into a half-recumbent attitude, found himself face to face with the unearthly visitor who drew them; as close to it as I am now to you, and I am standing in the spirit at your elbow.

It was a strange figure—like a child; yet not so like a child as like an old man, viewed through some supernatural medium, which gave him the appearance of having receded from the view, and being diminished to a child's proportions. Its hair, which hung about its neck and down its back, was white as if with age; and yet the face had not a wrinkle in it, and the tenderest bloom was on the skin. The arms were very long and muscular; the hands the same, as if its hold were of uncommon strength. Its legs and feet, most delicately formed, were, like those upper members, bare. It wore a tunic of the purest white; and round its waist was bound a lustrous belt, the sheen of which was beautiful. It held a branch of fresh green holly in its hand; and, in singular contradiction of that wintry emblem, had its dress trimmed with summer flowers.

But the strangest thing about it was that from the crown of its head there sprung a bright clear jet of light, by which all this was visible; and which was doubtless the occasion of its using, in its duller moments, a great extinguisher for a cap, which it now held under its arm.

Even this, though, when Scrooge looked at it with increasing steadiness, was *not* its strangest quality. For as its belt sparkled and glittered, now in one part and now in another, and what was light one instant, at another time was dark, so the figure itself fluctuated in its distinctness, being now a thing with one arm, now with one leg, now with twenty legs, now a pair of legs without a head, now a head without a body; of which dissolving parts, no outline would be visible in the dense gloom wherein they melted away. And in the very wonder of this, it would be itself again; distinct and clear as ever.

"Are you the Spirit, sir, whose coming was foretold to me?" asked Scrooge.

"I am!"

The voice was soft and gentle. Singularly low, as if instead of being so close beside him, it were at a distance.

"Who and what are you?" Scrooge demanded.

"I am the Ghost of Christmas Past."

"Long Past?" inquired Scrooge, observant to its dwarfish stature.

"No. Your past."

Perhaps Scrooge could not have told anybody why, if anybody could have asked him, but he had a special desire to see the Spirit in his cap, and begged him to be covered.

"What!" exclaimed the Ghost. "Would you so soon put out, with worldly hands, the light I give? Is it not enough that you are one of those whose passions made this cap, and force me through whole trains of years to wear it low upon my brow?"

Scrooge reverently disclaimed all intention to offend or any knowledge of having willfully "bonneted" the Spirit at any period of his life. He then made bold to inquire what business brought him there.

"Your welfare!" said the Ghost.

Scrooge expressed himself much obliged, but could not help thinking that a night of unbroken rest would have been more conducive to that end.

The spirit must have heard him thinking, for it said, "Your reclamation, then. Take heed!"

It put out its strong hand as it spoke, and clasped him gently by the arm.

"Rise! And walk with me!"

It would have been in vain for Scrooge to plead that the weather and the hour were not adapted to pedestrian purposes; that bed was warm, and the thermometer a long way below freezing; that he was clad but lightly in his slippers, dressing gown, and nightcap; and that he had a cold upon him at the time. The grasp, though gentle as a woman's hand, was not to be resisted. He rose; but finding that the Spirit made toward the window, clasped its robe in supplication.

"I am mortal," Scrooge remonstrated, "and liable to fall."

"Bear but a touch of my hand there," said the Spirit, laying it upon his heart, "and you shall be upheld in more than this!"

As the words were spoken, they passed through the wall and stood upon an open country road, with fields on either hand. The city had entirely vanished. Not a vestige of it was to be seen. The darkness and the mist had vanished with it, for it was a clear, cold, winter day, with snow upon the ground.

"Good Heaven!" said Scrooge, clasping his hands together, as he looked about him. "I was bred in this place. I was a boy here!"

The Spirit gazed upon him mildly. Its gentle touch, though it had been light and instantaneous, appeared still present to the old man's sense of feeling. He was conscious of a thousand odors floating in the air, each one connected with a thousand thoughts and hopes and joys and cares, long, long forgotten.

"Your lip is trembling," said the Ghost. "And what is that upon your cheek?"

Scrooge muttered, with an unusual catching in his voice, that it was a pimple; and begged the Ghost to lead him where he would.

"You recollect the way?" inquired the Spirit.

"Remember it!" cried Scrooge with fervor. "I could walk it blindfold."

"Strange to have forgotten it for so many years!" observed the Ghost, "Let us go on."

They walked along the road, Scrooge recognizing every gate and post and tree, until a little market town appeared in the distance, with its bridge, its church, and winding river. Some shaggy ponies now were seen trotting toward them with boys upon their backs, who called to other boys in country gigs and carts, driven by farmers. All these boys were in great spirits and shouted to each other, until the broad fields were so full of merry music that the crisp air laughed to hear it.

"These are but shadows of the things that have been," said the Ghost. "They have no consciousness of us."

The jocund travelers came on; and as they came, Scrooge knew and named them every one. Why was he rejoiced beyond all bounds to see them? Why did his cold eye glisten, and his heart leap up as they went past? Why was he filled with gladness when he heard them give each other Merry Christmas, as they parted at crossroads and byways, for their several homes? What was merry Christmas to Scrooge? Out upon merry Christmas! What good had it ever done to him?

"The school is not quite deserted," said the Ghost. "A solitary child, neglected by his friends, is left there still."

Scrooge said he knew it. And he sobbed.

They left the highroad by a well-remembered lane, and soon approached a mansion of dull red brick, with a little weathercock-surmounted cupola on the roof, and a bell hanging in it. It was a large house, but one of broken fortunes, for the spacious offices were little used, their walls were damp and mossy, their windows broken, and their gates decayed. Fowls clucked and strutted in the stables, and the coach house and sheds were overrun with grass. Nor was it more retentive of its ancient state within; for entering the dreary hall and glancing through the open doors of many rooms, they found them poorly furnished, cold, and vast. There was an earthy savor in the air, a chilly bareness on the place, which associated itself somehow with too much getting up by candlelight, and not too much to eat.

They went, the Ghost and Scrooge, across the hall to a door at the back of the house. It opened before them and disclosed a long, bare, melancholy room, made barer still by lines of plain deal forms and desks. At one of these a lonely boy was reading near a feeble fire; and Scrooge sat down upon a form, and wept to see his poor forgotten self as he had used to be.

Not a latent echo in the house, not a squeak and scuffle from the mice behind the paneling, not a drip from the half-thawed waterspout in the dull yard behind, not a sigh among the leafless boughs of one despondent poplar, not the idle swinging on an empty storehouse door, no, not a clicking in the fire, but fell upon the heart of Scrooge with softening influence, and gave a freer passage to his tears.

The Spirit touched him on the arm and pointed to his younger self, intent upon his reading. Suddenly a man in foreign garments, wonderfully real and distinct to look at, stood outside the window, with an axe stuck in his belt, and leading by the bridle an ass laden with wood.

"Why, it's Ali Baba!" Scrooge exclaimed in ecstasy. "It's dear old honest Ali Baba! Yes, yes I know. One Christmas time, when yonder solitary child was left here all alone, he did come for the first time, just like that. Poor boy! And Valentine," said Scrooge, "and his wild brother, Orson; there they go! And what's his name, who was put down in his drawers, asleep, at the gate of Damascus; don't you see him? And the Sultan's groom turned upside down by the Genii, there he is upon his head! Serves him right. I'm glad of it. What business had he to be married to the Princess?"

To hear Scrooge expending all the earnestness of his nature on such subjects, in a most extraordinary voice between laughing and crying, and to see his heightened and excited face, would have been a surprise to his business friends in the city, indeed.

"There's the Parrot!" cried Scrooge. "Green body and yellow tail, with a thing like lettuce growing out of the top of his head; there he is! 'Poor Robin Crusoe,' he called him, when he came home again after sailing round the island. 'Poor Robin Crusoe, where have you been, Robin Crusoe?' The man thought he was dreaming, but he wasn't. It was the Parrot, you know. There goes Friday, running for his life to the little creek! Halloa! Hoop! Halloo!"

Then, with a rapidity of transition very foreign to his usual character, he said, in pity for his former self, "Poor boy," and cried again.

"I wish," Scrooge muttered, putting his hand in his pocket and looking about him, after drying his hands with his cuff, "but it's too late now."

"What is the matter?" asked the Spirit.

"Nothing," said Scrooge. "Nothing. There was a boy singing a Christmas carol at my door last night. I should like to have given him something; that's all."

The Ghost smiled thoughtfully and waved its hands, saying as it did so, "Let us see another Christmas!"

Scrooge's former self grew large at the words, and the room became a little darker and more dirty. The panels shrunk, the windows cracked; fragments of plaster fell out of the ceiling, and the naked laths were shown instead; but how all this was brought about, Scrooge knew no more than you do. He only knew that it was quite correct; that everything had happened so; that there he was alone again, when all the other boys had gone home for the jolly holidays.

He was not reading now, but walking up and down despairingly. Scrooge looked at the Ghost and, with a mournful shaking of his head, glanced anxiously toward the door.

It opened; and a little girl, much younger than the boy, came darting in, and putting her arms about his neck, and often kissing him, addressed him as her "Dear, dear brother."

"I have come to bring you home, Dear Brother!" said the child, clapping her tiny hands, and bending down to laugh. "To bring you home, home, home!"

"Home, little Fan?" returned the boy.

"Yes!" said the child, brimful of glee. "Home, for good and all. Home, forever and ever. Father is so much kinder than he used to be, that home's like Heaven. He spoke so gently to me one dear night when I was going to bed, that I was not afraid to ask him once more if you might come home; and he said 'Yes,' you should; and sent me in a coach to bring you. And you're to be a man," said the child, opening her eyes; "and are never to come back here; but first we're to be together all the Christmas long, and have the merriest time in all the world."

"You are quite a woman, little Fan!" exclaimed the boy.

She clapped her hands and laughed and tried to touch his head; but being too little, laughed again, and stood on tiptoe to embrace him. Then she began to drag him, in her childish eagerness, toward the door; and he, nothing loath to go, accompanied her.

A terrible voice in the hall cried, "Bring down Master Scrooge's box, there!" And in the hall appeared the schoolmaster himself, who glared on Master Scrooge with a ferocious condescension, and threw him into a dreadful state of mind by shaking hands with him. He then conveyed him and his sister into the veriest old well of a shivering best-parlor that ever was seen, where the maps upon the wall, and the celestial and terrestrial globes in the windows, were waxy with cold. Here he procured a decanter of curiously light wine and a block of curiously heavy cake, and administered installments of these dainties to the young people, at the same time sending out a meager servant to offer a glass of "something" to the postboy, who answered that he thanked the gentleman, but if it was the same tap as he had tasted before, he had rather not. Master Scrooge's trunk being by this time tied on to the top of the chaise, the children bade the schoolmaster good-by right willingly; and getting into it, drove gaily down the garden sweep, the quick wheels dashing the hoar frost and snow from off the dark leaves of the evergreens like spray.

"Always a delicate creature, whom a breath might have withered," said the Ghost. "But she had a large heart!"

"So she had," cried Scrooge. "You're right. I will not gainsay it, Spirit. God forbid!"

"She died a woman," said the Ghost, "and had, as I think, children."

"One child," Scrooge returned.

"True," said the Ghost. "Your nephew!"

Scrooge seemed uneasy in his mind, and answered briefly, "Yes."

Although they had but that moment left the school behind them, they were now in the busy thoroughfares of a city, where shadowy passengers passed and repassed, where shadowy carts and coaches battled for the way, and all the strife and tumult of a real city were. It was made plain enough, by the dressing of the shops, that here too it was Christmas time again; but it was evening, and the streets were lighted up.

The Ghost stopped at a certain warehouse door, and asked Scrooge if he knew it.

"Know it?" said Scrooge. "Was I apprenticed here?"

They went in. At sight of an old gentleman in a Welsh wig, sitting behind such a high desk, that if he had been two inches taller he must have knocked his head against the ceiling, Scrooge cried in great excitement, "Why, it's old Fezziwig! Bless his heart; it's Fezziwig alive again!"

Old Fezziwig laid down his pen and looked up at the clock, which pointed to the hour of seven. He rubbed his hands, adjusted his capacious waistcoat, laughed all over himself, from his shoes to his organ of benevolence, and called out in a comfortable, oily, rich, fat, jovial voice, "Yo ho, there! Ebenezer! Dick!"

Scrooge's former self, now grown a young man, came briskly in, accompanied by his fellow 'prentice.

"Dick Wilkins, to be sure!" said Scrooge to the Ghost. "Bless me, yes. There he is. He was very much attached to me, was Dick. Poor Dick! Dear, dear!"

"Yo ho, my boys!" said Fezziwig. "No more work tonight. Christmas Eve, Dick. Christmas, Ebenezer! Let's have the shutters up," cried old Fezziwig, with a sharp clap of his hands, "before a man can say 'Jack Robinson!'"

You wouldn't believe how those two fellows went at it! They charged into the street with the shutters—one, two, three—had 'em up in their places—four, five, six—barred 'em and pined 'em—seven, eight, nine—and came back before you could have got to twelve, panting like race horses.

"Hilli-ho!" cried old Fezziwig, skipping down from the high desk with wonderful agility. "Clear away, my lads, and let's have lots of room here! Hilli-ho, Dick! Chirrup, Ebenezer!"

Clear away! There was nothing they wouldn't have cleared away, or couldn't have cleared away, with old Fezziwig looking on. It was done in a minute. Every movable was packed off, as if it were dismissed from public life for evermore; the floor was swept and watered, the lamps were trimmed, fuel was heaped upon the fire; and the warehouse was as snug and warm and dry and bright a ballroom as you would desire to see upon a winter's night.

In came a fiddler with a music book and went up to the lofty desk and made an orchestra of it, and tuned like fifty stomach-aches. In came Mrs. Fezziwig, one vast, substantial smile. In came the three Miss Fezziwigs, beaming and lovable. In came the six young followers whose hearts they broke. In came all the young men and women employed in the business. In came the housemaid with her cousin, the baker. In came the cook with her brother's particular friend, the milkman. In came the boy from over the way, who was suspected of not having board enough from his master; trying to hide himself behind the girl from next door but one, who was proved to have had her ears pulled by her mistress. In they all came, one after another; some shyly, some boldly, some gracefully, some awkwardly, some pushing, some pulling; in they all came, anyhow and everyhow. Away they all went, twenty couples at once; hands half round and back again the other way; down the middle and up again; round and round in various stages of affectionate grouping; old top couple always turning up in the wrong place; new top couple starting off again, as soon as they got there; all top couples at last, and not a bottom one to help them! When this result was brought about, old Fezziwig, clapping his hands to stop the dance cried out, "Well done!" And the fiddler plunged his hot face into a pot of porter especially provided for that purpose. But, scorning rest, upon his reappearance he instantly began again, though there were no dancers yet, as if the other fiddler had been carried home, exhausted on a shutter, and he were a brand-new man resolved to beat him out of sight or perish.

There were more dances, and there were forfeits, and more dances, and there was cake, and there was negus, and there was a great piece of Cold Roast, and there was a great piece of Cold Boiled, and there were mince pies and plenty of beer. But the great effect of the evening came after the Roast and Boiled, when the fiddler (an artful dog, mind! The sort of man who knew his business better than you or I could have told it him!) struck up "Sir Roger de Coverley." Then old Fezziwig stood out to dance with Mrs. Fezziwig. Top couple, too, with a good stiff piece of work cut out for them, three or four and twenty pair of partners, people who were not to be trifled with, people who would dance, and had no notion of walking.

But if they had been twice as many—ah, four times—old Fezziwig would have been a match for them, and so would Mrs. Fezziwig. As to her, she was worthy to be his partner in every sense of the term. If that's not high praise, tell me higher, and I'll use it. A positive light appeared to issue from Fezziwig's calves. They shone in every part of the dance like moons. You couldn't have predicted, at any given time, what would become of them next. And when old Fezziwig and Mrs. Fezziwig had gone all through the dance—advance and retire, both hands to your partner, bow and curtsey, corkscrew, thread-the-needle, and back again to your place—

Fezziwig "cut"—cut so deftly that he appeared to wink with his legs, and came upon his feet again without a stagger.

When the clock struck eleven, this domestic ball broke up. Mr. and Mrs. Fezziwig took their stations, one on either side of the door, and shaking hands with every person individually as he or she went out, wished him or her a Merry Christmas. When everybody had retired but the two 'prentices, they did the same to them; and thus the cheerful voices died away, and the lads were left to their beds, which were under a counter in the back shop.

During the whole of this time Scrooge had acted like a man out of his wits. His heart and soul were in the scene, and with his former self. He corroborated everything, remembered everything, enjoyed everything, and underwent the strangest agitation. It was not until now, when the bright faces of his former self and Dick were turned from them, that he remembered the Ghost, and became conscious that it was looking full upon him, while the light upon its head burned very clear.

"A small matter," said the Ghost, "to make these silly folks so full of gratitude."

"Small!" echoed Scrooge.

The Spirit signed to him to listen to the two apprentices, who were pouring out their hearts in praise of Fezziwig; and when he had done so, said, "Why! Is it not? He has spent but a few pounds of your mortal money, three or four perhaps. Is that so much that he deserves this praise?"

"It isn't that," said Scrooge, heated by the remark and speaking unconsciously like his former, not his latter self. "It isn't that, Spirit. He has the power to render us happy or unhappy; to make our service light or burdensome; a pleasure or a toil. Say that his power lies in words and looks; in things so slight and insignificant that is it impossible to add and count 'em up; what then? The happiness he gives is quite as great as if it cost a fortune."

He felt the Spirit's glance, and stopped.

"What is the matter?" asked the Ghost.

"Nothing particular," said Scrooge.

"Something, I think?" the Ghost insisted.

"No," said Scrooge. "No. I should like to be able to say a word or two to my clerk just now. That's all."

His former self turned down the lamps as he gave utterance to the wish; and Scrooge and the Ghost again stood side by side in the open air.

"My time grows short," observed the Spirit. "Quick!"

This was not addressed to Scrooge, or to any one whom he could see, but it produced an immediate effect. For again Scrooge saw himself. He was older now, a man in the prime of life. His face had not the harsh and rigid lines of later years, but it had begun to wear the signs of care and avarice. There was an eager, greedy, restless motion in the eye, which showed the passion that had taken root, and where the shadow of the growing tree would fall.

He was not alone, but sat by the side of a fair young girl in a mourning dress, in whose eyes there were tears, which sparkled in the light that shone out of the Ghost of Christmas Past.

"It matters little," she said softly. "To you, very little. Another idol has displaced me; and if it can cheer and comfort you in time to come, as I would have tried to do, I have no just cause to grieve."

"What idol has displaced you?" he rejoined.

"A golden one."

"This is the evenhanded dealing of the world!" he said. "There is nothing on which it is so hard as poverty; and there is nothing it professes to condemn with such severity as the pursuit of wealth!"

"You fear the world too much," she answered, gently. "All your other hopes have merged into the hope of being beyond the chance of its sordid reproach. I have seen your nobler aspirations fall off one by one, until the master passion, Gain, engrosses you. Have I not?"

"What then?" he retorted. "Even if I have grown so much wiser, what then? I am not changed toward you."

She shook her head.

"Am I?"

"Our contract is an old one. It was made when we were both poor and content to be so, until, in good season, we could improve our worldly fortune by our patient industry. You are changed. When it was made you were another man."

"I was a boy," he said impatiently.

"Your own feeling tells you that you were not what you are," she returned. "I am. That which promised happiness when we were one in heart, is fraught with misery now that we are two. How often and how keenly I have thought of this, I will not say. It is enough that I have thought of it, and can release you."

"Have I ever sought release?"

"In words, no, never."

"In what, then?"

"In a changed nature, in an altered spirit, in another atmosphere of life, another Hope as its great end. In everything that made my move of any worth or value in your sight. If this had never been between us," said the girl, looking mildly but with steadiness upon him, "tell me, would you seek me out and try to win me now? Ah, no!"

He seemed to yield to the justice of this supposition, in spite of himself. But he said, with a struggle, "You think not."

"I would gladly think otherwise if I could," she answered, "Heaven knows! When I have learned a Truth like this, I know how strong and irresistible it must be. But if you were free today, tomorrow, yesterday, can even I believe that you would choose a dowerless girl—you who, in your very confidence with her, weigh every-thing by Gain; or choosing her, if for a moment you were false enough to your one guiding principle to do so, do I not know that your repentance and regret would surely follow? I do; and I release you. With a full heart, for the love of him you once were."

He was about to speak; but, with her head turned from him, she resumed.

"You may—the memory of what is past half makes me hope you will—have pain in this. A very, very brief time, and you will dismiss the recollection of it, gladly, as an unprofitable dream, from which it happened well that you awoke. May you be happy in the life you have chosen!"

She left him and they parted.

"Spirit!" said Scrooge. "Show me no more! Conduct me home. Why do you delight to torture me?"

"One shadow more!" exclaimed the Ghost.

"No more!" cried Scrooge. "No more. I don't wish to see it. Show me no more!"

But the relentless Ghost pinioned him in both arms, and forced him to observe what happened next.

They were in another scene and place, a room, not very large or handsome, but full of comfort. Near the winter fire sat a beautiful young girl, so like that last that Scrooge believed it was the same, until he saw her, now a comely matron, sitting opposite her daughter. The noise in this room was perfectly tumultuous, for there were more children there than Scrooge in his agitated state of mind could count; and, unlike the celebrated herd in the poem, they were not forty children conducting themselves like one, but every child was conducting itself like forty. The consequences were uproarious beyond belief, but no one seemed to care; on the contrary, the mother and daughter laughed heartily and enjoyed it very much, and the latter, soon beginning to mingle in the sports, got pillaged by the young brigands most ruthlessly. What would I not have given to be one of them! Though I never could have been so rude, no, no! I wouldn't for the wealth of all the world have crushed that braided hair, and torn it down; and for the previous little show, I wouldn't have plucked it off—God bless my soul!—to save my life. As to measuring her waist in sport, as they did, bold young brood, I couldn't have done it; I should have expected my arm to have grown round it for a punishment, and never come straight again. And yet I should have dearly liked, I own, to have touched her lips, to have questioned her, that she might have opened them, to have looked upon the lashes of her downcast eyes and never raised a blush, to have let loose waves of her hair, an inch of which would be a keepsake beyond price; in short, I should have liked to have had the lightest license of a child, and yet to have been man enough to know its value.

But now a knocking at the door was heard, and such a rush immediately ensued that she with laughing face and plundered dress was borne toward it in the center of a flushed and boisterous group, just in time to greet the father, who came home attended by a man laden with Christmas toys and presents. Then the shouting and the struggling, and the onslaught that was made on the defenseless porter! The scaling him, with chairs for ladders, to dive into his pockets, despoil him of brown paper parcels, hold on tight by his cravat, hug him round the neck, pommel his back, and kick his legs in irrepressible affection. The shouts of wonder and delight with which the development of every package was received! The terrible announcement that the baby had been taken in the act of putting a doll's frying pan into his mouth, and was more than suspected of having swallowed a fictitious turkey, glued on a wooden platter! The immense relief of finding this a false alarm! The joy, and gratitude, ecstasy! They are all indescribably alike. It is enough that, by degrees, the children and their emotions got out of the parlor, and, by one stair at a time, up to the top of the house, where they went to bed.

And now Scrooge looked on more attentively than ever, when the master of the house, having his daughter leaning fondly on him, sat down with her and her mother at his own fireside; and when he thought that such another creature, quite as graceful and as full of promise, might have called him Father, and been a springtime in the haggard winter of his life, his sight grew very dim indeed.

"Belle," said the husband, turning to his wife, with a smile, "I saw an old friend of yours this afternoon."

"Who was it?"

"Guess!"

"How can I? Tut, don't I know." She added, in the same breath, laughing as he laughed, "Mr. Scrooge."

"Mr. Scrooge it was. I passed his office window; and as it was not shut up, and he had a candle inside, I could scarcely help seeing him. His partner lies upon the point of death, I hear; and there he is alone. Quite alone in the world, I do believe."

"Spirit!" said Scrooge. "Remove me from this place."

"I told you these were shadows of the things that have been," said the Ghost. "That they are what they are, do not blame me!"

"Remove me!" Scrooge exclaimed. "I cannot bear it!"

He turned upon the Ghost, and seeing that it looked upon him with a face in which, in some strange way, there were fragments of all the faces it had shown him, wrestled with it.

"Leave me! Take me back. Haunt me no longer!"

In the struggle—if that can be called a struggle in which the Ghost, with no visible resistance on its own part was undisturbed by any effort of its adversary— Scrooge observed that its light was burning high and bright; and dimly connecting that with its influence over him, he seized the extinguisher-cap, and by a sudden action pressed it down upon its head.

The Spirit dropped beneath it, so that the extinguisher covered its whole form; but though Scrooge pressed it down with all his force, he could not hide the light, which streamed from under it, in an unbroken flood upon the ground.

He was conscious of being exhausted and overcome by an irresistible drowsiness and, further, of being in his own bedroom. He gave the cap a parting squeeze, in which his hand relaxed, and had barely time to reel to bed before he sank into a heavy sleep.

* * * * *

Awakening in the middle of a prodigiously tough snore, and sitting up in bed to get his thoughts together, Scrooge had no occasion to be told that the bell was again upon the stroke of one. He felt that he was restored to consciousness in the right nick of time, for the especial purpose of holding a conference with the second messenger despatched to him through Jacob Marley's intervention.

Now, being prepared for almost anything, he was not by any means prepared for nothing; and consequently, when the bell struck one and no shape appeared, he was taken with a violent fit of trembling. Five minutes, ten minutes, a quarter of an hour went by, yet nothing came. All this time he lay upon his bed, the very core and center of a blaze of ruddy light which streamed upon it when the clock proclaimed the hour, and which, being only light, was more alarming than a dozen ghosts, as he was powerless to make out what it meant, or would be at; and was sometimes apprehensive that he might be at that very moment an interesting case of spontaneous combustion, without having the consolation of knowing it. At least, however, he began to think—as you and I would have thought at first, for it is always the person not in the predicament who knows what ought to have been done in it, and would unquestionably have done it too—at last, I say, he began to think that the source and secret of this ghostly light might be in the adjoining room, from whence, on further tracing it, it seemed to shine. This idea taking full possession of his mind, he got up softly and shuffled in his slippers to the door.

The moment Scrooge's hand was on the lock, a strange voice called him by his name and bade him enter. He obeyed.

It was his own room. There was no doubt about that. But it had undergone a surprising transformation. The walls and ceiling were so hung with living green, that it looked a perfect grove, from every part of which bright gleaming berries glistened.

"Come in!" exclaimed the Ghost. "Come in and know me better, man!"

Scrooge entered timidly, and hung his head before this Spirit. He was not the dogged Scrooge he had been; and though the Spirit's eyes were clear and kind, he did not like to meet them.

"I am the Ghost of Christmas Present," said the Spirit. "Look upon me!"

Scrooge reverently did so. It was clothed in one simple deep green robe, or mantle, bordered with white fur. This garment hung so loosely on the figure that its capacious breast was bare, as if disclaiming to be warded or concealed by any artifice. Its feet, observable beneath the ample folds of the garment, were also bare, and on its head it wore no other covering than a holly wreath, set here and there with shining icicles. Its dark brown curls were long and free, free as its genial face, its sparkling eye, its open hand, its cheery voice, its unconstrained demeanor, and its joyful air. Girded round its middle was an antique scabbard, but no sword was in it.

"You have never seen the like of me before?" exclaimed the Spirit.

"Never," Scrooge made answer to it.

"Have never walked forth with the younger members of my family; meaning (for I am very young) my elder brothers born in these later years?" pursued the Phantom.

"I don't think I have," said Scrooge. "I am afraid I have not. Have you had many brothers, Spirit?"

"More than eighteen hundred," said the Ghost.

"A tremendous family to provide for," muttered Scrooge. The Ghost of Christmas Present rose.

"Spirit," said Scrooge submissively, "conduct me where you will. I went forth last night on compulsion, and I learned a lesson which is working now. Tonight, if you have aught to teach me, let me profit by it."

"Touch my robe!"

Scrooge did as he was told, and held it fast.

Holly, mistletoe, red berries, ivy, turkeys, geese, game, poultry, brawn, meat, pigs, sausages, oysters, pies, puddings, fruit, and punch, all vanished instantly. So did the room, the fire, the ruddy glow, the hour of night, and they stood in the city streets on Christmas morning, where (for the weather was severe) the people made a rough but brisk and not unpleasant kind of music, in scraping the snow from the pavement in front of their dwellings, and from the tops of their houses, whence it was mad delight to the boys to see it come plumping down into the road below, and splitting into artificial little snowstorms.

The house fronts looked black enough, and the windows blacker, contrasting with the smooth white sheet of snow upon the roofs and with the dirtier snow upon the ground, which last deposit had been plowed up in deep furrows by the heavy wheels of carts and wagons, furrows that crossed and recrossed each other hundreds of times where the great streets branched off, and made intricate channels, hard to trace, in the thick yellow mud and icy water. The sky was gloomy, and the shortest streets were choked up with a dingy mist, half thawed, half frozen, whose heavier particles descended in a shower of sooty atoms, as if all the chimneys in Great Britain had, by one consent, caught fire and were blazing away to their dear hearts' content. There was nothing very cheerful in the climate or the town, and yet was there an air of cheerfulness abroad that the clearest summer air and brightest summer sun might have endeavored to diffuse in vain.

In time the bells ceased, and the bakers were shut up; and yet there was a genial shadowing forth of all these dinners and the progress of their cooking, in the thawed blotch of wet above each baker's oven, where the pavement smoked as if its stones were cooking too.

"Is there a peculiar flavor in what you sprinkle from your torch?" asked Scrooge.

"There is. My own."

"Would it apply to any kind of dinner on this day?" asked Scrooge.

"To any kindly given. To a poor one most."

"Why to a poor one most?" asked Scrooge.

"Because it needs it most."

"Spirit," said Scrooge, after a moment's thought, "I wonder you, of all the beings in the many worlds about us, should desire to cramp these people's opportunities of innocent enjoyment."

"I!" cried the Spirit.

"You would deprive them of their means of dining every seventh day, often the only day on which they can be said to dine at all," said Scrooge; "wouldn't you?"

"I!" cried the Spirit.

"You seek to close these places on the Seventh Day," said Scrooge. "And it comes to the same thing."

"I seek!" exclaimed the Spirit.

"Forgive me if I am wrong. It has been done in your name, or at least in that of your family," said Scrooge.

"There are some upon this earth of yours," returned the Spirit, "who lay claim to know us, and who do their deeds of passion, pride, ill will, hatred, envy, bigotry, and selfishness in our name, who are as strange to us, and all our kith and kin, as if they had never lived. Remember that, and charge their doings on themselves, not us."

Scrooge promised that he would; and they went on, invisible, as they had been before, into the suburbs of the town. It was a remarkable quality of the Ghost (which Scrooge had observed at the baker's) that notwithstanding his gigantic size, he could accommodate himself to any place with ease; and that he stood beneath a low roof quite as gracefully and like a supernatural creature as it was possible he could have done in any lofty hall.

And perhaps it was the pleasure the good Spirit had in showing off this power of his, or else it was his own kind, generous, hearty nature, and his sympathy with all poor men, that led him straight to Scrooge's clerk's; for there he went, and took Scrooge with him, holding to his robe; and on the threshold of the door the Spirit smiled, and stopped to bless Bob Cratchit's dwelling with the sprinklings of this torch. Think of that! Bob had but fifteen bob a week himself; he pocketed on Saturdays but fifteen copies of his Christian name; and yet the Ghost of Christmas Present blessed his four-roomed house!

Then up rose Mrs. Cratchit, Cratchit's wife, dressed out but poorly in a twice-turned gown, but brave in ribbons, which are cheap and make a goodly show for sixpence; and she laid the cloth, assisted by Belinda Cratchit, second of her daughters, also brave in ribbons; while Master Peter Cratchit plunged a fork into the saucepan of potatoes, and getting the corners of his monstrous shirt collar (Bob's private property, conferred upon his son and heir in honor of the day) into his mouth, rejoiced to find himself so gallantly attired, and yearned to show his linen in the fashionable peaks. And now two smaller Cratchits, boy and girl, came tearing in, screaming that outside the baker's they had smelled the goose and known it for their own; and basking in luxurious thoughts of sage and onion, these young Cratchits danced about the table and exalted Master Peter Cratchit to the skies, while he (not proud, although his collar nearly choked him) blew the fire until the slow potatoes bubbling up, knocked loudly at the saucepan lid to be let out and peeled.

"What has ever got your precious father, then?" said Mrs. Cratchit. "And your brother, Tiny Tim! And Martha warn't as late last Christmas Day by half an hour!"

"Here's Martha, Mother!" said a girl appearing as she spoke.

"Here's Martha, Mother!" cried the two young Cratchits. "Hurrah! There's such a goose, Martha!"

"Why, bless your heart alive, my dear, how late you are!" said Mrs. Cratchit, kissing her a dozen times, and taking off her shawl and bonnet for her with officious zeal.

"We'd a deal of work to finish up last night," replied the girl, "and had to clear away this morning, Mother!"

"Well! Never mind, so long as you are come," said Mrs. Cratchit. "Sit ye down before the fire, my dear, and have a warm, Lord bless ye!"

"No, no! There's Father coming," cried the two young Cratchits, who were everywhere at once. "Hide, Martha, hide!"

So Martha hid herself, and in came little Bob, the father, with at least three foot of comforter exclusive of the fringe hanging down before him, and his threadbare clothes darned up and brushed, to look seasonable, and Tiny Tim upon his shoulder. Alas for Tiny Tim, he bore a little crutch, and had his limbs supported by an iron frame!

"Why, where's our Martha?" cried Bob Cratchit, looking round.

"Not coming," said Mrs. Cratchit.

"Not coming!" said Bob, with a sudden declension in his high spirits; for he had been Tim's blood horse all the way from church, and had come home rampant. "Not coming upon Christmas Day!"

Martha didn't like to see him disappointed, if it were only in joke, so she came out prematurely from behind the closet door and ran into his arms, while the two young Cratchits hustled Tiny Tim and bore him off into the washhouse, that he might hear the pudding singing in the copper.

"And how did little Tim behave?" asked Mrs. Cratchit, when she had rallied Bob on his credulity, and Bob had hugged his daughter to his heart's content.

"As good as gold," said Bob, "and better. Somehow he gets thoughtful, sitting by himself so much, and thinks the strangest things you ever heard. He told me, coming home, that he hoped the people saw him in the church, because he was a cripple, and it might be pleasant to them to remember upon Christmas Day who made lame beggars walk, and blind men see."

There never was such a goose. Bob said he didn't believe there ever was such a goose cooked. Its tenderness and flavor, size and cheapness, were the themes of universal admiration. Eked out by apple sauce and mashed potatoes, it was sufficient dinner for the whole family; indeed, as Mrs. Cratchit said with great delight (surveying one small atom of a bone upon the dish), they hadn't eaten it all at last! Yet every one had had enough, and the youngest Cratchits, in particular, were steeped in sage and in onion to the eyebrows! But now the plates being changed by Miss Belinda, Mrs. Cratchit left the room—too nervous to bear witness—to take the pudding up and bring it in.

Suppose it should not be done enough! Suppose it should break in turning out! Suppose somebody should have got over the wall of the back yard, and stolen it, while they were merry with the goose—a supposition at which the two young Cratchits became livid! All sorts of horrors were supposed.

Hallo! A great deal of steam! The pudding was out of the copper. A smell like a washing day! That was the cloth. A smell like an eating house and a pastry cook's next door to each other, with a laundress's next to that! That was the pudding! In half a minute Mrs. Cratchit entered—flushed, but smiling proudly—with the pudding, like a speckled cannon ball, so hard and firm, blazing in half-a-quartern of ignited brandy, and bedight with Christmas holly stuck into the top.

Oh, a wonderful pudding! Bob Cratchit said, and calmly, too, that he regarded it as the greatest success achieved by Mrs. Cratchit since their marriage. Mrs. Cratchit said that now the weight was off her mind, she would confess she had her doubts about the quantity of flour. Everybody had something to say about it, but nobody said or thought it was at all a small pudding for a large family. It would have been flat heresy to do so. Any Cratchit would have blushed to hint at such a thing.

At last the dinner was all done, the cloth was cleared, the hearth swept, and the fire made up. The compound in the jug being tasted, and considered perfect, apples and oranges were put upon the table, and a shovel full of chestnuts on the fire. Then all the Cratchit family drew round the hearth, in what Bob Cratchit called a circle, meaning half a one; and at Bob Cratchit's elbow stood the family display of glass: two tumblers and a custard cup without a handle.

These held the hot stuff from the jug, however, as well as golden goblets would have done; and Bob served it out with beaming looks, while the chestnuts on the fire sputtered and cracked noisily. Then Bob proposed, "A Merry Christmas to us all, my dears. God bless us!"

Which all the family re-echoed.

"God bless us every one!" said Tiny Tim, the last of all.

He sat very close to his father's side, upon his little stool. Bob held his withered little hand in his, as if he loved the child and wished to keep him by his side and dreaded that he might be taken from him.

"Spirit," said Scrooge, with an interest he had never felt before, "tell me if Tiny Tim will live."

"I see a vacant seat," replied the Ghost, "in the poor chimney corner, and a crutch without an owner, carefully preserved. If these shadows remain unaltered by the Future, the child will die."

"No, no," said Scrooge. "Oh, no, kind Spirit! Say he will be spared."

"If these shadows remain unaltered by the Future, none other of my race," returned the Ghost, "will find him here. What then? If he be like to die, he had better do it, and decrease the surplus population."

Scrooge hung his head to hear his own words quoted by the Spirit, and was overcome with penitence and grief.

"Man," said the Ghost, "if man you be in heart, not adamant, forbear that wicked cant until you have discovered What the surplus is, and Where it is. Will you decide what men shall live, what men shall die? It may be that, in the sight of Heaven, you are more worthless and less fit to live than millions like this poor man's child. Oh, God! To hear the Insect on the leaf pronouncing on the too much life among his hungry brothers in the dust!"

Scrooge bent before the Ghost's rebuke and, trembling, cast his eyes upon the ground. But he raised them on hearing his own name.

"Mr. Scrooge!" said Bob; "I'll give you Mr. Scrooge, the Founder of the Feast!"

"The Founder of the Feast, indeed!" cried Mrs. Cratchit, reddening. "I wish I had him here. I'd give him a piece of my mind to feast upon, and I hope he'd have a good appetite for it."

"My dear," said Bob; "The children! Christmas Day."

"It should be Christmas Day, I am sure," said she, "on which one drinks the health of such an odious, stingy, hard, unfeeling man as Mr. Scrooge. You know he is, Robert! Nobody knows it better than you do, poor fellow!"

"My dear," was Bob's mild answer. "Christmas Day."

"I'll drink his health for your sake and the Day's," said Mrs. Cratchit, "not for his. Long life to him! A merry Christmas and a happy New Year! He'll be very merry and very happy, I have no doubt!"

The children drank the toast after her. It was the first of their proceedings which had no heartiness in it. Tiny Tim drank it last of all, but he didn't care twopence for it. Scrooge was the Ogre of the family. The mention of his name cast a dark shadow on the party, which was not dispelled for full five minutes.

After it had passed away, they were ten times merrier than before, from the mere relief of Scrooge the Baleful being done with. Bob Cratchit told them how he had a situation in his eye for Master Peter's being a man of business; and Peter himself looked thoughtfully at the fire from between his collar, as if he were deliberating what particular investments he should favor when he came into the receipt of that bewildering income. Martha, who was a poor apprentice at a milliner's, then told them what kind of work she had to do, and how many hours she worked at a stretch, and how she meant to lie abed tomorrow morning for a good long rest; tomorrow being a holiday she passed at home. Also how she had seen a countess and a lord some days before, and how the lord "was much about as tall as Peter"; at which Peter pulled up his collar so high that you couldn't have seen his head if you had been there.

All this time the chestnuts and the jug went round and round; and by the by they had a song about a lost child traveling in the snow, from Tiny Tim, who had a plaintive little voice, and sang it very well indeed.

There was nothing of high mark in this. They were not a handsome family; they were not well dressed; their shoes were far from being waterproof; their clothes were scanty; and Peter might have known, and very likely did, the inside of a pawnbroker's. But they were happy, grateful, pleased with one another, and contented with the time; and when they faded, and looked happier yet in the bright sprinklings of the Spirit's torch at parting, Scrooge had his eye upon them, and especially on Tiny Tim, until the last.

By this time it was getting dark, and snowing pretty heavily; and, as Scrooge and the Spirit went along the streets, the brightness of the roaring fires in kitchens, parlors, and all sorts of rooms, was wonderful. Here, the flickering of the blaze showed preparations for a cozy dinner, with hot plates baking through and through before the fire, and deep red curtains, ready to be drawn to shut out cold and darkness. There, all the children of the house were running out into the snow to meet their married sisters, brothers, cousins, aunts, and to be the first to greet them. Here, again, were shadows on the window blinds of guests assembling, and there, a group of handsome girls, all hooded and fur-booted, and all chattering at once, tripped lightly off to some near neighbor's house, where, woe upon the single man who saw them enter—artful witches, well they knew it—in a glow.

But if you had judged from the numbers of people on their way to friendly gatherings, you might have thought that no one was at home to give them welcome when they got there, instead of every house expecting company, and piling up its fires half-chimney high. Blessings on it, how the Ghost exulted! How it bared its breadth of breast, and opened its capacious palm, and floated on, outpouring, with a generous hand, its bright and harmless mirth on everything within its reach! The very lamplighter, who ran on before, dotting the dusky streets with specks of light, and who was dressed to spend the evening somewhere, laughed out loudly as the Spirit passed, though little kenned the lamplighter that he had any company but Christmas!

And now, without a word of warning from the Ghost, they stood upon a bleak and desert moor, where monstrous masses of rude stone were cast about as though it were the burial of giants; and water spread itself wheresoever it listed; or would have done so, but for the frost that held it prisoner; and nothing grew but moss and furze and coarse, rank grass. Down in the west the setting sun had left a streak of fiery red, which glared upon the desolation for an instant like a sullen eye, and frowning lower, lower, lower yet, was lost in the thick gloom of darkest night.

"What place is this?" asked Scrooge.

"A place where miners live, who labor in the bowels of the earth," returned the Spirit. "But they know me. See!"

A light shone from the window of the hut, and swiftly they advanced toward it. Passing through the wall of mud and stone, they found a cheerful company assembled round a glowing fire. An old, old man and woman, with their children and their children's children, and another generation beyond that, all decked out gaily in their holiday attire. The old man, in a voice that seldom rose above the howling of the wind upon the barren waste, was singing them a Christmas song; it had been a very old song when he was a boy; and from time to time they all joined in the chorus. So surely as they raised their voices, the old man got quite blithe and loud; and so surely as they stopped, his vigor sank again.

Again the Ghost sped on, above the black and heaving sea—on, on—until, being far away, as he told Scrooge, from any shore, they lighted on a ship.

It was a great surprise to Scrooge, while listening to the moaning of the wind and thinking what a solemn thing it was to move on through the lonely darkness over an unknown abyss, whose depths were secrets as profound as Death, it was a great surprise to Scrooge, while thus engaged, to hear a hearty laugh. It was a much greater surprise to Scrooge to recognize it as his nephew's, and to find himself in a bright dry, gleaming room, with the Spirit smiling by his side, and looking at the same nephew with approving affability!

"Ha! Ha!" laughed Scrooge's nephew. "Ha, ha, ha!"

If you should happen, by any unlikely chance, to know a man more blessed in a laugh than Scrooge's nephew, all I can say is, I should like to know him too. Introduce him to me, and I'll cultivate his acquaintance.

It is a fair, evenhanded, noble adjustment of things, that while there is infection in disease and sorrow, there is nothing in the world so irresistibly contagious as laughter and good humor. When Scrooge's nephew laughed in this way, holding his sides, rolling his head, and twisting his face into the most extravagant contortions, Scrooge's niece, by marriage, laughed as heartily as he. And their assembled friends being not a bit behindhand, roared out lustily.

"Ha, ha! Ha, ha, ha ha!"

"He said that Christmas was a humbug, as I live!" cried Scrooge's nephew. "He believed it, too!"

"More shame for him, Fred!" said Scrooge's niece, indignantly. Bless these women! They never do anything by halves. They are always in earnest.

She was very pretty, exceedingly pretty. With a dimpled, surprised-looking, capital face, a ripe little mouth that seemed made to be kissed—as no doubt it was; all kinds of good little dots about her chin that melted into one another when she laughed, and the sunniest pair of eyes you ever saw in any little creature's head. Altogether she was what you would have called provoking, you know, but satisfactory, too. Oh, perfectly satisfactory.

"He's a comical fellow," said Scrooge's nephew, "that's the truth; and not so pleasant as he might be. However, his offenses carry their own punishment and I have nothing to say against him."

"I'm sure he is very rich, Fred," hinted Scrooge's niece. "At least you always tell *me* so."

"What of that, my dear!" said Scrooge's nephew. "His wealth is of no use to him. He don't do any good with it. He don't make himself comfortable with it. He hasn't the satisfaction of thinking—ha, ha, ha!—that he is ever going to benefit Us with it."

"I have no patience with him," observed Scrooge's niece. Scrooge's niece's sister and all the other ladies expressed the same opinion.

"Oh, I have!" said Scrooge's nephew. "I am sorry for him; I couldn't be angry with him if I tried. Who suffers by his ill whims! Himself, always. Here he takes it into his head to dislike us, and he won't come and dine with us. What's the consequence? He don't lose much of a dinner."

"Indeed, I think he loses a very good dinner," interrupted Scrooge's niece. Everybody else said the same, and they must be allowed to have been competent judges, because they had just had dinner, and with the dessert upon the table, were clustered round the fire, by lamplight.

"Well! I am very glad to hear it," said Scrooge's nephew, "because I haven't any great faith in these young housekeepers. What do *you* say, Topper?"

Topper had clearly got his eyes upon one of Scrooge's niece's sisters, for he answered that a bachelor was a wretched outcast, who had no right to express an opinion on the subject. Whereat Scrooge's niece's sister—the plump one with the lace tucker, not the one with the roses—blushed.

"Do go on, Fred," said Scrooge's niece, clapping her hands. "He never finishes what he begins to say! He is such a ridiculous fellow!"

Scrooge's nephew reveled in another laugh, and as it was impossible to keep the infection off, though the plump sister tried hard to do it with aromatic vinegar, his example was unanimously followed.

"I was only going to say," said Scrooge's nephew, "that the consequence of his taking a dislike to us, and not making merry with us, is, I think, that he loses some pleasant moments which could do him no harm. I am sure he loses pleasanter companions than he can find in his own thoughts, either in his moldy old office or his dusty chambers. I mean to give him the same chance every year, whether he likes it or not, for I pity him. He may rail at Christmas till he dies, but he can't help thinking better of it—I defy him—if he finds me going there, in good temper, year after year, and saying, 'Uncle Scrooge, how are you?' If it only puts him in the vein to leave his poor clerk fifty pounds, that's something; and I think I shook him yesterday."

After a while they played at forfeits, for it is good to be children sometimes, and never better than at Christmas, when its mighty Founder was a child Himself. Stop! There was first a game at blindman's buff. Of course there was. And I no more believe Topper was really blind than I believe he had eyes in his boots. My opinion is that it was a done thing between him and Scrooge's nephew, and that the Ghost of Christmas Present knew it. The way he went after that plump sister in the lace tucker was an outrage on the credulity of human nature. Knocking down the fire irons, tumbling over the chairs, bumping up against the piano, smothering himself among the curtains, wherever she went, there went he! He always knew where the plump sister was. He wouldn't catch anybody else. If you had fallen up against him (as some of them did) on purpose, he would have made a feint of endeavoring to seize you, which would have been an affront to your understanding, and would instantly have sidled off in the direction of the plump sister. She often cried out that it wasn't fair, and it really was not. But when at last he caught her, when, in spite of all her silken rustlings, and her rapid flutterings past him, he got her into a corner whence there was no escape, then his conduct was the most execrable. For his pretending not to know her, his pretending that it was necessary to touch her headdress, and further to assure himself of her identity by pressing a certain ring upon her finger and a certain chain about her neck, was vile, monstrous! No doubt she told him her opinion of it when, another blindman being in office, they were so confidential together, behind the curtains.

Scrooge's niece was not one of the blindman's buff party, but was made comfortable with a large chair and a footstool, in a snug corner where the Ghost and Scrooge were close behind her. But she joined in the forfeits, and loved her love to admiration with all the letters of the alphabet.

Likewise at the game of How, When, and Where, she was very great, and, to the secret joy of Scrooge's nephew, beat her sisters hollow, though they were sharp girls too, as Topper could have told you. There might have been twenty people there, young and old, but they all played, and so did Scrooge, for, wholly forgetting in the interest he had in what was going on that his voice made no sound in their ears, he sometimes came out with his guess quite loud, and very often guessed right, too; for the sharpest needle, best Whitechapel, warranted not to cut in the eye, was not sharper than Scrooge, blunt as he took it in his head to be.

The Ghost was greatly pleased to find him in this mood, and looked upon him with such favor that he begged like a boy to be allowed to stay until the guests departed. But this the Spirit said could not be done.

"Here is a new game," said Scrooge. "One half-hour, Spirit, only one!"

It was a game called "Yes and No," where Scrooge's nephew had to think of something, and the rest must find out what; he only answering to their questions yes or no, as the case was. The brisk fire of questioning to which he was exposed, elicited from him that he was thinking of an animal, a live animal, rather a disagreeable animal, a savage animal, an animal that growled and grunted sometimes, and talked sometimes, and lived in London, and walked about the streets, and wasn't made a show of, and wasn't led by anybody, and didn't live in a menagerie, and was never killed in a market, and was not a horse, or an ass, or a cow, or a bull, or a tiger, or a dog, or a pig, or a cat, or a bear. At every fresh question that was put to him, this nephew burst into a fresh roar of laughter and was so inexpressibly tickled, that he was obliged to get up off the sofa and stamp.

At last the plump sister, falling into a similar state, cried out, "I have found it out! I know what it is, Fred! I know what it is!"

"What is it?" cried Fred.

"It's your Uncle Scro-o-o-oge!"

Which it certainly was. Admiration was the universal sentiment, though some objected that the reply to "Is it a bear?" ought to have been "Yes"; inasmuch as an answer in the negative was sufficient to have diverted their thoughts from Mr. Scrooge, supposing they had ever had any tendency that way.

"He has given us plenty of merriment, I am sure," said Fred, "and it would be ungrateful not to drink his health. Here is a glass of mulled wine ready to our hand at the moment; and I say, 'Uncle Scrooge!'"

"Well! Uncle Scrooge!" they cried.

"A Merry Christmas and a Happy New Year to the old man, wherever he is!" said Scrooge's nephew. "He wouldn't take it from me, but may he have it, nevertheless. Uncle Scrooge!"

Uncle Scrooge had imperceptibly become so gay and light of heart that he would have pledged the unconscious company in return, and thanked them in an inaudible speech if the Ghost had given him time. But the whole scene passed off in the breath of the last word spoken by his nephew; and he and the Spirit were again upon their travels.

Much they saw, and far they went, and many homes they visited, but always with a happy end. The Spirit stood beside sick beds, and they were cheerful; on foreign lands, and they were close at home; by struggling men, and they were patient in their greater hope; by poverty, and it was rich. In almshouse, hospital and jail, in misery's every refuge, where vain man in his little brief authority had not made fast the door, and barred the Spirit out, he left his blessing, and taught Scrooge his precepts.

It was a long night, if it were only a night; but Scrooge had his doubts of this, because the Christmas holidays appeared to be condensed into the space of time they passed together. It was strange, too, that while Scrooge remained unaltered in his outward form, the Ghost grew older, clearly older. Scrooge had observed this change, but never spoke of it, until they left a children's Twelfth Night party, when, looking at the Spirit as they stood together in an open place, he noticed that his hair was gray.

"Are spirits' lives so short?" asked Scrooge.

"My life upon this globe is very brief," replied the Ghost. "It ends tonight."

"Tonight!" cried Scrooge.

"Tonight at midnight. Hark! The time is drawing near."

The chimes were ringing the three quarters past eleven.

"Forgive me if I am not justified in what I ask," said Scrooge, looking intently at the Spirit's robe, "but I see something strange, and not belonging to yourself, protruding from your skirts. Is it a foot or a claw?"

"It might be a claw, for the flesh there is upon it," was the Spirit's sorrowful reply. "Look here."

From the foldings of its robe it brought two children wretched, abject, frightful, hideous, miserable. They knelt down at its feet and clung upon the outside of its garment.

"Oh, Man! Look here. Look, look, down here!" exclaimed the Ghost.

They were a boy and girl. Yellow, meager, ragged, scowling, wolfish; but prostrate, too, in their humility.

"Spirit! Are they yours?" Scrooge could say no more.

"They are Man's," said the Spirit, looking down upon them. "And they cling to me, appealing from their fathers. This boy is Ignorance. This girl is Want. Beware of them both, and all of their degree, but most of all beware this boy, for on his brow I see that written which is Doom, unless the writing be erased. Deny it!" cried the

Spirit, stretching out its hand toward the city. "Slander those who tell it ye! Admit it for your factious purposes, and make it worse! And bide the end!"

"Have they no refuge or resource?" cried Scrooge.

"Are there no prisons!" said the Spirit, turning on him for the last time with his own words. "Are there no workhouses?"

The bell struck twelve.

Scrooge looked about him for the Ghost, and saw it not. As the last stroke ceased to vibrate, he remembered the prediction of old Jacob Marley, and lifting up his eyes, beheld a solemn Phantom, draped and hooded, coming like a mist along the ground toward him.

* * * * *

The Phantom slowly, gravely, silently approached. When it came near him, Scrooge bent down upon his knee, for in the very air through which this Spirit moved it seemed to scatter gloom and mystery.

It was shrouded in a deep black garment, which concealed its head, its face, its form, and left nothing of it visible save one outstretched hand. But for this it would have been difficult to detach its figure from the night, and separate it from the darkness by which it was surrounded.

He felt that it was tall and stately when it came beside him, and that its mysterious presence filled him with a solemn dread. He knew no more, for the Spirit neither spoke nor moved.

"I am in the presence of the Ghost of Christmas Yet To Come?" said Scrooge.

The Spirit answered not, but pointed onward with its hand.

"You are about to show me shadows of the things that have not happened, but will happen in the time before us," Scrooge pursued. "Is that so, Spirit?"

The upper portion of the garment was contracted for an instant in its folds, as if the Spirit had inclined its head. That was the only answer he received.

It gave him no reply. The hand was pointed straight before them.

"Lead on!" said Scrooge. "Lead on! The night is waning fast, and it is precious time to me, I know. Lead on, Spirit!"

The phantom moved away as it had come toward him. Scrooge followed in the shadow of its dress, which bore him up, he thought, and carried him along.

The Spirit stopped beside one little knot of business men. Observing that the hand was pointed to them, Scrooge advanced to listen to their talk.

"No," said a great fat man with a monstrous chin, "I don't know much about it either way. I only know he's dead."

"When did he die?" inquired another.

"Last night, I believe."

"Why, what was the matter with him?" asked a third, taking a vast quantity of snuff out of a very large snuffbox. "I thought he'd never die."

"God knows," said the first, with a yawn.

"What has he done with his money?" asked a red-faced gentleman with a pendulous excrescence on the end of his nose, that shook like the gills of a turkey cock.

"I haven't heard," said the man with the large chin, yawning again. "Left it to his company, perhaps. He hasn't left it to me. That's all I know."

This pleasantry was received with a general laugh.

"It's likely to be a very cheap funeral," said the same speaker, "for upon my life I don't know of anybody to go to it. Suppose we make up a party and volunteer?"

"I don't mind going if a lunch is provided," observed the gentleman with the excrescence on his nose. "But I must be fed, if I make one."

Another laugh.

"Well, I am the most disinterested among you, after all," said the first speaker, "for I never wear black gloves, and I never eat lunch. But I'll offer to go, if anybody else will. When I come to think of it, I'm not at all sure that I wasn't his most particular friend; for we used to stop and speak whenever we met. By, by!"

Speakers and listeners strolled away and mixed with other groups. Scrooge knew the men, and looked toward the Spirit for an explanation.

The Phantom glided on into a street. Its finger pointed to two persons meeting. Scrooge listened again, thinking that the explanation might lie here.

He knew these men, also, perfectly. They were men of business, very wealthy, and of great importance.

He had made a point always of standing well in their esteem in a business point of view.

"How are you?" said one.

"How are you?" returned the other.

"Well!" said the first. "Old Scratch has got his own at last, hey?"

"So I am told," returned the second. "Cold, isn't it!"

"Seasonable for Christmas time. You are not a skater, I suppose?"

"No. No. Something else to think of. Good morning!"

Not another word. That was their meeting, their conversation, and their parting.

Scrooge was at first inclined to be surprised that the Spirit should attach importance to conversations apparently so trivial, but feeling assured that they must have some hidden purpose, he set himself to consider what it was likely to be. They could scarcely be supposed to have any bearing on the death of Jacob, his old partner, for that was Past, and this Ghost's province was the Future. Nor could he think of any one immediately connected with himself, to whom he could apply them. But nothing doubting that to whomsoever they applied they had some latent moral for his own improvement, he resolved to treasure up every word he heard, and everything he saw, and especially to observe the shadow of himself when it appeared. For he had an expectation that the conduct of his future self would give him the clue he missed, and would render the solution of these riddles easy.

He looked about in that very place for his own image, but another man stood in his accustomed corner, and though the clock pointed to his usual time of day for being there, he saw no likeness of himself among the multitudes that poured in through the porch. It gave him little surprise, however, for he had been revolving in his mind a change of life, and thought and hoped he saw his newborn resolutions carried out in this.

They left the busy scene and went into an obscure part of the town, where Scrooge had never penetrated before, although he recognized its situation and its bad repute. The ways were foul and narrow, the shops and houses wretched, the people half-naked, drunken, slipshod, ugly. Alleys and archways, like so many cesspools, disgorged their offenses of smell and dirt and life upon the straggling streets; and the whole quarter reeked with crime, with filth, and misery.

Far in this den of infamous resort, there was a low-browed, beetling shop, below a penthouse roof, where iron, old rags, bottles, bones, and greasy offal were brought. Upon the floor within were piled up heaps of rusty keys, nails, chains, hinges, files, scales, weights, and refuse of all kinds. Secrets that few would like to scrutinize were bred and hidden in mountains of unseemly rags, masses of corrupted fat, and sepulchers of bones. Sitting in among the wares he dealt in, by a charcoal stove made of old bricks, was a gray-haired rascal, nearly seventy-five years of age, who had screened himself from the cold air without, by a frozen curtaining of miscellaneous tatters hung upon a line, and smoked his pipe in all the luxury of calm retirement.

Scrooge and the Phantom came into the presence of this man, just as a woman with a heavy bundle slunk into the shop. But she had scarcely entered, when another woman, similarly laden, came in too; and she closely followed by a man in faded black, who was no less startled by the sight of them, than they had been upon the recognition of each other. After a short period of blank astonishment, in which the old man with the pipe had joined them, they all three burst into a laugh.

"Let the charwoman alone to be the first!" cried she who had entered first. "Let the laundress alone to be the second; and let the undertaker's man alone to be the third. Look here, old Joe, here's a chance! If we haven't all three met here without meaning it!"

"You couldn't have met in a better place," said old Joe, removing his pipe from his mouth. "Come into the parlor. You were made free of it long ago, you know; and the other two ain't strangers. Stop till I shut the door of the shop. Ah! How it skreeks! There ain't such a rusty bit of metal in the place as its own hinges, I believe; and I'm sure there's no such old bones here, as mine. Ha, ha! We're all suitable to our calling, we're well matched. Come into the parlor. Come into the parlor."

The parlor was the space behind the screen of rags. The old man raked the fire together with an old stair rod, and having trimmed his smokey lamp (for it was night) with the stem of his pipe, put it into his mouth again.

While he did this, the woman who had already spoken threw her bundle on the floor and sat down in a flaunting manner on a stool, crossing her elbows on her knee, and looking with a bold defiance at the other two.

"What odds then! What odds, Mrs. Dilber?" said the woman. "Every person has a right to take care of themselves. He always did!"

"That's true, indeed!" said the laundress. "No man more so."

"Why, then, don't stand staring as if you was afraid, woman. Who's the wiser? We're not going to pick holes in each other's coats, I suppose?"

"No, indeed!" said Mrs. Dilber and the man together. "We should hope not."

"Very well, then!" cried the woman. "That's enough. Who's the worse for the loss of a few things like these? Not a dead man, I suppose."

"No, indeed," said Mrs. Dilber, laughing.

"If he wanted to keep 'em after he was dead, a wicked old screw," pursued the woman, "why wasn't he natural in his lifetime? If he had been, he'd have had somebody to look after him when he was struck with Death, instead of lying gasping out his last there, alone by himself."

"It's the truest word that ever was spoke," said Mrs. Dilber. "It's a hard judgment on him."

"I wish it was a little heavier judgment," replied the woman; "and it should have been, you may depend upon it, if I could have laid my hands on anything else. Open that bundle, old Joe, and let me know the value of it. Speak out plain. I'm not afraid to be the first, nor afraid for them to see it. We knew pretty well that we were helping ourselves, before we met here, I believe. It's no sin. Open the bundle, Joe."

But the gallantry of her friends would not allow of this; and the man in faded black, mounting the breach first, produced his plunder. It was not extensive. A seal or two, a pencil case, a pair of sleeve buttons, and a brooch of no great value, were all. They were severally examined and appraised by old Joe, who chalked the sums he was disposed to give for each upon the wall, and added them up into a total when he found that there was nothing more to come.

"That's your account," said Joe, "and I wouldn't give another sixpence, if I was to be boiled for not doing it. Who's next?"

Mrs. Dilber was next. Sheets and towels, a little wearing apparel, two old-fashioned silver teaspoons, a pair of sugar tongs, and a few boots. Her account was stated on the wall in the same manner.

"I always give too much to ladies. It's a weakness of mine, and that's the way I ruin myself," said old Joe. "That's your account. If you ask me for another penny, and made it an open question, I'd repent of being so liberal, and knock off half-a-crown."

"And now undo my bundle, Joe," said the first woman.

Joe went down on his knees for the greater convenience of opening it, and having unfastened a great many knots, dragged out a large heavy roll of some dark stuff.

"What do you call this?" said Joe. "Bed curtains!"

"Ah!" returned the woman, laughing and leaning forward on her crossed arms. "Bed curtains!"

"You don't mean to say you took 'em down, rings and all, with him lying there?" said Joe.

"Yes, I do," replied the woman. "Why not?"

"You were born to make your fortune," said Joe, "and you'll certainly do it."

"I certainly shall hold my hand, when I can get anything in it by reaching it out, for the sake of such a man as he was, I promise you, Joe," returned the woman, coolly. "Don't drop that oil upon the blankets, now."

"His blankets?" asked Joe.

"Whose else's do you think?" replied the woman. "He isn't likely to take cold without 'em, I dare say."

"I hope he didn't die of anything catching? Eh?" said old Joe, stopping in his work and looking up.

"Don't you be afraid of that," returned the woman. "I ain't so fond of his company that I'd loiter about him for such things, if he did. Ah! You may look through that shirt till your eyes ache; but you won't find a hole in it, nor a threadbare place. It's the best he had, and a fine one, too. They'd have wasted it, if it hadn't been for me."

"What do you call wasting of it?" asked old Joe.

"Putting it on him to be buried in to be sure," replied the woman with a laugh. "Somebody was fool enough to do it, but I took it off again. If calico ain't good enough for such a purpose, it isn't good enough for anything. It's quite as becoming to the body. He can't look uglier than he did in that one."

Scrooge listened to this dialogue in horror. As they sat grouped about their spoil, in the scanty light afforded by the old man's lamp, he viewed them with a detestation and disgust which could hardly have been greater, though they had been obscene demons, marketing the corpse itself.

"Ha, ha!" laughed the same woman, when old Joe producing a flannel bag with money in it, told out their several gains upon the ground. "This is the end of it, you see? He frightened every one away from him when he was alive, to profit us when he was dead! Ha, ha, ha!"

"Spirit!" said Scrooge, shuddering from head to foot. "I see, I see. The case of this unhappy man might be my own. My life tends that way, now. Merciful Heaven, what is this!"

He recoiled in terror, for the scene had changed, and now he almost touched a bed, a bare, uncurtained bed, on which, beneath a ragged sheet, there lay something covered up which, though it was dumb, announced itself in awful language.

The room was very dark, too dark to be observed with any accuracy, though Scrooge glanced round it in obedience to a secret impulse, anxious to know what kind of room it was. A pale light rising in the outer air fell straight upon the bed, and on it, plundered and bereft, unwatched, unwept, uncared for, was the body of this man.

He lay, in the dark, empty house, with not a man, a woman, or a child to say, "He was kind to me in this or that, and for the memory of one kind word I will be kind to him." A cat was tearing at the door, and there was a sound of gnawing rats beneath the hearthstone. What they wanted in the room of death, and why they were so restless and disturbed, Scrooge did not dare to think.

"Spirit!" he said. "This is a fearful place. In leaving it I shall not leave its lesson, trust me. Let us go!"

Still the Ghost pointed with unmoved finger to the head.

"I understand you," Scrooge returned, "and would do it if I could. But I have not the power, Spirit. I have not the power."

Again it seemed to look upon him.

"If there is any person in the town who feels emotion caused by this man's death," said Scrooge, quite agonized, "show that person to me, Spirit, I beseech you!"

The Phantom spread its dark robe before him for a moment, like a wing, and withdrawing it, revealed a room by daylight, where a mother and her children were.

She was expecting someone, and with anxious eagerness, for she walked up and down the room, started at every sound, looked out from the window, glanced at the clock, tried, but in vain, to work with her needle, and could hardly bear the voices of her children in their play.

At length the long-expected knock was heard. She hurried to the door and met her husband, a man whose face was careworn and depressed, though he was young. There was a remarkable expression in it now, a kind of serious delight of which he felt ashamed, and which he struggled to repress.

He sat down to the dinner that had been hoarding for him by the fire, and when she asked him faintly what news (which was not until after a long silence), he appeared embarrassed how to answer.

"Is it good," she said, "or bad?"—to help him.

"Bad," he answered.

"We are quite ruined?"

"No. There is hope yet, Caroline."

"If he relents," she said, amazed, "there is! Nothing is past hope, if such a miracle has happened."

"He is past relenting," said her husband. "He is dead."

She was a mild and patient creature, if her face spoke truth, but she was thankful in her soul to hear it, and she said so, with clasped hands. She prayed forgiveness the next moment, and was sorry; but the first was the emotion of her heart.

"What the half-drunken woman, whom I told you of last night, said to me when I tried to see him and obtain a week's delay, and what I have thought was a mere excuse to avoid me, turns out to have been quite true. He was not only very ill, but dying then."

"To whom will our debt be transferred?"

"I don't know. But before that time we shall be ready with the money. And even though we were not, it would be bad fortune indeed to find so merciless a creditor in his successor. We may sleep tonight with light hearts, Caroline!"

Yes. Soften it as they would, their hearts were lighter. The children's faces, hushed and clustered round to hear what they so little understood, were brighter; and it was a happier house for this man's death! The only emotion that the Ghost could show him, caused by the event, was one of pleasure.

"Let me see some tenderness connected with a death," said Scrooge; "or that dark chamber, Spirit, which we left just now, will be forever present to me."

The Ghost conducted him through several streets familiar to his feet; and as they went along, Scrooge looked here and there to find himself, but nowhere was he to be seen. They entered poor Bob Cratchit's house; the dwelling he had visited before; and found the mother and the children seated round the fire.

Quiet. Very quiet. The noisy little Cratchits were as still as statues in one corner, and looking up at Peter, who had a book before him. The mother and her daughters were engaged in sewing. But surely they were very quiet!

"'And He took a child, and set him in the midst of them.'"

Where had Scrooge heard these words? He had not dreamed them. The boy must have read them out as he and the Spirit crossed the threshold. Why did he not go on?

The mother laid her work upon the table, and put her hand up to her face.

"The color hurts my eyes," she said.

The color? Ah, poor Tiny Tim!

"They're better now again," said Cratchit's wife. "It makes them weak by candle-light; and I wouldn't show weak eyes to your father when he comes home, for the world. It must be near his time."

"Past it rather," Peter answered, shutting up his book. "But I think he has walked a little slower than he used to, these few last evenings, Mother."

They were very quiet again. At last she said, in a steady, cheerful voice that only faltered once, "I have known him walk with—I have known him walk with Tiny Tim upon his shoulder, very fast, indeed."

"And so have I," cried Peter. "Often."

"And so have I," exclaimed another. So had all.

"But he was very light to carry," she resumed, intent upon her work, "and his father loved him so, that it was no trouble; no trouble. And there is your father at the door!"

She hurried out to meet him; and little Bob in his comforter—he had need of it, poor fellow—came in. His tea was ready for him on the hob, and they all tried who should help him to it most. Then the two young Cratchits got upon his knees and laid, each child, a little cheek against his face, as if they said, "Don't mind it, Father. Don't be grieved!"

Bob was very cheerful with them, and spoke pleasantly to all the family. He looked at the work upon the table, and praised the industry and speed of Mrs. Cratchit and the girls. They would be done long before Sunday, he said.

"Sunday! You went today, then, Robert?" said his wife.

"Yes, my dear," returned Bob. "I wish you could have gone. It would have done you good to see how green a place it is. But you'll see it often. I promised him that I would walk there on a Sunday. My little, little child!" cried Bob. "My little child!"

He broke down all at once. He couldn't help it. If he could have helped it, he and his child would have been farther apart perhaps than they were.

He left the room and went upstairs into the room above, which was lighted cheerfully, and hung with Christmas. There was a chair set close beside the child and there were signs of someone having been there lately. Poor Bob sat down in it, and when he had thought a little and composed himself, he kissed the little face. He was reconciled to what had happened, and went down again quite happy.

They drew about the fire, and talked, the girls and mother working still. Bob told them of the extraordinary kindness of Mr. Scrooge's nephew, whom he had scarcely seen but once, and who, meeting him in the street that day, and seeing that he looked a little—"just a little down, you know," said Bob, inquired what had happened to distress him. "On which," said Bob, "for he is the pleasantest-spoken gentleman you ever heard, I told him. 'I am heartily sorry for it, Mr. Cratchit,' he said, 'and heartily sorry for your good wife.' By the by, how he ever knew that I don't know."

"Knew what, my dear?"

"Why, that you were a good wife," replied Bob.

"Everybody knows that!" said Peter.

"Very well observed, my boy!" cried Bob. "I hope they do. 'Heartily sorry,' he said, 'for your good wife. If I can be of service to you in any way,' he said, giving me his card, 'that's where I live. Pray come to me.' Now, it wasn't," cried Bob, "for the sake of anything he might be able to do for us, so much as for his kind way, that this was quite delightful. It really seemed as if he had known our Tiny Tim, and felt with us."

"I'm sure he's a good soul!" said Mrs. Cratchit.

"You would be sure of it, my dear," returned Bob, "if you saw and spoke to him. I shouldn't be at all surprised—mark what I say!—if he got Peter a better situation."

"Only hear that, Peter," said Mrs. Cratchit.

"And then," cried one of the girls, "Peter will be keeping company with some one, and setting up for himself."

"Get along with you!" retorted Peter, grinning.

"It's just as likely as not," said Bob, "one of these days, though there's plenty of time for that, my dear. But however and whenever we part from one another, I am sure we shall none of us forget poor Tiny Tim—shall we—or this first parting that there was among us?"

"Never, Father!" cried they all.

"And I know," said Bob, "I know, my dears, that when we recollect how patient and how mild he was, although he was a little, little child, we shall not quarrel easily among ourselves, and forget poor Tiny Tim in doing it."

"No, never, Father!" they all cried again.

"I am very happy," said little Bob; "I am very happy!"

Mrs. Cratchit kissed him, his daughters kissed him, the two young Cratchits kissed him, and Peter and himself shook hands. Spirit of Tiny Tim, thy childish essence was from God!

"Specter," said Scrooge, "something informs me that our parting moment is at hand. I know it, but I know not how. Tell me what man that was whom we saw lying dead?"

The Ghost of Christmas Yet To Come conveyed him, as before—though at a different time, he thought, indeed, there seemed no order in these latter visions, save that they were in the Future—into the resorts of businessmen, but showed him not himself. Indeed, the Spirit did not stay for anything, but went straight on, as to the end just now desired, until besought by Scrooge to tarry for a moment.

"This Court," said Scrooge, "through which we hurry now, is where my place of occupation is, and has been for a length of time. I see the house. Let me behold what I shall be in days to come."

The Spirit stopped. The hand was pointed elsewhere.

"The house is yonder," Scrooge exclaimed. "Why do you point away?"

The inexorable finger underwent no change.

Scrooge hastened to the window of his office and looked in. It was an office still, but not his. The furniture was not the same, and the figure in the chair was not himself. The Phantom pointed as before.

He joined it once again, and wondered why and whither he had gone, accompanied it until they reached an iron gate. He paused to look around before entering.

A churchyard. Here, then, the wretched man whose name he had now to learn, lay underneath the ground. It was a worthy place. Walled in by houses, overrun by grass and weeds, the growth of vegetations' death, not life, choked up with too much burying, fat with repleted appetite. A worthy place!

The Spirit stood among the graves, and pointed down to one. He advanced toward it, trembling. The Phantom was exactly as it had been, but he dreaded that he saw new meaning in its solemn shape.

"Before I draw nearer to that stone to which you point," said Scrooge, "answer me one question. Are these the shadows of the things that Will be, or are they shadows of the things that May be, only?"

Still the Ghost pointed downward to the grave by which it stood.

"Men's courses will foreshadow certain ends, to which, if persevered in, they must lead," said Scrooge. "But if the courses be departed from, the ends will change. Say it is thus with what you show me!"

The Spirit was immovable as ever. Scrooge crept toward it, trembling as he went, and following the finger, read upon the stone of the neglected grave his own name. *Ebenezer Scrooge.*

"Am I that man who lay upon the bed?" he cried, upon his knees.

The finger pointed from the grave to him, and back again.

"No, Spirit! Oh, no, no!"

The finger still was there.

"Spirit!" he cried, tight clutching at his robe. "Hear me! I am not the man I was. I will not be the man I must have been but for this intercourse. Why show me this, if I am past all hope!"

For the first time the hand appeared to shake.

"Good Spirit," he pursued, as down upon the ground he fell before it. "Your nature intercedes for me, and pities me. Assure me that I yet may change these shadows you have shown me by an altered life?"

The kind hand trembled.

"I will honor Christmas in my heart, and try to keep it all the year. I will live in the Past, the Present, and the Future. The Spirits of all three shall strive within me. I will not shut out the lessons that they teach. Oh, tell me I may sponge away the writing on this stone?"

In his agony he caught the spectral hand. It sought to free itself, but he was strong in his entreaty, and detained it. The Spirit, stronger yet, repulsed him.

Holding up his hands in a last prayer to have his fate reversed, he saw an alteration in the Phantom's hood and dress. It shrunk, collapsed, and dwindled down into a bedpost.

* * * * *

Yes! And the bedpost was his own. The bed was his own, the room was his own. Best and happiest of all, the Time before him was his own, to make amends in!

"I will live in the Past, the Present, and the Future!" Scrooge repeated, as he scrambled out of bed. "The Spirits of all three shall strive within me. Oh, Jacob Marley! Heaven, and the Christmas time be praised for this! I say it on my knees, old Jacob, on my knees!"

He was so fluttered and so glowing with his good intentions, that his broken voice would scarcely answer to his call. He had been sobbing violently in his conflict with the Spirit, and his face was wet with tears.

"They are not torn down," cried Scrooge, folding one of his bed curtains in his arms; "they are not torn down, rings and all. They are here—I am here—the shadows of the things that would have been may be dispelled. They will be. I know they will!"

His hands were busy with his garments all this time, turning them inside out, putting them on upside down, tearing them, mislaying them, making them parties to every kind of extravagance.

"I don't know what day of the month it is," said Scrooge. "I don't know how long I have been among the Spirits. I don't know anything. I'm quite a baby. Never mind. I don't care. I'd rather be a baby. Hallo! Whoop! Hallo here!"

He was checked in his transports by the churches ringing out the lustiest peals he had ever heard. Clash, clang, hammer; ding, dong, bell. Bell, dong, ding; hammer, clang, clash! Oh, glorious, glorious!

Running to the window, he opened it and put out his head. No fog, no mist; clear, bright, jovial, stirring, cold; cold, piping for the blood to dance to; golden sunlight; heavenly sky; sweet fresh air; merry bells. Oh, glorious. Glorious!

"What's today?" cried Scrooge, calling downward to a boy in Sunday clothes, who perhaps had loitered in to look about him.

"Eh?" returned the boy, with all his might of wonder.

"What's today, my fine fellow?" said Scrooge.

"Today!" replied the boy. "Why, Christmas Day."

"It's Christmas Day!" said Scrooge to himself. "I haven't missed it. The Spirits have done it all in one night. They can do anything they like. Of course they can. Of course they can. Hallo, my fine fellow!"

"Hallo!" returned the boy.

"Do you know the poulterer's in the next street but one, at the corner?" Scrooge inquired.

"I should hope I did," replied the lad.

"An intelligent boy!" said Scrooge. "A remarkable boy! Do you know whether they've sold the prize turkey that was hanging up there? Not the little prize turkey, the big one?"

"What, the one as big as me?" returned the boy.

"What a delightful boy!" said Scrooge. "It's a pleasure to talk to him. Yes, my buck!"

"It's hanging there now," replied the boy.

"Is it?" said Scrooge. "Go and buy it, and tell 'em to bring it here, that I may give them the direction where to take it. Come back with the man, and I'll give you a shilling. Come back with him in less than five minutes, and I'll give you half a crown!"

The boy was off like a shot. He must have had a steady hand at a trigger who could have got a shot off half so fast.

"I'll send it to Bob Cratchit's," whispered Scrooge, rubbing his hands and splitting with a laugh. "He shan't know who sends it. It's twice the size of Tiny Tim. Joe Miller never made such a joke as sending it to Bob's will be!"

The hand in which he wrote the address was not a steady one, but write it he did, somehow, and went downstairs to open the street door, ready for the coming of the poulterer's man. As he stood there, waiting his arrival the knocker caught his eye.

"I shall love it as long as I live!" cried Scrooge, patting it with his hand. "I scarcely ever looked at it before. What an honest expression it has in its face! It's a wonderful knocker! Here's the turkey. Hallo! Whoop! How are you! Merry Christmas!"

It was a turkey. He never could have stood upon his legs, that bird. He would have snapped 'em short off in a minute, like sticks of sealing wax.

"Why, it's impossible to carry that to Camden Town," said Scrooge. "You must have a cab."

The chuckle with which he said this, and the chuckle with which he paid for the turkey, and the chuckle with which he paid for the cab, and the chuckle with which he recompensed the boy, were only to be exceeded by the chuckle with which he sat down, breathless, in his chair again, and chuckled till he cried.

Shaving was not an easy task, for his hand continued to shake very much; and shaving requires attention, even when you don't dance while you are at it. But if he had cut the end of his nose off, he would have put a piece of sticking plaster over it and been quite satisfied.

He dressed himself "all in his best," and at last got out into the streets. The people were by this time pouring forth, as he had seen them with the Ghost of Christmas Present; and walking with his hands behind him, Scrooge regarded everyone with a delighted smile. He looked so irresistibly pleasant, in a word, that three or four good-humored fellows said, "Good morning, sir! A Merry Christmas to you!" And Scrooge said often afterward, that of all the blithe sounds he had ever heard, those were the blithest in his ears.

He had not gone far, when coming on toward him he beheld the portly gentleman who had walked into his countinghouse the day before and said, "Scrooge and Marley's, I believe?" It sent a pang across his heart to think how this old gentleman would look upon him when they met, but he knew what path lay straight before him and he took it.

"My dear sir," said Scrooge, quickening his pace and taking the old gentleman by both hands. "How do you do? I hope you succeeded yesterday. It was very kind of you. A Merry Christmas to you, sir!"

"Mr. Scrooge?"

"Yes," said Scrooge. "That is my name, and I fear it may not be pleasant to you. Allow me to ask your pardon. And will you have the goodness—" Here Scrooge whispered in his ear.

"Lord bless me!" cried the gentleman, as if his breath were taken away. "My dear Mr. Scrooge, are you serious?"

"If you please," said Scrooge. "Not a farthing less. A great many back payments are included in it, I assure you. Will you do me that favor?"

"My dear sir," said the other, shaking hands with him. "I don't know what to say to such munifi—"

"Don't say anything, please," retorted Scrooge. "Come and see me. Will you come and see me?"

"I will!" cried the old gentleman. And it was clear he meant to do it.

"Thank'ee," said Scrooge. "I am much obliged to you. I thank you fifty times. Bless you!"

He went to church, and walked about the streets, and watched the people hurrying to and fro, and patted the children on the head, and questioned beggars, and looked down into the kitchens of houses, and up to the windows, and found that everything could yield him pleasure. He had never dreamed that any walk—that anything—could give him so much happiness. In the afternoon he turned his steps toward his nephew's house.

He passed the door a dozen times before he had the courage to go up and knock. But he made a dash, and did it.

"Is your master at home, my dear?" said Scrooge to the girl. Nice girl! Very.

"Yes, sir."

"Where is he, my love?" said Scrooge.

"He's in the dining-room, sir, along with mistress. I'll show you upstairs, if you please."

"Thank'ee. He knows me," said Scrooge, with his hand already on the dining-room lock. "I'll go in here, my dear."

He turned it gently, and sidled his face in round the door. They were looking at the table (which was spread out in great array); for these young housekeepers are always nervous on such points, and like to see that everything is right.

"Fred!" said Scrooge.

Dear heart alive, how his niece by marriage started. Scrooge had forgotten, for the moment, about her sitting in the corner with the footstool, or he wouldn't have done it, on any account.

"Why, bless my soul!" cried Fred. "Who's that?"

"It's I. Your Uncle Scrooge. I have come to dinner. Will you let me in, Fred?"

Let him in! It is a mercy he didn't shake his arm off. He was at home in five minutes. Nothing could be heartier. His niece looked just the same. So did Topper when he came. So did the plump sister when she came. So did every one when they came. Wonderful party, wonderful games, wonderful unanimity, wonderful happiness!

But he was early at the office next morning. Oh, he was early there. If he could only be there first and catch Bob Cratchit coming late! That was the thing he had set his heart upon.

And he did it; yes, he did! The clock struck nine. No Bob. A quarter past. No Bob. He was full eighteen minutes and a half behind his time. Scrooge sat with his door wide open, that he might see him come into the tank.

His hat was off before he opened the door, his comforter too. He was on his stool in a jiffy, driving away with his pen, as if he were trying to overtake nine o'clock.

"Hallo" growled Scrooge, in his accustomed voice as near as he could feign it. "What do you mean by coming here at this time of day?"

"I am very sorry, sir," said Bob. "I am behind my time."

"You are!" repeated Scrooge. "Yes, I think you are. Step this way, sir, if you please."

"It's only once a year, sir," pleaded Bob, appearing from the tank. "It shall not be repeated. I was making rather merry yesterday, sir."

"Now, I'll tell you what, my friend," said Scrooge. "I am not going to stand this sort of thing any longer. And therefore," he continued, leaping from his stool and giving Bob such a dig in the waistcoat that he staggered back into the tank again, "and therefore I am about to raise your salary!"

Bob trembled, and got a little nearer to the ruler. He had a momentary idea of knocking Scrooge down with it, holding him, and calling to the people in the court for help and a straight waistcoat.

"A Merry Christmas, Bob!" said Scrooge, with an earnestness that could not be mistaken, as he clapped him on the back. "A merrier Christmas, Bob, my good fellow, than I have given you for many a year! I'll raise your salary and endeavor to assist your struggling family, and we will discuss your affairs this very afternoon, over a Christmas bowl of smoking bishop, Bob! Make up the fires and buy another coal scuttle before you dot another i, Bob Cratchit!"

Scrooge was better than his word. He did it all, and infinitely more; and to Tiny Tim, who did not die, he was a second father. He became as good a friend, as good a master, and as good a man, as the good old city knew, or any other good old city, town, or borough, in the good old world. Some people laughed to see the alteration in him, but he let them laugh, and little heeded them, for he was wise enough to know that nothing ever happens on this globe, for good, at which some people did not have their fill of laughter in the outset; and knowing that such as these would be blind anyway, he thought it quite as well that they should wrinkle up their eyes in grins, as have the malady in less attractive forms. His own heart laughed; and that was quite enough for him.

He had no further intercourse with Spirits, but lived upon the Total Abstinence Principle, ever afterward; and it was always said of him, that he knew how to keep Christmas well, if any man alive possessed the knowledge. May that be truly said of us, and all of us! And so, as Tiny Tim observed, God Bless Us, Every One!

Charles Dickens (1812–1870) experienced great poverty as a child in England, a theme that often appears in his classic stories. An English aristocrat, Lord Jeffrey, once told Dickens that he had done "more good by ["A Christmas Carol"], fostered more kindly feelings, and prompted more positive acts of beneficence than can be traced to all the pulpits in Christendom since Christmas 1842."

The Adventure of the Blue Carbuncle

Sir Arthur Conan Doyle

How does Sherlock Holmes celebrate the holiday season? By getting to the bottom of a mysterious misdeed, of course! Here is one of the classic Holmes stories—with a Christmas setting, no less. The goose that figures prominently in this tale was, of course, a staple of the late nineteenth-century Christmas celebration in many households.

I had called upon my friend Sherlock Holmes upon the second morning after Christmas, with the intention of wishing him the compliments of the season. He was lounging upon the sofa in a purple drawing gown, a pipe-rack within his reach upon the right, and a pile of crumpled morning papers, evidently newly studied, near at hand. Beside the couch was a wooden chair, and on the angle on the back hung a very seedy and disreputable felt hat, much the worse for the wear, and cracked in several places. A lens and forceps lying upon the seat of the chair suggested that the hat had been suspended in this manner for the purpose of examination.

"You are engaged," said I; "perhaps I interrupt you."

"Not at all. I am glad to have a friend with whom I can discuss my results. The matter is a perfectly trivial one"—he jerked his thumb in the direction of the old hat—"but there are points in connection with it which are not entirely devoid of interest and even of instruction."

I seated myself in his armchair and warmed my hands before his crackling fire, for a sharp frost had set in, and the windows were thick with the ice crystals. "I suppose," I remarked, "that, homely as it looks, this thing has some deadly story linked on to it—that it is the clue which will guide you in the solution of some mystery and the punishment of some crime."

"No, no. No crime," said Sherlock Holmes, laughing. "Only one of those whimsical little incidents which will happen when you have four million human beings all jostling each other within the space of a few square miles. Amid the action and reaction of so dense a swarm of humanity, every possible combination of events may be expected to take place, and many a little problem will be presented which may be striking and bizarre without being criminal. We have already had experience of such."

"So much so," I remarked, "that of the last six cases which I have added to my notes, three have been entirely free of any legal crime."

"Precisely. You allude to my attempt to recover the Irene Adler papers, to the singular case of Miss Mary Sutherland, and to the adventure of the man with the twisted lip. Well, I have no doubt that this small matter will fall into the same innocent category. You know Peterson, the commissionaire?"

"Yes."

"It is to him that this trophy belongs."

"It is his hat?"

"No, no; he found it. Its owner is unknown. I beg that you will look upon it not as a battered billycock but as an intellectual problem. And, first, as to how it came here. It arrived upon Christmas morning, in company with a good fat goose, which is, I have no doubt, roasting at this moment in front of Peterson's fire. The facts are these: about four o'clock on Christmas morning, Peterson, who as you know, is a very honest fellow, was returning from some small jollification and was making his way homeward down Tottenham Court Road. In front of him he saw, in the gaslight, a tallish man, walking with a slight stagger, and carrying a white goose hung over his shoulder. As he reached the corner of Goodge Street, a row broke out between this stranger and a little knot of roughs. One of the latter knocked off the man's hat, on which he raised his stick to defend himself and, swinging it over his head, smashed the shop window behind him. Peterson had rushed forward to protect the stranger from his assailants; but the man, shocked at having broke the window, and seeing an official-looking person in uniform rushing toward him, dropped his goose, took to his heels, and vanished amid the labyrinth of small streets which lie at the back of Tottenham Court Road. The roughs had also fled at the appearance of Peterson, so that he was left in possession of the field of battle, and also of the spoils of victory in the shape of this battered hat and a most unimpeachable Christmas goose."

"Which surely he restored to their owner?"

"My dear fellow, there lies the problem. It is true that 'For Mrs. Henry Baker' was printed upon a small card which was tied to the bird's left leg, and it is true that the initials 'H.B.' are legible upon the lining of this hat; but as there are some thousands of Bakers, and some hundreds of Henry Bakers in this city of ours, it is not easy to restore lost property to any one of them."

"What, then, did Peterson do?"

"He brought round both hat and goose to me on Christmas morning, knowing that even the smallest problems are of interest to me. The goose we retained until this morning, when there were signs that, in spite of the slight frost, it would be well that it should be eaten without unnecessary delay. Its finder has carried it off, therefore, to fulfill the ultimate destiny of a goose, while I continue to retain the hat of the unknown gentleman who lost his Christmas dinner."

"Did he not advertise?"

"No."

"Then, what clue could you have as to his identity?"

"Only as much as we can deduce."

"From his hat?"

"Precisely."

"But you are joking. What can you gather from this old battered felt?"

"Here is my lens. You know my methods. What can you gather yourself as to the individuality of the man who has worn this article?"

I took the tattered object in my hands and turned it over rather ruefully. It was a very ordinary black hat of the usual round shape, hard and much the worse for wear. The lining had been of red silk, but was a good deal discolored. There was a maker's name; but, as Holmes had remarked, the initials "H.B." were scrawled upon one side. It was pierced in the brim for a hat-securer, but the elastic was missing. For the rest, it was cracked, exceedingly dusty, and spotted in several places, although there seemed to have been some attempt to hide the discolored patches by smearing them with ink.

"I can see nothing," said I, handing it back to my friend.

"On the contrary, Watson, you can see everything. You fail, however, to reason from what you see. You are too timid in drawing your inferences."

"Then pray tell me what it is that you can infer from this hat?"

He picked it up and gazed at it in the peculiar introspective fashion which was characteristic of him. "It is perhaps less suggestive than it might have been," he remarked, "and yet there are a few inferences which are very distinct, and a few others which represent at least a strong balance of probability. That the man was highly intellectual is of course obvious upon the face of it, and also that he was fairly well-to-do within the last three years, although he has now fallen upon evil days. He had foresight, but has less now than formerly, pointing to a moral regression, which, when taken with the decline of his fortunes, seems to indicate some evil influence, probably drink, at work upon him. This may account also for the obvious fact that his wife has ceased to love him."

"My dear Holmes!"

"He has, however, retained some degree of self respect," he continued, disregarding my remonstrance. "He is a man who leads a sedentary life, goes out little, is out of training entirely, is middle-aged, has grizzled hair which he has had cut within the last few days, and which he anoints with lime cream. These are the more patent facts which are to be deduced from his hat. Also, by the way, that it is extremely improbable that he has gas laid on in his house."

"You are certainly joking, Holmes."

"Not in the least. Is it possible that even now, when I give you these results, you are unable to see how they are attained?"

"I have no doubt that I am very stupid, but I must confess that I am unable to follow you. For example, how did you deduce that this man was intellectual?"

For answer Holmes clapped the hat upon his head. It came right over the forehead and settled upon the bridge of his nose. "It is a question of cubic capacity," said he; "a man with so large a brain must have something in it."

"The decline of his fortunes, then?"

"This hat is three years old. These flat brims curled at the edge came in then. It is a hat of the very best quality. Look at the band of ribbed silk and the excellent lining. If this man could afford to buy so expensive a hat three years ago, and has had no hat since, then he has assuredly gone down in the world."

"Well, that is clear enough, certainly. But how about the foresight and the moral regression?"

Sherlock Holmes laughed. "Here is the foresight," said he, putting his finger upon the little disc and loop of the hat-securer. "They are never sold upon hats. If this man ordered one, it is a sign of a certain amount of foresight, since he went out of his way to take this precaution against the wind. But since we see that he has broken the elastic and has not troubled to replace it, it is obvious that he has less foresight now than formerly, which is a distinct proof of a weakening nature. On the other hand, he has endeavored to conceal some of these stains upon the felt by daubing them with ink, which is a sign that he has not entirely lost his self-respect."

"Your reasoning is certainly plausible."

"The further points, that he is middle-aged, that his hair is grizzled, that it has been recently cut, and that he uses lime-cream, are all to be gathered from a close examination of the lower part of the lining. The lens discloses a large number of hair-ends, clean cut by the scissors of the barber. They all appear to be adhesive, and there is a distinct odor of lime-cream. This dust, you will observe, is not the gritty, gray dust of the street but the fluffy brown dust of the house, showing that it has been hung up indoors most of the time; while the marks of moisture upon the inside are proof positive that the wearer perspired very freely, and could, therefore, hardly be in the best of training."

"But his wife—You said that she had ceased to love him."

"This hat has not been brushed for weeks. When I see you, my dear Watson, with a week's accumulation of dust upon your hat, and when your wife allows you to go out in such a state, I shall fear that you have also been unfortunate enough to lose your wife's affection."

"But he might be a bachelor."

"Nay, he was bringing home the goose as a peace-offering to his wife. Remember the card upon the bird's leg."

"You have an answer to everything. But how on earth do you deduce that the gas is not laid on in his house?"

"One tallow stain, or even two, might come by chance; but when I see no less than five, I think that there can be little doubt that the individual must be brought into frequent contact with burning tallow—walks upstairs at night probably with his hat in one hand and a guttering candle in the other. Anyhow, he never got tallow-stains from a gas-jet. Are you satisfied?"

"Well, it is very ingenious," said I, laughing; "but since, as you said just now, there has been no crime committed, and no harm done save the loss of a goose, all this seems to be rather a waste of energy."

Sherlock Holmes had opened his mouth to reply, when the door flew open, and Peterson, the commissionaire, rushed into the apartment with flushed cheeks and the face of a man who is dazed with astonishment.

"The goose, Mr. Holmes! The goose, sir!" he gasped.

"Eh? What of it, then? Has it returned to life and flapped off through the kitchen window?" Holmes twisted himself round upon the sofa to get a fairer view of the man's excited face.

"See here, sir! See what my wife found in its crop!" He held out his hand and displayed upon the center of the palm a brilliantly scintillating blue stone, rather smaller than a bean in size, but of such purity and radiance that it twinkled like an electric point in the dark hollow of his hand.

Sherlock Holmes sat up with a whistle. "By Jove, Peterson!" said he, "this is treasure trove indeed. I suppose you know what you have got?"

"A diamond, sir? A precious stone. It cuts into glass as though it were putty."

"It's more than a precious stone. It is *the* precious stone."

"Not the Countess of Morcar's blue carbuncle!" I ejaculated.

"Precisely so. I ought to know its size and shape, seeing that I have read the advertisement about it in the *Times* every day lately. It is absolutely unique, and its value can only be conjectured, but the reward offered of a thousand pounds is certainly not within a twentieth part of the market price."

"A thousand pounds! Great Lord of mercy!" The commissionaire plumped down into the chair and stared from one to the other of us.

"That is the reward, and I have reason to know that there are sentimental considerations in the background which would induce the Countess to part with half her fortune if she could but recover the gem."

"It was lost, if I remember aright, at the Hotel Cosmopolitan," I remarked.

"Precisely so, on December 22nd, just five days ago. John Horner, a plumber, was accused of having abstracted it from the lady's jewel case. The evidence against him was so strong that the case has been referred to the Assizes. I have some account of this matter here, I believe." He rummaged amid his newspaper, glancing over the dates, until at last he smoothed one out, doubled it over, and read the following paragraph:

Hotel Cosmopolitan Jewel Robbery. John Horner, 26, plumber, was brought up upon the charge of having upon the 22nd inst., abstracted from the jewel-case of the Countess of Morcar the valuable gem known as the blue carbuncle. James Ryder, upper-attendant at the hotel, gave his evidence to the effect that he had shown Horner up to the dressing-room of the Countess of Morcar upon the day of the robbery in order that he might solder the second bar of the grate, which was loose. He had remained with Horner some little time, but had finally been called away. On returning, he found that Horner had disappeared, that the bureau had been forced open, and the small morocco casket in which, as it afterwards transpired, the Countess was accustomed to keep her jewel, was lying empty upon the dressing-table. Ryder instantly gave the alarm, and Horner was arrested the same evening; but the stone could not be found either upon his person or in his rooms. Catherine Cusack, maid to the Countess, deposed to having heard Ryder's cry of dismay on discovering the robbery, and to have rushed into the room, where she found matters as described by the last witness. Inspector Bradstreet, B division, gave evidence as to the arrest of Horner, who struggled frantically, and protested his innocence in the strongest terms. Evidence of a previous conviction for robbery having been given against the prisoner, the magistrate refused to deal summarily with the offense, but referred it to the Assizes. Horner, who had shown signs of intense emotion during the proceedings, fainted away at the conclusion and was carried out of the court.

"Hum! So much for the police-court," said Holmes thoughtfully, tossing aside the paper. "The question for us now to solve is the sequence of events leading from a rifled jewel-case at one end to the crop of a goose in Tottenham Court Road at the other. You see, Watson, our little deductions have suddenly assumed a much more important and less innocent aspect. Here is the stone; the stone came from the goose, and the goose came from Mr. Henry Baker, the gentleman with the bad hat and all the other characteristics with which I have bored you. So now we must set ourselves very seriously to finding this gentleman and ascertaining what part he has played in this little mystery. To do this, we must try the simplest means first, and these lie undoubtedly in an advertisement in all the evening papers. If this fails, I shall have recourse to other methods."

"What will you say?"

"Give me a pencil and that slip of paper. Now then:

Found at the corner of Goodge Street, a goose and a black felt hat. Mr. Henry Baker can have the same by applying at 6:30 this evening at 221B Baker Street."

"That is clear and concise."

"Very. But will he see it?"

"Well, he is sure to keep an eye on the papers, since, to a poor man, the loss was a heavy one. He was clearly so scared by his mischance in breaking the window and by the approach of Peterson that he thought nothing but flight, but since then he must have bitterly regretted the impulse which caused him to drop his bird. Then, again, the introduction of his name will cause him to see it, for everyone who knows him will direct his attention to it. Here you are, Peterson, run down to the advertising agency and have this put in the evening papers."

"In which, sir?"

"Oh, in the *Globe*, *Star*, *Pall Mall*, *St. James*, *Evening News*, *Standard*, *Echo*, and any others that occur to you."

"Very well, sir. And this stone?"

"Ah, yes, I shall keep the stone. Thank you. And, I say, Peterson, just buy a goose on your way back and leave it here with me, for we must have one to give to this gentlemen in place of the one which your family is now devouring."

When the commissionaire had gone, Holmes took up the stone and held it against the light. "It's a bonny thing," said he. "Just see how it glints and sparkles. Of course it is a nucleus and focus of crime. Every good stone is. They are the devil's pet baits. In the larger and older jewels every facet may stand for a bloody deed. This stone is not yet twenty years old. It was found in the banks of the Amoy River in southern China and is remarkable in having every characteristic of the carbuncle, save that it is blue in shade instead of ruby red. In spite of its youth, it has already a sinister history. There have been two murders, a vitriol-throwing, a suicide, and several robberies brought about for the sake of this forty-grain weight of crystal-lized charcoal. Who would think that so pretty a toy would be a purveyor to the gallows and the prison? I'll lock it up in my strong box now and drop a line to the Countess to say that we have it."

"Do you think that this man Horner is innocent?"

"I cannot tell."

"Well, then, do you imagine that this other one, Henry Baker, had anything to do with the matter?"

"It is, I think, much more likely that Henry Baker is an absolutely innocent man, who had no idea that the bird which he was carrying was of considerably more value than if it were made of solid gold. That, however, I shall determine by a very simple test if we have an answer to our advertisement."

"And you can do nothing until then?"

"Nothing."

"In that case I shall continue my professional round. But I shall come back in the event at the hour you have mentioned, for I should like to see the solution of so tangled a business."

"Very glad to see you. I dine at seven. There is a woodcock, I believe. By the way, in view of recent occurrences, perhaps I ought to ask Mrs. Hudson to examine its crop."

I had been delayed at a case, and it was a little after half-past six when I found myself in Baker Street once more. As I approached the house I saw a tall man in a Scotch bonnet with a coat which was buttoned up to his chin waiting outside in the bright semicircle which was thrown from the fanlight. Just as I arrived the door opened, and we were shown up together to Holmes's room.

"Mr. Henry Baker, I believe," said he, rising from his armchair and greeting his visitor with the easy air of geniality which he could so readily assume. "Pray take this chair by the fire, Mr. Baker. It is a cold night, and I observe that your circulation is more adapted for summer than for winter. Ah, Watson, you have just come at the right time. Is that your hat, Mr. Baker?"

"Yes sir, that is undoubtedly my hat."

He was a large man with rounded shoulders, a massive head, and a broad, intelligent face, sloping down to a pointed beard of grizzled brown. A touch of red in nose and cheeks, with a slight tremor of his extended hand, recalled Holmes's surmise as to his habits. His rusty black frock-coat was buttoned right up in front, with the collar turned up, and his lank wrists protruded from his sleeves without a sign of cuff or shirt. He spoke in a slow staccato fashion, choosing words with care, and gave the impression generally of a man of learning and letters who had ill-usage at the hands of fortune.

"We have retained these things for some days," said Holmes, "because we expected to see an advertisement from you giving your address. I am at a loss to know now why you did not advertise."

Our visitor gave a rather shamefaced laugh. "Shillings have not been so plentiful with me as they once were," he remarked. "I had no doubt that the gang of roughs who assaulted me had carried off both my hat and the bird. I did not care to spend more money in a hopeless attempt at recovering them."

"Very naturally. By the way, about the bird, we were compelled to eat it."

"To eat it!" Our visitor half rose from his chair in his excitement.

"Yes, it would have been of no use to anyone had we not done so. But I presume that this other goose upon the sideboard, which is about the same weight and perfectly fresh, will answer your purpose equally well?"

"Oh, certainly, certainly," answered Mr. Baker with a sigh of relief.

"Of course, we still have the feathers, legs, crop, and so on of your own bird, so if you wish—"

The man burst into a hearty laugh. "They might be useful to me as relics of my adventure," said he, "but beyond that I can hardly see what use the *disjecta membra* of my late acquaintance are going to be to me. No, sir, I think that, with your permission, I will confine my attentions to the excellent bird which I perceive upon the sideboard."

Sherlock Holmes glanced sharply across at me with a slight shrug of his shoulders.

"There is your hat, then, and there is your bird," said he. "By the way, would it bore you to tell me where you got the other one from? I am somewhat of a fowl fancier, and I have seldom seen a better grown goose."

"Certainly sir," said Baker, who had risen and tucked his newly gained property under his arm. "There are a few of us who frequent the Alpha Inn, near the Museum—we are to be found in the Museum itself during the day, you understand. This year our good host, Windigate by name, instituted a goose club, by which, on consideration of some few pence every week, we were each to receive a bird at Christmas. My pence were duly paid, and the rest is familiar to you. I am much indebted to you, sir, for a Scotch bonnet is fitted neither to my years nor my gravity." With a comical pomposity of manner he bowed solemnly to both of us and strode off upon his way.

"So much for Mr. Henry Baker," said Holmes when he had closed the door behind him. "It is quite certain that he knows nothing whatsoever about the matter. Are you hungry, Watson?"

"Not particularly."

"Then I suggest that we turn our dinner into a supper and follow up this clue while it is still hot."

"By all means." It was a bitter night, so we drew on our ulsters and wrapped cravats about our throats. Outside, the stars were shining coldly in a cloudless sky, and the breath of the passers-by blew out into smoke like so many pistol shots. Our foot-falls rang out crisply and loudly as we swung through the doctors' quarter, Wimpole Street, Harley Street, and so through Wigmore Street into Oxford Street. In a quarter of an hour we were in Bloomsbury at the Alpha Inn, which is a small public-house at the corner of one of the streets which runs down into Holborn. Holmes pushed open the door of the private bar and ordered two glasses of beer from the ruddy-faced, white-aproned landlord.

"Your beer should be excellent if it is as good as your geese," said he.

"My geese!" The man seemed surprised.

"Yes. I was speaking only half an hour ago to Mr. Henry Baker, who was a member of your goose club."

"Ah! Yes, I see. But you see, sir, them's not our geese."

"Indeed! Whose, then?"

"Well, I got the two dozen from a salesman in Covent Garden."

"Indeed? I know some of them. Which was it?"

"Breckinridge is his name."

"Ah! I don't know him. Well, here's your good health, landlord, and prosperity to your house. Goodnight."

"Now for Mr. Breckinridge," he continued, buttoning up his coat as we came out into the frosty air. "Remember, Watson, that though we have so homely a thing as a goose at one end of this chain, we have at the other a man who will certainly get seven years' penal servitude unless we can establish his innocence. It is possible that our inquiry may but confirm his guilt; but, in any case, we have a line of investigation which has been missed by the police, and which a singular chance has placed in our hands. Let us follow it out to the bitter end. Faces to the south, then, and quick march!"

We passed across Holborn, down Endell Street, and so through a zigzag of slums to Covent Garden Market. One of the largest stalls bore the name of Breckinridge upon it, and the proprietor, a horsy-looking man, with a sharp face and trim side-whiskers, was helping a boy to put up the shutters.

"Good-evening. It's a cold night," said Holmes.

The salesman nodded and shot a questioning glance at my companion.

"Sold out of geese, I see," continued Holmes, pointing at the bare slabs of marble.

"Let you have five hundred to-morrow morning."

"That's no good."

"Well, there are some on the stall with the gas-flare."

"Ah, but I was recommended to you."

"Who by?"

"The landlord of the Alpha."

"Oh, yes; I sent him a couple of dozen."

"Fine birds they were, too. Now where did you get them from?"

To my surprise the question provoked a burst of anger from the salesman.

"Now, then, mister," said he, with his head cocked and his arms akimbo, "what are you driving at? Let's have it straight, now."

"It is straight enough. I should like to know who sold you the geese which you supplied to the Alpha."

"Well, then, I shan't tell you. So now!"

"Oh, it is a matter of no importance; but I don't know why you should be so warm over such a trifle."

"Warm! You'd be as warm, maybe, if you were as pestered as I am. When I pay good money for a good article there should be an end of the business; but it's 'Where are the geese?' and 'Who did you sell the geese to?' and 'What will you take for the geese?' One would think they were the only geese in the world, to hear the fuss that is made over them."

"Well, I have no connection with any other people who have been making inquiries," said Holmes carelessly. "If you won't tell us the bet is off, that is all. But I'm always ready to back my opinion on a matter of fowls, and I have a fiver on it that the bird I ate is a country bred."

"Well, then, you've lost your fiver, for it's town bred," snapped the salesman. "It's nothing of the kind."

"I say it is."

"I don't believe it."

"D'you think you know more about fowls than I, who have handled them ever since I was a nipper? I tell you, all those birds that went to the Alpha were town bred."

"You'll never persuade me to believe that."

"Will you bet, then?"

"It's merely taking your money, for I know that I am right. But I'll have a sovereign on with you, just to teach you not to be so obstinate."

The salesman chuckled grimly. "Bring me the books, Bill," said he.

The small boy brought round a small thin volume and a great greasy-backed one, laying them out together beneath the hanging lamp.

"Now, then, Mr. Cocksure," said the salesman, "I thought that I was out of geese, but before I finish you'll find that there is still one left in my shop. You saw this little book?"

"Well?"

"That's the list of the folk from whom I buy. D'you see? Well, then, here on this page are the country folk, and the numbers after their names are where their accounts are in the big ledger. Now, then! You see this other page in red ink? Well, that is a list of my town suppliers. Now, look at that third name. Just read it out to me."

"Mrs. Oakshott, 117, Brixton Road—249," read Holmes.

"Quite so. Now turn that up in the ledger."

Holmes turned to the page indicated. "Here you are, 'Mrs. Oakshott, 117, Brixton Road, egg and poultry supplier.'"

"Now, then, what's the last entry?"

"'December 22nd. Twenty-four geese at 7s.6.'"

"Quite so. There you are. And underneath?"

"'Sold to Mr. Windigate of the Alpha, at 12s.'"

"What have you to say now?"

Sherlock Holmes looked deeply chagrined. He drew a sovereign from his pocket and threw it down upon the slab, turning away with the air of a man whose disgust is too deep for words. A few yards off he stopped under a lamp-post and laughed in the hearty, noiseless fashion which was peculiar to him.

"When you see a man with whiskers of that cut and the 'Pink 'un' protruding out of his pocket, you can always draw him out of a bet," said he. "I dare say that if I had put a hundred pounds down in front of him, that man would not have given me such complete information as was drawn from him by the idea that he was doing me on a wager. Well, Watson, we are, I fancy, nearing the end of our quest, and the only point which remains to be determined is whether we should go on to this Mrs. Oakshott tonight, or whether we should reserve it for to-morrow. It is clear from what that surly fellow said that there are others besides ourselves who are anxious about the matter, and I should—"

His remarks were suddenly cut short by a loud hubbub which broke out from the stall which we had just left. Turning round we saw a little rat-faced fellow standing in the center of the circle of yellow light which was thrown by the swinging lamp, while Breckinridge, the salesman, framed in the door of his stall, was shaking his fists fiercely at the cringing figure.

"I've had enough of you and your geese," he shouted. "I wish you were all at the devil together. If you come pestering me any more with your silly talk I'll set the dog at you. You bring Mrs. Oakshott here and I'll answer her, but what have you to do with it? Did I buy the geese off you?"

"No; but one of them was mine all the same," whined the little man.

"Well, then, ask Mrs. Oakshott for it."

"She told me to ask you."

"Well, you can ask the King of Proosia, for all I care. I've had enough of it. Get out of this!" He rushed fiercely forward, and the inquirer flitted away into the darkness.

"Ha! This may save us a visit to Brixton Road," whispered Holmes. "Come with me, and we will see what is to be made of this fellow." Striding through the scattered knots of people who lounged round the flaring stalls, my companion speedily overtook the little man and touched him upon the shoulder. He sprang round, and I could see in the gas-light that every vestige of color had been driven from his face.

"Who are you, then? What do you want?" he asked in a quavering voice.

"You will excuse me," said Holmes blandly, "but I could not help overhearing the questions which you put to the salesman just now. I think that I could be of assistance to you."

"You? Who are you? How could you know anything of this matter?"

"My name is Sherlock Holmes. It is my business to know what other people don't know."

"But you can know nothing of this?"

"Excuse me, I know everything of it. You are endeavoring to trace some geese which were sold by Mrs. Oakshott, of Brixton Road, to a salesman named Breckinridge, by him in turn to Mr. Windigate, of the Alpha, and by him to his club, of which Mr. Henry Baker is a member."

"Oh, sir, you are the very man whom I have longed to meet," cried the little fellow with outstretched hands and quivering fingers. "I can hardly explain to you how interested I am in this matter."

Sherlock Holmes hailed a four-wheeler which was passing. "In that case we had better discuss it in a cosy room rather than in this wind-swept marketplace," said he. "But pray tell me, before we go farther, who it is that I have the pleasure of assisting."

The man hesitated for an instant. "My name is John Robinson," he answered with a sidelong glance.

"No, no; the real name," said Holmes sweetly. "It is always awkward doing business with an alias."

A flush sprang to the white cheeks of the stranger. "Well, then," said he, "my real name is James Ryder."

"Precisely so. Head attendant at the Hotel Cosmopolitan. Pray step into the cab, and I shall soon be able to tell you everything which you wish to know."

The little man stood glancing from one to the other of us with half-frightened, half-hopeful eyes, as one who is not sure whether he is on the verge of a windfall or of a catastrophe. Then he stepped into the cab, and in half an hour we were back in the sitting-room at Baker Street. Nothing had been said during our drive, but the high, thin breathing of our new companion, and the claspings, and unclaspings of his hands, spoke of the nervous tension within him.

"Here we are!" said Holmes cheerily as we filed into the room. "The fire looks very seasonable in this weather. You look cold, Mr. Ryder. Pray take the basket-chair. I will just put on my slippers before we settle this little matter of yours. Now, then! You want to know what became of those geese?"

"Yes, sir."

"Or rather, I fancy, of that goose. It was one bird, I imagine, in which you were interested—white, with a black bar across the tail."

Ryder quivered with emotion. "Oh, sir," he cried, "can you tell me where it went to?"

"It came here."

"Here?"

"Yes, and a most remarkable bird it proved. I don't wonder that you should take an interest in it. It laid an egg after it was dead—the bonniest, brightest little blue egg that ever was seen. I have it here in my museum."

Our visitor staggered to his feet and clutched the mantelpiece with his right hand. Holmes unlocked the strong-box and held up the blue carbuncle, which shone out like a star, with a cold, brilliant, many-pointed radiance. Ryder stood glaring with a drawn face, uncertain whether to claim or disown it.

"The game's up, Ryder," said Holmes quietly. "Hold up, man, or you'll be into the fire! Give him an arm back into his chair, Watson. He's not got blood enough to go in for felony with impunity. Give him a dash of brandy. So! Now he looks a little more human. What a shrimp it is, to be sure!"

For a moment he had staggered and nearly fallen, but the brandy brought a tinge of color into his cheeks, and he sat staring with frightened eyes at his accuser.

"I have almost every link in my hands, and all the proofs which I could possibly need, so there is little which you need tell me. Still, that little may as well be cleared up to make the case complete. You had heard, Ryder, of this blue stone of the Countess of Morcar's?"

"It was Catherine Cusack who told me of it," said he in a crackling voice.

"I see—her ladyship's waiting-maid. Well, the temptation of sudden wealth so easily acquired was too much for you, as it has been for better men before you; but you were not very scrupulous in the means you used. It seems to me, Ryder, that there is the making of a very pretty villain in you. You knew that this man Horner, the plumber, had been concerned in some such matter before, and that suspicion would rest the more readily upon him. What did you do, then? You made some small job in my lady's room—you and your confederate Cusack—and you managed that he should be the man sent for. Then, when he had left, you rifled the jewel-case, raised the alarm, and had this unfortunate man arrested. You then—"

Ryder threw himself down suddenly upon the rug and clutched at my companion's knees. "For God's sake, have mercy!" he shrieked. "Think of my father! Of my mother! It would break their hearts. I never will again. I swear it. I'll swear it on a Bible. Oh, don't bring it into court! For Christ's sake, don't!"

"Get back into your chair!" said Holmes sternly. "It is very well to cringe and crawl now, but you thought little enough of this poor Horner in the dock for a crime of which he knew nothing."

"I will fly, Mr. Holmes. I will leave the country, sir. Then the charges against him will break down."

"Hum! We will talk about that. And now let us hear a true account of the next act. How came the stone into the goose, and how came the goose into the open market? Tell us the truth, for there lies your only hope of safety."

Ryder passed his tongue over his parched lips. "I will tell you just as it happened, sir," he said. "When Horner had been arrested, it seemed to me that it would be best for me to get away with the stone at once, for I did not know at what moment the police might take it into their heads to search me and my room. There was no place about the hotel where it would be safe. I went out, as if on some commission, and I made for my sister's house. She had married a man named Oakshott, and lived on Brixton Road, where she fattened fowls for the market. All the way there every man I met seemed to me to be a policeman or a detective; and, for all that it was a cold night, the sweat was pouring down my face before I came to the Brixton Road. My sister asked me what was the matter, and why I was so pale; but I told her that I had been upset by the jewel robbery at the hotel. Then I went into the backyard and smoked a pipe, and wondered what it would be best to do.

"I had a friend once called Maudsley, who went to the bad, and has just been serving his time in Pentonville. One day he had met me, and fell into talk about the ways of thieves, and how they could get rid of what they stole. I knew that he would be true to me, for I knew one or two things about him; so I made up my mind to go right on to Kilburn, where he lived, and take him into my confidence. He would show me how to turn the stone into money. But how to get to him in safety? I thought of the agonies I had gone through in coming from the hotel. I might at any moment be seized and searched, and there would be the stone in my waistcoat pocket. I was leaning against the wall at the time and looking at the geese which were waddling round my feet, and suddenly an idea came into my head which showed me how I could beat the best detective that ever lived.

"My sister had told me some weeks before that I might have the pick of her geese for a Christmas present, and I knew that she was always as good as her word. I would take my goose now, and in it I would carry the stone to Kilburn. There was a little shed in the yard, and behind this I drove one of the birds—a fine big one, white, with a barred tail. I caught it, and, prying its bill open, I thrust the stone down its throat, as far as my finger could reach. The bird gave a gulp, and I felt the stone pass along its gullet and down into its crop. But the creature flapped and struggled, and out came my sister to know what was the matter. As I turned to speak to her the brute broke loose and fluttered among the others.

"'Whatever were you doing with that bird, Jem?' says she.

"'Well,' said I, 'you said you'd give me one for Christmas, and I was feeling which was the fattest.'

"'Oh,' says she, 'we've set yours aside for you—Jem's bird, we call it. It's the big white one over yonder. There's twenty-six of them, which makes one for you, and one for us, and two dozen for the market.'

"'Thank you, Maggie,' says I; 'but if it is all the same to you, I'd rather have that one I was handling just now.'

"'The other is a good three pound heavier,' said she, 'and we fattened it expressly for you.'

"'Never mind. I'll have the other, and I'll take it now,' said I.

"'Oh, just as you like' said she, a little huffed. 'Which is it you want, then?'

"'That white one with the barred tail, right in the middle of the flock.'

"'Oh, very well. Kill it and take it with you.'

"Well, I did what she said, Mr. Holmes, and I carried the bird all the way to Kilburn, I told my pal what I had done, for he was a man that it was easy to tell a thing like that to. He laughed until he choked, and we got a knife and opened the goose. My heart turned to water, for there was no sign of the stone, and I knew that some terrible mistake had occurred. I left the bird, rushed back to my sister's, and hurried into the back yard. There was not a bird to be seen there.

"'Where are they all, Maggie?' I cried.

"'Gone to the dealer's, Jem.'

"'Which dealer's?'

"'Breckinridge, of Covent Garden.'

"'But was there another with a barred tail?' I asked, 'the same as the one I chose?'

"'Yes, Jem; there were two barred-tailed ones, and I could never tell them apart.'

"Well, then, of course I saw it all, and I ran off as hard as my feet would carry me to this man Breckinridge; but he had sold the lot at once, and not one word would he tell me as to where they had gone. You heard him yourselves to-night. Well, he has always answered me like that. My sister thinks that I am going mad. Sometimes I think that I am myself. And now—and now I am myself a branded thief, without ever having touched the wealth for which I sold my character. God help me! God help me!" He burst into convulsive sobbing, with his face buried in his hands.

There was a long silence, broken only by his heavy breathing, and by the measured tapping of Sherlock Holmes's finger-tips upon the edge of the table. Then my friend rose and threw open the door.

"Get out!" said he.

"What, sir! Oh, Heaven bless you!"

"No more words. Get out!"

And no more words were needed. There was a rush, a clatter upon the stairs, the bang of a door, and the crisp rattle of running footfalls from the street.

"After all, Watson," said Holmes, reaching up his hands for his clay pipe, "I am not retained by the police to supply their deficiencies. If Horner were in danger it would be another thing; but this fellow will not appear against him, and the case must collapse. I suppose that I am committing a felony, but it is just possible that I am saving a soul. This fellow will not go wrong again; he is too terribly frightened. Send him to jail now, and you make him a jail-bird for life. Besides, it is the season for forgiveness. Chance has put in our way a most singular and whimsical problem, and its solution is its own reward. If you will have the goodness to touch the bell, Doctor, we will begin another investigation, in which, also a bird will be the chief feature."

One of the founders of the modern mystery story, Sir Arthur Conan Doyle (1859–1930) was born in Scotland and trained as a medical doctor, writing stories in his spare time. Eventually, his detective Sherlock Holmes became so popular that he was able to leave his medical practice completely.

The Elves and the Shoemaker

The Brothers Grimm

*Jacob and Wilhelm Grimm—German university professors of linguistics—were also
known as the Brothers Grimm, producing books full of fairy tales that have long
entranced both children and adults. While "The Elves and the Shoemaker" stands on
its own as one of these fairy tales, it is also an example of how an act of selfless giving
has the power to change lives for the better.*

Once upon a time there was a poor shoemaker. He made excellent shoes and
worked quite diligently, but even so he could not earn enough to support himself
and his family. He became so poor that he could not even afford to buy the leather
he needed to make shoes; finally he had only enough to make one last pair. He cut
them out with great care and put the pieces on his workbench, so that he could
sew them together the following morning.

"Now, I wonder," he sighed, "will I ever make another pair of shoes? Once I've sold
this pair I shall need all the money to buy food for my family. I will not be able to
buy any new leather."

That night, the shoemaker went to bed a sad and distraught man.

The next morning, he awoke early and went down to his
workshop. On his bench he found an exquisite pair of
shoes! They had small and even stitches, formed so
perfectly that he knew he couldn't have produced
a better pair himself. Upon close examination, the
shoes proved to be made from the very pieces of
leather he had set out the night before. He immediately put the fine pair of shoes in the window
of his shop and drew back the blinds.

"Who in the world could have done this service for me?" he asked himself. Even before he
could make up an answer, a rich man strode
into his shop and bought the shoes—and for a
fancy price.

The shoemaker was ecstatic; he immediately went out and purchased plenty of food for his family—and some more leather. That afternoon he cut out two pairs of shoes and, just as before, laid all the pieces on his bench so that he could sew them the next day. Then he went upstairs to enjoy a good meal with his family.

"My goodness!" he cried the next morning when he found two pairs of beautifully finished shoes on his workbench. "Who could make such fine shoes—and so quickly?" He put them in his shop window, and before long some wealthy people came in and paid a great deal of money for them. The happy shoemaker went right out and bought even more leather.

For weeks, and then months, this continued. Whether the shoemaker cut two pairs or four pairs, the fine new shoes were always ready the next morning. Soon his small shop was crowded with customers. He cut out many types of shoes: stiff boots lined with fur, delicate slippers for dancers, walking shoes for ladies, tiny shoes for children. Soon his shoes had bows and laces and buckles of fine silver. The little shop prospered as never before, and its proprietor was soon a rich man himself. His family wanted for nothing.

As the shoemaker and his wife sat by the fire one night, he said, "One of these days, I shall learn who has been helping us."

"We could hide behind the cupboard in your workroom," she said. "That way, we would find out just who your helpers are." And that is just what they did. That evening, when the clock struck twelve, the shoemaker and his wife heard a noise. Two tiny men, each with a bag of tools, were squeezing beneath a crack under the door. Oddest of all, the two elves were stark naked!

The two men clambered onto the workbench and began working. Their little hands stitched and their little hammers tapped ceaselessly the whole night through.

"They are so small! And they make such beautiful shoes in no time at all!" the shoemaker whispered to his wife as dawn rose. (Indeed, the elves were about the size of his own needles.)

"Quiet!" his wife answered. "See how they are cleaning up now." And in an instant, the two elves had disappeared beneath the door.

The next day, the shoemaker's wife said, "Those little elves have done so much good for us. Since it is nearly Christmas, we should make some gifts for them."

"Yes!" cried the shoemaker. "I'll make some boots that will fit them, and you make some clothes." They worked until dawn. On Christmas Eve the presents were laid out upon the workbench: two tiny jackets, two pairs of trousers, and two little woolen caps. They also left out a plate of good things to eat and drink. Then they hid once again behind the cupboard and waited to see what would happen.

Just as before, the elves appeared at the stroke of midnight. They jumped onto the bench to begin their work, but when they saw all the presents they began to laugh and shout with joy. They tried on all the clothes, then helped themselves to the food and drink. Then they jumped down, danced excitedly around the workroom, and disappeared beneath the door.

After Christmas, the shoemaker cut out his leather as he always had—but the two elves never returned. "I believe they may have heard us whispering," his wife said. "Elves are so very shy when it comes to people, you know."

"I know I will miss their help," the shoemaker said, "but we will manage. The shop is always so busy now. But my stitches will never be as tight and small as theirs!"

That shoemaker did indeed continue to prosper, but he and his family always remembered the good elves who had helped them during the hard times. And each and every Christmas Eve from that year onward, they gathered around the fire to drink a toast to their tiny friends.

Although Jacob (1785–1863) and Wilhelm (1786–1859) Grimm devoted their lives to the study of literature, they didn't actually write any of the stories that won them world renown. The tales that made them famous, Der Kinder-und Hausmarchen (The Children and the House of Fairy Tales)*, were collected from the European folklore and legends of the time.*

The Gift of the Magi

O. Henry

"The Gift of the Magi" is probably the best known of all O. Henry's works, and it's not hard to see why. The story, which features a classic example of the ironic endings that made the author famous, captures the essence of the spirit of Christmas. The poor young couple in the story, like their Biblical counterparts, leave an unforgettable impression, thanks to the pureness of their intent, the selflessness of their giving, and the power of their love.

One dollar and eighty-seven cents. That was all. And sixty cents of it was in pennies. Pennies saved one and two at a time by bulldozing the grocer and the vegetable man and the butcher until one's cheeks burned with the silent imputation of parsimony that such close dealing implied. Three times Della counted it. One dollar and eighty-seven cents. And the next day would be Christmas.

There was clearly nothing to do but flop down on the shabby little couch and howl. So Della did it. Which instigates the moral reflection that life is made up of sobs, sniffles, and smiles, with sniffles predominating.

While the mistress of the home is gradually subsiding from the first stage to the second, take a look at the home. A furnished flat at eight dollars per week. It did not exactly beggar description, but it certainly had that word on the lookout for the mendicancy squad.

In the vestibule below was a letter-box into which no letter would go, and an electric button from which no mortal finger could coax a ring. Also appertaining thereunto was a card bearing the name "Mr. James Dillingham Young."

The "Dillingham" had been flung to the breeze during a former period of prosperity when its possessor was being paid thirty dollars per week. Now, when the income was shrunk to twenty dollars, the letters of "Dillingham" looked blurred, as though they were thinking seriously of contracting to a modest and unassuming D. But whenever Mr. James Dillingham Young came home and reached his flat above he was called "Jim" and greatly hugged by Mrs. James Dillingham Young, already introduced to you as Della. Which is all very good.

Della finished her cry and attended to her cheeks with a powder puff. She stood by the window and looked out dully at a gray cat walking a gray fence in a gray back yard. Tomorrow would be Christmas Day, and she had only $1.87 to buy Jim a present. She had been saving every penny she could for months, with this result. Twenty dollars a week doesn't go far. Expenses had been greater than she had calculated. They always are. Only $1.87 to buy a present for Jim. Her Jim. Many a happy hour she had spent planning for something nice for him. Something fine and rare and sterling—something just a little bit near to being worthy of the honor of being owned by Jim.

There was a pier glass between the windows of the room. Perhaps you have seen a pier glass in an eight dollar flat. A very thin and very agile person may, by observing his reflection in a rapid sequence of longitudinal strips, obtain a fairly accurate conception of his looks. Della, being slender, had mastered the art.

Suddenly she whirled from the window and stood before the glass. Her eyes were shining brilliantly, but her face had lost its color within twenty seconds. Rapidly she pulled down her hair and let it fall to its full length.

Now, there were two possessions of the James Dillingham Youngs in which they both took a mighty pride. One was Jim's gold watch that had been his father's and his grandfather's. The other was Della's hair. Had the Queen of Sheba lived in the flat across the airshaft, Della would have let her hair hang out the window some day to dry just to depreciate Her Majesty's jewels and gifts. Had King Solomon been the janitor with all his treasures piled up in the basement, Jim would have pulled out his watch every time he passed, just to see him pluck at his beard from envy.

So now Della's beautiful hair fell about her, rippling and shining like a cascade of brown waters. She did it up again nervously and quickly. Once she faltered for a minute while a tear splashed on the worn red carpet.

On went her old brown jacket; on went her old brown hat. With a whirl of skirts and with the brilliant sparkle still in her eyes, she fluttered out the door and down the stairs to the street.

Where she stopped the sign read: "Mme. Sofronie. Hair Goods of All Kinds." One flight up Della ran, and collected herself, panting. Madame, large, too white, chilly, hardly looked the "Sofronie."

"Will you buy my hair?" asked Della. "I buy hair," said Madame. "Take yer hat off and let's have a sight at the looks of it." Down rippled the brown cascade. "Twenty dollars," said Madame, lifting the mass with a practiced hand. "Give it to me quick," said Della. Oh, and the next two hours tripped on rosy wings. Forget the hashed metaphor. She was ransacking the stores for Jim's present.

She found it at last. It surely had been made for Him and no one else. There was no other like it in any of the stores, and she had turned all of them inside out. It was a platinum watch-chain, simple and chaste in design, properly proclaiming its value by substance alone and not by meretricious ornamentation—as all good things should do. It was even worthy of The Watch. As soon as she saw it she knew that it must be Jim's. It was like him. Quietness and value—the description applied to both. Twenty-one dollars they took from her for it, and she hurried home with the eighty-seven cents. With that chain on his watch Jim might be properly anxious about the time in any company. Grand as the watch was, he sometimes looked at it on the sly on account of the shabby old leather strap that he used in place of a proper gold chain.

When Della reached home her intoxication gave way a little to prudence and reason. She got out her curling-irons and lighted the gas and went to work repairing the ravages made by generosity added to love. Which is always a tremendous task, dear friends—a mammoth task.

Within forty minutes her head was covered with tiny close-lying curls that made her look wonderfully like a truant schoolboy. She looked at her reflection in the mirror long, carefully, and critically.

"If Jim doesn't kill me," she said to herself, "before he takes a second look at me, he'll say I look like a Coney Island chorus girl. But what could I do—oh! What could I do with a dollar and eighty-seven cents?"

At seven o'clock the coffee was made and the frying pan was on the back of the stove, hot and ready to cook the chops. Jim was never late, Della doubled the watch chain in her hand and sat on the corner of the table near the door that he always entered. Then she heard his step on the stair away down on the first flight, and she turned white for just a moment. She had a habit of saying little silent prayers about the simplest everyday things, and now she whispered: "Please, God, make him think I am still pretty."

The door opened and Jim stepped in and closed it. He looked thin and very serious. Poor fellow, he was only twenty-two—and to be burdened with a family! He needed a new overcoat and he was without gloves.

Jim stepped inside the door, as immovable as a setter at the scent of quail. His eyes were fixed upon Della, and there was an expression in them that she could not read, and it terrified her. It was not anger, nor surprise, nor disapproval, nor horror, nor any of the sentiments that she had been prepared for. He simply stared at her fixedly with that peculiar expression on his face.

Della wriggled off the table and went for him. "Jim, darling," she cried, "don't look at me that way. I had my hair cut off and sold it because I couldn't have lived through Christmas without giving you a present. It'll grow out again—you won't mind, will you? I just had to do it. My hair grows awfully fast. Say 'Merry Christmas!' Jim, and let's be happy. You don't know what a nice—what a beautiful gift I've got for you."

"You've cut off your hair?" asked Jim, laboriously, as if he had not arrived at that patent fact yet even after the hardest mental labor.

"Cut if off and sold it," said Della. "Don't you like me just as well, anyhow? I'm me without my hair, ain't I?" Jim looked about the room curiously. "You say your hair is gone?" he said, with an air almost of idiocy. "You needn't look for it," said Della. "It's sold, I tell you—sold and gone, too. It's Christmas Eve, boy. Be good to me, for it went for you. Maybe the hairs of my head were numbered," she went on with a sudden serious sweetness, "but nobody could ever count my love for you. Shall I put the chops on, Jim?"

Out of his trance Jim seemed to quickly wake. He enfolded his Della. For ten seconds let us regard with discreet scrutiny some inconsequential object in the other direction. Eight dollars a week or a million a year—what is the difference? A mathematician or a wit would give you the wrong answer. The Magi brought valuable gifts, but that was not among them. This dark assertion will be illuminated later on.

Jim drew a package from his overcoat pocket and threw it upon the table. "Don't make any mistake, Dell," he said, "about me. I don't think there's anything in the way of a haircut or a shave or a shampoo that could make me like my girl any less. But if you'll unwrap that package you may see why you had me going awhile at first."

White fingers and nimble tore at the string and paper. And then an ecstatic scream of joy; and then, alas! A quick feminine change to hysterical tears and wails, necessitating the immediate employment of all the comforting powers of the lord of the flat.

For there lay The Combs—the set of combs that Della had worshiped for long in a Broadway window. Beautiful combs, pure tortoise shell, with jeweled rims—just the shade to wear in the beautiful vanished hair. They were expensive combs, she knew, and her heart had simply craved and yearned over them without the least hope of possession. And now they were hers, but the tresses that should have adorned the coveted adornments were gone.

But she hugged them to her bosom, and at length she was able to look up with dim eyes and a smile and say: "My hair grows so fast, Jim!"

And then Della leaped up like a little singed cat and cried, "Oh, oh!" Jim had not yet seen his beautiful present. She held it out to him eagerly upon her open palm. The dull precious metal seemed to flash with a reflection of her bright and ardent spirit.

"Isn't it a dandy, Jim? I hunted all over town to find it. You'll have to look at the time a hundred times a day now. Give me your watch. I want to see how it looks on it."

Instead of obeying, Jim tumbled down on the couch and put his hands under the back of his head and smiled. "Dell," said he, "let's put our Christmas presents away and keep 'em awhile. They're too nice to use just at present. I sold the watch to get money to buy your combs. And now suppose you put the chops on."

The Magi, as you know, were wise men—wonderfully wise men—who brought gifts to the Babe in the manger. They invented the art of giving Christmas presents. Being wise, their gifts were no doubt wise ones, possibly bearing the privilege of exchange in case of duplication. And here I have lamely related to you the uneventful chronicle of two foolish children in a flat who most unwisely sacrificed for each other the greatest treasures of their house. But in a last word to the wise of these days let it be said that of all who give gifts these two were the wisest. Of all who give and receive gifts, such as they are the wisest. Everywhere they are the wisest. They are the Magi.

Writer O. Henry (1862–1910) is best known for his short stories—more than 600 of them, in fact—which often come with a surprise twist at the end. He was born William Sydney Porter, but changed his name after a three-year stint in prison after being convicted of embezzlement (possibly unfairly). Although he was writing before prison, it was there that he began his short stories.

One Young Laddie's Christmas

Kate Whiting Patch

Patch's story—set in the Boston of nearly a century ago—is a particularly touching portrayal of the power of a child's unshakable faith. It is also an unapologetically sentimental look at the man who may be the world's most lovable figure—Santa Claus.

It was the day before Christmas, and the hurrying, busy crowd of happy people filled the Boston streets and shops. A very small atom in that crowd was Sandy Martin, but he carried a large share of the Christmas happiness, although his hands were mittenless and his pockets full of holes. How could one help being light-hearted and glad in the midst of all that joyous bustle and flurry? It made Sandy feel as if he were going to have a glorious big Christmas himself, and he quite forgot to sigh because he was not. He stood by the big toy-shop window, flattening his little purple nose against the glass, and watching the people go in and out. He wondered what they were buying and what boy and girl was to be made glad with the contents of those mysterious parcels.

But by and by he began to grow cold, and the coldness set him to thinking; and as he walked along, up past the Common, he began to wonder, just a little, why it was that Santa Claus should have so much to do with all these people and so little to do with him. The puzzled look had not disappeared from his small, freckled face, when he looked across the street and could hardly believe his own eyes—for there was Santa Claus himself, walking through the Common!

Sandy stopped short, and stared and stared until his eyes couldn't open any wider. Yes, that was surely Santa Claus. He did not have his reindeer and sleigh, to be sure, for there was no snow; but nobody but Santa could own such a jolly face and long white beard and nice furry clothes and big boots. Then he had a good many toys about him, too; and he carried a great sign, with something in big letters on it, which told people that the rarest treasures for Christmas stockings were to be found at a certain big store on Washington Street.

But Sandy could not read and he did not bother with the letters. He just stared and stared.

Santa was evidently tired; for while Sandy was looking at him, the old saint paused in his walk and sat down on one of the benches.

"It *is* Santa Claus," said Sandy to himself. "I'm going over to talk with him, and I'll ask him why he doesn't come down our chimney, too."

No sooner said than done. Across the street Sandy hurried, and marching up to the old man, he said, in a friendly way, "How do you do, Mr. Santa Claus?"

Santa looked up, a little surprised, but smiled good naturedly at the ragged urchin before him, and remarked affably, "Well, young man, how do you do? And what may be your name?"

"I'm Sandy Martin," was the prompt answer. And with that, Sandy Martin, waiting for no further invitation, proceeded to pull himself up on the seat beside Mr. Santa Claus. "I've come over here to ask you a question," he began at once. "I want to know why you don't come to our house Chris'mus; we've got jus' as good a chimney as any one, and there's an ole lightning rod beside it fer you to tie your reindeer to."

Santa seemed immensely pleased, and chuckled to himself.

"You see," said he to Sandy, "I have so many places to go to, it is very hard to find 'em all. Where do you live, any way?"

"Up in Gower Street, No. 65. I thought you might have forgotten."

At this point Sandy became conscious that a third person was listening to the conversation. A tall, dark lady in deep mourning had come up to where the two were sitting, and stood near, waiting for a street-car. Her face was very pale and sad, and it quite surprised Sandy to think that any one could look so at Christmas-time, and before the very eyes of Santa Claus, too. As he stared up at her, the sadness was chased away for an instant by an amused smile. Sandy, who stood in awe of no one, smiled back at her, and said cheerfully, "Merry Christmas, ma'am."

The lady smiled, but sighed too.

"Thank you, my dear," she said, in a sweet, sad voice. "I hope that you may have a merry Christmas, but the day cannot be a merry one for me."

Sandy was surprised again, and gazed in bewilderment from Santa to the lady.

"Why? Don't grown-up people have merry Christmases?" he asked.

"Sometimes," answered the lady sadly. "I thought," continued Sandy, "that it was even more fun for the grown-up people than for the children; 'cause I thought

The Everything Family Christmas Book

you all knew Santa Claus and had secrets with him. All the other people I've seen looked jolly and glad, an' I thought every one was happy 'cause they was all thinkin' how they'd surprise some other one."

A shadow fell across Sandy's little face, and the lady saw it.

"My dear little boy," she said, with something like tears in her voice, although her eyes were smiling again, "don't let me spoil your thought of Christmas happiness. You are right, and I have been wrong; every one should be happy at this blessed season, and I am going to have a secret with Santa Claus, and a merry Christmas, too."

Sandy looked happy again, and began to slide off the seat.

"I've got to go home now, for it's getting dark," he said; "but I'm ever so glad I met you, Mr. Santa Claus, and I hope you'll find your way tonight all right. If you can, I wish you'd bring Maggie a doll with blue eyes, and Benny a sled, and mother a new shawl; and, Mr. Santa Claus," he added in a loud whisper, "I hope you'll give that lady there something she likes and make her have a good time."

Then Sandy trudged away, and when he looked back he was delighted to see the sad lady and Santa talking earnestly together.

While they ate their supper that night, Sandy excited the whole family with his story of meeting Santa Claus. His mother, tired out with her day's work, sighed, and tried to persuade him that it was not really Santa Claus he had seen—in vain; before they went to bed, each child hung up a ragged stocking back of the kitchen stove.

Mrs. Martin looked at them, and then sank down in her chair and had a good cry. She had been sewing hard all day, poor soul; but the money she had earned was no more than enough to keep a roof over their heads and procure food for the hungry little mouths—there was nothing to spare for Christmas stockings.

"Oh, what will they say in the morning," she wept, "when they find them empty! I can't bear it; no, I can't."

She looked about the room, and finally rose and took her shawl down from the peg.

"It's no use," she said, "I can't have them disappointed; I'll go out and pawn this and get a few things to put in them stockings."

She walked across the room and opened the door, but she did not go out, for someone was standing there.

"How do you do, ma'am?" he said, walking into the room. "I am Santa Claus, and as I couldn't very well get down the chimney I took the liberty of coming in at the door. I've a few things here for the little folks, and I promised your boy I'd come; I see he is ready for me."

With that, Santa Claus went to work, and Mrs. Martin dropped into her chair and uttered never a word; she felt as if she were dreaming. Had the myths of her childhood come back again? Was there really a Santa Claus, and had Sandy met him that afternoon? Surely it could be no one else who stood there before her; and had not this bluff, kindly old man with his own lips declared his identity?

Mrs. Martin sat perfectly dazed, and watched him as he crammed full the ragged stockings, twined a wreath of evergreen here and there and piled up a number of packages and a big basket on the table. Then, before she could utter a word, he had disappeared with a "Merry Christmas" leaving her to wonder if she had not indeed awakened from a dream.

Before light, next morning, great was the joyful excitement and noise at 65 Gower Street; and this only settled into momentary awe when mother told the children, that she herself had seen Santa Claus fill the stockings!

"But I thought you said there wasn't a Santa Claus," said Sandy, reproachfully.

"Well, I didn't believe there was," answered his mother helplessly; "but if that wasn't Santa Claus I don't know who it was."

"Course it was Santa Claus!" exclaimed Maggie; "didn't Sandy tell him to bring me a doll with blue eyes?" (Sandy nodded solemnly.) "Well, and he did bring her, didn't he?—the pretty darling! See, ma, she's got lace-edged clothes clear through, and buttoned boots."

"And didn't Sandy tell him to bring me a sled?" broke in Benny. (Sandy nodded solemnly again.) "And ain't the sled right here? And didn't the snow come, too, last night? And ain't I going coasting on the Common this very day?" Saying which Benny flung himself upon the shiny sled and tried to coast across the kitchen floor.

As if these arguments were not enough, Sandy turned to his mother again.

"And didn't I ask him to bring you a new shawl?" he said.

Mrs. Martin laid her hand on the soft thick shawl which Maggie had spread across the rocking-chair, and then she patted Sandy's shoulder gently.

"What did you tell him to bring to *you*?" she asked.

Sandy looked up in sudden surprise.

"Why, I never told him about me!" he exclaimed. "It was getting late, and I just remembered about the doll and the sled and the shawl. I forgot all about me; but now I'm sure it was Santa Claus, for he brought just the things I wanted."

"So he did!" said Maggie wonderingly. "There is the tool-chest, and the harmonica, and the big picture-book."

Benny had been peeping into the market-basket. "Whew!" he cried. "There's nuts and oranges and 'nanas and grapes; and there's red jelly and a turkey!"

"I see crackers and bread an 'taters," exclaimed Maggie from the other side of the basket. "Oh, ma! Ma! We can have a regular dinner, can't we!"

It is needless to tell of all the comfort and joy that happy Christmas brought to Sandy and his home. But his faith in Santa Claus is firm and sure and even Mrs. Martin half believes that the good old saint does somewhere exist, and was drawn down to their humble home by little Sandy's Christmas spirit.

American author Kate Whiting Patch (1870–1909) left behind many well-loved stories in her short life, for both adults and children (her "The Big Red Apple" is considered a children's classic). Her fiction appeared in Harper's *magazine,* The New England Magazine, Ladies' Home Journal, Smith's Magazine, *and* National Magazine.

A Letter from Santa Claus

Mark Twain

The father of young Susie Clemens, Samuel Langhorne Clemens (also known as Mark Twain) once took pen in hand to craft an unforgettable Christmas offering. His trademark wit is combined in this story with a child-like whimsy and an understanding of the special place that Santa Claus has in the hearts of children.

PALACE OF ST. NICHOLAS IN THE MOON

CHRISTMAS MORNING

MY DEAR SUSIE CLEMENS:

I have received and read all the letters which you and your little sister have written me by the hand of your mother and your nurses; I have also read those which you little people have written me with your own hands—for although you did not use any characters that are in grown people's alphabet, you used the characters that all children in all lands on earth and in the twinkling stars use; and as all my subjects in the moon are children and use no character but that, you will easily understand that I can read your and your baby sister's jagged and fantastic marks without any trouble at all. But I had trouble with those letters which you dictated through your mother and the nurses, for I am a foreigner and cannot read English writing well. You will find that I made no mistakes about the things which you and the baby ordered in your own letters—I went down your chimney at midnight when you were asleep and delivered them all myself—and kissed both of you, too, because you are good children, well trained, nice mannered, and about the most obedient little people I ever saw. But in the letter which you dictated there were some words which I could not make out for certain, and one or two small orders which I could not fill because we ran out of stock. Our last lot of kitchen furniture for dolls has just gone to a very poor little child in the North Star away up in the cold country above the Big Dipper. Your mama can show you that star and you will say: "Little Snow Flake" (for that is the child's name), "I'm glad you got that furniture, for you need it more than I." That is, you *must* write that, with your own hand, and Snow Flake will write you an answer. If you only spoke it she wouldn't hear you. Make your letter light and thin, for the distance is great and the postage very heavy.

There was a word or two in your mama's letter which I couldn't be certain of. I took it to be "a trunk full of doll's clothes." Is that it? I will call at your kitchen door about nine o'clock to inquire. But I must not see anybody and I must not speak to anybody but you. When the kitchen doorbell rings, George must be blindfolded and sent to open the door. Then he must go back to the dining room or the china closet and take the cook with him. You must tell George he must walk on tiptoe and not speak—otherwise he will die someday. Then you must go up to the nursery and stand on a chair or the nurse's bed and put your ear to the speaking tube that leads down to the kitchen and when I whistle through it you must speak in the tube and say, "Welcome, Santa Claus!" Then I will ask whether it was a trunk you ordered or not. If you say it was, I shall ask you what *color* you want the trunk to be.

Your mama will help you to name a nice color and then you must tell me every single thing in detail which you want the trunk to contain. Then when I say "Good-by and a merry Christmas to my little Susie Clemens," you must say "Good-by, good old Santa Claus, I thank you very much and please tell that little Snow Flake I will look at her star tonight and she must look down here—I will be right in the west bay window; and every fine night I will look at her star and say, 'I know somebody up there and *like* her, too.'" Then you must go down into the library and make George close all the doors that open into the main hall, and everybody must keep still for a little while. I will go to the moon and get those things and in a few minutes I will come down the chimney that belongs to the fireplace that is in the hall—if it is a trunk you want—because I couldn't get such a thing as a trunk down the nursery chimney, you know.

People may talk if they want, until they hear my footsteps in the hall. Then you tell them to keep quiet a little while till I go back up the chimney. Maybe you will not hear my footsteps at all—so you may go now and then and peep through the dining-room doors, and by and by you will see that thing which you want, right under the piano in the drawing room—for I shall put it there.

If I should leave any snow in the hall, you must tell George to sweep it into the fireplace, for I haven't time to do such things. George must not use a broom, but a rag—else he will die someday. You must watch George and not let him run into danger. If my boot should leave a stain on the marble, George must not holystone it away. Leave it there always in memory of my visit; and whenever you look at it or show it to anybody you must let it remind you to be a good little girl. Whenever you are naughty and somebody points to that mark which your good old Santa Claus's boot made on the marble, what will you say, little sweetheart?

Good-by for a few minutes, till I come down to the world and ring the kitchen doorbell.

Your loving SANTA CLAUS

Whom people sometimes call "The Man in the Moon"

Humorist Mark Twain (1835–1910) is well known to readers around the world for his classic novels The Adventures of Tom Sawyer *and* Huckleberry Finn, *but the former Mississippi steamboat pilot and newspaperman was a prolific lecturer and traveler as well. With a keen eye for observing his surroundings and a keen intellect with which to interpret them, he is one of America's most-loved authors.*

7

Christmas Poems

From William Shakespeare to Robert Frost, some of the most notable poets in history have written about Christmas. In this chapter, you'll find unforgettable verse that was written to evoke the holiday atmosphere. You might recognize some of the poems—after all, who could forget "'Twas the Night Before Christmas"—but you might discover some new favorites, too. Whether you choose to read the selections aloud or enjoy them in a quiet moment, you're sure to get a big dose of the season's special spirit!

The Holly and the Ivy

Traditional

In English lore, holly and ivy were often personified as male and female, which made them popular topics for carols. In the words to this carol, however—which reads wonderfully as a poem—the holly represents the Virgin Mary, while the berry stands for the infant Jesus.

The holly and the ivy,
When they are both full grown,
Of all the trees that are in the wood,
The holly bears the crown.

The rising of the sun,
And the running of the deer,
The playing of the merry organ,
Sweet singing in the choir.

The holly bears a blossom
As white as the lily flower,
And Mary bore sweet Jesus Christ
To be our sweet Savior.

The holly bears a berry
As red as any blood,
And Mary bore sweet Jesus Christ
To do poor sinners good.

The holly bears a prickle
As sharp as any thorn
And Mary bore sweet Jesus Christ
On Christmas day in the morn.

The holly bears a bark
As bitter as any gall,
And Mary bore sweet Jesus Christ
For to redeem us all.

The holly and the ivy,
When they are both full grown,
Of all the trees that are in the wood
The holly bears the crown.

Merry Christmas, Everyone!

Anonymous

The author of this poem is, unfortunately, unknown. Simple and beautiful, "Merry Christmas, Everyone!" provides a memorable picture of childhood innocence and anticipation at Christmas time.

In the rush of the merry morning,
When the red burns through the gray,
And the wintry world lies waiting
For the glory of the day,
Then we hear a fitful rushing
Just without, upon the stair,
See two white phantoms coming,
Catch the gleam of sunny hair.

Rosy feet upon the threshold,
Eager faces peeping through,
With the first red ray of sunshine
Chanting cherubs come in view;
Mistletoe and gleaming holly,
Symbols of a blessed day,
In their chubby hands they carry,
Streaming all along the way.

Well we know them, never weary
Of their innocent surprise;
Waiting, watching, listening always
With full hearts and tender eyes,
While our little household angels,
White and golden in the Sun,
Greet us with the sweet old welcome—
"Merry Christmas, everyone!"

Mistletoe

Walter de la Mare

In years past, mistletoe wasn't just an excuse for kissing—people also believed that it brought good luck. While mistletoe can be found hanging above the doorways of many homes today (as a gesture of welcome as well as an excuse for a smooch), it has historically been prohibited from church premises because of its status as an old-world charm.

Sitting under the mistletoe
(Pale-green, fairy mistletoe),
One last candle burning low,
All the sleepy dancers gone,
Just one candle burning on,
Shadows lurking everywhere:
Some one came, and kissed me there.

Tired I was; my head would go
Nodding under the mistletoe
(Pale-green, fairy mistletoe),
No footsteps came, no voice, but only,
Just as I sat there, sleepy, lonely,
Stooped in the still and shadowy air
Lips unseen—and kissed me there.

Walter De La Mare (1873–1956) grew up in Kent, a county known as the "garden of England" for its lovely countryside. After attending school in London, he worked as an accountant for an oil company, which is when he began writing. He's known for his poetry, which often has an air of the supernatural.

Christmas Trees

Robert Frost

Robert Frost, perhaps the single most popular American poet, gained a worldwide audience by writing about nature and life in the country, so it's very appropriate that he chose to write about the Christmas tree. His offering gently explores the tension between commercialism and the natural way of life.

The city had withdrawn into itself
And left at last the country to the country;
When between whirls of snow not come to lie
And whirls of foliage not yet laid, there drove
A stranger to our yard, who looked the city,
Yet did in country fashion in that there
He sat and waited till he drew us out,
A-buttoning coats, to ask him who he was.
He proved to be the city come again
To look for something it had left behind
And could not do without and keep its Christmas.
He asked if I would sell my Christmas trees;
My woods—the young fir balsams like a place
Where houses all are churches and have spires.
I hadn't thought of them as Christmas trees.
I doubt if I was tempted for a moment
To sell them off their feet to go in cars
And leave the slope behind the house all bare,
Where the sun shines now no warmer than the moon.
I'd hate to have them know it if I was.
Yet more I'd hate to hold my trees except
As others hold theirs or refuse for them,
Beyond the time of profitable growth,
The trial by market everything must come to.
I dallied so much with the thought of selling.

Then whether from mistaken courtesy
And fear of seeming short of speech, or whether
From hope of hearing good of what was mine,
I said, "There aren't enough to be worth while."
"I could soon tell how many they would cut,
You let me look them over."

"You could look.
But don't expect I'm going to let you have them."
Pasture they spring in, some in clumps too close
That lop each other of boughs, but not a few
Quite solitary and having equal boughs
All round and round. The latter he nodded "Yes" to,
Or paused to say beneath some lovelier one,
With a buyer's moderation, "That would do."
I thought so, too, but wasn't there to say so.
We climbed the pasture on the south, crossed over,
And came down on the north.

He said, "A thousand."

"A thousand Christmas trees!—at what apiece?"

He felt some need of softening that to me:
"A thousand trees would come to thirty dollars."

Then I was certain I had never meant
To let him have them. Never show surprise!
But thirty dollars seemed so small beside
The extent of pasture I should strip, three cents
(For that was all they figured out apiece),
Three cents so small beside the dollar friends
I should be writing to within the hour
Would pay in cities for good trees like those.
Regular vestry trees whole Sunday Schools
Could hang enough on to pick off enough.

A thousand Christmas trees I didn't know I had!
Worth three cents more to give away than sell
As may be shown by a simple calculation.
Too bad I couldn't lay one in a letter.
I can't help wishing I could send you one,
In wishing you herewith a Merry Christmas.

Perhaps best known for his poem, "The Road Not Taken," American poet Robert Frost (1874–1963) won four Pulitzer prizes for his work. While much of his poetry describes his surroundings in New England, it also explores the themes of life, loss, and the ways of nature.

The Oxen

Thomas Hardy

Although most of his work focuses on characters who live in the fictitious Wessex county of England, Thomas Hardy also wrote about Christmas. In "The Oxen," he puts into verse a centuries-old legend: that at midnight on the eve of Christ's birth, and every Christmas Eve thereafter, the oxen fall to their knees in honor of the Lord.

Christmas Eve, and twelve of the clock.
  "Now they are all on their knees,"
An elder said as we sat in a flock
  By the embers in hearthside ease.

We pictured the meek mild creatures where
  They dwelt in their strawy pen,
Nor did it occur to one of us there
  To doubt they were kneeling then.

So fair a fancy few would weave
  In these years! Yet, I feel,
If someone said on Christmas Eve,
  "Come; see the oxen kneel

"In the lonely barton by yonder coomb
  Our childhood used to know,"
I should go with him in the gloom,
  Hoping it might be so.

Many readers of English literature will recognize Thomas Hardy (1840–1928) as the author of novels such as Far From the Madding Crowd, Return of the Native, *and* Tess of the d'Urbervilles. *The author actually trained as an architect, but was able to give up his practice as his novels became more successful.*

Poems for Christmas

Marie Irish

Marie Irish specialized in poems, songs, and plays for children to perform at Christmas time. Here are a few examples of her delightful work.

Christmas Lights

Bright Christmas stars shine on high,
Golden stars in the wint'ry sky;
Christmas candles in windows brought
Send a greeting into the night;
While in our hearts the Christmas flame,
Glows with a love like His who came,
The infant Christ of lowly birth,
To bring good will and peace to earth.

Merry Christmas

I like Christmas day,
With its wreaths of holly,
I like Santa Claus
With his smile so jolly;
I like the Christmas tree,
Shining straight and tall,
And my pretty presents,
I surely like them all.
I like the smiles and cheer,
And how I like to hear
The happy people say
"Merry Christmas" in such a pleasant way.

The Merry Day

Mother Nature robes herself
In her snowy gown of white,
Father Winter scatters frost
That glistens with a sparkling light.

Old December lags along
With reluctant footsteps slow,
Until Miss Christmas comes at last,
With the jolliest hours we know.

Santa Claus, the bountiful,
Helps her in his lavish way—
December, Christmas, Santa Claus,
O, what a merry, merry day!

Christmas Secrets

Think of the thousands of secrets
That are tucked securely away,
All sorts of wonderful secrets
To be revealed on Christmas day.

Secrets large and secrets small,
Secrets short and secrets tall,
Secrets thick and secrets thin—
Won't the folks who get them grin?

There are secrets flat on their backs,
There are others hanging up high,
Some are standing smack on their heads,
Some in pitchy-black corners lie.

Secrets round and secrets square,
Secrets dark and secrets fair,
Secrets sour and secrets sweet,
Secrets to wear and secrets to eat.

And if all these secrets were one
And laid out on a long, long shelf,
I think it would surely surprise
Dear old jolly Santa himself.

One of Marie Irish's books, titled Choice Christmas Entertainments, *was published in 1922 by Paine Publishing Co. of Dayton, Ohio. The book's cover shows a charming picture of Santa Claus standing on a roof, about to head down the chimney with a big sack of toys over his shoulder.*

Christmas—1863

Henry Wadsworth Longfellow

Although describing a specific Christmas during the Civil War, Longfellow stresses in this poem a theme that applies to every era: Even though life is full of hardship, the goodness of God will always prevail.

I hear the bells on Christmas day
The old familiar carols play,
And wild and sweet,
The words repeat
Of peace on earth, good-will to men.

Then from each black, accursed mouth
The cannon thundered in the South;
And with that sound
The carols drowned
Of peace on earth, good-will to men.

It was as if an earthquake rent
The hearthstones of a continent,
And made forlorn
The household born
Of peace on earth, good-will to men.

And in despair I bowed my head,
"There is no peace on earth," I said,
"For hate is strong
And mocks the song
Of peace on earth, good-will to men."

Then pealed the bells more loud and deep;
"God is not dead, nor doth He sleep;
The Wrong shall fail,
The Right prevail,
With peace on earth, good-will to men."

Henry Wadsworth Longfellow (1807–1882) was hugely popular during the nineteenth century, particularly for his narrative poetry. These story poems, describing characters and events from America's history, include "The Song of Hiawatha" and "Evangeline" (about a young couple who were torn apart during the expulsion of Acadian settlers from eastern Canada).

A Visit from St. Nicholas
('Twas the Night Before Christmas)

Clement C. Moore

On Christmas Eve, 1822, Dr. Clement Clarke Moore unveiled what is arguably the most popular Christmas poem of all time, "A Visit from Saint Nicholas." Also known as "'Twas the Night Before Christmas," the poem was written strictly for the enjoyment of Moore's children, but a listener present at the reading was impressed enough to send the poem to The Troy Sentinel, *where it was published the following December.*

'Twas the night before Christmas, when all through the house
Not a creature was stirring, not even a mouse;
The stockings were hung by the chimney with care,
In hopes that Saint Nicholas soon would be there;

The children were nestled all snug in their beds,
While visions of sugarplums danced in their heads;
And Mama in her kerchief, and I in my cap,
Had just settled our brains for a long winter's nap—

When out on the lawn there arose such a clatter,
I sprang from my bed to see what was the matter.
Away to the window I flew like a flash,
Tore open the shutters and threw up the sash.

The moon on the breast of the new-fallen snow
Gave a lustre of midday to objects below;
When what to my wondering eyes should appear,
But a miniature sleigh and eight tiny reindeer.

With a little old driver, so lively and quick
I knew in a moment it must be Saint Nick!
More rapid than eagles his coursers they came,
And he whistled and shouted and called them by name:

"Now, Dasher! Now, Dancer! Now, Prancer and Vixen!
On, Comet! On, Cupid! On, Donner and Blitzen!
To the top of the porch, to the top of the wall!
Now dash away, dash away, dash away all!"

As dry leaves that before the wild hurricane fly,
When they meet with an obstacle, mount to the sky,
So up to the housetops the coursers they flew,
With a sleigh full of toys—and Saint Nicholas, too.

And then in a twinkling I heard on the roof
The prancing and pawing of each little hoof.
As I drew in my head, and was turning around,
Down the chimney Saint Nicholas came with a bound.

He was dressed all in fur from his head to his foot,
And his clothes were all tarnished with ashes and soot;
A bundle of toys he had flung on his back,
And he looked like a peddler just opening his pack.

His eyes, how they twinkled! His dimples, how merry!
His cheeks were like roses, his nose like a cherry;
His droll little mouth was drawn up like a bow,
And the beard on his chin was as white as the snow.

The stump of a pipe he held tight in his teeth,
And the smoke it encircled his head like a wreath.
He had a broad face and a little round belly
That shook, when he laughed, like a bowl full of jelly.

He was chubby and plump—a right jolly old elf;
And I laughed, when I saw him, in spite of myself.
A wink of his eye and a twist of his head
Soon gave me to know I had nothing to dread.

He spoke not a word, but went straight to his work,
And filled all the stockings; then turned with a jerk,
And laying his finger aside of his nose,
And giving a nod, up the chimney he rose.

He sprang in his sleigh, to his team gave a whistle,
And away they all flew like the down of a thistle;
But I heard him exclaim, ere he drove out of sight:
"Happy Christmas to all, and to all a good-night!"

Clement Moore (1779–1863), a professor of Biblical Learning at the New York General Theological Seminary, liked to dabble in rhymes and poetry, but was too embarrassed by "A Visit" to take public credit for it. The poem was published anonymously until 1844, when Moore, presumably encouraged by the poem's success, included it in a collection of his other works.

The Everything Family Christmas Book

A Christmas Carol

Christina Rossetti

Christina Rossetti is one of a very few popular female poets of the nineteenth century. Her poem and the classic story from Charles Dickens share not only a title, but also a reverence for Christmas and the spirit that surrounds it. The last stanza of this poem is often published alone under the title "My Gift." Whether excerpted or whole, the poem reminds us that it is the desire to give, and not the gift itself, that is the essence of the Christmas spirit.

In the bleak mid-winter
Frosty wind made moan,
Earth stood hard as iron,
Water like a stone;
Snow had fallen, snow on snow,
Snow on snow,
In the bleak mid-winter
Long ago.

Our God, Heaven cannot hold Him
Nor earth sustain;
Heaven and earth shall flee away
When He comes to reign;
In the bleak mid-winter
A stable-place sufficed
The Lord God Almighty
Jesus Christ.

Enough for Him, whom cherubim
Worship night and day,
A breastful of milk
And a mangerful of hay;

Enough for Him, whom angels
Fall down before,
The ox and ass and camel
Which adore.

Angels and archangels
May have gathered there,
Cherubim and seraphim
Thronged the air;
But only His mother
In her maiden bliss
Worshipped the Beloved
With a kiss.

What can I give Him
Poor as I am?
If I were a shepherd
I would bring a lamb,
If I were a Wise Man
I would do my part,—
Yet what I can I give Him,
Give my heart.

The Victorian poet Christina Rossetti (1830–1894) was born in London into an Italian family that was deeply involved in the arts, including writing. She published her first poems at the age of twelve. Her work is often religious in nature, but also deals with fantasy and fairy tales.

Bird of Dawning

William Shakespeare

What would a collection of Christmas literature be without a contribution from the Bard himself? This extract, from Act One, Scene One of Hamlet, *conveys in a few brief lines the essential sacredness of the season.*

Some say that ever 'gainst that season comes
Wherein our Saviour's birth is celebrated,
The bird of dawning singeth all night long;
And then, they say, no spirit dare stir abroad;
The nights are wholesome; then no planets strike,
No fairy takes, nor witch hath power to charm,
So hallow'd and so gracious is that time.

William Shakespeare (1564–1616) covered the full range of the human condition—from history to tragedy to comedy—in his work, which features a rhythm called iambic pentameter. Although the language of Elizabethan England can initially be daunting, Shakespeare's themes and observations have remained current for centuries.

8

Christmas Carols

Few holidays on the calendar are as closely associated with music and singing as Christmas. From choirs that fill cathedrals and churches with song to grade-school concerts that fill parents with pride, Christmas is linked with lyrics that celebrate the season. You'll find the words for some of the most popular traditional carols in this chapter (including all of the gifts from the "Twelve Days of Christmas"). Why not gather some friends, plan your route around the neighborhood, and start singing?

Angels We Have Heard on High

Lyrics and Music: Traditional French

1. Angels we have heard on high,
Sweetly singing o'er the plains,
And the mountains in reply,
Echoing their joyous strains.
Refrain: Gloria in excelsis Deo!
   Gloria in excelsis Deo!

2. Shepherds, why this jubilee?
Why your joyous strains prolong?
What the gladsome tidings be,
Which inspire your heav'nly song?
(Refrain)

3. Come to Bethlehem and see,
Him whose birth the angels sing;
Come, adore on bended knee,
Christ the Lord, the newborn King.
(Refrain)

The Everything Family Christmas Book

As Joseph Was A-Walking

Lyrics and Music: Appalachian Spiritual

1. As Joseph was a-walking, he heard an angel sing:
"This night shall be the birthnight of Christ, the heav'nly King." (repeat)

2. "He neither shall be bornéd in house nor in the hall,
Nor in a king's palace, but in an oxen's stall." (repeat)

3. "He neither shall be washen in white wine nor in red,
But in the clear spring water with which we were christenéd." (repeat)

4. "He neither shall be clothéd in purple nor in pall,
But in the fair white linen that usen babies all." (repeat)

5. "He neither shall be rockéd in silver nor in gold,
But in a wooden cradle that rocks upon the mold." (repeat)

6. "On the sixth day of January His birthday shall be,
When the stars and the elements shall tremble with glee." (repeat)

7. As Joseph was a-walking, thus did the angel sing,
And Mary's Son at midnight was born to be our King. (repeat)

Away in a Manger

Lyrics: Anonymous

1. A - way in a man - ger no crib for his bed, The lit - tle Lord

Je - sus laid down His sweet head. The stars in the sky___ looked

down where He lay, The lit - tle lord je - sus a - sleep on the hay.

1. Away in a manger, no crib for His bed,

The little Lord Jesus laid down His sweet head.

The stars in the sky looked down where He lay,

The little Lord Jesus asleep on the hay.

2. The cattle are lowing, the Baby awakes,

But little Lord Jesus, no crying He makes.

I love thee, Lord Jesus, look down from the sky,

And stay by my cradle till morning is nigh.

Deck the Halls with Boughs of Holly

Lyrics and Music: Traditional Welsh

1. Deck the halls with boughs of hol - ly, Fa - la - la - la - la, - la - la - la - la;

'Tis the sea son to be jol - ly Fa - la - la - la - la, - la - la - la - la.

Don we now our gay ap - par - el, Fa - la - la - la - la - la la - la - la

Troll the an - cient Yule - tide car - ol Fa - la - la - la - la, - la - la - la - la.

1. Deck the halls with boughs of holly,
Falalalala, lalalala;
'Tis the season to be jolly,
Falalalala, lalalala.
Don we now our gay apparel,
Falala, falala, lalala.
Troll the ancient yuletide carol,
Falalalala, lalalala.

2. See the blazing Yule before us,
Falalalala, lalalala;
Strike the harp and join the chorus,
Falalalala, lalalala.

Follow me in merry measure,
Falala, falala, lalala.
While I sing of Christmas treasure,
Falalalala, lalalala.

3. Fast away the old year passes,
Falalalala, lalalala;
Hail the new, ye lads and lasses,
Falalalala, lalalala.
Sing we joyous songs together,
Falala, falala, lalala.
Heedless of the wind and weather,
Falalalala, lalalala.

The First Noël

Lyrics and Music: Traditional

1. The first Noël The angel did say was to certain poor shepherds in fields where they lay; In fields where they lay keeping their sheep on a cold winter's night that was so deep. No-ël, No-ël, No-ël No-ël, Born is the King of Is-ra-el.

1. The first Noël, the angel did say,
Was to certain poor shepherds in fields as they lay,
In fields where they lay keeping their sheep,
On a cold winter's night that was so deep.
Refrain: Noël, Noël, Noël, Noël
Born is the King of Israel

2. They looked up and saw a star
Shining in the east, beyond them far,
And to the earth it gave great light,
And so it continued both day and night.
(Refrain)

3. And by the light of that same star
Three wise men came from country far;
To see the King was their intent,
And to follow the star where e'er it went.
(Refrain)

4. This star drew nigh to the northwest,
O'er Bethlehem it took its rest;
And there it did both stop and stay,
Right over the place where Jesus lay.
(Refrain)

5. Then entered in those wise men three,
Full reverently upon the knee,
And offered there, in His presence,
Their gold and myrrh and frankincense.
(Refrain)

6. Then let us all with one accord
Sing praises to our heav'nly Lord;
That hath made heaven and earth of naught,
And with His blood mankind hath bought.
(Refrain)

The Everything Family Christmas Book

God Rest You Merry, Gentlemen

Lyrics and Music: Traditional English

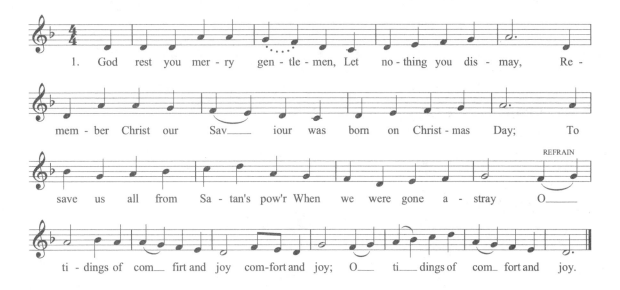

1. God rest you merry gentlemen, Let nothing you dismay, Remember Christ our Saviour was born on Christmas Day; To save us all from Satan's pow'r When we were gone astray O tidings of comfirt and joy comfort and joy; O tidings of comfort and joy.

1. God rest you merry, gentlemen,

Let nothing you dismay

Remember Christ our Savior

Was born on Christmas Day;

To save us all from Satan's pow'r

When we were gone astray.

Refrain: O tidings of comfort and joy, comfort and joy;

O tidings of comfort and joy

2. From God our heav'nly Father

The blessed angel came

And unto certain shepherds

Brought tidings of the same

How that in Bethlehem was born

The Son of God by name.

(Refrain)

3. "Fear not, then," said the angel

"Let nothing you affright,

This day is born a Savior

Of a pure Virgin bright,

To free all those who trust in Him

From Satan's pow'r and might."

(Refrain)

4. The shepherds at those tidings

Rejoiced much in mind,

And left their flocks a-feeding

In tempest, storm, and wind,

And went to Bethlehem straightway

This blessed Babe to find.

(Refrain)

Continued . . .

5. But when to Bethlehem they came,
Whereat this Infant lay,
They found Him in a manger,
Where oxen feed on hay;
His mother Mary kneeling
Unto the Lord did pray.
(Refrain)

6. Now to the Lord sing praises,
All you within this place,
And with true love and brotherhood
Each other now embrace;
This holy tide of Christmas
All others doth deface.
(Refrain)

Good King Wenceslas

Lyrics: John Mason Neale (1818–1866)

Music: *Piae Cantiones*, 1582

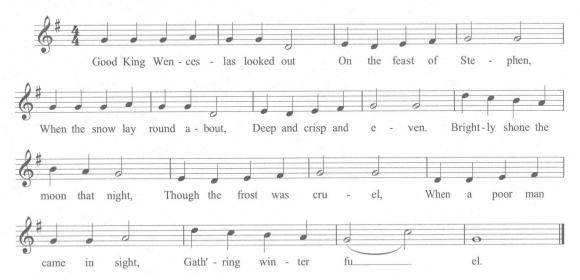

Good King Wen - ces - las looked out   On the feast of Ste - phen,

When the snow lay round a - bout,   Deep and crisp and   e - ven.   Bright-ly shone the

moon that night,   Though the frost was   cru - el,   When a   poor man

came in sight,   Gath' - ring win - ter   fu_____   el.

1. Good King Wenceslas looked out
On the feast of Stephen,
When the snow lay round about,
Deep and crisp and even.
Brightly shone the moon that night,
Though the frost was cruel,
When a poor man came in sight,
Gath'ring winter fuel.

2. "Hither, page, and stand by me,
If though know'st it telling,
Yonder peasant, who is he?
Where and what his dwelling?"
"Sire, he lives a good league hence,
Underneath the mountains,
Right against the forest fence,
By Saint Agnes' fountain."

3. "Bring me flesh, and bring
me wine,
Bring me pine logs hither
Thou and I shall see him dine,
When we bear them thither."
Page and monarch, forth they went,
Forth they went together;
Through the rude wind's wild lament
And the bitter weather.

4. "Sire the night is darker now,
And the wind blows stronger,
Fails my heart, I know not how;
I can go no longer."
"Mark my footsteps, my good page,
Tread thou in them boldly;
Thou shalt find the winter's rage
Freeze thy blood less coldly."

5. In his master's steps he trod,
Where the snow lay dinted;
Heat was in the very sod
Which the Saint had printed.
Therefore Christian men, be sure,
Wealth or rank possessing.
Ye who now will bless the poor
Shall yourselves find blessing.

Hark! The Herald Angels Sing

Lyrics: Charles Wesley (1707–1788)
Music: Felix Mendelssohn (1809–1847)

1. Hark! The herald angels sing,
"Glory to the newborn King;
Peace on earth, and mercy mild,
God and sinners reconciled!"
Joyful, all ye nations, rise,
Join the triumph of the skies;
With th'angelic host proclaim,
"Christ is born in Bethlehem!"
Refrain: Hark! The herald angels sing,
    "Glory to the newborn King."

2. Christ by highest heav'n adored;
Christ the everlasting Lord;
Come, desire of nations, come,
Fix in us thy humble home.

Veiled in flesh the Godhead see;
Hail th'Incarnate Deity,
Pleased as man with man to dwell;
Jesus, our Emmanuel.
(Refrain)

3. Hail, the heav'n-born Prince of Peace!
Hail, the Son of Righteousness!
Light and life to us He brings,
Ris'n with healing in His wings;
Mild He lays his glory by,
Born that man no more may die,
Born to raise the sons of earth,
Born to give them second birth.
(Refrain)

The Holly and the Ivy

Lyrics and Music: Traditional English

1. The hol - ly and the i - vy, When they are both full grown, Of____ all the trees that are in the wood, The____ hol - ly bears the crown; O the ris - ing of the sun____ and the run - ning of the deer, The____ play - ing of the mer - ry or - gan, Sweet sing - ing in the choir.

1. The holly and the ivy,
When they are both full grown,
Of all the trees that are in the wood
The holly bears the crown.
Refrain: O the rising of the sun,
   And the running of the deer,
   The playing of the merry organ,
   Sweet singing in the choir.

2. The holly bears a blossom,
As white as the lily flower,
And Mary bore sweet Jesus Christ
To be our sweet Savior.
(Refrain)

3. The holly bears a berry,
As red as any blood,
And Mary bore sweet Jesus Christ
To do poor sinners good.
(Refrain)

4. The holly bears a prickle,
As sharp as any thorn,
And Mary bore sweet Jesus Christ
On Christmas Day in the morn.
(Refrain)

5. The holly bears a bark,
As bitter as any gall,
And Mary bore sweet Jesus Christ
For to redeem us all.
(Refrain)

6. The holly and the ivy,
When they are both full grown,
Of all the trees that are in the wood
The holly bears the crown.
(Refrain)

I Saw Three Ships

Lyrics and Music: Traditional English

1. I saw three ships come sail - ing in, On Christ - mas Day, on
Christ-mas Day, I saw three ships come sail - ing in, on Christ-mas Day in the morn - ing.

1. I saw three ships come sailing in,
On Christmas Day, on Christmas Day,
I saw three ships come sailing in,
On Christmas Day in the morning.

2. And what was in those ships all three?
On Christmas Day, on Christmas Day,
And what was in those ships all three?
On Christmas Day in the morning.

3. Our Savior Christ and His lady,
On Christmas Day, on Christmas Day,
Our Savior Christ and His lady,
On Christmas Day in the morning.

4. Pray, whither sailed those ships all three?
On Christmas Day, on Christmas Day,
Pray, whither sailed those ships all three?
On Christmas Day in the morning.

5. O, they sailed into Bethlehem,
On Christmas Day, on Christmas Day,
O, they sailed into Bethlehem,
On Christmas Day in the morning.

6. And all the bells on earth shall ring,
On Christmas Day, on Christmas Day,
And all the bells on earth shall ring,
On Christmas Day in the morning.

7. And all the angels in heaven shall sing,
On Christmas Day, on Christmas Day,
And all the angels in heaven shall sing,
On Christmas Day in the morning.

8. And all the souls on earth shall sing,
On Christmas Day, on Christmas Day,
And all the souls on earth shall sing,
On Christmas Day in the morning.

9. Then let us all rejoice again!
On Christmas Day, on Christmas Day,
Then let us all rejoice again!
On Christmas Day in the morning.

It Came Upon a Midnight Clear

Lyrics: Edmund Sears (1810–1876)
Music: Richard S. Willis (1819–1900)

It came up-on a mid-night clear, That glo rious song of Old, From an-gels bend ing near the earth to touch their harps of gold, "Peace on the earth, good will to men, From heav'-n's all gra cious King." The world in sol emn still-ness lay To hear the an gels sing.

1. It came upon a midnight clear,
That glorious song of old,
From angels bending near the earth
To touch their harps of gold;
"Peace on the earth, good will to men,
From heav'n's all-gracious King."
The world in solemn stillness lay
To hear the angels sing.

2. Still through the cloven skies they come,
With peaceful wings unfurled,
And still their heav'nly music floats
O'er all the weary world.
Above its sad and lowly plains
They bend on hov'ring wing,
And ever o'er its Babel sounds
The blessed angels sing.

3. O ye, beneath life's crushing load
Whose forms are bending low,
Who toil along the climbing way
With painful steps and slow,
Look now, for glad and golden hours
Come swiftly on the wing:
O rest beside the weary road,
And hear the angels sing!

4. For lo, the days are hast'ning on,
By prophets seen of old,
When with the ever-circling years,
Shall come the time foretold,
When the new heav'n and earth shall own
The Prince of Peace their King,
And the whole world send back the song
Which now the angels sing.

Jingle Bells

Lyrics and Music: John Pierpont (1785–1866)

Dash-ing through the snow, In a one-horse o-pen sleigh, O'er the fields we go, Laugh-ing all the way; Bells on bob-tail ring, Mak-ing spi-rits bright. What fun it is to ride and sing a sleigh-ing song to-night Jin-gle bells, jin-gle bells, Jin-gle all the way! Oh, what fun it is to ride in a one-horse o-pen sleigh! Jin-gle bells, jin-gle bells, Jin-gle all the way! Oh, what fun it is to ride in a one-horse o-pen sleigh!

Dashing through the snow,
In a one-horse open sleigh,
O'er the fields we go,
Laughing all the way;
Bells on bobtail ring,
Making spirits bright,
What fun it is to ride and sing
A sleighing song tonight!

Jingle bells, jingle bells,
Jingle all the way!
Oh, what fun it is to ride
In a one-horse open sleigh!

Jingle bells, jingle bells,
Jingle all the way!
Oh, what fun it is to ride
In a one-horse open sleigh!

Jolly Old Saint Nicholas

Anonymous

Jol - ly old Saint Ni - cho - las Lean your ear this way! Don't you tell a sin - gle soul What I'm going to say. Christ-mas Eve is com - ing soon Now, you dear old man, Whis-per what you'll bring to me; Tell me if you can.

1. Jolly old Saint Nicholas,
lean your ear this way!
Don't you tell a single soul
what I'm going to say:
Christmas Eve is coming soon;
now, you dear old man
Whisper what you'll bring to me;
tell me if you can.

2. When the clock is striking twelve,
when I'm fast asleep
Down the chimney, broad and black,
with your pack you'll creep.
All the stockings you will find

hanging in a row
Mine will be the shortest one,
you'll be sure to know

3. Bobby wants a pair of skates,
Suzy wants a sled
Nellie wants a picture book,
yellow, blue, and red.
Now I think I'll leave to you
what to give the rest
Choose for me, dear Santa Claus;
you will know the best.

Joy to the World

Lyrics: Isaac Watts (1674–1748)

Music: unknown

1. Joy to the world! the Lord is come; Let earth re - ceive her King; Let ev___ 'ry___ heart___ pre - pare___ Him___ room,___ And heav'n and na - ture___ sing, And heav'n and na - ture___ sing, And heav'n___ And heav'n___ and na - ture sing.

1. Joy to the world! the Lord is come;

Let earth receive her King;

Let ev'ry heart prepare Him room,

And heav'n and nature sing,

And heav'n and nature sing,

And heav'n, and heav'n and nature sing.

2. Joy to the world! the Savior reigns;

Let men their songs employ;

While fields and floods, rocks, hills, and plains

Repeat the sounding joy,

Repeat the sounding joy,

Repeat, repeat the sounding joy.

3. He rules the world with truth and grace,

And makes the nations prove

The glories of His righteousness,

And wonders of His love,

And wonders of His love,

And wonders, and wonders of His love.

O Christmas Tree

Lyrics and Music: Traditional German

1. O Christmas Tree,

O Christmas Tree,

How steadfast are

your branches!

Your boughs are green

in summer's clime

And through the snows

of wintertime.

O Christmas Tree,

O Christmas Tree,

How steadfast are

your branches!

2. O Christmas Tree,

O Christmas Tree,

What happiness befalls me

When oft at

joyous Christmas-time

Your form inspires

my song and rhyme.

O Christmas Tree,

O Christmas Tree,

What happiness befalls me

3. O Christmas Tree,

O Christmas Tree,

Your boughs can

teach a lesson

That constant faith

and hope sublime

Lend strength and

comfort through all time.

O Christmas Tree,

O Christmas Tree,

Your boughs can

teach a lesson

O Come, All Ye Faithful *(Adeste Fidelis)*

Lyrics: (?)John Francis Wade (1712–1786)
Music: (?)John Reading (d. 1692)

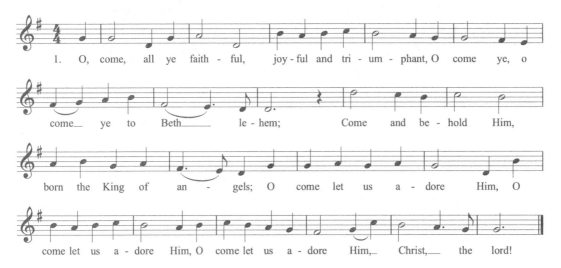

1. O come, all ye faithful, joyful and triumphant,

O come ye, o come ye to Bethlehem;

Come and behold Him, born the King of angels;

Refrain: O come, let us adore Him,

    O come, let us adore Him,

    O come, let us adore Him, Christ the Lord!

2. Sing, choirs of angels, sing in exultation,

O sing, all ye citizens of heaven above!

Glory to God, all glory in the highest;

(Refrain)

3. Yea, Lord, we greet Thee, born this happy morning,

Jesus, to Thee be all glory giv'n;

Word of the Father, now in flesh appearing;

(Refrain)

O Come, O Come, Emmanuel

Lyrics: Latin, 12th century, translated by John M. Neale (1818–1866)

Music: Plainsong, 12th century

1. O come, O come, Emmanuel
And ransom captive Israel,
That mourns in lonely exile here,
Until the Son of God appear.
Refrain: Rejoice! Rejoice! Emmanuel
Shall come to thee, O Israel!

2. O come, Thou Dayspring, come and cheer
Our spirits by Thine advent here;
Disperse the gloomy clouds of night,
And death's dark shadows put to flight.
(Refrain)

O Holy Night

Lyrics: Cappeau de Roquemaure
Music: Adolph Charles Adam (1803–1856)

1. O holy night! the stars are brightly shining,

It is the night of our dear Savior's birth!

Long lay the world, in sin and error pining,

'Til He appear'd, and the soul felt its worth.

A thrill of hope the weary world rejoices,

For yonder breaks a new and glorious morn!

Fall on your knees! O hear the angel voices!

O night divine, O night when Christ was born!

O night divine, O night, O night divine!

2. Led by the light of faith serenely beaming,

With glowing hearts by His cradle we stand.

So, led by light of a star sweetly gleaming,

Here came the wise men from the Orient land.

The King of Kings lay thus in lowly manger,

In all our trials born to be our friend;

He knows our need, to our weakness no stranger;

Behold your King! Before the Lowly bend!

Behold your King! your King! before Him bend!

O Little Town of Bethlehem

Lyrics: Phillips Brooks (1835–1893)
Music: Lewis H. Redner (1831–1908)

1. O lit-tle town of Beth-le-hem, How still we see thee lie! A-
bove thy deep and dream-less sleep the si-lent-stars go by; Yet
in the dark streets shi-neth The ev-er-last-ing Light; The
hopes and fears of all the years Are met in thee to-night.

1. O little town of Bethlehem,
How still we see thee lie!
Above thy deep and dreamless sleep
The silent stars go by;
Yet in thy dark streets shineth
The everlasting Light;
The hopes and fears of all the years
Are met in thee tonight.

2. For Christ is born of Mary,
And gathered all above,
While mortals sleep, the angels keep
Their watch of wond'ring love.
O morning stars, together
Proclaim the holy birth,
And praises sing to God the King,
And peace to all the earth.

3. How silently, how silently,
The wondrous gift is giv'n!
So God imparts to human hearts
The blessings of His heav'n.
No ear may hear His coming,
But in this world of sin,
Where meek souls will receive Him still,
The Dear Christ enters in.

4. O holy child of Bethlehem,
Descend to us, we pray,
Cast out our sin and enter in;
Be born in us today!
We hear the Christmas angels
The great glad tidings tell;
O come to us, abide with us
Our Lord Emmanuel!

Rise Up, Shepherd and Follow

Lyrics and Music: African American Spiritual

There's a star in the East on Christmas morn,

Rise up, shepherd, and follow!

It will lead to the place where the Savior's born;

Rise up, shepherd, and follow!

Leave your sheep and leave your lambs;

Rise up, shepherd, and follow!

Leave your ewes and leave your rams;

Rise up, shepherd, and follow!

Follow, follow!

Rise up, shepherd, and follow!

Follow the star of Bethlehem;

Rise up, shepherd, and follow!

Silent Night

Lyrics: Joseph Mohr (1792–1848)
Music: Franz Xavier Gruber (1787–1863)

1. Silent night, holy night!
All is calm, all is bright
Round yon Virgin Mother and Child
Holy Infant, so tender and mild,
Sleep in heavenly peace,
Sleep in heavenly peace.

2. Silent night, holy night!
Shepherds quake at the sight,
Glories stream from heaven afar,
Heav'nly hosts sing alleluia!
Christ the Savior is born!
Christ the Savior is born!

3. Silent night, holy night!
Wondrous star, lend thy light!
With the angels, let us sing
Alleluia to our King!
Christ the Savior is here,
Jesus the Savior is here.

The Twelve Days of Christmas

Lyrics and Music: Traditional English

1. On the first day of Christmas my true love sent to me
A partridge in a pear tree.

2. On the second day of Christmas my true love sent to me
Two turtle doves and a partridge in a pear tree.

3. On the third day of Christmas my true love sent to me
Three French hens, two turtle doves, and a partridge in a pear tree.

4. On the fourth day of Christmas my true love sent to me
Four calling birds, three French hens, two turtle doves, and a partridge in a pear tree.

5. On the fifth day of Christmas my true love sent to me
Five gold rings, four calling birds, three French hens, two turtle doves, and a partridge in a pear tree.

6. On the sixth day of Christmas my true love sent to me
Six geese a-laying, five gold rings, four calling birds . . .

7. On the seventh day of Christmas my true love sent to me
Seven swans a-swimming, six geese a-laying . . .

8. On the eighth day of Christmas my true love sent to me
Eight maids a-milking . . .

9. On the ninth day of Christmas my true love sent to me
Nine ladies dancing . . .

10. On the tenth day of Christmas my true love sent to me
Ten lords a-leaping . . .

11. On the eleventh day of Christmas my true love sent to me
Eleven pipers piping . . .

12. On the twelfth day of Christmas my true love sent to me
Twelve drummers drumming . . .

We Three Kings of Orient Are

Lyrics and Music: John Henry Hopkins, Jr. (1820–1891)

1. We three Kings of Or - i - ent are, Bear - ing gifts we tra - verse a - far, Field and foun - tain, moor and moun - tain, Fol - low - ing yon - der star, O,___ Star of won - der, star of night, Star of roy - al beau - ty bright, West - ward lead - ing, still pro - ceed - ing, Guide us to the per - fect light.

1. We three kings of Orient are,
Bearing gifts we traverse afar,
Field and fountain, moor and mountain,
Following yonder star.
Refrain: O, star of wonder, star of night,
Star of royal beauty bright,
Westward leading, still proceeding,
Guide us to thy perfect light.

2. Born a King on Bethlehem's plain,
Gold I bring to crown Him again,
King forever, ceasing never
Over us all to reign.
(Refrain)

3. Frankincense to offer have I,
Incense owns a Deity nigh:
Prayer and praising
All men raising,
Worship Him, God on high.
(Refrain)

4. Myrrh is mine; its bitter perfume
Breathes a life of gathering gloom;
Sorrowing, sighing, bleeding, dying,
Sealed in the stone-cold tomb.
(Refrain)

5. Glorious now, behold Him arise,
King, and God, and sacrifice;
Heaven sings alleluia:
Alleluia the earth replies.
(Refrain)

We Wish You a Merry Christmas

Lyrics and Music: Traditional English

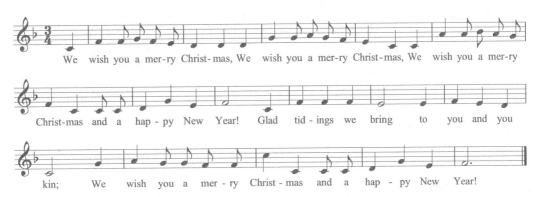

We wish you a mer-ry Christ-mas, We wish you a mer-ry Christ-mas, We wish you a mer-ry Christ-mas and a hap-py New Year! Glad tid-ings we bring to you and you kin; We wish you a mer-ry Christ-mas and a hap-py New Year!

We wish you a Merry Christmas,
We wish you a Merry Christmas,
We wish you a Merry Christmas
And a Happy New Year!
Glad tidings we bring,
To you and your kin!
We wish you a Merry Christmas
And a Happy New Year!

What Child Is This?

Lyrics: William Chatterton Dix (1837–1898)
Music: Sixteenth-century English

What Child is this,__ Who laid to rest__ on Ma-ry's lap__ is sleep ing? Whom

an - gels greet__ with an - thems sweet,__While shep-herds watch__ are keep - ing?

This, this - is Christ the King,__Whom shep-herds guard__ and an - gels sing:

This, this - is Christ the King,__ The Babe,__ the Son__ of Ma - ry.

1. What Child is this, Who, laid to rest,
On Mary's lap is sleeping?
Whom angels greet with anthems sweet,
While shepherds watch are keeping?
Refrain: This, this is Christ the King,
  Whom shepherds guard and angels sing:
  This, this is Christ the King,
  The Babe, the Son of Mary.

2. Why lies He in such mean estate,
Where ox and ass are feeding?
Good Christian, fear: for sinners here
The silent Word is pleading.
(Refrain)

3. So bring Him incense, gold, and myrrh,
Come, peasant, king, to own Him;
The King of Kings salvation brings,
Let loving hearts enthrone Him.
(Refrain)

While Shepherds Watched Their Flocks

Lyrics: Nahum Tate (1652–1715)
Music: George Frederick Handel (1685–1759)

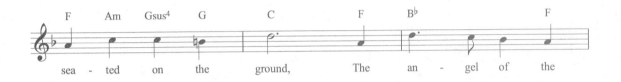

1. While shepherds watched their flocks by night,
All seated on the ground,
The angel of the Lord came down,
And glory shone around.
"Fear not," said he, for mighty dread
Had seized their troubled mind,
"Glad tidings of great joy I bring
To you and all mankind."

2. "To you, in David's town this day,
Is born of David's line
The Savior who is Christ the Lord,
And this shall be the sign:

The heavenly Babe you there shall find
To human view displayed,
All meanly wrapped in swathing bands,
And in a manger laid."

3. Thus spake the seraph, and forthwith
Appeared a shining throng
Of angels praising God and thus
Addressed their joyful song:
"All glory be to God on high
And on the earth be peace,
Goodwill henceforth from heaven to men
Begin and never cease."

9

Christmas on the Silver Screen

When you think of Christmas, you may think of the joy that's brought each season by television, music, and the movies. The Grinch, George Bailey, Rudolph the Red-Nosed Reindeer, and a host of other figures who came to prominence after World War II now play an important part in our celebration of the holiday. While some of them have little connection to the origins of Christmas, they nonetheless provide a window into the holiday and how you recognize it today.

It's a Wonderful Life

If you asked twenty people to name their top-ten Christmas films of all time, odds are that nineteen of them would find a place on the list for Frank Capra's 1946 Christmas classic, *It's a Wonderful Life*. It graces our television screens every season, to the point where the season wouldn't be quite the same without it.

The Movie Background

During World War II, Capra, who had scored with such hits as *It Happened One Night*, *Mr. Smith Goes to Washington*, and *Mr. Deeds Goes to Town*, headed the government's Office of War Information, and directed the powerful *Why We Fight* series of documentaries. When the war ended, Capra returned to Hollywood and, with William Wyler, George Stevens, and Samuel Briskin, formed Liberty Pictures—an independent production company in an era of big-studio moviemaking.

For Capra's first Liberty Pictures project, he bought the rights to a short piece by Philip Van Doren Stern called "The Greatest Gift." It told the tale of a man who was afforded the opportunity to see what life would have been like if he had never been born.

Capra asked Jimmy Stewart, who had returned from active duty as an Air Force pilot, to be his leading man in *It's a Wonderful Life*. To win Stewart's commitment before any script existed, Capra had to give a verbal summary of the plot he had in mind. According to Stewart, the account was a rambling one that had to do with an angel who didn't have any wings yet, a good man named George Bailey who wanted to see the world but never got to, a savings and loan company, a small town, and a misplaced wad of money—among many, many other things. Although Capra's summary left Stewart more baffled than ever about what the film was actually about, he agreed to do the picture. Donna Reed, Lionel Barrymore, and Thomas Mitchell also signed on.

The picture was filmed over the summer of 1946. All the snow in the winter scenes is fake; all the actors in overcoats and mittens were sweltering. When the movie was released in late December 1946, it received generally positive critical notices, but not such a positive welcome at the box office.

A Movie Flop

One argument goes that the film failed because it was Capra's darkest effort to date. *It's a Wonderful Life* includes a child-beating scene, a suicide attempt, and a nightmarish tour of a very seedy, very depressing outpost that could no longer call itself Bedford Falls. It may well be that the many down moments of the film just weren't in tune with the mood of the moviegoing public shortly after World War II. Even though the film features what may be the happiest (or, depending on your perspective, corniest) ending in movie history, that ending is a long time coming, and a war-weary audience may simply have been looking for more upbeat entertainment in late 1946 and early 1947.

Another line of reasoning has it that Liberty Films had trouble competing with bigger, better-promoted, and better-distributed studio films. This may well have been the case; even though RKO was handling the distribution of the picture, the number of theaters initially showing the film seems quite low for a major release, and Liberty apparently had trouble collecting from theaters.

The third theory suggests that bad timing was the film's undoing. It was released to a few dozen theaters very late in December 1946, with broader distribution coming only late the following January. Not, perhaps, the best way to launch a Christmas movie. Another obstacle may have been the weather: A major blizzard put a huge hole in East Coast movie attendance during the film's run.

Whether it was because of the tone of the film, the competitive pressures from the big studios, the timing, or a combination of all three, *It's a Wonderful Life* was anything but a wonderful experience for the fledgling Liberty Films studio. By the end of the year, that project and others like it had brought the company into serious financial trouble. To avoid personal responsibility for Liberty's debts, Capra and his partners dissolved the studio—and, in so doing, paved the way for the remarkable revival of the story of George Bailey of Bedford Falls.

A Television Revival

The irony is that if Liberty hadn't failed, *It's a Wonderful Life* might never have become a holiday tradition—television, not the movies, was the medium through which Capra's film became widely known and loved. This was largely because the company's failure allowed the film's copyright to enter the public domain at a time when broadcasters were hungry for cheap holiday-oriented programming. If you had a copy of the film, you could show it, period. (You could also delete as many scenes from it as you pleased in order to accommodate television's appetite for commercial breaks, a fact that has frustrated many a Capra purist.)

Thankfully, the official, original, and unedited version of the film is available on DVD (Turner Entertainment, which obtained the RKO library, has the original negative). Head down to your local movie rental or retail outlet and check out a copy of the crystal clear, uncut *It's a Wonderful Life* for holiday viewing. But get there early—you'll have some competition!

Whoops!

Even the experts aren't perfect all the time. Watch for these film flubs in Capra's holiday masterpiece.

- In the dinner scene before the big dance, when Harry Bailey says, "Annie, my sweet, have you got those pies?" the water-pitcher on the table is about one-third full. Later in the scene, without anyone's assistance, the level has mysteriously risen to about one-half.
- Shortly after Mary loses her bathrobe and dashes into a nearby bush, she tells George that she's hiding in the hydrangea bush. It's hard to tell what the set designer was getting at with this "plant," but one thing's for certain: It isn't a hydrangea.
- Watch very closely after George tosses the robe onto the bush; the robe vanishes in the next shot!
- In the scene in which George walks into the Building and Loan carrying a holiday wreath, the wreath magically appears and disappears on his arm in various shots.
- After George leaves Mr. Martini's on the night he attempts to commit suicide, he crashes his car into an old tree. Before the car hits the tree, the car has no snow to speak of on it, but in the very next shot, noticeable snowdrifts have suddenly appeared on the car's body.
- Right before George's line "I wish I'd never been born," Clarence Oddbody is standing with his arms at his sides. But in the very next shot, Clarence's arms are crossed.
- Near the end of the long final scene of the film, Zuzu reaches for the pocket watch before the stocky man pulls it out of her coat to surprise her with it.

If you can spot them all, give yourself an extra cup of eggnog!

Four Decades of Holiday Viewing

Ever since television became a focal point of our living rooms in the early 1960s, we've gathered in front of the smaller silver screen on Christmas Eve, often with family members. Here's what we've been watching since 1962.

Christmas Eve, 1962

The Bing Crosby Show
Mary Martin joins Bing in a special holiday celebration.

Black Nativity
A children's special featuring, in the words of a newspaper listing of the day, an "all-Negro cast."

It's a Wonderful Life
Countless broadcasts of Frank Capra's film—about a good man who learns the value of his time on earth—give viewers a dose of holiday spirit.

Christmas Eve, 1963

The Red Skelton Hour
Red spends a special hour in celebration, complete with carols, comedy, and ballet. In a pantomime sketch, a hobo finds a ragged toy doll that magically comes to life.

Petticoat Junction
The plans for Christmas festivities in Hooterville are in trouble—until a railroad magnate pays a visit to the local folks.

Telephone Hour
Hostess Jane Wyatt welcomes Bill Baird's Marionettes to her Christmas show.

Christmas Eve, 1964

Hazel
Hazel tries to find a way to keep George from acting like Scrooge.

The Burke Family Singers
The Burkes pay a visit to Baroness Maria von Trapp for a special Christmas Eve celebration.

Dr. Kildare
Rip Torn guest stars as a patient whose generosity on Christmas Eve brings unexpected results.

Christmas Eve, 1965

The Smothers Brothers Comedy Hour
The Brothers celebrate their first network Christmas broadcast.

Gomer Pyle
Gomer and Sergeant Carter learn a lesson about the spirit of the season.

Sing Along with Mitch Miller
Mitch hosts a festive family reunion.

Christmas Eve, 1966

Bing Crosby's Hollywood Palace Christmas Special
Bing's special guests include Kate Smith, Cyd Charisse, and Bob Newhart.

The Lawrence Welk Show
Welk's Christmas show is a homey affair, with performances of classic Christmas songs by members of his family.

Heart of Christmas
The program features seasonal music from host/conductor Skitch Henderson and harpist Robert Maxwell.

Christmas Eve, 1967

The Ed Sullivan Show
Ed celebrates the holiday season with his guests Arthur Godfrey, Bobbie Gentry, and the Cowsills.

The GI's Christmas Eve Special
American servicemen send messages to their loved ones and show how the season is being observed in Vietnam.

And on Earth, Peace
An hour of Christmas music native to Central and Eastern Europe, hosted by Margaret Truman.

Christmas Eve, 1968

Julia
In the first American network television series to feature a nonwhite protagonist, star Diahann Carroll is joined by Marc Copage and Michael Link in an episode entitled "I'm Dreaming of a Black Christmas."

That's Life
Robert Morse, Leslie Uggams, and the Doodletown Pipers share thoughts on "Our First Christmas."

60 Minutes
Harry Reasoner offers his essay "What Christ Looked Like."

Christmas Eve, 1969

The Flying Nun
Sally Field stars in the Christmas episode "Winter Wonderland."

Music Hall
Wayne Newton hosts a seasonal celebration with his guests Julie Budd and the Singing Angels.

Space Cantata
A musical special set to official NASA footage from the *Apollo 8* mission.

Christmas Eve, 1970

The Flip Wilson Show
Flip and his guests Burl Ives and Sha-Na-Na present a holiday program of comedy and music.

Boughs of Holly
Host Pete Seeger shares some memorable Christmas songs.

Story Theater
Five fairy tales from the works of the Brothers Grimm, staged by the Yale Repertory Theater Company.

Christmas Eve, 1971

J.T.
Jane Wagner and Kevin Hooks star in this drama about a shy youngster whose closest friends are a cat and a transistor radio.

The Odd Couple
Tony Randall and Jack Klugman star in the Christmas episode "Scrooge Gets an Oscar."

Beethoven's Birthday
Leonard Bernstein and the Vienna Philharmonic celebrate the anniversary of the composer's birth.

Christmas Eve, 1972

Christmas with the King Family
The Kings offer an evening of wholesome musical fun and seasonal celebration.

The Miracles of Christmas
The Mormon Tabernacle Choir offers traditional Christmas favorites.

The Wonderful World of Disney
The Christmas episode "A Present for Donald" is featured.

Christmas Eve, 1973

Gunsmoke
James Arness and Amanda Blake star in the episode "P.S., Murry Christmas."

An American Christmas in Words and Music
Burt Lancaster hosts this celebration of the American Christmas, with guests James Earl Jones, Peter Yarrow, and Linda Lavin.

A Dream of Christmas
A southern minister has trouble adjusting to his new home in Los Angeles.

Christmas Eve, 1974

Holy Year Jubilee
Pope Paul VI celebrates Midnight Mass in St. Peter's Basilica.

Christmas at Pops
Arthur Fiedler and the Boston Pops Orchestra celebrate the season with the Tanglewood Festival Chorus.

The Joy of Christmas
The Westminster Ensemble joins the Mormon Tabernacle Choir for an evening of seasonal music.

Christmas Eve, 1975

Tony Orlando and Dawn
Carroll O'Connor and the International Children's Choir are guests on the Christmas episode of the popular variety show.

A Bicentennial Christmas
The American Christmas tradition is reviewed in anticipation of the nation's 200th birthday.

The Oral Roberts Christmas Special
Roberts offers inspirational messages for the season.

Christmas Eve, 1976

Donny and Marie
Guests Sonny and Cher, Edgar Bergen, and Paul Lynde help the duo celebrate the season.

The Homecoming: A Christmas Story
Patricia Neal stars as the mother of a rural American family in the 1930s.

The Sounds of Christmas
Doc Severinsen and his orchestra play holiday favorites.

Christmas Eve, 1977

The Jeffersons
In this holiday episode, George is sending gifts and cash to a mysterious address.

A Special Christmas with Mr. Rogers
The children's television personality and his friends—including King Friday and Mr. McFeely—celebrate the season.

Christmas around the World
Seasonal celebrations from several countries are broadcast live via satellite.

Christmas Eve, 1978

The Nutcracker
Mikhail Baryshnikov and Gelsey Kirkland star in Tchaikovsky's classic ballet.

It Happened One Christmas
Cloris Leachman and Wayne Rogers play supporting roles in this remake of Frank Capra's holiday classic, *It's a Wonderful Life*.

Amahl and the Night Visitors
Teresa Stratas stars in a new rendition of Menotti's holiday operetta.

Christmas Eve, 1979

A Christmas Special . . . With Love, Mac Davis
Mac is joined by Dolly Parton, Kenny Rogers, Robert Urich, and the choir of St. Mary's Church in Van Nuys, California.

Christmas Eve on Sesame Street
Big Bird and the rest of the gang get together for a celebration of the season.

Family
The holiday spirit takes a turn for the worse when Kate learns that Doug is keeping something from her.

Christmas Eve, 1980

The House without a Christmas Tree
A young girl's desire for a Christmas tree meets with opposition from her no-nonsense father.

A Fat Albert Christmas
The Cosby kids help a family in distress.

Real People
The program profiles "the nation's official Santa Claus." Also: a woman who dresses up as a Christmas tree; and the story of Hanukkah as told by hand puppets.

Christmas Eve, 1981

High Hopes: The Capra Years
Lucille Ball, Carl Reiner, and Burt Reynolds review the career of the man who directed *It's a Wonderful Life* and other classic films.

20/20
Hugh Downs offers a profile on the Salvation Army.

The Man in the Santa Claus Suit
Fred Astaire stars in this film about a mysterious man who changes the lives of three people.

Christmas Eve, 1982

Pinocchio's Christmas
This animated holiday special is based on the classic tale.

The Nativity
Princess Grace of Monaco hosts this recorded musical-drama production set in St. Patrick's Cathedral.

The Muppet Movie
Kermit and Miss Piggy star in a special holiday broadcast of the popular film.

Christmas Eve, 1983

Diff'rent Strokes
Arnold invites a street-corner Santa home to share the holiday.

Christmas with Luciano Pavarotti
The world-famous tenor sings Christmas classics.

The Love Boat
On Christmas Eve, Mickey Rooney makes an otherworldly visit to the ship's passengers.

Christmas Eve, 1984

Sleeping Beauty
Christopher Reeve and Bernadette Peters star in a made-for-cable adaptation.

Cagney and Lacey
Chris, Mary Beth, and company search for a quick exit from work on Christmas Eve.

Scarecrow and Mrs. King
Amanda and Lee find themselves spending the night before Christmas with Soviet agents.

Christmas Eve, 1985

Sing-It-Yourself Messiah
Three thousand San Franciscans join the Conservatory of Music Orchestra at Louise Davies Symphony Hall.

The Black Stallion
Mickey Rooney stars in the network broadcast premiere of this popular family film.

Joyeux Noël: A Cajun Christmas
A celebration of the holiday season, New Orleans style.

Christmas Eve, 1986

The Night They Saved Christmas
Art Carney and Jaclyn Smith strive to keep the North Pole from being blown sky-high.

St. Elsewhere
A rented Santa suffers a coronary while entertaining at the hospital.

Robert Shaw's Christmas Special
Shaw offers two hours of song and celebration.

Christmas Eve, 1987

Bugs Bunny's Looney Christmas Tales
The Warner Bros. gang blows off some holiday steam.

The Magic Flute
David Hockney presents a new rendition of Mozart's classic.

Oprah!
Oprah reviews the year's holiday entertainment offerings.

Christmas Eve, 1988

A Claymation Christmas Celebration
The California Raisins perform in a series of skits ranging from Dickensian London to the Cathedral of Notre Dame in Paris.

Christmas Comes to Willow Creek
Citizens of a poverty-stricken Alaska town learn the true meaning of the season.

The Garfield Christmas Special
The world's most popular cat stars in a half-hour animated special.

Christmas Eve, 1989

A Christmas Carol
George C. Scott delivers the definitive Scrooge of our time in this rebroadcast of the popular special.

A Muppet Family Christmas
Kermit, Miss Piggy, Big Bird, and the rest of the gang celebrate the holiday.

Bill Cosby Salutes Alvin Ailey
Roberta Flack, Anthony Quinn, and others join Bill in a salute to the world-famous choreographer.

Christmas Eve, 1990

A Very Retail Christmas
Ed O'Neill stars as a nasty toymaker.

The New Visions Christmas Special
VH-1, the music video channel, welcomes Dr. John for an evening of holiday song.

A Child's Christmas in Wales
The Disney Channel presents a new version of Dylan Thomas's classic.

Christmas Eve, 1991

The Little Match Girl
F. Murray Abraham narrates this animated adaptation of the Hans Christian Andersen tale, now set in New York City in 1999.

The Tailor of Gloucester
A musical adaptation of Beatrix Potter's story about a mouse who helps a tailor on Christmas Eve.

Die Fledermaus
The Royal Opera presents this production of the Strauss opera about a maid who masquerades as a countess at a ball. Starring Marilyn Horne, Joan Sutherland, and Luciano Pavarotti.

Christmas Eve, 1992

The Night Before Christmas
Joel Grey narrates a half-hour animated musical version of Clement Moore's poem.

Christmas in Vienna
An hour-long concert of seasonal favorites by José Carreras, Diana Ross, and Placido Domingo.

It's a Wonderful Life
The much-beloved classic is still gracing the Christmas season.

Christmas Eve, 1993

Disney's Christmas Fantasy on Ice
Mickey, Minnie, Donald, Pluto, and the rest of the gang prove that—no matter what shape or size feet come in—there are skates for them all, as well as exciting routines choreographed to everybody's favorite holiday music.

Scrooge
Albert Finney and Alec Guinness give three-star performances in this movie about Dickens's beloved miser.

The Christmas Star
Edward Asner and René Auberjonois star in this film about a con man who escapes from prison in a Santa Claus suit and meets two children who believe in him.

Christmas Eve, 1994

National Football League Playoffs
The New England Patriots played the Chicago Bears in Chicago in the final game of the regular season, while the Kansas City Chiefs fought the Los Angeles Raiders in Los Angeles in their final game. (The Patriots won 13-3, and the Chiefs won 19-9.)

Christmas Carol
Alastair Sim stars in this highly regarded, often-replayed, black-and-white take on the Dickens classic.

Hallelujah
Dennis Haysbert and James Earl Jones star in this drama about members of a Washington, D.C., church who want their new minister to work miracles three days before Christmas.

Christmas Eve, 1995

Cincinnati Pops Orchestra
A gala Christmas Eve concert led by conductor Erich Kunzel, and featuring special guest Mel Tormé.

Seasons Greetings from the Honeymooners
Ralph is a street-corner Santa; Joe the Bartender, Reginald Van Gleason III, and the Poor Soul visit; the Kramdens meet Tommy and Jimmy Dorsey.

The Honeymooner's First Christmas
Ralph (Jackie Gleason) and Alice (Pert Kelton) share their first Christmas; other Gleason characters are featured in sketches.

Christmas Eve, 1996

Angel of Pennsylvania Avenue
This Hallmark TV movie starring Robert Urich, based on a true story, focused on three children who ask U.S. President Hoover to help free their innocent Dad from jail.

Unlikely Angel
Dolly Parton stars as a singer who's sent back to Earth in order to earn a second chance at Heaven by doing good deeds.

Mrs. Santa Claus
The big red guy takes a back seat in this TV movie about Mrs. Santa Claus and her adventures with the sleigh.

Christmas Eve, 1997

Holiday in Your Heart
Based on LeAnn Rimes's autobiographical novel, this Lifetime movie also stars the country singer, as she chooses between her dreams of the Grand Ole Opry and her grandmother.

Frosty the Snowman
Jimmy Durante narrated this perennial favorite about the chilly guy and his black top hat, first released in 1969.

Christmas in My Hometown
A 1996 TV movie from Lifetime, with Melissa Gilbert and Tim Matheson, features an executive who's supposed to cut jobs at a tractor factory.

Christmas Eve, 1998

The Christmas Wish
Neil Patrick Harris is a grandson who, with grandmother Debbie Reynolds, deciphers a Christmas family mystery.

Santa Claus is Comin' to Town
Another seasonal chestnut, this animated family musical is narrated by Fred Astaire, and was released in 1970.

I'll Be Home for Christmas
Jonathan Taylor Thomas is Jake Wilkinson, a college student who makes a few discoveries about Christmas as he tries to get home for the holiday.

Christmas Eve, 1999

A Charlie Brown Christmas
The 1965 animated feature has given us the image of a limp, sparsely needled Christmas tree that nevertheless warms everyone's hearts.

One Special Night
Julie Andrews and James Garner are trapped overnight by a blizzard in a mountain cabin.

A Song for the Season
It's Bethlehem, Kentucky, in this movie starring Gerald McRaney as a school administrator who must fire music-teacher Naomi Judd.

Christmas Eve, 2000

Friends
Ross wants to teach his son, Ben, about Hanukkah, but accepts that Ben still needs Santa. Too late to find a Santa suit, Ross ends up in a "holiday" armadillo costume.

How the Grinch Stole Christmas
Nevermind the Jim Carrey movie—the original animated version launched in 1966, and is still a heartfelt Whoville treasure.

Trading Spaces Christmas Marathon
TLC airs back-to-back episodes of the home-decorating show in which two sets of friends decorate a room in each other's homes—as a surprise!

Christmas Eve, 2001

The Simpsons
Corporate sponsors help to rebuild the church after Homer and Bart burn it down, but their advertising inside the church prompts a crisis of faith for Lisa.

Rudolph's Shiny New Year
Rudolph gets another chance to shine in this cartoon adventure, released in 1976, in which he has to find Happy, the baby New Year.

Mickey's Twice Upon a Christmas
Disney released this movie straight to video in 1999, with Donald Duck, Goofy, and Mickey and Minnie all starring in their own stories.

Christmas Eve, 2002

The West Wing
The White House staffers head into the Christmas season by promoting peace in the Middle East and supporting a funding initiative to combat infant mortality.

Silent Night
Based on a true story, this Hallmark movie, set on Christmas Eve in 1944, stars Linda Hamilton as a German mother who convinces six warring American and German soldiers to declare a truce.

The Man Who Saved Christmas
The true story of toy manufacturer A. C. Gilbert, played by Jason Alexander, who convinces the U.S. government to resume toy production for Christmas during World War I.

Christmas Eve, 2003

Jack Frost
Michael Keaton comes back to life as a snowman in this family film from 1998.

Stealing Christmas
Will Tony Danza—as a bank robber—hit the local bank at Christmas, or is love and the holiday spirit enough to turn him away from crime?

Recess Christmas: Miracle on Third Street
Disney full-length animated movie about what happens when Principal Prickly gets his car stuck in a snowdrift.

Christmas Eve, 2004

Miracle on 34th Street
Released in 1947, there are few more heartwarming stories than this one about believing in Santa and in hope.

How I Met Your Mother
The sitcom gang head out in style (that is, a rented limo) to find the perfect New Year's Eve party.

Angel in the Family
A Hallmark movie in which a family experiences a holiday miracle when a wife and mother returns to them as an angel.

Christmas Eve, 2005

The White House Christmas 2005
HGTV peeks inside the White House to see how it's decorated for the holidays.

The Berenstein Bears' Christmas Tree
The furry family first headed into the woods to find a Christmas tree in 1979, but the TV cartoon is just as cute now as it was then.

ER
Doctors Pratt and Weaver are hoping for a miracle when they operate on a young girl who's suffering from gunshot wounds on Christmas Eve.

Christmas Eve, 2006

The Happy Elf
Harry Connick Jr. has his work cut out for him to bring holiday happiness to Bluesville.

The Polar Express
The 2004 movie shines even on the smaller screen, with Tom Hanks as a train conductor en route to Santa and the North Pole.

Rudolph the Red-Nosed Reindeer
Burl Ives is the distinctive voice behind the animated gem from 1964 about a reindeer who saves the day for Santa.

The Everything Silver Screen Christmas Trivia Quiz

How much do you know about holiday-season viewing? Here's the ultimate trivia quiz about the Christmas songs, films, television programs, and movies you're likely to come across. Grab a sheet of paper and jot down your answers—or turn it into a Christmas-party trivia game!

1. What role does Cary Grant play in 1947's *The Bishop's Wife?*
   (a) A hard-boiled newsroom editor
   (b) A befuddled collector of dinosaur bones
   (c) A dashing, sophisticated man about town who is being pursued by a sinister international espionage ring
   (d) A debonair angel

2. What is it that the little girl wants for Christmas in the 1991 film *All I Want for Christmas?*
   (a) Her two front teeth
   (b) A life-size poster of Keanu Reeves
   (c) For her divorced parents to get back together
   (d) An end to the blood feud that has set her town against itself for seven years

3. In what year was the Gian-Carlo Menotti operetta *Amahl and the Night Visitors*, in which a young boy encounters the Three Wise Men on the eve of Christ's birth, first broadcast on network television?
   (a) 1950
   (b) 1951
   (c) 1955
   (d) 1968

4. In the movie *A Christmas Story*, why is the boy's mother afraid to let him have a BB gun?
   (a) She's afraid he'll forget all about his other Christmas toys.
   (b) She's afraid he'll shoot his eye out.
   (c) She's afraid he'll run away from home, secure in his newfound power.
   (d) She's afraid he'll have an accident while cleaning the gun.

5. How did *Amahl and the Night Visitors* come to be written?
   (a) It was composed by a medieval monk who left the score behind a stone wall in a monastery, where it would rest undisturbed for two-and-a-half centuries.
   (b) It was written at the request of His Royal Highness, King Edward II.
   (c) It was commissioned for a special Christmas television broadcast.
   (d) It was composed for the London stage in the early 1930s.

6. Who plays Bob Cratchit in 1992's *The Muppet Christmas Carol*?
   (a) Michael Caine
   (b) John Denver
   (c) Bob Denver
   (d) Kermit the Frog

7. Charles Dickens himself makes an appearance in *The Muppet Christmas Carol*. Who plays him?
   (a) Hunter S. Thompson
   (b) Michael J. Fox
   (c) George C. Scott
   (d) The Great Gonzo

8. In the 1949 classic *Holiday Affair,* which two actors played suitors to Janet Leigh?
   (a) Robert Mitchum and Wendell Corey
   (b) Dean Martin and Jerry Lewis
   (c) Bud Abbott and Lou Costello
   (d) Bob Hope and Bing Crosby

9. Why does Ernest want to find a replacement for Santa in 1988's *Ernest Saves Christmas*?
   (a) Ernest has it on good authority that Santa's best days are behind him, although the old man refuses to face it.
   (b) Santa has decided that it's time to retire.
   (c) The reindeer won't work on Christmas Eve anymore because Santa refuses to pay them time and a half.
   (d) Santa is missing.

10. Who plays the handyman in 1984's *Christmas Lilies of the Field*?
    (a) Billy Dee Williams
    (b) Sidney Poitier
    (c) Clarence Williams III
    (d) Carroll O'Connor

11. For which of the following films did Irving Berlin compose the song "White Christmas"?
    (a) *White Christmas*
    (b) *Holiday Inn*
    (c) *It's a Wonderful Life*
    (d) *Last Tango in Paris*

12. What is the request made to heaven by a recently dead police officer (played by Mickey Rooney) in 1984's *It Came Upon a Midnight Clear*?
    (a) That he be allowed to put on one last show in the barn
    (b) That peace on earth and goodwill among men by made manifest
    (c) That Santa be allowed to make his annual trip despite the evil designs of the Anti-Christmas League
    (d) That he be allowed to spend one final Christmas with his grandson

13. Who played the hapless slogan composer in 1940's *Christmas in July*?
    (a) Ronald Reagan
    (b) Jimmy Stewart
    (c) Preston Sturges
    (d) Dick Powell

14. Of the following, which was a slogan that was actually used in *Christmas in July*?
    (a) "If you can't sleep, it's not the coffee, it must be the bunk."
    (b) "Make it a special Christmas. Make it a regular Christmas. Chew Simu-lax tablets."
    (c) "Coffee the way it was meant to be."
    (d) "Good to the last drop."

15. In what year was *A Charlie Brown Christmas* first broadcast?
    (a) 1963
    (b) 1964

(c) 1965

(d) 1966

16. In the 1954 movie *White Christmas*, why was the old New England inn in such desperate financial straits?
    (a) The previous owner had been subject to a lawsuit, but had concealed this fact from prospective buyers.
    (b) The town suffered a major blow when a local shoe factory closed.
    (c) The inn was a ski resort, and there hadn't been any snow for a year.
    (d) The tourist guides had their doubts about the kitchen help.

17. Which of the following Christmas personages did not appear in an eponymous animated Christmas special?
    (a) Linus van Pelt
    (b) Rudolph the Red-Nosed Reindeer
    (c) Frosty the Snowman
    (d) The Little Match Girl

18. What's the name of the character Bing Crosby plays in *Holiday Inn*?
    (a) Winston Smith
    (b) Jim Hardy
    (c) Charles Foster Kane
    (d) Mike Cleary

19. Why was Macaulay Culkin exiled to his room in 1990's *Home Alone*?
    (a) He set an elaborate trap in his smug older-brother's room.
    (b) He was discovered attempting to tape his weird uncle while the uncle was taking a shower.
    (c) He had been watching too many old movies on video.
    (d) He was being punished for a disastrous kitchen spill.

20. Name the two bad guys in the *Home Alone* movies who eventually became famous as the "Wet Bandits."
    (a) Joe and Ratso
    (b) Harry and Marv
    (c) Harry and Tonto
    (d) Melvin and Howard

21. In the first *Home Alone* movie, where was the family headed for Christmas?
    (a) Paris
    (b) Barcelona
    (c) Florida
    (d) San Juan

22. How is Joe Pesci disguised as he scopes out the neighborhood in the early scenes of the first *Home Alone* movie?
    (a) As a mobster
    (b) As a policeman
    (c) As a mailman
    (d) As an exterminator

23. In the first *Home Alone* movie, why did Macaulay Culkin butt his head into his older brother's stomach?
    (a) The brother wouldn't let him have a turn with the Nintendo game.
    (b) The brother took the last of the cheese pizza.
    (c) The brother was threatening to squeal about a lousy grade on a spelling test.
    (d) The brother was choking on something.

24. What is the name of Macaulay Culkin's character in the *Home Alone* movies?
    (a) Kevin McAllister
    (b) Kevin McReynolds
    (c) Kevin MacArthur
    (d) Kevin McCall

25. What is the name of the scary old guy in the first *Home Alone* movie?
    (a) Cratchit
    (b) Bob
    (c) Marley
    (d) Marlon

26. Who does Macaulay Culkin go to in order to plead for the return of his family in the first *Home Alone* movie?
    (a) The pigeon lady
    (b) Santa Claus

(c) A hotel employee

(d) A policeman

27. In *Home Alone II*, where was the family headed for Christmas?

   (a) Paris

   (b) Barcelona

   (c) Florida

   (d) San Juan

28. Which of the following occurs in *Home Alone II*?

   (a) Joe Pesci's hair is set on fire.

   (b) A rope Joe Pesci is climbing is doused with kerosene and set on fire.

   (c) Joe Pesci is struck in the head by a huge lead pipe.

   (d) All of the above.

29. What is the first image, after the opening credits, in Frank Capra's 1946 classic *It's a Wonderful Life?*

   (a) A sky full of stars, three of which blink as a number of angels speak

   (b) George Bailey sledding down a hill on a snow shovel

   (c) George's younger brother, Harry Bailey, sledding down a hill on a snow shovel

   (d) A sign reading "You Are Now in Bedford Falls"

30. What is the name of the angel who is assigned the task of saving George Bailey's life in *It's a Wonderful Life?*

   (a) Lumen Phosphor

   (b) Fluor Candle

   (c) Clarence Oddbody

   (d) Tom Sawyer

31. Which two characters have this exchange in *It's a Wonderful Life?*

   "A lot of these people are out of work!"

   "Well, then, foreclose."

   "I can't do that. These families have children."

   "They're not my children."

   "They're somebody's children . . ."

   "Are you running a business or a charity ward?"

   (a) George Bailey and Henry Potter

(b) George Bailey and Uncle Billy

(c) Peter Bailey and Henry Potter

(d) George Bailey and Mr. Gower

32. Had George Bailey, the main character in *It's a Wonderful Life,* never been born, what would Bedford Falls have been called?

(a) Morgantown

(b) Pottersville

(c) Gowerville

(d) Robinwood

33. In *It's a Wonderful Life*, why was young George Bailey hit by his boss?

(a) He was late for work.

(b) He'd been neglecting his duties, paying too much attention to the girls at the soda counter.

(c) He hadn't delivered a prescription as he'd been specifically ordered to do.

(d) He kept daydreaming about traveling to foreign lands.

34. What are the names of the policeman and the taxi driver in *It's a Wonderful Life*?

(a) Bert and Ernie

(b) Tom and Jerry

(c) Mike and Terry

(d) Billy and Rick

35. Which of the following A-level Hollywood scriptwriters toiled on early drafts of *It's a Wonderful Life*, only to have his work rejected?

(a) Dalton Trumbo

(b) Marc Connelley

(c) Clifford Odets

(d) All of the above

36. In *It's a Wonderful Life,* what is the nickname of the little girl whose flower-petals wind up in George Bailey's pocket on the night he considers killing himself?

(a) Daisy

(b) Zuzu

(c) Pitter-Pat

(d) Bunkadoodle

37. What, according to a child in the Bailey family, does it mean when you hear bells ringing?

(a) You've been knocked out.

(b) You've just won the final round of *Jeopardy*.

(c) You have tinnitus.

(d) An angel has just gotten his wings.

38. Who played the lead role in *It Happened One Christmas*, the 1977 television remake of *It's a Wonderful Life*?

(a) Henry Winkler

(b) Marlo Thomas

(c) Jimmy Stewart

(d) John Denver

39. What actor who would later portray the captain on the pilot episode of *Star Trek*, also played Jesus in the controversial 1961 film *King of Kings*, now often aired during the holiday season?

(a) Jeffrey Hunter

(b) William Shatner

(c) Patrick Stewart

(d) DeForest Kelley

40. In December 1968, James Mason portrayed Franz Gruber in a network television special. Who was Franz Gruber?

(a) He was a poor German immigrant who brought the tradition of the decorated Christmas tree to the United States.

(b) He was an Austrian immigrant to the United States who wrote dozens of classic Christmas carols.

(c) He was a Swiss war hero who spirited hundreds of Jewish children to safety on Christmas Eve, 1943.

(d) He was an Austrian organist.

41. How did Edmund Gwenn (in the role of Kris Kringle in *Miracle on 34th Street*) come to the notice of the management at Macy's?

(a) He answered an advertisement for a department-store Santa.

(b) He saw that the Santa in the store's holiday float was so drunk that he couldn't stand up, and volunteered to replace him.

(c) He started handing out presents to children in the store.

(d) He showed up at the personnel office dressed in a Santa Claus costume.

42. Name the child star whose career was launched by her appearance in *Miracle on 34th Street*.
    (a) Shirley Temple
    (b) Elizabeth Taylor
    (c) Judy Garland
    (d) Natalie Wood

43. When was *Miracle on 34th Street* first released in movie theaters?
    (a) The late autumn of 1947
    (b) The winter of 1948
    (c) The late autumn of 1948
    (d) The summer of 1947

44. In *Miracle on 34th Street*, whom did Edmund Gwenn list as next of kin on his Macy's employment application form?
    (a) His invaluable colleague, Anna Botelho
    (b) Clarence Oddbody
    (c) The children of the world
    (d) Reindeer

45. In *Miracle on 34th Street*, what precipitated Edmund Gwenn's being committed to Bellevue?
    (a) He declared that he was not Santa after all, but rather the Tooth Fairy.
    (b) He struck a psychiatrist on the head with a cane.
    (c) He wandered the streets of New York without apparent purpose.
    (d) He failed a polygraph test administered by the New York City Police Department.

46. Name four actors who have portrayed Ebenezer Scrooge in the movies or on television.

47. Who plays Marley's ghost in *Scrooge*, the 1970 adaptation of *A Christmas Carol*?
    (a) John Gielgud
    (b) Alec Guinness
    (c) Jason Robards
    (d) Martin Sheen

48. When does the opening sequence of the 1959 classic *Ben-Hur* take place?
    (a) A.D. 33
    (b) A.D. 30
    (c) A.D. 112
    (d) A.D. 1

49. Red Skelton and Vincent Price teamed up in a classic restaurant sketch in the hour-long Christmas special *Red Skelton's Christmas Diner*. What were the names of the characters they played?
    (a) Max and Dan
    (b) Freddy the Freeloader and Professor Humperdue
    (c) Dracula and Dr. Frankenstein
    (d) Bud and Lou

50. Who are Santa's incompetent assistants in the 1934 film *Babes in Toyland*?
    (a) Charlie Chaplin and Buster Keaton
    (b) W. C. Fields and Mae West
    (c) Groucho, Chico, and Harpo Marx
    (d) Stan Laurel and Oliver Hardy

51. In the 1945 film *Christmas in Connecticut*, how does Barbara Stanwyck, as part of a promotional gimmick, convince the world that she's an ideal housewife?
    (a) She rents a house, hires a secret chef, and talks Reginald Gardiner into pretending to be her husband.
    (b) She takes out an ad in the *New York Times* that is supposed to have been written by her husband.
    (c) She hires her sister-in-law to impersonate her.
    (d) She has her picture taken with the children of her neighbor, Shirley Booth.

52. Who directed the cable-TV remake of *Christmas in Connecticut*?
    (a) Richard Lester
    (b) Bernardo Bertolucci
    (c) Jonathan Demme
    (d) Arnold Schwarzenegger

53. In 1946, David Lean directed a memorable version of *Great Expectations* that has become a holiday broadcast staple. What is the name of the film's orphan hero?
    (a) Pip Pirrip
    (b) David Copperfield
    (c) Nicholas Nickleby
    (d) Oliver Twist

54. Finish this sentence from the animated classic *The Grinch Who Stole Christmas*. "Maybe Christmas," he thought, "doesn't come from a store. Maybe Christmas, perhaps . . ."
    (a) ". . . means cruising in a convertible with four on the floor."
    (b) ". . . is a mail-order package from Land's End at your door."
    (c) ". . . is a new pair of socks in a shade you abhor."
    (d) ". . . means a little bit more."

55. From what town did the Grinch attempt to steal Christmas?
    (a) Bedford Falls
    (b) Whoville
    (c) Schenectady
    (d) Smallville

56. Whom did the Grinch encounter during his trip?
    (a) Cindy Lou Who
    (b) Horton the Elephant
    (c) The Cat in the Hat
    (d) The Lorax

57. In the 1982 animated feature *The Snowman*, who is the main attraction at the party to which the Snowman brings his young friend?
    (a) An elf
    (b) The Snow Queen

(c) A baby in swaddling clothes

(d) Santa Claus

58. How do the characters played by Jason Robards and Julie Harris meet in the 1988 HBO special *The Christmas Wife*?

(a) By bumping into one another on a street corner

(b) By being seated in adjoining seats to watch a performance of *The Nutcracker*

(c) Through a lonely hearts agency

(d) Via office e-mail

59. What member of the cast of M*A*S*H also appears in Fred Astaire's classic holiday television movie, *The Man in the Santa Claus Suit*?

(a) Gary Burghoff

(b) Alan Alda

(c) Robert Duvall

(d) Bud Cort

60. In the 1989 *Married . . . with Children* sendup of *It's a Wonderful Life* called *It's a Bundyful Life,* who played Al Bundy's guardian angel?

(a) Howard Stern

(b) Bobcat Goldthwait

(c) Sam Kinison

(d) Vincent Price

61. On which classic Christmas story is 1987's *A Miracle Down Under* loosely based?

(a) The Gift of the Magi

(b) The Little Drummer Boy

(c) A Christmas Carol

(d) A Christmas Memory

62. The 1990 syndicated movie *The Kid Who Loved Christmas* tells the story of a jazz musician (Michael Warren) who, after becoming a widower, fights to retain custody of his foster child. Which entertainment legend made his final film appearance in this movie?

(a) Michael Landon

(b) Sammy Davis Jr.

(c) Cary Grant

(d) James Cagney

63. In what year was *Mr. Magoo's Christmas Carol* first broadcast?
    (a) 1962
    (b) 1963
    (c) 1964
    (d) 1965

64. Whose voice narrated the animated special *Frosty the Snowman*?
    (a) Boris Karloff
    (b) Gene Autry
    (c) Fred Astaire
    (d) Jimmy Durante

65. Name the actress who played a mannequin who comes to life in the 1990 made-for-TV Christmas movie *A Mom for Christmas*. No multiple-choice here, but we will give you a big, big hint: She starred in the most successful movie musical of all time.

66. Name the members of the group that scored a hit that featured the chorus "Christmas, don't be late" in the early 1960s.
    (a) John, Paul, George, and Ringo
    (b) Mick, Keith, Charlie, Bill, and Ron
    (c) Pete, Roger, John, and Keith
    (d) Simon, Theodore, and Alvin

67. Which unlikely duet crooned "The Little Drummer Boy" for a holiday television special?
    (a) Janet Jackson and Frank Sinatra
    (b) David Bowie and Bing Crosby
    (c) Paul McCartney and Elvis Costello
    (d) Pat Boone and Little Richard

68. Which group recorded the novelty songs "Plenty of Jam Jars," "Everywhere It's Christmas," and "Christmas Time (Is Here Again)" for special Christmas disks meant for limited distribution to the official members of their fan club?
    (a) Spike Jones and His City Slickers
    (b) The Beatles

(c) The Partridge Family

(d) The Cowsills

69. Name the lead vocalist on the '80s Christmas hit "2000 Miles."

(a) Deborah Harry

(b) Pat Benatar

(c) Joan Jett

(d) Chrissie Hynde

70. Who recorded the only antiwar holiday song to achieve chart status in the U.S. during the Vietnam War? What was the song?

71. Name the rock star who organized the benefit recording "Do They Know It's Christmas," and won praise for his work on behalf of famine victims.

(a) Bob Geldof

(b) Elton John

(c) Mark Knopfler

(d) Sting

72. This song, composed for a children's Christmas program in the 1940s, sold over a million copies in seven weeks when it was released nationally, thereby becoming one of the fastest-selling records in history. Name the song.

(a) "Frosty, the Snowman"

(b) "Winter Wonderland"

(c) "All I Want for Christmas Is My Two Front Teeth"

(d) "Silver Bells"

73. Who recorded the original version of "I Saw Mommy Kissing Santa Claus"?

(a) Jimmy Boyd

(b) Herman Hasswell

(c) Pinky Lee

(d) Michael Jackson

74. How old was this artist when he recorded "I Saw Mommy Kissing Santa Claus"?

(a) 11

(b) 12

(c) 9

(d) 44

75. In what year was Bing Crosby's recording of Irving Berlin's "White Christmas" released?

(a) 1942

(b) 1943

(c) 1944

(d) 1945

76. Who recorded the immortal holiday classic "Grandma Got Run Over by a Reindeer"?

(a) Weird Al Yankovic

(b) Barnes & Barnes

(c) Elmo and Patsy

(d) The Nurk Twins

77. One of the following recordings is fictitious. Which is it?

(a) "Santa Bring My Baby Back to Me," by Elvis Presley

(b) "Santa Claus Is Coming to Town," by Bruce Springsteen

(c) "Away in a Manger," by the Brady Bunch

(d) "Santa's Got a Brand New Bag," by James Brown

(e) "Winter Wonderland Experience," by Jimi Hendrix

78. Who was the artist who recorded a chorus of barking dogs singing "Jingle Bells"?

(a) Don Charles

(b) Dr. Demento

(c) David Gilmour

(d) Philip Glass

79. Who recorded "Santa Claus and His Old Lady"?

(a) John Cougar Mellencamp

(b) John Mellencamp

(c) John Cougar

(d) Cheech and Chong

80. Who wrote the song "Rudolph the Red-Nosed Reindeer"?
    (a) Gene Autry
    (b) Johnny Marks
    (c) Kurt Weill
    (d) Harry Warren

81. When was Rudolph's song first released commercially?
    (a) 1947
    (b) 1948
    (c) 1949
    (d) 1950

82. Who wrote the book about Rudolph that is said to have inspired the song?
    (a) E. B. White
    (b) Theodore Geisel
    (c) Robert L. May
    (d) Watty Piper

83. Which figure comes closest to the actual number of "Rudolph the Red-Nosed Reindeer" recordings sold, by all artists recording it, since the song was first released?
    (a) 20 million
    (b) 50 million
    (c) 80 million
    (d) 100 million

84. In the animated special *Rudolph the Red-Nosed Reindeer,* who utters the immortal line "His beak blinks like a blinkin' beacon!"?
    (a) Santa
    (b) Prancer
    (c) Comet
    (d) Donner

85. What is the name of Rudolph's dentist friend?
    (a) Marvin
    (b) Newton
    (c) Irving
    (d) Herbie

86. What is the name of Rudolph's explorer friend?
    (a) Barry Lyndon
    (b) Yukon Cornelius
    (c) Yukon Jack
    (d) Jumping Jack Flash

87. What do Bumbles do?
    (a) Bounce
    (b) Make honey
    (c) Rumble
    (d) The Froog

88. This made-for-TV movie was not only the highest-rated Christmas special of
    the 1988 season—it was the highest-rated TV movie of the year for the net-
    work that broadcast it. What was it?
    (a) *The Homecoming at Walton's Mountain*
    (b) *Adventure at Space Mountain: A Christmas Saga*
    (c) *Michael Landon Presents a Little House Christmas*
    (d) *A Very Brady Christmas*

89. Who plays Mary Steenburgen's guardian angel in 1985's *One Magic Christmas*?
    (a) Dennis Hopper
    (b) Harry Dean Stanton
    (c) Burgess Meredith
    (d) Walter Matthau

90. In 1985's *Santa Claus: The Movie,* what did the evil toymaker B.Z. attempt to
    foist upon the world's children?
    (a) A lollipop that would supposedly allow them to fly, but that would be
        likely to explode when used
    (b) The Everlasting Gobstopper
    (c) Poisoned candy canes
    (d) Fruitcake

91. What is the name of Chevy Chase's character in *National Lampoon's Christ-
    mas Vacation*?
    (a) Frank Appleton
    (b) Clark Griswold

(c) Brad Majors

(d) Ward Cleaver

92. Who plays the Ghost of Christmas Present in 1988's *Scrooged*?
   (a) Jack Nicholson
   (b) David Johansen
   (c) Carol Kane
   (d) Jason Robards

93. How does the Ghost of Christmas Present highlight Bill Murray's lesson in *Scrooged*?
   (a) Gives him a cookie for every correct answer
   (b) Allows him a glimpse at his own gravestone
   (c) Causes the headlines in the *Wall Street Journal* to change to odd messages only the two of them would understand
   (d) Attacks him with a toaster

94. What is Bill Murray's job in *Scrooged*?
   (a) He is a stock-market tycoon.
   (b) He is president of the IBC television network.
   (c) He is chief executive officer of the world's largest toy company.
   (d) He is a writer.

95. In *Scrooged,* how does Bill Murray suggest that mice decked out as reindeer should be outfitted?
   (a) With antlers stapled to their heads
   (b) With tiny candy canes
   (c) With fake sleigh bells that don't ring
   (d) With forty red, white, and blue shoestrings

96. Which of the following animated characters starred in a Christmas holiday special or video?
   (a) Bart Simpson
   (b) The Jetsons
   (c) The Flintstones
   (d) Tom & Jerry
   (e) All of the above

97. How many feature-length, Christmas-related films had been released by Walt Disney Studios before 1985's *One Magic Christmas*?
    (a) Four
    (b) Three
    (c) Two
    (d) Zero

98. Who played Jesus in 1965's *The Greatest Story Ever Told*?
    (a) Patrick McGoohan
    (b) David McCallum
    (c) Robert Reed
    (d) Max Von Sydow

99. Jack Jones and Mel Torme joined Judy Garland on her 1963 network television Christmas special. Name the future Academy-Award winner who also made an appearance on that program.

100. Who starred in the 1982 American Ballet Theatre production of *The Nutcracker,* now broadcast seemingly every holiday season on PBS?
    (a) Mikhail Baryshnikov and Gelsey Kirkland
    (b) Rudolf Nureyev and Margot Fonteyn
    (c) Leslie Collier and Anthony Dowell
    (d) Shari Lewis and Lamb Chop

101. In the episode of *The Brady Bunch* entitled "The Voice of Christmas," why does young Cindy Brady ask Santa to restore her mother's voice?
    (a) So Carol Brady can sing at Christmas church services
    (b) So Carol Brady can audition for a community production of *The Sound of Music*
    (c) So Carol Brady can recite "A Visit from St. Nicholas" to the Brady family as she always does at Christmas time
    (d) So Carol Brady can sing about Wesson Oil

102. In the film *Prancer,* what happens when little Jessica first walks within sight of an above-street display of Santa's reindeer?
    (a) She has a near-death experience.
    (b) She sees the ghost of her mother.

(c) She watches as one of the reindeer falls to the ground and nearly strikes an automobile.

(d) She makes a wish.

103. In *Prancer*, why does Jessica's father want to shoot the real reindeer after he sees it standing in the middle of the road?
    (a) It's wounded and he wants to put it out of its misery.
    (b) It's strikingly similar in appearance to an old girlfriend.
    (c) He's a warped, frustrated old man.
    (d) He's hallucinating.

104. Which Christmas song does Judy Garland sing in *Meet Me in St. Louis*?
    (a) "Have Yourself a Merry Little Christmas"
    (b) "Winter Wonderland"
    (c) "Rudolph the Red-Nosed Reindeer"
    (d) "The Christmas Song"

105. How does a Christmas tree figure into the plot of 1973's *The Poseidon Adventure?*
    (a) Ernest Borgnine uses it to stop an attacking shark.
    (b) Terrified passengers climb it in an attempt to reach the bottom of the capsized ship.
    (c) Leslie Nielsen trips on it, causing a concussion that keeps him from responding effectively to the tidal wave bearing down on the ship.
    (d) Shelley Winters wears a gown that is ripped by it as she passes one of the ornaments.

106. Which characters end up dressing as Santa Claus in the Christmas episode of *I Love Lucy* in which the object is to cheer up a distraught Little Ricky?
    (a) Lucy
    (b) Lucy and Ethel
    (c) Lucy, Ethel, and Ricky
    (d) Lucy, Ethel, Ricky, and Fred

The Everything Quiz Answers and Scoring

1. d

2. c

3. b

4. b

5. c

6. d

7. d

8. a

9. b

10. a (Poitier appeared in 1963's *Lilies of the Field*, which preceded this feature.)

11. b

12. d

13. d

14. a

15. c

16. c

17. a (This was a trick question; "eponymous" means that the special bears the same name as the character. A futuristic animated version of *The Little Match Girl* aired in 1991.)

18. b

19. d

20. b

21. a

22. b

23. b

24. a

25. c

26. b

27. c

28. d

29. d

30. c

31. c (Peter was George's father.)

32. b

33. c

34. a

35. d

36. b

37. d

38. b

39. a (Hunter played Captain James T. Kirk's predecessor.)

40. d (Another trick question. Gruber's only music credit is the immortal "Silent Night.")

41. b

42. d

43. d

44. d

45. b

46. Here are six: Reginald Owen (1938), Alistair Sim (1951), Mr. Magoo (1962), Albert Finney (1970), George C. Scott (1982), and Michael Caine (1992). Okay, okay, Magoo is a bit of a stretch. (By the way, Bill Murray is not a correct answer; his character's name in *Scrooged* is Frank Cross.)

47. b

48. d (*Ben-Hur* opens with an account of the Nativity.)

49. b

50. d

51. a

52. d

53. a

54. d

55. b

56. a

57. d

58. c

59. a

60. c

61. c

62. b

63. a

64. d

65. Olivia Newton-John (The megahit musical was, of course, *Grease*.)

66. d

67. b

68. b

69. d

70. "Happy Xmas (War Is Over)" by John Lennon and the Plastic Ono Band

71. a

72. c

73. a

74. b

75. a

76. c

77. e

78. a

79. d

80. b

81. c

82. c

83. b

84. d (Donner is Rudolph's dad)

85. d

86. b

87. a

88. d

89. b

90. a

91. b

92. c

93. d

94. b

95. a

96. e

97. d

98. d

99. Judy's seventeen-year-old daughter, Liza Minnelli, of course. Liza's siblings, Joey Luft and Lorna Luft, also appeared.

100. a

101. a

102. c

103. a

104. a

105. b

106. d

Scoring

How do you (or your group) rate?

- *20 or fewer correct:* As a general rule, you've been doing something other than watching television at Christmas over the past thirty or forty years. Congratulations on that, but don't pick "Holiday Films" as a *Jeopardy* category.
- *21 to 40 correct:* Okay. You got the easy ones. You've been rocking to "Jingle Bell Rock," but you could probably stand to rent *It's a Wonderful Life* a time or two.
- *41 to 60 correct:* You've definitely got the holiday spirit, but Andy Williams still thinks you can do better.
- *61 to 80 correct:* Nice work. You can probably recite the lyrics to "White Christmas" without batting an eye. Spread the good cheer!
- *81 to 100 correct:* Nat King Cole is crooning "The Christmas Song" just for you.
- *101 to 106 correct:* You can probably recite the entire script of *The Grinch Who Stole Christmas* verbatim—from deep sleep. Take a bow.

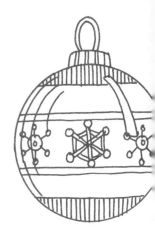

10

A Century of the American Christmas

Although its roots extend back for centuries, the Christmas that North Americans know and love is fundamentally a twentieth-century phenomenon. Take Santa, for example: It wasn't until a nationwide ad campaign for Coca-Cola in the 1920s that he came with a consistent look. In fact, Christmas wasn't an official holiday throughout the United States until 1890—and even at that time, New Year's Day was a strong competitor for the honor of prime gift-giving holiday. The following surveys and excerpts from published accounts of Christmases past offer a glimpse of the holiday's evolution.

Christmas in the 1900s

In the first decade of the 1900s, technology was making its influence known, as the automobile rolled onto the roads in earnest and the Wright brothers made their first flight at Kitty Hawk, North Carolina. Many Americans shopped by catalog from Sears Roebuck and Montgomery Ward, and the toy teddy bear made its first appearance, thanks to a cartoon that showed Theodore Roosevelt sparing the life of a bear.

Your Christmas Budget in the 1900s

Wondering what you might have bought for friends and family at the beginning of the twentieth century? Here are some popular items from the 1900s, with their prices, taken from contemporary newspapers and magazine ads:

- Men's smoking jacket: $5.00
- Women's corset ("All popular sizes"): $1.59
- Sheet-music cabinet: $6.25
- Phonograph: $150.00
- China candlestick: 50 cents
- Boys' worsted sweater: $2.00
- Toy sewing machine: $1.00
- Toy automobile "with rubber tire wheels": $2.50
- Elevated railroad set: $5.00
- Clothbound copy of *Peck's Bad Boy*: 39 cents

Festive Fact

Peck's Bad Boy was Henry Peck, a fictional boy created by author George Peck. Henry wasn't very enthusiastic about rules, and gained huge popularity around the turn of the century for the pranks that he played. The stories, which appeared in newspapers and books, were even made into movies in the 1920s and 1930s.

In the News in the 1900s

Morgan Celebrates the Season

NEW YORK, December 23—Ten clerks employed by J. Pierpont Morgan are reported to have each received from the banker a present of a $5,000 gold certificate. A messenger for Mr. Morgan drew the bills from the subtreasury.

For the benefit of those who are not on intimate terms with $5,000 gold certificates, it may be explained that they are among the most beautiful examples of the printer's art. In color they are a most effective blending of orange, black, and green.

—1901 *Boston Globe* account

An Act of Benevolence

Pay the Boy a Nickel!

To the Editor:

Every person purchasing a paper [on Christmas Eve] should pay the newsboy therefor five cents [instead of the customary two]. The amount will not be missed by the giver and a great good will result.

—Letter appearing in the *Boston Globe*

A Poem Suitable for the Season

The merry halls may jingle in the good, old-fashioned way;
In merriment we mingle, with the music holding sway.
The "Gloria in Excelsis" is sounding everywhere.
But, really, tisn't Christmas, if Mother isn't there.

She hangs a newer halo round the mistletoe on high;
A spirit of bravado drew away the weary sigh—
For sorrow is no mistress, and life lets go its fear
Amid the joys of Christmas, when Mother, dear, is here.

The fire upon the hearthstone lights up with ruddier glow;
The laughter is more mirthsome, bubbling forth in frolic flow;
The Christ Child truly comes to us, in all His heavenly cheer,
If the advent of old Christmas finds Mother, also, here.

—William Hopkins

A Thought for the Holiday Season

On the seamy side there comes at Christmas a feeling that the word is, to those who are not of the elect, most unkind; and it is the experience of police that most of the injudicious, unlimited drinking . . . is not caused so much by the exuberance of people wanting to celebrate Christmas, as by the efforts of those who would forget.

—*Boston Globe* editorial in support of the growing movement toward prohibition of liquor

Christmas Advertising in the 1900s

Dependable Goods, Fair Prices, and Your Goodwill are responsible for the throngs which have filled out stores and the marked enthusiasm displayed during these Xmas holidays. Although the buying has been beyond expectation and our assortments are yet complete, still each day makes a large hole in the stock. In order not to carry over Xmas Goods, from now on goods will be marked at prices that will be simply irresistible. Come and profit during these last two days.

—Gilchrist Department Store advertisement

Christmas in the 1910s

The industrial age and mass production were the hallmarks of this decade, with the one millionth Model T Ford in production and names such as Chevrolet and Dodge making an appearance. Popular toys included Lincoln Logs, Tinker Toys, and the Erector Set. From 1914 to 1918, however, our attention was firmly focused on Europe, where World War I was being fought by soldiers from Canada and other countries around the world, and from 1917–1918, soldiers from the United States as well.

Your Christmas Budget in the 1910s

It's amazing to think that you can still buy a folding umbrella for under $10.00—but the $1,250.00 automobile today might not be such a smart buy.

- Women's leather handbag: $3.50
- Folding umbrella ("indispensable when traveling"): $4.00
- Opera glasses: $5.00
- French plume: $1.95

- Singer "sewmachine": $24.50
- "Self-starting" Everett automobile: $1,250.00
- Girls' wool dress: $2.95

In the News in the 1910s

A Plea

Dear Santa, I've got to go
To bed—it's late, you see—
So listen, please, for you must know
Just what to bring to me.
I want a pair of skates, a knife,
A pony that can trot;
I want a nice big drum and fife
And all the books you've got.
I want a kite with miles of string
And several Christmas trees
But when you come this year, don't bring
Another baby, please.

—Anonymous poem, circa 1915

Better Late Than Never

It occurred to a Pittsfield man yesterday that Christmas was coming. In that merry relation, a thought struck him. Glancing up at a shelf in the office where he is employed, he saw thereon a package [addressed to a friend], which just one year ago his wife had given him to mail . . . He sent the package along . . .

—From the *Berkshire Evening Eagle*, 1911

Christmas Advertising in the 1910s

Churchill's Wonderful Christmas Review, "Cornell's Follies"
For the entertainment of our many guests, and in keeping with the Christmas Spirit of Gladness and Good-will, we present this extraordinary review headed by the "Cornells" and assisted by a chorus of *twenty beautiful girls*. . . . We promise an evening of delightful entertainment, bewildering in the variety of its enjoyment.
Churchill's: More than a restaurant—a Broadway institution.
Broadway at 49th St.

Christmas in the 1920s

The 1920s bring to mind the age of flapper fashion and jazz music, but the years also brought new fashions in art and architecture, from art deco to modernism. Frank Lloyd Wright was active in this decade, and in 1927, Charles Lindbergh made the first solo flight across the Atlantic in the *Spirit of St. Louis*. Hot toys included die-cast metal toys, the Raggedy Ann doll, and, toward the end of the decade, the yo-yo.

Your Christmas Budget in the 1920s

At less than $40.00 (even in 1920s dollars), a Persian rug would have made a good investment in both décor and value.

- Winter overcoat: $18.50
- Fountain pen: $2.50
- Silk hat: $7.50
- Victrola brand phonograph: $99.80
- RCA Radiola ("musical quality unsurpassed"): $115.00
- RCA Radiola with loudspeaker: $150.00
- Persian rug: $38.75
- One-pound box of chocolates: $6.50
- Ladies' silk umbrella: $10.00
- Toy tool chest: $1.55
- "Juvenile model" bicycle: $48.75
- Girls' ice skates: $5.00
- "Beautiful stately jointed doll" with wig, dress, shoes, and stockings: $1.95

In the News in the 1920s

"Peace on Earth" Near Fulfillment

> —*Boston Globe* headline, December 25, 1921, lead story referring to progress in a Washington peace conference of major international powers

Prohibition Makes Its Presence Felt

Shortly after the Volstead Act went into effect, federal authorities issued an announcement, apparently meant for inclusion in Christmas Eve editions of the nation's newspapers, that the use of "fermented wines for sacramental purposes" during religious services would be forbidden. The substitution of a "specially pre-pared fruit juice" was said to be under consideration by major religious leaders.

At an elite Christmas party attended by Channing H. Cox, the governor of Massachusetts, prohibition agent Harold Wilson seized four bottles of White Horse Cellar whiskey. A major scandal ensued, and the bottles disappeared under mysterious circumstances.

Way of Women at Christmas Puzzles a Woman

Why Not Start List Now (December 5) and Do Your Christmas Giving Sensibly, with Regard to Feelings of Others, as well as for Time, Strength, and Money? Leaving Everything until Last Minute Makes Season Harder for Clerks and Spoils Holiday!

—Headline of an article in the December 5, 1926, *Providence Journal*, urging procrastinating wives to show a little more thought during the holiday season. The article is accompanied by an illustration of an unnamed acquaintance of the author's who "used to dread Christmas and spent the whole holiday in bed, utterly spent, and with ice-bags at her head and feet."

A Christmas Card Suggestion of the Era
To a Stout Lady in a Short Skirt
May your silk hose be filled to overflowing
With all the gifts that Santa's shops comprise
And may you have the joy that comes of knowing
It takes so much to fill a hose your size.

—Anonymous poem, circa 1925

Christmas Advertising in the 1920s

With the approach of the world's greatest holiday, the question of Seasonable Clothing and Suitable Gifts for family and friends absorbs the attention of the majority of the people. How to satisfy this very laudable ambition is the question. Let us help you. Go to the JOYCE STORE nearest you . . . You don't need to pay cash for your Xmas clothing! We will gladly charge your purchases and you may pay for them in easy partial payments—next year!

—Joyce Store advertisement

Christmas in the 1930s

The Thirties were a time of great hardship for many people, as the Great Depression took hold of the continent. By the end of the decade, as World War II began in Europe, social programs and work projects such as those tackled by the Civilian Conservation Corps had been launched. Even the toys reflect the times: Board games such as Monopoly, which was introduced in 1935, became popular partially because they were less expensive than many other forms of entertainment.

Two significant Christmas traditions find their roots in the 1930s. At this time, people began buying their Christmas trees from Christmas-tree farms rather than finding them in forests. This decade also saw the widespread practice of leaving out cookies for Santa Claus.

Your Christmas Budget in the 1930s

The child's red wagon in the following list remains a staple of childhood play even today.

- "Satin or metallic" men's pajamas: $10.95
- Pullman men's slippers: $4.00
- Quart bottle of Monopole champagne: $5.00
- Westinghouse radio: $21.00
- Boys' knickers: $1.49
- Child's wagon (red): $3.49
- Doll, layette, and basket: $4.94
- Dollhouse: $5.00

- Toy airplane: 65 cents
- Toy typewriter: $1.95

In the News in the 1930s

The President Rejects the Idea of a Long Weekend

In 1931, back in the days of the six-day work week, President Hoover granted federal workers the day off for December 26, a Saturday, but denied them the day after New Year's Day. In less than a year, weary Depression-era voters would grant Hoover some time off.

Little Orphan Annie on Christmas During the Great Depression

ANNIE (after hearing two society ladies complain elaborately about the hectic holiday shopping season): Well, I haven't but two or three folks to give to, and only a buck or so to spend—I guess in some ways it's a cinch to be poor! Anyway, it's lots simpler . . .

—From the December 24, 1936 syndicated comic strip by Harold Gray

A Bread-Line Christmas

In 1931, roughly 5,000 unemployed men showed up to eat a free Christmas dinner of turkey and mulligan stew at one site in Manhattan. The total number of New York City families receiving charity food baskets or free meals that year is not known, but it was clearly in the tens of thousands. An unspecified number of men took part in a Christmas dinner for "the city's hoboes" at the Hobo College on East Fourth Street. Nationwide, six million people—perhaps 8 percent of the adult population of the country—were looking for work.

Mail Early—Postal Workers Need the Hours

A plea to "mail early" during the Xmas season, in order to aid the local unemployed, was issued last night over station WBZ by Postmaster William E. Hurley, who urged that Xmas cards and packages be sent this week.

"During the Xmas season," said Postmaster Hurley, "the mail increases about 300 percent, and the handling of this enormous quantity of mail taxes the facilities of the Postal Service to the limit. It has been necessary to augment our regular force with a large number who are unskilled in Post Office work, but we cannot give them more than two days unless you give us your Christmas mail at once."

—*Boston Globe*, December 20, 1931

Christmas Spirit

Brooklyn salesman Sam Coplon, a Spanish Civil War veteran who recuperated from his wounds at a hospital in North Creek, New York, was eager to find a way to express his gratitude. For twenty years—most notably at the height of the Great Depression—he delivered toys to the impoverished children of the Adirondacks at Christmastime. In one year alone, Coplon delivered more than 12,000 toys with the help of local clergy and charitable organizations.

Christmas Advertising in the 1930s

Christmas Greetings That Are Spoken Ring True

Spreading over far horizons, Xmas voices will soon be bringing joy into millions of hearts and homes throughout the land.

Somewhere there is someone who would like to hear you say, "Merry Christmas"; someone whose happily surprised answer *"The same to you and many of them"* will brighten the day for you.

Although miles apart, the telephone will quickly bridge the gap, sending and bringing back holiday greetings with all the warmth and sincerity that only voices can give.

—A New York Telephone Company ad from the early 1930s

Christmas in the 1940s

World War II defined the first half of the 1940s, associated with images of Rosie the Riveter as women went to work to replace the men who'd left for the war. Television arrived later in the decade, as did the very first computer and the traditional American diner. Forties-era toys included the Slinky, Tonka trucks, and Silly Putty.

Your Christmas Budget in the 1940s

Representative prices for items popular during the decade are difficult to establish with certainty, because many prices fluctuated wildly during the war. These appeared in newspaper and magazine ads during the '40s.

- Cigarette case: $9.95
- Zippered rayon ladies' robe: $6.98
- Upright vacuum cleaner: $49.90
- Electric iron: $2.49
- Electric coffee maker: $6.98
- Roller skates: $9.95
- Magnetized soldier doll with American flag: $4.00
- Tiddlywinks game: 39 cents

In News in the 1940s

Pearl Harbor Brings a Different Kind of Christmas

While preparations are going on here, in a mild way to be sure, due to wartime conditions, our little British cousins across the seas have not been overlooked. Old Santa, that kindly bewhiskered man, will pay them a visit through the thoughtfulness of the relief agencies here. . . . Of the many thousands (of) toys of various types and descriptions sent across the seas by Bundles for Britain, most of them are soft dolls and animals made from scraps of materials in the sewing looms . . .

—*New York Times*, December 21, 1941

The Power of Christmas Across the Centuries

From the centuries between [the first Christmas] and now, come stories of holy men, of bishops and peasant-saints, and of brave men who preached…Christ to the Vikings of the north or on Iona's isle. As in popular belief, with each returning eve of the Nativity the miracles of the first Christmas happen again, so in these tales the thorn-tree blossoms anew and wonderful roses bloom in the bleak forest.

—From the foreword to *The Christmas Book of Legends and Stories*, a popular 1944 release

Enter Bing Crosby, Singing

There's a lot to be said against a White Christmas. It is awkward, trying to fit an old-fashioned Christmas on a new-fashioned, hard-surfaced world, obliterating its familiar signposts, cunningly disguising its modern dangers, hiding its unpleasantness under a soft veil.

But here it is, the enchanted world you looked out on as a kid, white, mystic, beautiful, through which jovial creature half fat man, half spirit came riding, a transformed world in which anything could happen. All you had to do was believe hard enough that it could.

Listen! Sleigh bells? Do you suppose there is such a spirit, after all?

—*Providence Journal*, December 24, 1947

Christmas Advertising in the 1940s

More than 3 million faces testify!

The Schick Shaver is a gift men really use! *Swell* for service men! Soldiers, sailors, or marines . . . because they can be plugged in at camp or on a boat—and work!

—Ad appearing shortly after the Japanese attack on Pearl Harbor

Christmas in the 1950s

Television became perhaps the greatest influence during the 1950s, bringing programs such as *The Honeymooners* and *Father Knows Best* into living rooms across the nation, first in black and white, and then in color. Rock and roll arrived on the music scene, as did a polio vaccine on the health front. Mr. Potato Head, Frisbees, and Barbie dolls made names for themselves in the toy departments.

Your Christmas Budget in the 1950s

With items such as slide projectors becoming more available, everyone could be treated to pictures of the family vacation!

- Slide projector: $43.95
- Men's topcoat: $18.00
- Quilted rayon and taffeta robe: $8.95
- Pipe and lighter set: $1.94
- Television set with "lifesize seventeen-inch screen": $229.95
- Donald Duck xylophone: $2.65
- Mickey Mouse train set: $1.59
- Musical milk mug: $6.95

In the News in the 1950s

A Message from Independence

"Our hearts are saddened on this Christmas Eve by the suffering and the sacrifice of our brave men and women in Korea. We miss our boys and girls who are out there . . . they are trying to prevent another world war. We pray to the Prince of Peace for their success and safety."

—President Harry Truman in Independence, Missouri, December 24, 1951

Forsaking the White House tradition of sending formal Christmas cards, President and Mrs. Eisenhower commissioned cards that feature drawings of them in caricature, wearing bright red suits with white trimming and wishing the recipient a merry Christmas. Clearly, observers note, this is a First Couple that does not mind letting down its guard now and then.

The Choice

If Western civilization dies in a rain of nuclear explosions, it will be written in a later day that the tragedy of our century was the inability of man to apply to the problems of peace the genius that loosed a most fearful Armageddon. "Peace on earth," the angels sang 2,000 years ago, but peace today is as tremulous as thin fog at dawn along the shore. . . . Today is a day for happiness . . . but we shall end by trading that happiness for horror if we cannot recapture the humility, the simplicity, the understanding, the faith, the affection, and the lack of fear that marked the shepherds who saw His tiny fists wave in the lamplight of a stable at Bethlehem.

—From an editorial in the *Providence Journal*, December 25, 1957

Christmas Advertising in the 1950s

Hectic Xmas Shopping Give You Gas, Indigestion, "Hurry-Worry Stomach"?
You shop too fast, eat on the run, worry. No wonder your stomach gets upset! But you can now get immediate long-lasting relief—with AMITONE! Only AMITONE contains GLYCINE, that automatically regulates excess stomach acids. Minty tablets melt on your tongue. At drugstores.

—An ad from the early 1950s

Christmas in the 1960s

A pivotal decade, the 1960s were marked by the Civil Rights movement, the rise of the hippies, the Bay of Pigs, the Vietnam War, and the race to be the first nation to reach the moon. Postwar baby boomers began to transition from teenagers to adults against a background of toys that included Easy Bake Ovens, the Etch-a-Sketch, and GI Joe.

Your Christmas Budget in the 1960s

Kitchen convenience was offered in style in the 1960s—never mind the refrigerator, check out the lazy Susans and the electric can openers!

- Lazy Susan: $4.76
- Electric can opener: $7.77
- Ladies' stretch slacks: $3.97
- Aluminum Christmas tree and stand: $2.99
- Monaural copy of Ray Conniff's LP *Memories Are Made of This*: $2.40
- Stereophonic copy of Ray Conniff's LP *Memories Are Made of This*: $2.90
- "Your kiddie's Polaroid picture taken with Santa himself": 49 cents
- Viewmaster stereo viewer in "rugged, shock-resistant plastic": $1.75
- Sled: $3.00
- "Poor Pitiful Pearl" doll and "change of clothes that makes her a princess": $8.00

In the News in the 1960s

Trading Stamps to the Rescue

Mrs. Phyllis Stephens, 20, of Scotia, New York, said she faced a gloomy holiday when she learned that neither she nor her husband, Corporal Luther C. Stephens, could afford the $146 round-trip fare from his station at the U.S. Marine Training School at Memphis, Tenn. Then she remembered that she had collected 80 books of trading stamps. The young wife knew the stamps were redeemable for gifts and in desperation sent a telegram to the Triple S Blue Stamps company in Hackensack, New Jersey. The firm decided to play Santa Claus. It told Mrs. Stephens it would supply a plane ticket to bring her Marine home Friday and return him to Memphis Christmas night.

—United Press International report, December 21, 1961

The animated television special *A Charlie Brown Christmas* premiered in December 1965, with Charles Schulz's memorable cartoon-strip characters and the sad little Christmas tree that manages to brighten up the whole season. Reviews and ratings were both excellent, and the show became a staple holiday broadcast in every following year.

A Christmas Greeting with an Interesting Perspective

. . . And God called the dry land Earth; and the gathering together of the waters called He seas; and God saw that it was good. And from the crew of *Apollo 8*, we close with good night, good luck, a merry Christmas, and God bless all of you—all of you on the good Earth.

—Message from *Apollo 8* astronauts, Christmas Eve, 1968

Christmas Advertising in the 1960s

If He Has Everything: Bottled Portable Radio, $35.00

Would you ever guess that there is an eight-transistor radio tucked inside this bottle of "Ballantine's Whisky"? Its quality components give it a fine full sound and selectivity. Runs on penlight batteries!

—From a 1966 ad for a department store

Christmas in the 1970s

Protests against the Vietnam War increased as the decade opened; it would close with the capture of hostages at the U.S. Embassy in Tehran, after seeing the end of the war and the resignation of a president. North American families took to the highways in station wagons, sporting mood rings and playing with Rubik's Cubes, skateboards, and Matchbox cars.

Your Christmas Budget in the 1970s

Ah, the 8-track cassette player! Music technology has come a long way since the 1970s, but the 8-track was an innovation in its own time.

- Stereo set with turntable and 8-track player: $199.95
- AM radio mounted in headphones: $14.95
- Lava lamp: $45.00
- "25-function" calculator: $49.95
- CB radio: $89.95
- Bionic Man action figure: $6.66
- Baby Thataway: $8.88
- Ten-speed bicycle: $99.50
- Evel Knievel stunt cycle: $9.96

In the News in the 1970s
Pining for the PreWatergate Christmas

New York Times columnist Russell Baker, writing in December, 1974—the first Christmas of the Ford administration—recorded his wistful observations of the gray holidays of his immediate Washington past. Baker wrote solemnly that, back then, white Christmases were out; gray ones were much more fashionable, because that was the color that could get you past security. "Several days before Christmas," Baker recalled, "everyone in the Government seemed to leave town, and we would be left alone in the great empty city with only the wiretap police, the undercover CIA agents, and the holdup men. . . ."

Understanding Santa Is Troublesome for Laotians on Their First American Yule

Khamchanh Chantarangsy was preparing about a dozen of his fellow Laotians for their first American Christmas . . . They had never heard of Santa Claus . . . Now that the refugees are in America, he said, "We try to do everything like American . . . ."

Khamchanh interpreted [for his friend Xiong Ton]: "He says it is quite strange, quite interesting but quite impossible for this man to penetrate the roof of his house with such a large sack of toys."

—From the *Providence Journal*, December 24, 1976

Christmas Advertising in the 1970s

Santa, Conserve Your Energy!

No need to shop around . . . just one stop at Azuma—thousands of gift ideas for everyone on your list—their huge selection will "sleigh" you!

—Ad for a New York store during the height of the oil crisis

Christmas in the 1980s

The beginning of the end for the Cold War marked the close of this decade, as the Berlin Wall fell in Germany. Here at home, the drive toward space continued with the first reusable space vehicle, the Space Shuttle, in 1981. Computers arrived in homes and schools, while video games such as Nintendo and Pac Man gained huge followings. Shoppers flocked to stores in search of Cabbage Patch Dolls, while other hot toys included Trivial Pursuit and the Teenage Mutant Ninja Turtles.

Your Christmas Budget in the 1980s

Technology is seen increasingly in homes, exemplified by this list of items.

- Microwave oven: $227.00
- Videocassette recorder (1980): $1,395
- Videocassette recorder (1989): $299
- Garfield telephone: $44.70
- Space Invaders video game cassette: $24.88
- Your favorite Care Bear: $13.99
- Castle Greyskull, from the Masters of the Universe Collection: $23.99
- Lazer tag game kit: $29.99
- Rambo Rocket water launcher: $14.96

In the News in the 1980s

And Then What?

Highlights from columnist Ellen Goodman's tongue-in-cheek 1981 *Boston Globe* column "Ways to Lose Weight During the Holidays" included giving birth, "the only surefire way to drop seven pounds overnight between Christmas and New Year's"; joining a cult that consumes only food of a certain shade; hiring a food stylist to assemble beautiful, but inedible, meals; and getting a divorce.

Christmas, USA

- Bethlehem: 838
- Holly: 542
- Joy: 145
- Holiday: 110
- Christmas: 89
- Noël: 30
- Carol: 17
- Mistletoe: 12
- Santa Claus: 7

—From a 1985 U.S. Geological Survey report of places, including local landmarks, bearing names reminiscent of Christmas themes

A Yuppified Christmas

"Ghost," said Jeremy, "tell me, please, what do I have to do to become president— or at least managing director?"

—From Michael Lewis's 1989 *New York Times* column "A Christmas Bonus," a parody of *A Christmas Carol* in which a Wall Streeter ponders his awful fate in years to come: a door bearing the words "Jeremy Gaunt, Vice President"

The Brady Bunch, Revisited

Debuting on Sunday, December 18, 1988, *A Very Brady Christmas* was CBS's highest-rated TV movie of that year. Following its premiere broadcast, the telepicture elevated CBS's third-place ranking to the number-two spot for the first time that season in the weekly ratings.

Says (producer) Sherwood (Schwartz), "The success of it was a combination of two things. One was the fact that it was Christmas time, which is family time, so it was a perfect opportunity to bring them back. And number two, many people wanted to know what they looked like. There was a great longing to see what happens. It's like with any family reunion."

—From Elizabeth Moran's book *Bradymania*

Christmas Advertising in the 1980s

Hot Shirt for Berzerk Fans

Straight from Atari's latest home video challenge comes this sharp-looking official Berzerk T-shirt. Captures all the fast-blasting action of this all-time favorite. $7.95

—From the Atari Club Christmas Catalog 1982, from *www.gamingsteve.com*

Christmas in the 1990s

The 1990s brought an unsettling decade, as we coped with the first Gulf War and the bombings of the World Trade Center in New York City and the Alfred P. Murrah Federal Building in Oklahoma City. On the economic side, however, the nation was booming, alongside advances in technology that brought the World Wide Web to homes and businesses, connecting people around the world like never before. Popular toys included Beanie Babies and Tickle Me Elmo, and a move from skateboards to Rollerblades.

Your Christmas Budget in the 1990s

- Sony Walkman: $69.99
- Transformer toy figure: $15.00
- Girl's bicycle: $150.00
- Hardcover book: $25.00
- Music CD: $19.99
- Cordless power drill: $95.00
- Polar fleece scarf: $9.99
- DVD Player: $525

In the News in the 1990s

Vatican Text of Pope John Paul II's Message to Children for Christmas 1994

People cannot live without love. They are called to love God and their neighbor, but in order to love properly they must be certain that God loves them.

God loves you, dear children! This is what I want to tell you at the end of the Year of the Family and on the occasion of these Christmas feast days, which in a special way are your feast days.

I hope that they will be joyful and peaceful for you; I hope that during them you will have a more intense experience of the love of your parents, of your brothers and sisters, and of the other members of your family.

This love must then spread to your whole community, even to the whole world, precisely through you, dear children. Love will then be able to reach those who are most in need of it, especially the suffering and the abandoned.

What joy is greater than the joy brought by love? What joy is greater than the joy which you, O Jesus, bring at Christmas to people's hearts, and especially to the hearts of children?

Raise your tiny hand, Divine Child, and bless these young friends of yours, bless the children of all the earth.

—John-Paul P.P. II, December 13, 1994

In 1999, a 100-foot Norway spruce made history at the Rockefeller Center, when it became the tallest tree to grace the Center during the Christmas season, an annual tradition since 1933. The tree came from the yard of a couple from Killingworth, Connecticut.

Christmas Advertising in the 1990s

New online ordering from L.L. Bean lets customers wrap up holiday shopping.

L.L. Bean Inc., the Maine based outdoors catalog company is pleased to offer customers the option of shopping online this holiday season.

Building upon an 84 year tradition of customer commitment, L.L. Bean now offers on-line ordering for customers who prefer the convenience of shopping from their computers. Customers may now order and send L.L. Bean merchandise to everyone on their Christmas list while visiting the company's Web site. . . . For Christmas, customers will find a Product Guide that offers over 300 of L.L. Bean's most popular products for the holidays in all of L.L. Bean's product categories: Clothing, Home and Camp, Sporting Goods, LL Kids and Gift Certificates. The order process is simple and expedient. Each detailed product display contains the illustrative photos and informational copy that customers are accustomed to finding in the L.L. Bean catalogs. Upon selection the customer will immediately know if the item is in-stock, and will receive prompt confirmation of the order via e-mail.

—L.L. Bean

Christmas in the 2000s

Although the decade opened with the hope brought by the turn of the millennium, emotions turned to shock at the events of September 11, 2001 in the United States, with conflict ensuing in countries around the world. As the decade continued, however, further advances in technology, health, and environmental research provided hope again—in the battles for wellness, quality of life, and climate change. Toys based on cartoon characters remained very popular, from Buzz Lightyear to Spider-man, along with ever-more-sophisticated computer-simulation games.

Your Christmas Budget in the 2000s

A century later, here's how your very first Christmas-budget list looks, updated to keep up with the times.

- Men's sport jacket (smoking optional): $99.95
- TV cabinet: $450.00
- Portable MP3 player: $109.99
- China candlestick: $35.00
- Boys' worsted sweater: $30.00
- Toy sewing machine: $29.99
- Toy automobile: $9.99
- Railroad set: $34.00
- Paperbound copy of *Peck's Bad Boy*: $19.95

In the News in the 2000s

Green Christmas: Tips for an Eco-Friendly Holiday

Between Thanksgiving and New Year's day, Americans throw away a million extra tons of garbage each week, including holiday wrapping and packaging, according to Robert Lilienfeld. Lilienfield is coauthor of the book *Use Less Stuff: Environmental Solutions for Who We Really Are.*

So why not recycle holiday gift wrap? Lilienfield, who has published a newsletter on reducing waste since 1996, notes that if every family reused just 2 feet of holiday ribbon, the 38,000 miles of ribbon saved could tie a bow around the entire planet.

And not all gifts need wrapping. "Think back to your three favorite holiday memories," Lilienfeld said. "I'm willing to bet that they all involve time you spent with your family and friends."

By giving gifts that can be experienced, like tickets to a baseball game or a home-made dinner, you can minimize wrapping and still win points with the receiver. "People like these gifts just as much," he said.

—Cameron Walker for *National Geographic News*, December 20, 2004

Trees for Troops

Christmas Tree growers donated more than 11,000 Christmas Trees to U.S. troops and their families during the 2006 holiday season. The Trees for Troops Program, sponsored by the Christmas SPIRIT Foundation (and FedEx Corp., which donated the shipping for all of the trees), kicked off on Nov. 14, 2006, with the collection of trees in Columbus, Ohio and Indianapolis, Indiana. These trees were shipped overseas to Afghanistan, Iraq, the Middle East and sailors in the 5th fleet in the Gulf.

Additional Christmas Trees were delivered to U.S. troops and their families at military bases across the United States.

—*www.christmastree.org*

Christmas Advertising in the 2000s

Fantasy Gifts

Neiman Marcus revealed its annual list of fantasy gifts in 2005 to include a private Elton John concert for $1.5 million, a prototype M400 Skycar (a personal vertical take-off and landing aircraft) for $3.5 million, and a designer tree house by artist Roderick Wolgamott Romero for $50,000.

—CNN

11

Christmas Around the World

Christmas is observed in all kinds of places around the world—from the privacy of a single home to public worship in a cathedral, in the smallest villages and the largest cities, in the jungles and in the deserts. In many places, however, it looks much different than a North American Christmas. Do they have Santa Claus in China, for example? What's for Christmas dinner in Sweden? What happens when Christmas arrives during summer vacation? Here's a sampling of global traditions, to answer these questions and more.

Christmas in Europe

As a general rule, the Christmas season in Europe begins in early December and lasts through January 6. The celebration is marked by beautiful and expansive Nativity scenes, delicious feasts, and the observance of Epiphany. Though each culture has its unique customs and rituals, there are elements that unify the holiday for all within a given country.

France

For the French, the winter holiday (known as Noël, from an expression meaning "day of birth") begins on December 6, St. Nicholas's Day. St. Nicholas's Day is celebrated most heartily in the provinces, particularly in Lorraine, as it is believed that the Virgin Mary gave Lorraine to Nicholas as a gift; he is its patron saint. He is also, of course, the patron saint of children; little ones throughout France leave out their shoes in the hope that St. Nicholas will leave gifts of nuts and candy during his night visit.

Festive Fact

Unlike the American Santa, Père Noël is tall, dresses in a long red robe, and travels with a sack and a donkey. Though Père Noël is not seen in department stores as often as Santa is in the United States, he too can be contacted by sending letters to the North Pole.

French homes are known for their crèches, or Nativity displays, which are meant to look as realistic and beautiful as possible. Some contain *santons* (little saints) representing people in the Nativity. Santons came to France in the 1800s from Italy, by way of Italian merchants. The figures are made of clay, and in most cases, are clothed with fabric.

Flowers are another staple decoration in the French home during the holiday season. Lush arrangements of roses, gladioli, carnations, and snapdragons are often found on the table or next to the fireplace, as are poinsettias, hyacinths, azaleas, and Christmas begonia plants. Some houses assign a special place on the table a bouquet the hellebore, or Christmas Rose.

The arrival of Christmas Eve sees the infant Jesus taking his place in the family crèche after a small ceremony. Little children are put to bed, hoping that the gifts they ask for will be left by Père Noël. Previously, Petit Jesus, or Little Jesus, was the one who came to children on Christmas Eve. Later, the visitor was the spirit of Christmas, Père Noël. In present-day France, most children believe Jesus sends Père Noël in his place.

After the children are in bed, the older members of the family head off to midnight Mass. Along the way there are often processions re-enacting the Nativity, some of which end in living crèches (where people play out the manger scene). The midnight Mass itself is very important in France, and almost everyone attends.

At the Mass's conclusion, all head home to begin the *reveillon* (awakening), which is the grand Christmas Eve feast. The feast may have as many as fifteen courses, ranging from soups, fruits, salads, meats, fish, and chicken to cheese, breads, nuts, pastry, and candy. The reveillon often lasts the entire night, with no time for the adults to sleep before the children wander down to open their gifts. The adults wait to exchange their gifts on New Year's Day, though some villages near the Spanish border mix Spanish and French traditions and open gifts on January 6.

Belgium

Gift giving in Belgium traditionally takes place on December 6. In French-speaking areas, it's Père Noël who brings the gifts, while in Walloon-speaking areas, it's more likely to be St. Nicholas himself, who makes a quick visit two days beforehand to take a look around and gauge children's behavior. On December 6, good children can expect special treats, while bad ones can look for sticks in the shoes that they've left out to be filled.

An area of the country known as Flanders is famous for its Nativity plays, which are performed with great care and attention to tradition. Three men who are chosen for their good behavior during the year dress as Magi and walk through the town. They sing songs at each house and are rewarded with snacks. Belgium is also known for its processions on Christmas Eve, which wind through town until they reach the church for midnight mass.

Italy

Italy is the birthplace of the manger scene, or *presepio*, which is filled with clay figures called *pastori*. It rightfully holds a place of distinction in the Italian Christmas, dating back almost eight centuries to the time of St. Francis of Assisi.

The *ceppo* is an Italian version of the Christmas tree. Made of wood, the ceppo gives the appearance of a ladder, with shelves linking two sides. The bottom shelf contains a presepio; other shelves contain gifts and decorations.

Italian children receive gifts twice during this season. The Christ Child is said to bring small gifts on Christmas Eve, but the more anticipated gift giving is from La Befana, who comes down the chimney on Epiphany Eve to leave goodies in shoes. Legend has it that La Befana was the woman who declined the Wise Men's offer to accompany them on their journey to see the Christ Child. Regretting her decision later, she set out to bring the Child gifts, but, as she never found Him, she leaves gifts for other children instead. (The tradition has variants in many other countries as well.) Santa Claus is also a familiar figure in Italy, where he's known as Babbo Natale.

As part of an older tradition, shepherds (*pifferai*) often come in from neighboring villages to play their horns and bagpipes before the holy shrines. In a role similar to that of the American Santa Claus, women dressed as La Befana collect for charities like the Red Cross.

Spain

The Christmas season in Spain begins on December 8 with the Feast of the Immaculate Conception. This includes *Los Seises*, the Dance of Six, an ancient custom whereby six boys (now ten) perform a dance that symbolizes Christ's birth and life. This is celebrated annually at Seville's cathedral.

The manger scene, or *nacimiento,* has a place of reverence in the Spanish Christmas. This manger scene contains all the traditional elements, along with a few distinctly Spanish ones, including a Spanish bull and a stream of water. Sometimes bullfighters are part of the onlookers. These scenes are set up in public squares and in homes, taking precedence over Christmas trees, which are not common.

The Spanish refer to Christmas Eve as *Noche Buena* (Good Night). On Christmas Eve, family members gather in the room containing the nacimiento to sing hymns and pray. Late in the evening, the *Misa de Gallo* (Mass of the Rooster) is attended. Many Hispanic countries refer to midnight Mass as the Mass of the Rooster; it has been said that the only time a rooster ever crowed at midnight was the moment when Christ was born. After Mass, a big meal is consumed.

A fast for the twenty-four hours preceding Christmas Eve ends with a festive meal, along with the tradition of the "Urn of Fate," a bowl filled with both presents and empty boxes. Each person picks to see whether he or she is fated to receive a gift—although no one ever really goes away empty-handed.

Adults exchange gifts on Christmas Day. Another treat is the Urn of Fate, a bowl filled with the names of everyone present. Two names are picked out at the same time; those whose names are chosen together are supposed to enjoy a lasting friendship or romance.

There is much dancing and other festivities through Epiphany, the day that children receive presents in their shoes from the Three Wise Men. (There is no Santa Claus figure.)

England

In England, the Christmas tree has been widespread since Prince Albert introduced the custom in 1841. Caroling and bell ringing are very popular as well, and the land that gave us the Christmas card is still sending them by the millions. Father Christmas, so similar in many ways to the American Santa Claus, leaves gifts for children. Letters to him were traditionally thrown in the fire (a little more difficult now that many houses no longer have an open fireplace) so that their lists could fly up the chimney.

House decorations of holly, ivy, and mistletoe and children hanging up their stockings are also traditional elements of Christmas in England. Christmas Eve might see people attending church services. Many families open their gifts Christmas morning, sitting down to a meal of turkey or roast beef in the afternoon. For dessert, sweet mince pies and brandy-laced plum pudding are still favorites, and pulling crackers is looked forward to throughout the meal. Many people make time to listen to the Queen's annual message, which is aired on television in the afternoon.

Christmas crackers—which first appeared in London in 1846—are cardboard tubes covered with bright paper that's twisted to close up both ends. When the crackers are pulled apart they make a small "bang" or "crack," and release little toys, jokes, and tissue-paper hats hidden within the tubes.

An additional observance, or day off, at this time of year is Boxing Day, held on December 26. The name is taken from the old custom of opening the alms boxes in church the day after Christmas to give money to the needy. The idea expanded to servants and tradesmen, who expected to be tipped for the year's service.

Wales

Carol singing, or *eisteddfodde,* in Wales has become an art form. Nowhere in the world are Christmas carols more carefully crafted and lovingly sung. Many churches retain a carol-singing service known as Plygain at Christmas. Once a Christmas-morning service that began as early as 3:00 A.M., it now tends to be an evening service.

The Christmas season is also the time for the Mari Lwyd, or Grey Mare, to appear. This odd creature is represented by a man wearing a sheet and carrying a horse's skull or imitation horse's head. The creature dances around in public and tries to bite people with the horse's jaws. If he manages to bite you, you must give him money!

Pulling (making) taffy, which is a chewy toffee candy, is one way to spend the day; in Wales, taffy is as much a part of Christmas fare as candy canes are in America.

Ireland

Christmas in Ireland takes on quite a religious tone, although decorations and gift giving (and shopping) are popular, too. Lit candles (often replaced now with electric lights) are left in the windows on Christmas Eve to light the Holy Family's way, with church services attended on Christmas Eve or Christmas morning.

Father Christmas is the gift giver here, with presents traditionally given out on Christmas morning, followed by a big holiday meal later in the day. For a treat, three special puddings are made during this season: one for Christmas, one for New Year's, and one for Twelfth Night, the latter of which is also known as Little Christmas.

On the day after Christmas (St. Stephen's Day), many once engaged in "hunting the wren." This old tradition called for the killing of a wren to symbolize the death of the old year and the birth of the new. The dead wren was carried by the hunters from house to house, singing carols. The homeowner would give the hunters some goodies for their troubles, and they would give a feather for good luck in return. Areas that still observe this custom today use a fake stuffed wren, and money collected usually goes to charity.

Scotland

With Christmas celebrations banned after the sixteenth-century Reformation in Scotland, December 25 remained a regular working day until 1958, when it was finally declared a public holiday. Today, it has largely caught up with European traditions of gift giving and decorating, although it retains some of its own special superstitions—including the idea that the home's fire needs to be kept burning on Christmas Eve to keep mischievous elves from coming down the chimney and causing bad luck.

The Scots also celebrate Hogmanay, or New Year's Eve, as a major event, often gathering together friends and family to celebrate the coming of the new year. Cities such as Edinburgh host huge public celebrations.

Germany

Germany, perhaps more than any other country, has influenced the way Christmas is celebrated around the world. The tradition of the Christmas tree began in Germany, after all, and most modern families there would consider it unthinkable to pass the holiday without one. Advent wreaths and calendars (which mark the countdown to Christmas Day) make their appearance at the end of November. Germany is also one of the countries in which children leave a shoe out on the eve of St. Nicholas's Day (December 6) to be filled with candy.

There are more gifts after Mass or church on Christmas Eve. That's when the Christkind, or Kris Kringle—not to be confused with St. Nicholas or Santa Claus—brings the gifts. At first, the Christkind was meant to be the Baby

Jesus; later the name came to stand for a more angelic figure that embodies the spirit of the Christ Child. The Christkind wears a flowing white robe, a white veil, and gold wings, often entering by an open window and ringing a bell when gifts have been left.

Austria

St. Nicholas's Day opens the Christmas season in Austria as well, when the saint arrives with the devil (St. Nicholas often appears with a darker companion who deals with the children on the "misbehaving" list). Both figures test the children, and the good ones receive presents.

One of Austria's most important contributions to the celebration of Christmas is a song sung by church choirs and carolers around the world: "Silent Night." On Christmas Eve, 1818, organist Franz Gruber composed the music to accompany Josef Mohr's poem. The carol was Gruber's only published musical work.

The Nativity scene is displayed around the family tree, which is often decorated with small toys and candy as well as ornaments. There are processions known as "Showing the Christ Child," and Nativity plays are also performed; similar to the Spanish posadas, they dramatize the Holy Family's journey. On Christmas Eve, many enjoy music from the *Turmblasen*, a brass band that plays carols from church steeples or building towers.

Switzerland

Switzerland is populated by four distinct groups of people, all of whom tend to follow their own traditions: French, German, Italian, and Romansh. Regardless of nationality, however, manger scenes and trees are common themes, and on December 6, the Chlausjagen Festival, or Feast of St. Nicholas, is often celebrated.

In some parts of Switzerland, great care is taken to emphasize the holiday's religious significance before its festive side. Presents are brought by the Chriskindli: The angelic figure arrives to the sound of bells. In fact, churches in Switzerland are famous for their bells—bell-ringing competitions are held in some areas, such as Valais, on Christmas Eve.

Holland

Of all the countries in the world that celebrate St. Nicholas's Day, Holland is the one in which the saint can truly be said to reign supreme. Arriving by steamer on the last Saturday in November, he's greeted by huge crowds of people, including dignitaries. After parading through the streets in full bishop's regalia, Nicholas and his companion, Black Peter, take up residence in a hotel and begin preparations for St. Nicholas's Eve. In the time between his arrival and the holiday, St. Nicholas visits schools, hospitals, and shopping malls. The presents he leaves in children's shoes on St. Nicholas's Eve are disguised and come with catchy poems; Black Peter leaves switches for misbehaving children.

For Christmas, there are church services and much eating and merriment. Boiled chestnuts are among the popular snacks. The houses are decorated with holly and pine, and there are Christmas trees. December 26, also a legal holiday, is referred to as Second Christmas, but is usually an opportunity for resting up from the previous day's activities. One nice feature of this day is the abundance of music that can be heard from a variety of choirs, radio broadcasts, and other performances.

Denmark

' In Denmark, Santa is not alone. A mysterious creature lurks about during the Christmas season: the mischievous Julnisse. Dressed in gray with a red bonnet, red socks, and white clogs, the elf-like Julnisse hides in farmhouse lofts or barnyards. Unless appeased with a treat, he may play tricks; but if properly taken care of, he'll watch over the family's animals for the upcoming year. The figure is quite popular and is often featured on collector's plates made specially for Christmas.

The tradition of collecting such plates began years ago, when rich families would give their servants plates of goodies for the Christmas holiday. The servants set aside the plates, which they considered far better than their everyday dishes. The custom caught on, and now the Christmas plate—with or without a Julnisse—is a popular collectible.

Food is a major element of the Danish celebration, including the Christmas meal—which often features roast goose or turkey, red cabbage, potatoes, and pastry. One custom (common to other Scandinavian countries as well) involves hiding an almond in the rice pudding. The child who receives the portion with the almond gets a prize.

Norway

Norwegians, like other Scandinavian peoples, believe in sharing Christmas with the animals. On Christmas Eve day, a sheaf of grain, or "Bird Tree," is hung out in the yard so that the birds may feast, too.

By four o'clock on Christmas eve, all work has ceased; all are dressed in their best clothes to begin the festivities; and other Scandinavian customs are observed. The rice pudding is eaten, and whoever finds the magic almond is given a treat. Of course, some rice pudding must also be given to the barnyard elf to ensure he'll protect the animals and not pull pranks.

For the children, there is Julesvenn to bring gifts on Christmas Eve. Between Christmas and the season's end on January 13, there are many parties for children and adults, including the Julebukk, a Halloween-like celebration named after Thor's goat. Children wear costumes and knock on neighbors' doors asking for treats.

Sweden

Although St. Lucia's Day on December 13 is observed in other Scandinavian countries, it is celebrated on a grand scale in Sweden. St. Lucia, who was martyred in A.D. 304 for being a Christian, is important to the Swedes because, legend says, she brought food to Sweden during a time of famine. In the wee hours of December 13, thousands of young girls in white robes, acting the part of St. Lucia, serve pastry and coffee to their parents while they are in bed. Special buns are made with an "X" on them to symbolize Christ. There is also an official St. Lucia parade in Stockholm.

On Christmas Eve day, the family gathers in the kitchen for a ritual known *as doppa i grytan* ("dipping in the kettle"). A kettle is filled with drippings—corned beef, pork, and sausage—each person dips a piece of dark bread in the kettle until it is soaked through, then eats it. This ritual is meant to remind each family member of those who are less fortunate, and to encourage thankfulness.

Christmas Spirit

Because King Knut had once declared that Christmas should be celebrated for twenty days, the season doesn't officially end until January 13, Saint Knut's Day. (King Knut IV ruled from 1080–1086 and is honored as a saint for his virtue and generosity.) The days between Christmas and Saint Knut's Day are filled with parties for children and adults.

The Everything Family Christmas Book

The Swedish also have the Scandinavian tradition of rice pudding with the hidden almond, only here the finder of the almond is destined to be married within a year. And like other Scandinavians, the Swedes have their gnome, known as Jultomten, who must be appeased, and who puts presents under the tree on Christmas Eve, accompanied by poems.

Finland

Christmas in Finland encompasses most of the Scandinavian traditions already described, with some unique Finnish customs added for good measure. The period of Advent is known as Little Christmas, and is a time of preparation and celebration. Gingerbread is a favorite treat, as is *glögli,* a drink of red wine and spices. Another custom is visiting the steam baths before Christmas Eve, presumably to get squeaky clean for the holiday.

Greece

In the Greek tradition, Christmas is not as important a holiday as Easter, so the celebration is on a smaller scale than some might expect. December 6 marks St. Nicholas's Day, but emphasizes his role as the patron saint of sailors; December is a time of rough seas around Greece, so prayers are for safety rather than gifts.

Christmas itself is celebrated merrily, however: Children wander the streets singing carols and playing little drums or triangles and are rewarded with candy, nuts, or money. There are no Christmas trees, however, and gift giving is reserved for St. Basil's Day (January 1). Featured within the Christmas meal is the *Christopsomo,* or Christ Bread. The bread is usually decorated with a symbol indicating the family's occupation. Because the Greek Church is an Eastern church, it celebrates Christ's birth on January 6, which is also when the Blessing of the Water takes place. In this ceremony, a priest dips a crucifix in a lake, river, or stream. The water, called Baptismal Water, is now considered holy and is used by the faithful for its healing powers. This Blessing of the Water is also done in Syrian and Coptic churches, as well as in some parts of Russia and the United States.

Russia

Many of the Russian Christmas customs date back to prerevolutionary Russia, when Christianity flourished. Father Frost was a staple of the old tradition, and presents were brought by Babushka, Russia's version of the old woman who was supposed to have declined to join the Wise Men. There was also a girl dressed in white called Kolyada, who would visit houses, singing carols and giving treats. Some communities engaged in the Blessing of the Water; sometimes a priest would go through the village with this water to bless the houses.

Christmas returned to Russia in the early 1990s, and many of the older traditions did, too. These include several weeks of fasting—avoiding meat—until after church services on Christmas Eve (which, according to the Julian calendar, is January 6). Christmas Eve dinner often includes *kutya,* a porridge made of wheat berries, honey, and poppy seeds, symbolizing hope and happiness.

Poland

During the Christmas season, the letters "C," "M," and "B" are the most important in Poland. Representing the initials of the Three Wise Men (Caspar, Melchior, and Balthasar), the letters are painted on the doors of homes along with three crosses, in hopes of ensuring a good year.

Lucky children in Poland receive gifts twice during the Christmas season. St. Nicholas brings the first round on St. Nicholas's Day; the Star Man, accompanied by Star Boys, brings the second round on Christmas Eve.

The Star of Bethlehem is very important to the Poles. On Christmas Eve, after the first star has appeared in the sky, the head of the household breaks a wafer, called *oplatek,* and shares it with every person in the house. These wafers, which bear images of the Nativity, have been blessed by a priest.

Wigilia, the Christmas Eve meal, has thirteen courses—one for Jesus and each of the Apostles. Hay is placed under the tablecloth in some homes, as a reminder that Christ was born in a manger. The midnight Mass in Poland is called *Pasterka,* the Mass of the Shepherds. It is believed that on this night the animals bow in reverence and receive the power to speak.

The Czech Republic

The Czech Republic sets aside both December 25 and 26 for Christmas, which are known as First and Second Christmas. The season opens with Svatej Nikulus (St.

Nicholas's) Day on December 6 and ends with the visit of the Tri Kralu (Three Kings) on January 6. Svatej Nikulus has a bag of goodies for nice children; his companion for the trip is the devil, who carries switches for the bad ones.

The manger scene, or *Jeslicky*, is a must in churches and homes. There are Christmas trees, which are lit Christmas Eve. Dinner consists of carp, pudding, and fruit stew, and a seat at dinner is left empty for the Christ Child. Later, Pasterka (midnight Mass) will be attended.

Christmas in Central America and the West Indies

Christmas in Central America and the West Indies is characterized not by snow and sleigh bells, but warm weather and bright flowers. For the most part, the countries in this area follow the traditions of the midnight Mass and Nativity scenes.

Midnight Mass in many Spanish-speaking countries is known as *Miso de Gallo*, or mass of the rooster, because it's believed that the only time the rooster ever crowed at midnight was to mark the birth of Jesus. It's fitting, since the rooster's crow can also symbolize the birth of the day after the night.

On Christmas Eve, there are often processions with people wearing costumes and carrying the manger. Large festive meals are eaten on either Christmas Eve or Christmas Day. On Christmas Day, there are picnics, bullfights, and other good times. A small number of Christmas trees are imported from the United States, and Santa is seen on occasion, but not to bring gifts. Gifts are generally put in children's shoes by the Three Kings or the Christ Child on January 6th.

Mexico

The Christmas season in Mexico begins on December 16, the first day of *posadas*. *Posada* is the Mexican word for a tradition popular in many Spanish-speaking countries: the commemoration of the Holy Family's pilgrimage. Posadas take place over a period of nine days before Christmas and entail the faithful acting out Mary and Joseph's search for lodging. People travel to one another's homes, taking on the roles of pilgrims or innkeepers, with the ritual culminating in celebration and prayer around the family altar, on which is placed a crèche.

The houses are decorated with Spanish moss, evergreens, and paper lanterns. Also present are "The Flowers of the Holy Night," or poinsettias. After the religious portion of the posada is over, there is much merriment, with food, fireworks, and piñatas. The final, and most important, posada takes place on Christmas Eve. The Baby Jesus is placed in the cradle amid prayer and song. Afterward, everyone attends midnight Mass.

Honduras

Hondurans have their own version of posadas. For nine days before Christmas, the faithful act out Mary and Joseph's search for lodging. One house in the village is chosen to be the place of shelter, where people go to sing and pray. Tamales are served, dances and fireworks displays are held, and people visit each other's crèches.

Costa Rica

In Costa Rica, the Nativity scene is given its own room, not just a spot in a corner or on a table. In accordance with the climate, the decorations consist of brilliantly colored flowers and wreaths of cypress leaves and red coffee berries. Children put out their shoes for the Christ Child to fill, as their parents did, but Santa is beginning to show up more and more.

Nicaragua

By late November, festivities have started in Nicaragua. Children gather in the streets with bouquets to honor the Virgin Mary with song. This portion of the holiday ends on December 8, with the Feast of the Immaculate Conception. On December 16, the Novena to the Holy Child begins; another kind of posada, it concludes on Christmas Eve at midnight Mass. Children receive gifts from the Three Kings on January 6.

Panama

Schoolchildren in Panama engage in pre-Christmas activities much like the ones enjoyed by American children. Decorations and cards are made, gifts are exchanged, and there are plays. Christmas Eve and Christmas Day are celebrated, with the meal including chicken with rice and tamales. Once again, children receive gifts on Epiphany, King's Day.

Puerto Rico

Understandably, there is a large American influence on the Puerto Rican Christmas, which features a mixture of Spanish and American traditions. Puerto Ricans have Santa Claus and a tree, but receive gifts on both Christmas and Epiphany. A fun pre-Christmas tradition is *Asalto,* in which a band of people appear on someone's lawn to shout, sing carols, and plead for goodies. The owner usually opens up his or her house to them; after a small party, the group moves on to another house. Generally, Christmas in Puerto Rico lasts from early December to Las Octavitas, which is eight days after Epiphany.

Christmas in South America

The celebration of Christmas in South America is similar to that in Central America because of the warm climate and the religious aspects of the holiday. As with most countries of Hispanic origin, children receive gifts on Epiphany rather than Christmas; the *nacimiento* (crèche) and midnight Mass are essential, but posadas are not as popular as in other areas.

Chile

Christmas in Chile is observed in accordance with most of the region, including the midnight Mass of the Rooster, but the gift giver here is known as Viejo Pascuero, or Old Man Christmas. Oddly enough, he has reindeer, but of course, with a significant lack of big chimneys, he's forced to enter houses through windows instead. A notable part of the Christmas meal is *pan de pasqua,* a bread that contains candied fruit.

Peru

Markets become very busy in the days before Christmas, offering both gift items and decorations for the Nativity scenes, or nacimiento, that many families have. This is a time of song and music, although the Christmas Eve service is, as always, much quieter in nature. Children often receive gifts both on Christmas Day (as Santa becomes a more popular figure) and on January 6, which is the Feast of the Three Kings.

Colombia

Much of the Christmas season in Colombia begins in earnest nine days before Christmas Day, when the Novena, a prayer ritual, begins. The *pesebre,* or Nativity scene, is also important, with Jesus generally making his appearance on Christmas

Eve. Colombia is one of the rare Hispanic countries in which children receive gifts brought by the Christ Child on Christmas Eve, not Epiphany.

Venezuela

An interesting tradition in Venezuela is "The Standing Up of the Christ Child," or *La Paradura del Niño*. According to the rules, the figurine of the Child must be stood up on New Year's Day to indicate his maturity. Any Child found lying down in its manger at that time is likely to be "kidnapped" and kept in a special place of honor until the ransom is paid. Ransom is a *paradura* party. But before the party can begin, "godparents" must be chosen; later, they lead a procession to where the Child is kept. After the godparents return the figurine to the manger setting and stand it up, children offer gifts and there is much food and dancing.

Brazil

Brazil has incorporated some American ideas for Christmas, including a Santa equivalent called Papa Noël, lighted Christmas trees, and similar gift-giving traditions. The manger, or *pesebre,* is still very important, however. On Christmas Eve, a meal is laid out before the household attends midnight Mass, so that the Holy Family may eat if they wish. Children put out shoes for Papa Noël to fill. Because of the warm climate, Christmas Day is often filled with picnics and sport.

Christmas in Africa

In most African countries, Christians make up a relatively small part of the population, so Christmas is generally a lower-key affair than it is in many western countries. The emphasis is typically on charitable acts and simple presents, rather than the purchase of expensive gifts. Church services and often, caroling, are considered important. In Algiers, for example, there are a number of Catholic churches that celebrate midnight Mass, and streets are colorfully decorated for the holiday.

The Christian church in Ethiopia is the Coptic church. Believers there still abide by an older calendar, which places Christmas on January 7, when people break their traditional pre-Christmas fast from milk or meat products with a meal of rice and meat.

In Ghana, Christmas evergreen or palm trees are seen, and there is a Father Christmas who comes out of the jungle. Children have school pageants and there is more gift giving. Early Christmas morning, a group enacts the story of the shepherds and angels heralding Christ's birth, traveling the streets and singing songs. This band is often rewarded with gifts.

In Liberia, oil palm trees are often decorated with bells for Christmas, with a church service attended in the morning and Christmas dinner shared in the afternoon. It's similar in Nigeria, where Christmas is a time to visit family.

In South Africa, Christmas falls in the midst of summer vacation, so the activities are adapted to the warmer weather. Shops are decorated, streets are lit, and Father Christmas puts gifts in the children's stockings. After a church service on Christmas Day, however, the Christmas feast is eaten outside. Depending on their cultural heritage, South Africans may also celebrate Christmas with feasts, carnivals, and parades.

Christmas in the Middle East

Although much of the Middle East is devoted to Islam—or, in Israel, to Judaism— every year thousands of Christians from around the world make pilgrimages to the Holy Land, especially Bethlehem. They come to visit the place where, according to the Gospels, it all began. Not surprisingly, this is the time of the year when Bethlehem is most popular, although the scope of the celebrations often depends on the political climate at the time.

The festivities in the "little town" center on the Church of the Nativity and the Shepherds' Fields. The Church of the Nativity is believed to stand on the place where Christ was born; under the church, within a small cave, a star on the floor marks the place where Mary gave birth to Jesus. The Shepherds' Fields is said to represent the fields where the angels announced the arrival of Christ.

There are three Christian groups in Bethlehem. The Roman Catholics celebrate Christmas on December 25, the Greek Orthodox on January 6, and the Armenian Christians on January 18. Representatives protecting the interests of these three groups sit on a board that governs the Church of the Nativity, so that no group will be favored or slighted. No services are held within the church itself, but rather in an adjoining building. Services on Christmas Eve are by invitation only, but are televised to the crowds outside. Afterward, most venture to the Shepherds' Fields, which are also divided into three sections.

Christmas is also celebrated quite widely in Lebanon, with lights, carols, and midnight church services. Papa Noél brings presents to children, and the meal often includes a cake that's designed to resemble a Yule log.

Some of the more predominantly Muslim countries do have Christian sections, and in those sections Christmas is observed, although the observance is usually more strictly religious, as in Africa. Some countries, however, have Christian populations that have been celebrating Christmas for centuries.

In Armenia, it is believed that Christmas should be celebrated on the day of Christ's baptism, which is January 6 in most church calendars. However, the Armenian Church follows the old Julian calendar, which marks this date as January 18. One week before Christmas there is a fast, during which no meat, eggs, cheese, or milk may be eaten. Religious services are held on Christmas Eve and Christmas Day. Afterward, children go onto the roofs with handkerchiefs and sing carols; often the handkerchiefs are later filled with fruit, grain, or money.

In Iraq, where the Magi are believed to have traveled from, Christmas is known as the Little Feast (Easter being the Great Feast). Christians here fast from December 1 until Christmas Eve, consuming no meat, eggs, milk, or cheese. After the evening church service a great feast begins, but there is no gift exchange.

Syria celebrates Christmas longer than most Middle Eastern countries, beginning on December 4 (St. Barbara's Day) and lasting through Epiphany (January 6). Children receive gifts on New Year's Day from the Camel of Jesus. One tradition, left over from the days of religious persecution, is to lock the outside gate of the house on Christmas Eve. This is to remind all that they once had to practice their religion behind closed doors. The father lights a great fire in the courtyard, the youngest son reads from the Gospel, and hymns are sung. After the fire has been reduced to embers, family members make a wish and jump over them. Epiphany Eve is known in Syria as Lilat-al-Kadr (Night of Destiny). A magic mule brings presents to children on this night. The mule's magic powers come from when he was caught up as the trees bowed at midnight the night of Christ's birth.

In Pakistan, many aspects of the Christmas celebration are similar to those in America—there's even a Santa Claus. December 25 is a public holiday, although it honors not Jesus but Jinnah, the founder of Pakistan. Still, for Christians, the day is known as Bara Din, and is marked by church services, family visits, and delicious food.

In neighboring India, the Christmas trees for the churches are made out of straw. The straw is twisted into shape and coated with mud; later, greens are applied, and then candles. In some instances, banana trees are also decorated.

Christmas in the Far East

In the Far East, Christianity exists alongside such other faiths or ideologies as Buddhism, Confucianism, and Shintoism. While Christians celebrate the holiday for its traditional meanings, many of the other aspects, such as decorating and gift giving, have been adopted more widely.

China

China was only opened to the West 400 years ago, so—relatively speaking—Christians and Christmas have not been around for long. A very small portion of the Christian population celebrates a Christmas that's referred to as Sheng Dan Jieh, or the Holy Birth Festival. Christmas trees are called "trees of light," and paper lanterns are intermingled with holly for decoration. Stockings are hung, and there are versions of Santa known as Lam Khoong-Khoong (nice old father) and Dun Che Lao Ren (Christmas old man). Gift giving has some formal rules: Jewelry and other more-valuable gifts are only given to the immediate family; other gifts are given to relatives and friends.

More important to the majority of Chinese is the New Year, referred to as the Spring Festival, which is celebrated in late January. New toys and clothes are given and feasts are held. The spiritual aspects concern ancestor worship, and portraits of ancestors are displayed on New Year's Eve. This is not, strictly speaking, a Christmas celebration, but it is a festive and popular seasonal undertaking.

Japan

Christmas in Japan is celebrated by a large number of people—including a good many who follow other religions. For the Japanese, Christmas is a strictly secular celebration, considered a time for fun and gifts. There are Japanese versions of American Christmas carols; department stores have Christmas trees and special Christmas sales; holly, bells, and other decorations are everywhere. A Buddhist monk named Hotei-osho is a Santa-like figure who brings presents to children, but Santa is there as well, along with his red-nosed reindeer.

For those who celebrate the religious aspects of the Japanese Christmas, the holiday season is a time for services, hymns, children's pageants (with Japanese dress), visits to hospitals, and other services to the needy. Often, Japanese cakes are given out to those attending church.

Korea

Typical for this part of the world, Korea has a small pocket of Christians who celebrate Christmas with traditional religious services. Schoolchildren put on pageants, and there is a great effort put into helping the needy. For the actual Christmas service, a group of adults and children stay awake in the church on Christmas Eve. After midnight, they go out into the neighborhood singing, and they are often invited into homes for a treat. Religious services are held in the morning, and there is much caroling as people make their way there.

For the country as a whole, Christmas is a nonworking holiday, although the majority of the population is Buddhist. Some families have trees and children are given small gifts.

Christmas in Other Parts of the World

Christmas in Canada and Australia shares many customs handed down from European and North American celebrations of Christmas. The holidays are also, however, informed by both climate and geography.

Canada

Christmas is celebrated in many different ways in Canada, a result of the way that cultural and religious groups from many parts of the world have found a home there. Many Canadians of Ukrainian descent, for example, follow the Orthodox church's calendar, and celebrate Christmas on January 6. In French-speaking areas such as the province of Québec, the Roman Catholic traditions of displaying crèches, or Nativity scenes, as decorations remain very strong, as does attending midnight Mass on Christmas Eve, followed by a hearty meal that includes *tourtière* (a meat pie) and present opening.

The annual Santa Claus Parade in downtown Toronto began in 1905 as a way to celebrate the arrival of Santa at the Eaton's department store. The first parade featured Santa arriving at the train station and walking to the store. Today, the parade—with bands, clowns, and intricately decorated floats—features almost 2,000 participants and stretches for more than three miles.

The Everything Family Christmas Book

Along with the widespread North American traditions of decorating the home inside and out with lights, visiting Santa at local stores and malls to offer him a wish list, and decorating Christmas trees with ornaments and lights, many Canadian Christmas traditions depend on geography.

In the north, for example, the winter season was often celebrated before the arrival of Christmas with feasts, games, dogsled races, and gift exchanges. Known as *Quviasuvvik*, or the Happy Time, many of these traditions have now been wrapped into the church services and charitable causes that are part of Canadian customs throughout the country.

In Vancouver, on Canada's west coast, the Carol Ships are an annual tradition, as boats decorated with sparkling lights take to the harbor in a nightly parade throughout December.

Australia

As in South Africa, Christmas falls during summer vacation down under. Because of the climate, flowers are the most important Christmas decoration, particularly the Christmas Bush and the Christmas Bell. Father Christmas and Santa exist side by side—like siblings, which they certainly are. Gifts are exchanged on Christmas morning before attending church. Typically, the afternoon is spent at the beach or engaging in sports.

Australia is also the home of "Carols by Candlelight," a tradition started by radio announcer Norman Banks in 1937. After Banks saw a woman listening to carols alone by candlelight, he decided to do something to relieve the loneliness and isolation some feel during the holidays. He announced a community carol sing for anyone who wanted to join in. The concept has grown in popularity over the years, and the recorded program is now broadcast the world over.

12

Multicultural Celebrations

In addition to Christmas, there are other notable observances that may take place toward the end of the year, sometimes coinciding with Christmas or the lead-up to the holiday season. These include Hanukkah, Kwanzaa, Diwali, and Ramadan. Each of these is both meaningful and popular in this diverse world, with many schools around the world now including them—along with Christmas—in their multicultural celebrations.

Hanukkah

Hanukkah, meaning "dedication," is a Jewish holiday commemorating the rededication of the Temple in Jerusalem in 165 B.C. The eight-day "Festival of Light," or "Feast of Dedication," begins on the twenty-fifth day of the Hebrew month called Kislev, which usually falls in late November or December. Because Christmas and Hanukkah occur around the same time of the year, many people think of Hanukkah as a sort of Jewish Christmas, but that is far from the case.

The meaning and significance of Hanukkah is individual, steeped in Jewish tradition and experience. What the two holidays do have in common, however, is a complex history, and the use of ritual and symbolism in their celebration. Hanukkah, like Christmas, is a midwinter festival, and like Christmas, marks a single event but uses rituals and customs from other holidays and festivals.

The Roots of the Festival

More than 2,000 years ago, the people of Judea (Southern Palestine, including Jerusalem) were the subjects of various kings and empires. In time, the people of Judea became subjects of the Greek empire. When Alexander the Great came to rule his empire, he sought to spread Greek culture, known as Hellenic culture, to the world, beginning with his occupied territories. Thus began the so-called Hellenization of the Jewish people, a cultural exchange that was originally peaceful.

When Alexander died, his kingdom was divided up between his generals, one of whom was Seleucis. Seleucis's domain extended across, Asia Minor and Syria. It was under Seleucis that conditions changed, and laws were brought in forbidding the Jewish people from practicing their religion and forcing them to adopt Hellenic practices instead, enforced by an oppressive army campaign.

Then, in a small village called Modi'in, a priest named Mattathias, along with his five sons, mounted an opposition and managed to surprise and overcome the soldiers. The success of this band, known collectively as the Maccabees, gave their compatriots hope, and soon new recruits from all over were making their way to the hills to train.

Over the next three years, the Maccabees achieved victory after victory. When Mattathias died, his son Judah took over and led the Maccabees to the ultimate success: the defeat of the Syrian army and the reclaiming of the Temple in Jerusalem, in the year 165 B.C.

When worshipers went to light the Temple lamps as part of the rededication ceremony, however, they found only enough purified oil to burn for one day. Miraculously, the lamp continued to burn for eight days, which was enough time to prepare new oil.

The eight days of Hanukkah, therefore, commemorate the miracle of the oil, and also the miracle of the Maccabees' victory over a much larger, better-trained, and better-equipped army. Over time, that has come to symbolize victory and survival in the face of great odds, especially the survival of religious freedom.

The Evolution of the Festival

After that first celebration in the Temple, Judah decreed that the miracle of the Jewish victory should be commemorated every year in the same fashion. Over the centuries, borrowing a bit from other Jewish festivals and inspiring some customs of its own, Hanukkah has evolved into the holiday we recognize today.

There are several explanations for the festival's eight-day duration. The most widely accepted is that it commemorates the eight days that the lamps stayed lit. There is also a legend that Judah and his followers found eight enemy spears in the Temple, which they made into a lamp stand. Some observers think that the eight days are the result of combining the Hanukkah festivities with other Jewish festivals.

In the years immediately following the Maccabean victory, having these legends to fall back on became increasingly important to the survival of Hanukkah. Within thirty years, the Jewish lands came under Roman rule, and a holiday that rejoiced in Jewish battle success and nationalism would not have been tolerated. So the legend of the oil moved to the forefront, thereby masking the deeper reasons behind Hanukkah until it was safe for them to come to prominence again.

Hanukkah Today

Today in the United States, Hanukkah is celebrated for the most part quietly at home, with family and friends. Though observance of the holiday may vary from house to house, the Menorah—a candleholder with space for nine candles, including a central candle known as the *shamash,* or "servant," candle that lights all others—is the central element of any Hanukkah celebration. On the first night of Hanukkah, one candle on the candelabrum is lit by the shamash. Each night after the first an additional candle is lit, until all eight are aglow on the final night.

Hanukkah is a happy holiday, full of food and good cheer. On the fifth night of Hanukkah, many families engage in a formal gathering known as the Night of the Fifth Candle dinner. This is typically the time during the festival when family members and friends from far away make a special effort to gather with their loved ones. These days, this special gathering is not always restricted to the fifth night of Hanukkah, but may take place on the night during the festival that the most people can attend.

Over the course of the eight days, families usually entertain friends at home, eating, drinking, singing, and generally being merry. Songs echo through the halls and small gifts are exchanged on many nights. Depending on the family's preference, the custom of giving one small gift per night can be modified to one or two larger gifts given on only a few nights.

Hanukkah observances in the synagogue consist of reading passages from the Torah on each of the eight days. Psalms 113 through 118 and the prayer of Al Ha-Nissim may also be read. Many temples and synagogues sponsor Hanukkah festivals, as do schools and community centers. Most of the activity is geared toward children, featuring plays, concerts, parties, and food.

Though not the most important holiday on the Jewish calendar, Hanukkah stands out as a time of great merriment. Hanukkah is important to the Jewish people as a reminder of a miraculous time in their history, but it can be a valuable reminder to all of the potential of the human spirit.

Hanukkah Foods

While food selections for Passover and other Jewish holidays arise from strict observances of religious law and ritual, the specific items of Hanukkah fare have evolved, in no small measure, under the influence of later customs.

Often served with sour cream, potato latkes are made from grated potato combined with egg, onion, and flour. The mixture is fried in oil, which symbolizes the miracle oil that kept the Temple lamps burning for eight days.

The *sufganiyot*, or holeless jelly donuts, are another favorite Hanukkah delicacy, particularly in Israel. They're also cooked in hot oil, after which they might be coated with sugar or cinnamon.

Dairy products are also popular, as a result of the legend of Judith, daughter of the Maccabees. It is said that Judith once entertained an enemy leader by feeding him large quantities of cheese. The man became so thirsty that he had to drink more wine than he should have, which dulled his senses and made him easy to capture.

Hanukkah Games and Gifts

The dreidel, a top with four marked sides, is by far the most popular Hanukkah toy. Each side of the dreidel is marked with a Hebrew letter representing the words in the sentence, "A great miracle happened there." As the top spins and comes to rest, nuts, sweets, or pennies are traded among the players.

Money given during Hanukkah is called Hanukkah *gelt*. In older times, this money was given to children so they could buy a gift for their Hebrew school teacher. These days, they are allowed to keep most, if not all, of the money for themselves. Hanukkah gelt remains one of the more popular Hanukkah gifts.

Katowes are popular among older children. These brain twisters are puzzles and riddles of sorts; all of the answers to these puzzles must be in numbers that equal forty-four, which is the total number of candles lit during the Hanukkah festival. Adults may pass the time playing checkers or chess.

Kwanzaa

Kwanzaa, meaning "first fruits of the harvest" in Swahili, is a seven-day celebration of African-American and pan-African heritage, unity, and values which takes place from December 26 through New Year's Day. Founded in 1966 by Maulana Karenga—a professor at California State University—Kwanzaa is a nonreligious ceremony that strives to promote a feeling of pride and cultural awareness.

Though it more closely resembles the Jewish Hanukkah with its candles and duration, and the American Thanksgiving in tone and theme, many people incorrectly assume that Kwanzaa is meant to be an alternative to Christmas. While it does take place during the same season, Kwanzaa is in no way meant to replace Christmas, and many people celebrate both events.

Kwanzaa Symbolism

In Africa, many celebrations take place after the first fruits of the harvest are gathered, centered on five principles. These include the coming together of people; reverence and gratitude for the creator and what it has provided; a commemoration of the past and its lessons; a recommitment to cultural ideals; and celebration of life itself.

Kwanzaa has taken these fundamental ideas and developed them so that each of its seven days is assigned a principle that is explored on that day. The principles are known by both their English and Swahili names: *Umoja* (unity), *Kujichagulia* (self-determination), *Ujima* (collective work and responsibility), *Ujamaa* (cooperative economics), *Nia* (purpose), *Kuumba* (creativity), and *Imani* (faith). (Swahili is considered a pan-African language, and is widely understood throughout the continent.)

Kwanzaa has seven basic symbols:

- *Mazao,* or crops, represent the harvest.
- *Mkeka,* or the mat, represents the foundation formed by tradition and history.
- *Kinara,* or the seven-branched candleholder, represents the roots of the African people.
- *Muhindi,* or corn, represents children and the future.
- *Mishumma Saba,* or the seven candles, represents the seven principles.
- *Kikombe cha Umoja,* the unity cup, represents unity.
- *Zawadi,* or gifts, represent parents' love for their children.

On each night of Kwanzaa, a candle is lit on the kinara as a way to mark awareness of the principle. After the candle is lit, the prescribed part of the evening is over. As with most of Kwanzaa, it is up to the individual to decide how he or she would best like to explore the principles, and the festival as a whole. Some give examples of the principle at work in their daily life, others read stories or poems by African or African-American authors; still others play music or dance.

Kwanzaa Food

Fruits and vegetables are an important part of Kwanzaa, as they symbolize unified effort, as in harvesting. The week is also highlighted with special African or African-American foods, such as black-eyed peas salad, Yassa (chicken marinated in onion sauce), groundnut soup, sweet potato pie, collard greens, brown rice, cornbread, fish, and African stew.

Diwali

A five-day festival, Diwali (also known as Deepavali in southern India) is one of the biggest and most joyful festivals of the Hindu and Sikh years, taking place in October or November, depending on the lunar cycle. It shares with Christmas a tradition of candle lighting and gift giving, but of course celebrates something quite different.

The overwhelming significance of Diwali, or the Festival of Lights, comes from its name, which signifies the triumph of light over darkness, and thus of good over evil. This is celebrated particularly on the third day of the festival, which coincides with the complete waning of the moon (which creates a dark sky). Oil lamps (*diyas*) and candles are lit, and the Lakshmi Puja ceremony calls on the goddess of wealth to bless the house.

The festival also marks other significant events, according to the area that people come from. Some believe, for example, that it recognizes Lord Rama's return from a war in which he killed the demon Ravana. Others believe that it recognizes the death of another demon, named Narajasura, at the hands of Lord Krishna's wife. Others associate it with the god Vishnu's banishment of king Bali to the underworld.

In general, however, along with good over evil, Diwali is a time of rebirth, which is why you'll find many participants wearing a new set of clothes to symbolize the new beginning (which in some areas actually coincides with the beginning of a new year). Many people exchange gifts during Diwali, particularly sweets, and it's very common to hear firecrackers exploding in celebration. Diwali is also a time of worship and reflection on one's inner light, and is overwhelmingly a time for family and loved ones.

Ramadan

Ramadan is one of the most significant months—the ninth—of the Muslim calendar. It is believed that this is when the Holy Quran, the book that guides those who follow Islam, was sent to earth from heaven. Ramadan's date varies according to the cycles of the moon, which periodically puts the start of the holiday in December for several years running, but can occur any time during the year, including summer.

Also known as the holiest of months, Muslims use Ramadan as a time to worship and to renew their faith. To help them do that without the interferences of everyday life, they will observe a fast during daylight hours, during which they will refrain from eating and drinking and other activities, such as smoking. It's also important during this time to watch one's behavior: to avoid lying or gossiping or being angry or jealous. The focus is on being pure in thought, word, and deed.

The fast begins at daylight—defined as the earliest time of day in which you can distinguish a white thread from a black one—and can be broken with a meal called the *iftar* as soon as it is night. While the fast can be challenging in countries near the equator, where night and day are roughly equal, it can be even more difficult in northern countries where nights can be much longer than the days, depending on the time of year. In this case, the fasting schedule of other countries is often adopted.

Muslims have five prayers that they say daily, according to the time of day; Ramadan adds one more, called the Taraweeh, or night prayer. The night of the 27th day of Ramadan is considered especially holy, as is the Laylat-al-Qadr, or Night of Power, when the Holy Quran was revealed to Mohammed, and when God sets the world's course for the coming year.

The end of Ramadan is celebrated with a three-day festival to break the fast, called Eid ul-Fitr. It's a time to gather with family and friends, to eat and pray together, and to recognize those less fortunate with gifts of food. In an interesting echo of traditions from other cultures, new clothes are often worn during this festival—once again symbolizing a rebirth.

More Celebrations

This time of year is significant for other beliefs, too. Buddhists, for example, celebrate December 8 as Bodhi Day, the day on which Buddha achieved enlightenment and thus transcended beyond the earthly plane of birth, death, and rebirth.

And, of course, modern-day Druids and Wiccans celebrate December 21 as the winter solstice—the longest night of the year, when the sun appears to die and be reborn, offering the promise of renewal and rejuvenation.

From Ramadan to Bodhi Day, Kwanzaa to Hanukkah, this time of year is a very special one for many people around the world. As technology and the news media increasingly shrink our world, making it easier to communicate and to understand each other, it's worth taking time out to recognize the diversity of ways in which people choose to guide their lives.

13

Christmas Your Way: With Family and Friends

More than any other holiday, Christmas is a time for gathering together with family and friends—a time for red noses and chilly toes during skating and tobogganing parties, or the touch of a salt-tinged breeze at the ocean's edge . . . sitting down together over delicious meals, enjoying concerts and carol sings, or sharing holiday cheer at special parties. It can be a whirlwind of a season, but there are great ways to celebrate Christmas, make it meaningful for your family, and still be stress-free!

Create Your Own Christmas Traditions

Many Christmas traditions are passed down within families from generation to generation, but there's no reason why you can't create some special traditions of your own to mark the season. There's also no reason why those traditions can't adapt over the years as children get older and families change. The key is to make the traditions ones that are meaningful, enjoyable, and special for you and those close to you.

Decorating Traditions

Facing an entire house—or even just a tree—that needs decorating for Christmas can be a daunting task. Why not turn it into a family event or invite friends who might be spending the holidays on their own? If it's easier for you to decorate on your own, you could arrange for friends or family to "borrow" your children for their own shopping or decorating party, giving you time to get your house looking festive.

You can also turn buying your Christmas tree into an event, whether you're choosing one from a tree farm in the country or a tree lot in town. Find the tree as a family, armed with a Thermos of hot chocolate or another favorite drink.

Many families buy a special ornament for each child annually—they might have the year on them, or simply reflect the child's interests, from hockey to ballet. Ornaments are also available that tell the Biblical story of Christmas. You can also involve the family in putting together the Nativity scene, whether it's a large outdoor version or a smaller tabletop set. If your scene has great emotional value for you, it might be wise to buy another inexpensive set of figures that the kids can help with.

Advent calendars and wreaths not only add to the seasonal feel, but also provide children with a tangible, visual clue to how long it is until Christmas. You could make the calendars or wreaths as a family, or purchase them and create a little ceremony out of opening the calendar windows each day of December or lighting the candles in the wreath each Sunday before December 25. And every member of the family could use a stocking: Perhaps older children can help make stockings to welcome new family members or even pets.

Family Activity Traditions

The holiday season offers special events and activities pretty much every evening and weekend, so there's never any shortage of things to do. If your family has a favorite activity, then by all means indulge! Some families choose a different activity each year, perhaps even voting for it at a family meeting (helping to show how democracy works) or coming to a decision together (demonstrating consensus building in action).

Activities can range from those with a fee (local zoos, museums, sports facilities, and science centers, for example) to those that are likely completely free (such as carol services, tobogganing, and many neighborhood skating rinks). Christmas light displays can make for a great activity, too: Simply pile the kids into the car and head to your local display (many towns and cities feature a special light display)—or even take a stroll around your block to check out the neighboring houses.

Depending on the age of your children, you may want to involve them in holiday shopping, too. This is an opportunity to help them practice planning, budgeting, and decision-making skills. Or you could plan for them to enjoy an activity supervised by family or friends, while you head out with your shopping list unencumbered.

One of the best ways to both create a tradition and share your family's goodwill is to help families who might be less fortunate. Involving the kids, in an age-appropriate way, and even having them help make the decision about how you help others, can truly reflect the Christmas spirit. Consider donating time to a toy drive, food bank, or homeless shelter near you. You could also raise funds for a cause that's important to your family, or sponsor a child or family overseas.

Traditions Around the House

One favorite tradition that can take place well ahead of December 25 is writing a letter to Santa. Make it a festive occasion, to help little ones for whom tasks such as writing neatly and spelling correctly are a challenge: Special cookies may be a great incentive. After Christmas, make writing thank-you letters an equally enjoyable time for your children. Smaller children can draw pictures, while older children can print messages on cards or write proper letters. Let them know that the letters don't have to be perfect, but they do need to be sent.

If you're looking for a little quiet time around the house, especially on a busy day such as Christmas Eve, you could try instituting a tradition to match your mood. Try a Christmas-movie afternoon or time together reading Christmas books. Christmas Eve and Christmas Day also make great times to read the Christmas story aloud as a family.

Family traditions include parents! Consider creating a tradition of your own when the kids go to bed on Christmas Eve. If you're not off to midnight Mass, you might want to wrap presents together, or just enjoy a quiet moment in the midst of a sometimes hectic season.

Make your children feel special by including them in kitchen activities. Older children can help with baking and holiday food preparation; younger children will likely enjoy using colored icing to decorate cookies. At the dinner table, try including them in the festive atmosphere by serving them special juices or smoothies.

If you have family members who live too far away to visit at Christmas, make it a tradition to create a special family gift for them: Videotape the children playing, sending greetings, or singing carols, and then create a CD or DVD for them to play on their television set or computer. Software programs can also be used to design and print calendars with family photos for each month.

Welcoming Christmas Company

A full house at Christmas can be a very happy house, but it can also be more chaos than a barrel of monkeys—especially if some of those monkeys are children all keyed up at the prospect of a visit from Santa. A few preparations can make your guests feel welcome and help you cope with the extra people.

Setting the Stage

Whether your guest accommodation is a pull-out sofa bed or a separate bedroom, imagine that you're a guest in your own home. What do you need most, and what will make you feel comfortable, rested, and welcome?

Fresh linens and fluffy towels (with a place to hang them up) are always appreciated, along with extra blankets or pillows, just in case they're needed. A reading lamp beside the bed and a night light in the hall or bathroom can help light the way. Making space in bathrooms and closets also makes a big difference.

Really want to impress your guests? Consider adding bottled water, fresh flowers, a clock radio, books, magazines, or a little welcome basket of extra toiletries to their room. A coffee- or tea-making tray (think hotels and motels) can help guests whose sleep schedules might be different.

If children are among your prospective visitors, make sure you have toys, books, movies, or games on hand: You can buy them inexpensively at secondhand stores if you don't already have a stock of your own. Check ahead of time, too, to see if the children have favorite snacks.

Stress-Reducing Strategies

Being clear and upfront about expectations and schedules is always a good idea. If, for example, you're still heading to work every day, let your company know what your schedule is, so that you'll have that precious bathroom time to yourself in the morning. And also let them know that you don't expect them to be up with you and the larks!

Make sure that you introduce your guests to your home and any of its eccentricities, from keys to alarms to plumbing. To keep everyone safe, make sure that your guests know what your local emergency numbers are (or where they're kept) and any fire escape routes.

Especially if your company is staying longer than just a few days, it's a good idea to plan a few activities that you can enjoy together. Make sure it's something that you want to do, too, so that you're as enthusiastic about the activity as they are. You can also suggest activities or local attractions that they may wish to try on their own: Provide local tourist information and directions as needed.

Holiday Entertaining Made Easy

Whether it's a family gathering or an opportunity to welcome friends or work colleagues into your home during the Christmas season, the holidays are a great excuse for a party. It can be a busy season, though, so consider your timing carefully to make it as easy as possible for people to attend. Send your invitations early, whether they're going via e-mail or regular mail. Give your guests clear information, too, about what to expect, especially if you're doing something unique this year.

Party Ideas for Adults

Gear your party to your audience; you know best whether they'll appreciate Frank Sinatra or Frank Zappa, after all. That being said, the following ideas can be adapted to all ages and interests.

Decorating Party

If you have lots of house to decorate, or if you don't mind exactly what your Christmas tree looks like, considering inviting friends and family for a decorating party. Theme it for the holidays, with carols on the stereo, movies on DVD in case the kids get bored or tired, and plenty of eggnog and hot chocolate.

All for One

Do you have a cause that's near and dear to your heart? Consider hosting an event that raises awareness or funds (or both) for the cause. Let your guests know ahead of time what's happening, and whether they can bring along charitable donations such as food, toys, books, or even money to help out.

Songs for your Christmas party playlist might include: "Jingle Bell Rock" by Bill Haley and the Comets; "2000 Miles" by the Pretenders; "Happy Xmas (War Is Over)" by John Lennon and the Plastic Ono Band; and "Wonderful Christmastime," by Paul McCartney. Look for compilations of carols and classics in the stores, too.

Consider giving small gifts away, or holding a draw for a larger, donated door prize as a thank you to those who've attended. And be sure to offer receipts for tax purposes if your cause is a recognized charity.

Baking Away

Since holiday baking can often be a solitary endeavor, why not welcome company in the kitchen by inviting a few friends over to help? This works especially well if you have a double oven, but even if you don't, you might be able to juggle the cookie baking so that cookies that are quick to prepare get made and into the oven first. Or, stick to cookie recipes that can accommodate fridge or freezer time for the dough: You can all exchange dough and baking instructions and then bake a variety of cookies at home.

If your kitchen is too small to make this practical, consider making your party into a cookie exchange. The guidelines can vary, but one way to handle it is for everyone to bring a dozen cookies for each person—if you have six people, everyone goes home with six-dozen cookies!

Christmas Masquerade

Suggest that guests dress up as characters from famous holiday films and videos. Examples might include George Bailey from *It's a Wonderful Life*, Rudolph, or Frosty the Snowman. Have one person become Santa Claus for the evening and surprise your guests with inexpensive gifts, such as homemade bread or fudge. This could also be a good way to distribute Christmas favors to everybody in attendance.

Game On!

Charades might be an old chestnut, but it's great fun when you use elements that fit the season. Try Christmas movies; traditional Christmas figures such as Santa Claus, the Little Drummer Boy, or the reindeer; and the names of Christmas songs.

Another classic Christmas-party idea involves a memory game based on the song "The Twelve Days of Christmas." Gather the players into a circle; let each person review the lyrics for a few moments, and appoint one person as judge. The judge takes the lyrics and selects a person to start the song, beginning with the first day. From memory, each player must sing a single day—and all the days that preceded it! If you miss a day (or, depending on the harshness of the judge, if you hesitate unduly), you must leave the circle. The judge then reads the correct lyric for the remaining players. When the circle has been reduced to two players, the judge gives each the twelfth day. If both can recite it, the game ends in a tie. Otherwise, the person who gets furthest through the longest and most difficult day wins the game.

Secret Santa

Christmas is the season of giving (and receiving), so how about a Secret Santa gift exchange as a theme for your party? You can adjust the amount of money to be spent according to the income of the guests, but $10–$15 is usually a good maximum amount to spend on a gift.

Secret Santa can be done in a variety of ways, but the easiest is probably to have everyone bring a wrapped gift that will be good for either gender, then draw numbers at the party (number 1 picks a gift first). Or, if you know for certain who is coming, put all the names in a hat and match people up so that everyone has a special Secret Santa.

Party Ideas for Children

If you're looking for a good way to keep children occupied during those long days before the holiday, why not throw a Christmas party? Try a few of the following ideas for your festive gathering.

Banner Afternoon

Find a large roll of paper and roll it out across the floor. Assign each child an area and the tools to decorate, and have the group make a giant holiday banner for a children's hospital, nursing home, or other charitable institution.

Buy card and craft supplies and have the children make Christmas cards for parents or brothers and sisters. Not only does it keep children happily and creatively occupied, it's also a lovely surprise when parents come to pick up children from the party.

Festive Game Twists

Play a holiday version of "Pin the Tail on the Donkey" with "Pin the Nose on Rudolph" or "Pin the Star on the Tree." Just set up the appropriate poster, and place adhesive tape on the object the child tries to affix to it. Children can also play the old game of "Duck, duck, goose," as "Rudolph, Rudolph, reindeer."

"Rudolph in the Middle" is another fun game: Children form a circle with one child in the middle. The children hold hands and walk in a circle, singing "Rudolph the Red-Nosed Reindeer." On the word "glows," the children all drop to the floor. The child in the middle must tag someone on the outside before they sit down; if she succeeds, the tagged player goes to the middle.

These games easily lead into an all-time favorite: musical chairs, played with Christmas songs such as "Jingle Bells," "Santa Claus Is Coming to Town," or other

Christmas songs. When playing with very young children, have the number of chairs equal the number of children, so that nobody feels left out; for older children, it ups the fun factor to take away the chairs.

Stocking Stuffers

To borrow from another holiday, entertain with the "Christmas Stocking Hunt." Fill many small stockings with various candies, nuts, crayons, gum, or other small items and then create a Christmas version of an Easter egg hunt, with stockings hidden in various out-of-the way spots around the house.

The "Stocking Puzzle Game" is another great party activity for children. Using magazines, cut out pictures of toys and trinkets that would be appropriate to put in a stocking. Tape the pictures to cardboard, then cut the cardboard into irregular shapes like a puzzle. Put each puzzle into an envelope and put the envelopes into stockings. (Depending upon the size of the puzzle, you may wish to put more than one in each stocking.) Give each child a stocking and have them complete the puzzles; the one who finishes first gets to pick the first simple prize from a big stocking. (Have plenty of trinkets on hand—you don't want to leave a player unhappy!)

Quiet Time

For a quiet interlude or as a prelude to an afternoon nap, gather the children around for story time. Pick out a favorite Christmas reading that's both age and culture appropriate, and share some holiday fun.

Take the Stress Out of Christmas

It's so tempting to try to fit everything into the Christmas season: entertaining, quality time with family, concerts, decorating, baking, sending cards—it's no wonder that anticipation for the season can be tinged with a little trepidation, too. It can be a stressful time, simply because it's so busy, or because it reminds you of friends and family who can't be with you.

Think of what might be major stressors for you over the holiday season, and try to head them off well before the holiday approaches. Above all, remember that the Christmas season is about goodwill, togetherness, and hope. It's not about being everything to everyone, and it's not about perfection. Try these tips to help you cope.

Gift Giving

Gifts can be tricky things. We all love to give and receive over the holidays, but it's easy to go overboard or to feel overwhelmed at the sheer number of gifts that need to be purchased. If this is your situation, talk to friends and family members about changing the way that you approach gifts this year.

If you have a talent for arts or crafts—beadwork, jewelry, scrapbooking, painting, picture framing, carpentry, stained glass, knitting, embroidery, sewing, or metalwork, for example—home-made gifts may be part of the answer. Start well ahead of time, however, to avoid putting too much stress on yourself close to Christmas.

Options include setting price limits on gifts; buying only for the children in your extended family, rather than everyone; drawing names within a circle of friends or family to buy a gift for one person, rather than for everyone; and even agreeing to go out for a holiday meal (perhaps in January, when everyone needs a pick-me-up) in lieu of buying gifts. You can also suggest making contributions to charity instead of giving gifts.

Christmas morning can come way too early for many parents of young children. Keep them occupied first thing by letting them open their stockings while still in bed, as long as they know that the presents under the tree have to stay unmolested until you get up!

Shopping Strategies

Shop like Santa: Make a list and check it twice. If you start with a list and a budget, you can easily see how your budget divides between each person. To make things easier for yourself, choose the same kind of gift for certain people (e.g., teachers, letter carriers, etc.): gift cards to local coffee shops, for example, or small baskets from gourmet food stores.

Check store flyers, the Internet, and catalogs for ideas and prices so you can narrow down what you're looking for and figure out what's good value (and what's not). Once you're ready to shop, check that you have your list in hand, comfy shoes on your feet, and a place to take a break when you get tired. Shop the malls early in the day to beat the crowds, and stick to your list.

The same goes for grocery shopping: Make a list, double check it, and then hit the supermarket while it's still quiet. If it's faster for you to shop alone, make sure that you ask someone at home to be there when you return to help you unload.

Add batteries to your list, for toys, cameras, and other holiday items. And, if it's possible that people might present you with gifts that you're not expecting, add a couple of versatile "just-in-case" items that you can gift wrap. Gourmet food or chocolates work well for both men and women, and if you don't use them as gifts, you can enjoy them yourself in January!

Reduce Your Load

Do you really need to send cards to everyone on your list? Or invite twenty people to an elaborate holiday party? Take a look at what you expect of yourself during the holidays, and consider either cutting down on the volume or cutting certain items out completely.

For example, why not decorate only one room—say, the living room where the tree will be placed? And rather than spending a full day balancing on a ladder outside the house as you string lights, try using ground-based floodlights that make a small holiday display shine.

Don't be afraid to say no. After all, no one in your home will fully enjoy Christmas if you're exhausted. In the same vein, learn to delegate tasks that you don't need to do yourself. Every member of the family should be helping out, as age and abilities allow.

Be in the Moment

Whether you have your hands deep in cookie dough or tied up in ribbons and tape, try to enjoy the sensations of the moment, remembering what the Christmas season is all about. Do whatever's needed to maintain as much peace and joy as you can: Take breaks (short walks can be a great stress reliever); avoid overindulging in either food or alcohol (it just makes the stress worse in the end); and don't forget to breathe deeply (short, shallow breaths increase your stress levels).

Keep Christmas Safe

As thoughts turn to Christmas trees and holiday cheer, taking a few quick and simple precautions can keep your home and family happy through the holidays. When it comes to decorating, home security or entertaining, making health and safety a priority will help keep Christmas as stress-free as possible.

Decorating

To reduce fire risk, keep natural Christmas trees very well watered. Make a fresh diagonal cut on the bottom of the trunk before placing it in a sturdy holder, so that the tree doesn't seal itself and prevent the uptake of water. Check the holder's water level daily, and keep the tree away from sources of heat. Tether it, if necessary, to avoid pets and children knocking or pulling it over.

Check the manufacturer's recommendations for artificial trees. Some shouldn't be used with strings of electric lights because of a shock hazard. Test your smoke detectors monthly (especially just before houseguests arrive for Christmas) to make sure everything's working properly.

Check your lights for damaged cords or broken bulbs before you string them up. Replace damaged or burned-out bulbs promptly; too many broken ones can cause the others to overheat. Never leave a bulb socket empty. Use clips rather than staples to put up the outdoor lights, as the staples can penetrate the cord, causing a shock and potential fire.

All electrical components, including extension cords, should have the Underwriters Laboratory (UL) or Canadian Standards Association (CSA) label of approval, to ensure that they've been tested for safety. Do your part, and use them for their original purpose: Indoor cords and lights aren't sturdy enough for outdoor use, while outdoor lights may burn too warmly for indoor use.

Be careful when decorating stair railings, indoors and out. Make sure that garlands and other trimmings don't prevent people from getting a good grasp on the railing.

Breakable or potentially toxic tree decorations should be kept out of the reach of children and pets. Poinsettias aren't considered toxic plants, but holly and mistletoe are. For a complete list, call your local Poison Control Center, or check its Web site.

Never leave lit candles and fireplaces unattended, and closely supervise children and pets in such areas. A sturdy fireguard can be used to keep little ones from getting too close to the fireplace.

Security

It's a busy time for everyone at Christmas, and unfortunately that includes thieves. Keep houses and vehicles locked, garage doors closed, and valuables out of sight. Entrances should be well lit, and bushes shouldn't obscure windows (otherwise, thieves can use them to hide behind while they gain access to your home).

If you're going on vacation, take normal precautions: Light timers should be variable to have the best effect; driveways should be kept shoveled; and mail or newspaper delivery should be either stopped or picked up daily by a neighbor.

Be careful, too, when shopping. Busy shopping malls can offer opportunities for pickpockets and purse "dippers." Put presents in car trunks, or at least cover them so that passersby can't see that there's anything inside your vehicle to steal. Avoid transferring packages into your trunk and then going into a building: If someone's watching the parking lot, you've just let them know there's something potentially valuable in the trunk.

Entertaining

Avoid the dangers of food poisoning by observing cooking times and temperatures carefully, especially with turkey and stuffing. Be especially careful if you or someone you know has food allergies, particularly to nuts, which are used in many holiday foods.

Keep candies and nuts out of the way of small children, who might choke on them, and keep alcohol out of their reach, too. And if you're enjoying a little Christmas cheer, designate a sober driver: Never drink and drive, and never let anyone else drive while under the influence, either.

14

Decking the Halls

No matter where you live, whether you celebrate Christmas where there's snow on the hills or waves on the beaches, the holiday season just wouldn't feel right without certain decorations. There are some that families pass down between generations, and others that tempt you in the stores (soon to become your own heirlooms)—but they all seem to say "Christmas is really here" when you open up the boxes. Here are some more ideas for decorating the house, inside and out.

Light Up Christmas

Christmas lights have come a long, long way since the first string of electric lights was introduced for sale in 1903 (they hit the White House Christmas tree a little earlier, in 1895). Today, there are lights for indoors and out, lights that wink and blink, and lights that loop from roofs and drape in nets over bushes. One of the best innovations is also one of the most recent: LED lights. LED is short for light-emitting-diode, but what you really need to know is that they consume less than 10 percent of the electricity that conventional lights use: This is great news for both utility bills and the environment. Plus, they look great and tend to burn cooler than conventional bulbs, which makes them less of a fire risk.

Lights come in a stunning array of styles from traditional, classic, white mini-lights to strings of big multicolored bulbs to garlands of red-hot chili peppers to color-changing floodlights. There's definitely a style to fit your taste! To make hanging them easier, there are also all kinds of clips for windows, gutters, brickwork, and more.

Just remember to plan your lights carefully. If you need to use extension cords, make sure that they're in good shape, and that they're as short as possible. Don't run them under carpets or leave them where they could be a tripping hazard. Also check to make sure they're rated properly for where you're using them (don't use indoor cords outdoors, for example). Ensure that you don't overload any electrical circuits by plugging in too many strands of lights at the same time.

Detangling Christmas lights has to be one of the season's most finicky jobs. It's best if you have some room to work, so that you can lay lights out on a tabletop or the floor—you can then see where the tangles are and work them loose. When you put the lights away this year, wrap them around a sturdy piece of cardboard or a store-bought light holder to keep them from tangling up with themselves or other cords.

The best time to check the lights is before you hang them. Plug them in to see if they're working, make sure that the bulbs and the electrical wires between them are in good condition, and replace any burned-out bulbs. Then, if it's time to get the ladder out, be safe: Position the ladder carefully; have someone hold it for you; and don't over-reach (move the ladder instead).

The Christmas Tree

Whether you buy your tree from a roadside stand or store lot, trek to your own private grove to chop one down yourself, or unwrap it from a box purchased at a department store, you'll want to pick one that's right for your living space. Measure the floor-to-ceiling dimension before you select a tree, and be sure to leave a good bit of room at the top for the angel, star, or other tree-top ornament.

Assuming yours is a live tree, you should cut the base of the tree's trunk on a diagonal angle once you get it home, and immediately place it in water. If it's cold, the branches are likely quite tightly tucked against the trunk: Let the branches drop for a few hours, preferably overnight, by standing the tree inside the house (in water) before you try decorating it.

Look for a sturdy tree stand that will help steady the tree and provide a good water reservoir, to reduce the amount of watering you have to do. Some natural trees now come with a plastic bag that helps protect them on the journey to your house. Once the tree is up, slide the plastic bag down and leave it on the floor under the tree (it's also a good idea to put a layer of newspapers or other protective surface between the tree stand and the floor). When it's time to take the tree down, you can simply slide the plastic bag back up over the tree, catching most of the stray needles before they bury themselves in your carpet.

Once the tree is up and its branches have dropped, you can decorate to your heart's content, with Christmas-tree skirts, lights, garlands, and more. Indulge in a favorite theme or just decorate as your whims take you.

All Around the House

In many houses, the Christmas tree is the focal point of the decorations, but it's certainly not alone. Depending on your decorating style, available time, and budget, you can decorate the whole house, a single room, or just the main living area. You can even theme the areas, with a child-friendly style in the playroom, for example, and a more sophisticated look in the living room.

Sometimes it's the littlest touches that make a big difference. You could, for example, tie up cinnamon sticks with a holiday bow and place them on the stovetop or on the mantel. Their fragrance is lovely, and the look is one of old-fashioned charm.

Virtually every surface of the home has potential for decorating. Your usual wall art can be switched with special art that you only display at Christmas; you can add garland swags to stair rails and mantels; even china, glassware, and cutlery can be switched for festive fare. Nativity scenes and Christmas villages can be added to each year (which makes for a great gift idea, too).

Cards, of course, can be placed on tables and shelves, but they can also form part of the décor: Try hanging them by their folds over a piece of string that's pinned to a wall or ceiling (choose a place that won't show the pinhole when the cards come down). Cards can also be taped one beneath the other, with the top card pinned or taped to the wall, to create a cascade of cards down the wall.

Candles are always welcome at the holidays, but do keep safety in mind. Never put them where they could catch an item such as curtains alight, and never leave them unattended. They look very welcoming in windows, but it's best to use battery-operated electric candles there: The effect is almost the same, but it's much safer.

Keep in mind that less can be more when it comes to decorating. If you feel like indulging your inner Christmas diva, then go for it, but don't be afraid to stick with something simple. Remember: This is all about what makes you happiest when you step inside your home.

Take Christmas Outside

Thanks to the availability of lighted outdoor ornaments—life-sized, head-nodding deer, inflatable snowmen and Santas—you can easily turn your yard into the Christmas grotto of your dreams. Or, you could stick with something simple and classic: Either way, planning is essential, especially if you live in a cold climate where December will have you freezing your fingers as you try to manage clips and lights that are brittle with the cold.

If you're stringing lights, it really is best to get them up when you have a spell of decent weather. You don't have to turn them on right away; just get them up while you can still climb a ladder in relative comfort. Other items, such as lawn ornaments, are easier to add later, whatever the weather.

If ladders and lights don't appeal to you, don't feel obligated by the season to string up those house lights. Green garlands and red bows—even a single, huge red bow wrapped around the trunk of a big tree in your front yard—can make just as pretty an outdoor package for the season. Another idea to try includes wrapping doors and mailboxes with Christmas paper or fabric and ribbons so they look like gifts (without, of course, interfering with the operation of whatever it is that you've wrapped).

Consider the security of your outdoor decorations, especially if they might be easy—and appealing—to steal (stranger things have happened, unfortunately). If you can fasten them some-how, that would be best; otherwise, consider the display's value. If it has great sentimental value and you can't secure it, you may want to think twice about putting it out front.

Natural Trimmings

Shopping in your own backyard is one opportunity for great Christmas decorations. From evergreen branches and cones to berries and the seedpods of architectural plants such as purple coneflower and poppies, there's a hidden wealth of décor ideas out there to decorate windowsills, fireplace mantels, or other appropriate places in your home.

If your garden won't provide what you need, check out other sources: Christmas-tree lots often sell branches and boughs, while craft stores may offer holly, cones, and even dried berries. Be very cautious about gathering items from parks or wild areas: Removing natural items from many areas is prohibited, so check and follow the rules—and never disturb anyone's private property.

If your evergreens have been outside in freezing tempera-tures, give them at least overnight to warm up before you start working with them. Be sure to wear old clothes while handling them—their sticky resin comes off your hands readily with soap and water, but it can stain clothes.

Stock up on that traditional Christmas plant, the poinsettia, in the shades that you love most: bright red, pink, and even white. Place them anywhere or everywhere! Try using the rule of threes for best effect: Grouping three plants together rather than positioning them by themselves can create an impressive display. And don't forget a sprig of mistletoe in a handy doorway (this might be a good time to go artificial, however, as natural mistletoe can be quite challenging to obtain).

Drying Fruit Slices

Drying slices of fruit, such as apples, lemons, and oranges, fills your home with a seasonal scent and leaves you with long-lasting ornaments for decorating wreaths, swags, and other natural arrangements. Cut fruit into slices about one-quarter-inch thick, and bake in a single layer at 300°F for about six hours: Watch carefully, to ensure they don't crisp up.

Sugaring Fruit

Sugaring fruit lends a translucent quality to the brilliant reds, golds, and greens of apples, lemons, oranges, and other brightly colored fruits, making them a lovely addition to wreaths and centerpiece arrangements. Either dip the whole fruit into, or brush them with, a lightly beaten egg white, then roll in fine sugar and let dry.

Remember safety: Uncooked egg white can carry salmonella, so wash your hands and utensils well. As with other natural materials, including berries, keep your decorations out of reach of pets and children—and keep in mind that this fruit can't be eaten later.

Evergreen Chair Swag

Any surface is game for decorating, even the backs of dining room or kitchen chairs! To make an evergreen swag, tie a couple of cedar boughs together at one end (it often looks best if the boughs reach from the top of the chair back to the chair seat). Tie a ribbon around that end, leaving enough ribbon to tie the swag to the chair back. Tie another length of ribbon in the same place, to create a big bow, and use glue or wire to add cones, fruit slices, berries, or cinnamon sticks just below the ribbon.

Yule Log Centerpiece

All you need for this fast, easy centerpiece is a small log (a piece of firewood with its bark still on might be just the ticket, but because of the glue, don't burn it later) and some decorations: greenery, cones, berries, fruit slices, or cinnamon sticks. Start by gluing the greenery to the log. Different textures and shades of green look great together, while holly berries add lovely color. Then glue cones, fruit, or cinnamon sticks in place: You're done!

Home Decorating Ideas—Step by Step

Home decorating doesn't have to cost a fortune. Depending on the time you have available, you can make lovely seasonal trimmings and fun, child-friendly decorations without breaking the bank. Here are a few ideas to get you started.

Christmas Piñata

It takes a little work—and some cleanup time—but your children might enjoy taking whacks at a real piñata for the holidays, in keeping with Spanish tradition. This comes with a warning, however: This isn't a Christmas Eve craft; start early, as the papier-mâché piñata must dry for several days!

To make the piñata (try a donkey or a reindeer), combine one-third of a cup of flour with one-quarter of a cup of water; transfer the mixture to a plastic bag and knead it to make paste; then transfer it to a large bowl. Blow up a balloon and dip strips of newspaper into the paste and use them to cover the balloon.

Roll some newspaper into a tight ball to form the donkey's head, and tape it to the balloon. Cover the head with paper dipped in paste. For ears, use cardboard from an egg carton or a box. Tape them on the head and cover them with paper dipped in paste. Use four toilet-paper rolls for legs using the same method and tape them to the body.

Let the piñata dry for two days. With poster paints, paint with bright colors, adding eyes, mouth, and other elements to the head; let dry. Once it's dry, gently cut a small hole in the top of the body section (you'll pop the balloon in the process) and drop-in candy, gum, party favors, and other treats. Use string or yarn to hang the piñata from the ceiling.

Fabric Gift Wrap

Using inexpensive fabric instead of paper for gift wrapping not only saves you money (look for fun Christmas prints to go on sale starting with Boxing Day), it's also good for the environment: Fabric gift wrap and bags can be used again and again, reducing the amount of paper going into landfills.

You can get very fancy with fabric, but you don't need to, especially if you'd like to avoid sewing. Instead, use pinking shears (scissors with a jagged edge) to create a cut edge on the fabric that won't need to be sewn. Wrap the gift and secure the fabric with ribbon (a little tape can help hold the fabric in place).

To make bags, fold the right sides of an appropriately sized piece of fabric together and sew along three edges, leaving one side open to create the top of the bag. Turn right side out, hem the opening (or use pinking shears), and tie with ribbon.

Festive Pomanders

Cloves, cinnamon, oranges . . . all the scents that say, "It must be Christmastime." While traditional pomanders were entirely covered with cloves, your fingers and your schedule will be thankful to discover that covering the entire fruit is not necessary for impressive results—you can also try covering only part of the fruit, creating patterns instead.

You'll need one fresh, unblemished piece of citrus fruit (such as an orange, lemon, or lime) and approximately one ounce of whole cloves, plus a nut pick and enough ribbon to wrap around the fruit twice and form a hanging loop.

Start by running the ribbon around the fruit horizontally and then vertically, then hold the ribbon ends together at the top with a straight pin or two. Insert the cloves into the fruit in the areas not covered by the ribbon (use the nut pick to create holes for the cloves if it's easier this way). Using a glue gun, fasten the ribbon on the top, adding a hanging loop and, if desired, dried flowers and a bow.

Glass-Ball Ornaments

Why not decorate glass balls to hang on your tree or elsewhere in your home? Clear glass ornaments can be bought in craft stores, and they leave lots of room for personal touches. You can remove the top from the ball and fill it with potpourri, sparkles, dried flowers, or a mixture of all three. Put the top back on and tie with a colored ribbon or lace. You can also paint the glass with acrylic paint or use glue to write a name in fancy script and then sprinkle glitter over the glue.

To make the ball even more special, put a small favorite memento or a picture of a loved one inside. Making personalized glass balls for a child's first Christmas—and successive ones—is also a nice idea.

Homemade Garlands

Looking for an easy, fun way to spruce up your tree? Make a garland. All you need is a long piece of string, yarn, or twine, a needle, a kitchen, and your imagination. The classic, of course, is the popcorn-and-cranberry version, but garlands can be made out of anything: candy, raisins, or dried dates alternated with buttons or colored squares of construction paper. Kids love to help, but watch those needles! Best to select large, dull ones, and to monitor children closely during this activity.

Homemade Wrapping Paper

Making homemade wrapping paper is another fun—and inexpensive—decorating activity. You will need: one large roll of brown or white paper; crayons; markers; paint; pictures cut from magazines; glue; glitter; lace; ribbons; and anything else you think might look good as wrapping! Roll out some paper, then cut in appropriate-size sheets to wrap specific gifts.

Try to personalize your sheets; if the person who is to receive the gift is a sports enthusiast, for instance, adorn the wrapping paper with images clipped from *Sports Illustrated*. It's best to carefully glue the decorations and let the paper dry rather than using transparent tape. Customized wrapping, when prepared carefully, adds an unforgettable personal touch to gift giving.

Wreaths

Wreaths are very easy to build using a variety of frames, and they present virtually limitless possibilities when it comes to decorating. If you have Virginia creeper, willow, or grapevine available, you can weave the strands together in various shapes to make a wreath frame. You can also buy frames like these at craft stores, along with those made from wire and Styrofoam.

For an evergreen wreath, tie small branches of evergreen to the frame with wire, building around the wreath until it's as full as desired. Decorate with berries, pinecones, or a simple ribbon. You can also create wreaths using evergreen cones instead of branches.

Fabric works well, too. The simplest designs might involve wrapping ribbon or fabric strips around a Styrofoam wreath form. Or, cut out thin strips of material (try 1½" wide and 4" long) using pinking shears. Using a knitting needle, force the center of the material into a Styrofoam form: It will take quite a long time to fill the form, but the effect is nicely three-dimensional.

You might also want to try wreaths that feature dried and polished (lacquered) fruit and nuts; just fruit; just nuts; candy; cotton balls; dried flowers; berries; holly; bows; or any combination of these.

Christmas Crafts for Children

Children remember Christmas as a time filled with special activities and unexpected treats. Working on holiday craft projects will give kids something to remember—and make your house look bright and festive.

Since safety can't be stressed enough, here's another reminder to always carefully monitor crafts activities involving children and scissors. Safety scissors for all of the following activities are a must, and so is supervision.

Clothespin Ornaments

Clothespin decorations, made from long, thin, wooden clothespins with a knob on top, are always a hit on Christmas trees, and can be great fun for kids who want to make something for the holidays. Using pipe cleaners, red and green felt, cotton balls, paint, glue, and glitter, they can let their imaginations run wild. Try making reindeer, toy soldiers, and even Santa.

Construction-Paper Snowflake

The snowflake has a long and distinguished history in many families, and it's colorful and very easy to make. Just fold colored construction paper into quarters (or more times, depending on how intricate you want the snowflake) and cut little designs in the paper along the folds and edges. Loop a string through one of the holes and hang. (You can also tape the flakes to a poster or wall; they're beautiful on their own, too.)

Construction-Paper Stockings

These are a timeless classic, and all you need is: red construction paper; green felt; cotton balls; gold and silver glitter; glue; and scissors. Cut a stocking shape out of red construction paper. Brush some glue on the top portion of the stocking and paste down cotton balls, to give the impression of fur trim. Spread glue elsewhere on the stocking and decorate with glitter and felt as desired. Use a paper punch to poke a hole in the top of the ornament. Children can cut out names from different-colored paper or write them on with markers. String with yarn or ribbon to hang.

Construction-Paper Christmas Trees

To add to the snowflakes on the wall, many children like to make these green trees. You will need: green construction paper; glue; markers, felt; and small decorative items as desired. To make the shape, cut a green tree shape of the desired size from the construction paper. (Or cut three triangles—big, bigger, biggest—and show the child how to glue them, overlapping each to make a tree.) Decorate using felt and any other goodies you have handy.

Egg-Carton or Paper-Cup Ornaments

These are simple, but fun. Cut the individual compartments out of a paper egg carton, making a small hole at the top. (You'll thread this hole with string later on when it's time to hang the ornament.) Using markers, color the compartments. Some popular themes include faces, snowflakes, and stars. It's also fun to hang a little bell inside with ribbon or thread.

You can make similar crafts using paper cups: Since you have a larger area to work with, you can glue pictures cut out of old Christmas cards or magazines, or even fabric, to the cup.

Holiday Placemats

All you need are large pieces of white, red, or green construction paper, markers or crayons, stickers, and any other decorating goodies. Have children draw a large circle in the center of the paper to mark where the plate should go. Draw a smaller circle for a glass, and outlines of forks, spoons, and knives. Decorate the paper as desired until you have a set of festive placemats for your table.

You can then take the placemats to your local office supply store, many of which have laminating machines that will handle this size of paper. Laminating isn't necessary, but it does protect your child's handiwork from table spills.

Homemade Christmas Cards

These add a personal touch to the traditional exchange of cards. Depending on whether the card is from the family or from the child, you will need: white, red, or green construction paper; crayons or markers; pictures cut from magazines or old Christmas cards; family photos; and all the regular decorating goodies. Fold the paper in half and decorate both the outside and inside, leaving enough space to write a Christmas message.

If you're sending these cards through the mail, it's a good idea to use store-bought envelopes, to ensure that the postal service's sorting machines don't reject them. And keep in mind that they'll likely require extra postage if they're larger or heavier than regular cards.

Homemade envelopes can be made by using larger pieces of construction paper, folded and stapled or taped together on the sides. Decorate the envelopes with glitter, or use markers to make some Christmas designs.

Homemade Clay Ornaments

These can be a lot of fun, although they do involve some stovetop work—you can make things easier with store-bought clay if needed (skip ahead to the decorating part, and follow package instructions for baking).

To make your own clay, mix together three cups of cornstarch and six cups of baking soda in a big pan. Mix well; add three and three-quarters cups of water. Cook over low heat, stirring constantly, until the mixture is the consistency of mashed potatoes. Remove from the heat and cover with a damp dish towel. When cool, remove the clay from the pan and knead it until smooth. Cover a tabletop with waxed paper taped securely to the underside of the table. Roll the clay to a one-quarter-inch thickness.

Cut out shapes with Christmas-theme cookie cutters. When the shapes are completed, use a knitting needle or unsharpened pencil to poke a small hole in the top of the ornament; it should be big enough to fit yarn through. Mix acrylic paint with a little water and let the children paint their ornaments. Be sure to let them dry thoroughly! Once the ornaments are hard enough, you may want to date each one and write the name of the artist on the back: These pieces tend to become heirlooms.

Macaroni Ornaments

Another classic! Cut a wreath shape out of heavy paper or cardboard. Decorate with different pieces of uncooked macaroni, gluing them down in desired spots. For variety, use a number of different kinds of macaroni. When the glue is completely dry, spray the ornament with gold paint (probably a grownup job).

Use a paper punch to poke a hole in the top of the ornament and string with yarn to hang. You can customize this technique to make macaroni stockings, candy canes, trees, or whatever else you desire.

Paper-Plate Santas

The paper-plate Santa is another holiday favorite. You will need: red construction paper; a paper plate; cotton balls; colored markers or crayons; glue; and scissors. On the paper plate, draw Santa's eyes, nose, and mouth using markers or crayons. Brush some glue above his eyes and around his mouth, and paste down cotton balls to make bushy eyebrows and a beard. Cut a triangle out of red construction paper for Santa's hat. Glue the hat to the top of the drawing; then glue one cotton ball to the tip of the hat. Let dry.

Paper-Plate Wreath

Staying with the paper-plate theme, you'll need: a paper plate; crayons; other decorating goodies of your choice, such as small pieces of felt, buttons, glitter, confetti, or fabric scraps; and scissors. Cut out the center of the paper plate so that the rim creates a wreath. Color with crayons, glue bits of holiday magic to the wreath, and then hang in a place of honor.

Pinecone Ornaments

These ornaments have decorated many a tree year after year, showcasing the craft skills of family members when they were still quite young! One method is to pour a small amount of glue onto a paper plate. Roll the pinecone around in the glue, then sprinkle the cone with colored glitter and let dry. Use a pipe cleaner to create a loop or hook for hanging.

You can also glue a piece of ribbon to the base of the cone, and add little decorations such as tiny presents (available at craft stores), small pieces of evergreens, or bows. The cone itself can be left natural, or can be sprayed with artificial snow or paint.

Santa Mobile

Older children can make this colorful mobile to help younger siblings join in on the Christmas spirit. You will need: small Styrofoam balls; paper plates; black, yellow, and red construction paper; dental floss or yarn; cotton balls; glue; markers; and silver paper. Cut Santa's boots and hat out of construction paper, then cut a strip of black paper for the belt and a small square of yellow for the buckle. Draw or paint his eyes, nose, and mouth on a Styrofoam ball, then glue on his hat. Glue cotton balls to the tip and brim of the hat. Paint or color the paper plate red and glue on the paper belt and buckle.

Thread a large needle with dental floss (an adult job) and poke it through the top of the Styrofoam head and out the neck, tying a loop at the top of Santa's head. Tape the other end of the dental floss to the back of the paper plate to join the head and body, then connect the boots to the plate by taping floss to the back of each boot and the back of the plate. Hang from the loop at the top. (You can also substitute a smaller paper plate for Santa's head if necessary.)

15
Christmas Recipes

ood is central to the celebration of the Christmas holiday—it's part of every culture's traditions, setting the scene for gatherings of friends and family. Since holiday baking occupies many families' Christmas preparations, that's what's included here—along with some lip-smackingly good beverages to enjoy with the breads, cookies, and other assorted goodies. (And don't forget that many of these recipes, packaged in a Christmas basket or cookie tin, would make delicious gifts that are sure to be appreciated.) Bon appétit!

Apple Crisp

Topping:

3 tablespoons chilled butter
½ cup firmly packed brown
  sugar
⅓ cup all-purpose flour

Filling:

½ teaspoon nutmeg
½ teaspoon ground cinnamon
¼ cup water
2 tablespoons granulated
  sugar
4 cups apples, peeled, cored,
  and thinly sliced

*Exquisite on a cold December morning
with a good cup of coffee!*

1. To make the topping: In a medium bowl, use a pastry blender or 2 knives and mix together brown sugar, flour, and butter until coarse crumbs form.

2. For the filling: Preheat oven to 375°F.

3. Grease a 9" pie pan.

4. Place apples in prepared pan.

5. Mix together sugar, nutmeg, cinnamon, and water. Toss apples with sugar mixture.

6. Sprinkle topping over filling.

7. Cook until top is golden brown and crispy, approximately 30 minutes.

Applesauce Loaf

If you've never tried this, you're in for a special holiday treat.

1. Preheat oven to 350°F. Grease and flour a 9" × 5" loaf pan.

2. In a medium bowl, cream butter and sugar together until light and fluffy.

3. Beat in eggs.

4. In another bowl, mix together flour, baking soda, cinnamon, nutmeg, salt, and cloves. Gradually beat flour mixture into butter mixture.

5. Beat in applesauce.

6. Stir in raisins and nuts.

7. Pour batter into prepared pan.

8. Bake loaf for 1 hour, or until a toothpick inserted into the center comes out clean. Transfer pan to wire rack. Cool for 10 minutes. Remove loaf from pan and cool completely.

9. Dust with confectioners' sugar.

1 cup granulated sugar
½ cup butter, softened
1 large egg, room temperature
1½ cups all-purpose flour
1½ teaspoons baking soda
1 teaspoon ground cinnamon
¾ teaspoon nutmeg
½ teaspoon salt
½ teaspoon ground cloves
1½ cups unsweetened
  applesauce
½ cup dark raisins
½ cup coarsely chopped
  walnuts (optional)
Confectioners' sugar
  (for dusting)

Blueberry Bread

1 cup fresh (or thawed frozen)
  blueberries
1½ cups all-purpose flour
1 tablespoon flour
½ cup granulated sugar
⅔ cup milk
1 egg
1 heaping teaspoon baking
  powder

*Try this with a good cup of coffee on Christmas morning.
You'll get a great start on the big day—
and you'll probably be back for seconds.*

1. Preheat oven to 375°F. Grease and flour a 9" × 5" loaf pan.

2. Sift the dry ingredients together (leaving aside 1 tablespoon flour).

3. In a separate bowl, stir together the egg and milk.

4. Make a well in the center of the dry ingredients. Add milk mixture to the well all at once, tossing with a fork until just moistened.

5. Toss blueberries in 1 tablespoon flour. Add blueberries to batter.

6. Spoon batter into prepared pan.

7. Bake until a toothpick inserted into the center comes out clean, approximately 30 minutes.

8. Transfer to wire rack; let cool.

Cranberry Bread

A wholesome and delicious holiday treat—
and easy to make, too!

1. Preheat oven to 350°F. Grease a 9" × 5" loaf pan.

2. Sift together flour, sugar, baking powder, baking soda, and salt.

3. Using a pastry blender or 2 knives held together, cut in shortening until coarse crumbs form.

4. In a separate bowl, combine orange juice, orange peel, and eggs.

5. Make a well in the center of the dry ingredients. Add egg mixture all at once, tossing with a fork until just moistened.

6. Stir in the nuts and cranberries. Spread batter in prepared pan. Bake until a toothpick inserted in the center comes out clean, approximately 1 hour.

7. Remove bread from pan; cool completely.

2 cups all-purpose flour
1 cup granulated sugar
1½ teaspoons baking powder
½ teaspoon baking soda
1 teaspoon salt
1 cup fresh or frozen cranberries, chopped into halves
¼ cup shortening
½ cup orange juice
1 teaspoon grated orange peel
1 large egg, lightly beaten
½ cup chopped walnuts
(optional)

Cranberry Scones

1 cup dairy sour cream

1½ teaspoons grated fresh orange peel

2 cups all-purpose flour, sifted

½ cup granulated sugar

2 teaspoons baking powder

½ teaspoon baking soda

½ teaspoon salt

¼ cup butter or margarine, softened

1 large egg, at room temperature

¼ cup dried cranberries

Give these accompanied by a special jar of your favorite jam or jelly.

1. Preheat oven to 375°F.

2. In a small bowl, combine sour cream and grated orange peel. Set aside.

3. In a large bowl, mix together the flour, baking powder, granulated sugar, and salt.

4. Using a pastry blender or 2 knives held together, cut butter into the flour mixture until coarse crumbs form.

5. Break the egg in a small dish and beat well with a fork. Add the egg to the flour mixture and beat together until blended.

6. Add the sour cream and orange-peel mixture and heat until just well blended.

7. Prepare a smooth surface (the kitchen counter is fine) by sprinkling it lightly with flour. Turn the dough out of the bowl. Using floured hands, knead the dough for about 30 seconds, or until smooth.

8. Taking only half the dough at a time, roll it out with a floured rolling pin until it is about ½" thick. Using a 3" round cookie cutter, or even the opening to a similarly sized empty can, cut out rounds of dough.

9. Place the rounds 1" apart on a greased or nonstick cookie sheet. Before putting them in the oven, push 5 dried cranberries into the top of each one.

10. Bake until the tops are just barely browned, 12–18 minutes.

11. Let cool on wire racks. Makes 1 dozen scones.

German Coffee Cake

A classic favorite.

1. Preheat oven to 350°F. Grease a 9" × 13" baking pan.

2. In a large mixing bowl, cream together margarine and sugar.

3. Add eggs, sour cream, baking soda, and vanilla.

4. Beat in flour and baking powder. Stir in nuts.

5. Pour half of batter into the greased pan.

6. Sprinkle half of topping over batter; run a knife once through batter.

7. Pour remaining batter into the pan, then run a knife once through batter.

8. Bake until a toothpick inserted into the center comes out clean, approximately 40–45 minutes.

9. Transfer baking pan to a wire rack. Cool for 30 minutes.

1 cup margarine, softened
2 cups granulated sugar
4 large eggs, at room temperature
1 pint sour cream
2 teaspoons vanilla extract
2 teaspoons baking soda
1½ cups all-purpose flour
3 teaspoons baking powder
½ cup walnuts (optional)

Topping:
½ cup granulated sugar and 2 teaspoons cinnamon, mixed together in small bowl

Holiday Lemon Nut Bread

2½ cups all-purpose flour
1 cup granulated sugar
3½ teaspoons baking powder
½ teaspoon baking soda
½ teaspoon salt
½ teaspoon grated lemon peel
½ cup water
⅓ cup shortening, melted
2 large eggs, lightly beaten
½ cup fresh lemon juice
1 cup chopped walnuts
   (or ½ cup nuts and
   ½ cup raisins)

A zesty change of pace for Christmas morning!

1. Preheat oven to 350°F. Grease and flour a 9" × 5" × 3" loaf pan.

2. In a large bowl, sift together flour, sugar, baking powder, baking soda, lemon peel, and salt.

3. Combine water, shortening, eggs, and juice. Make a well in the center of the dry ingredients. Pour egg mixture into well, tossing with a fork until dry ingredients are just moistened. Stir in nuts and raisins.

4. Spread batter into prepared pan.

5. Bake bread until a toothpick inserted into the center comes out clean, approximately 60–75 minutes.

6. Let cool for 10 minutes; remove from pan. Cool on wire rack for 5 minutes. Wrap in plastic and refrigerate until ready to serve.

Triple Lemon Butter

For gift-giving, wrap the butter roll in waxed paper and tie at the ends with holiday ribbons. Add an antique silver butter knife and the latest cookbook if you like. Other butters can also be made by mixing similar amounts of just about any herb to 1 stick of butter.

1. Wash herbs and set them aside on paper towels until all excess water has evaporated.

2. Combine herbs in a small bowl, using a wooden spoon. Reserving 1 teaspoon of the fresh herb mixture, or ½ teaspoon of the dry, mix herbs into the butter.

3. Using your hands, shape the butter into a log, dipping each end into the herb mixture set aside in the previous step. Gently score the sides with a fork, using horizontal strokes.

4. Store in the refrigerator.

2 tablespoons fresh lemon balm leaves, chopped or 2 teaspoons dried lemon balm, crumbled

1 tablespoon fresh lemon verbena leaves, chopped or 1 teaspoon dried lemon verbena, crumbled

1 stick butter, softened

1 teaspoon lemon juice

Brandy Rings

2½ cups all-purpose flour, sifted
1 cup butter or margarine
2 tablespoons brandy

A festive and delicious braided pastry.

1. Preheat oven to 350°F.

2. Grease 2 large baking sheets.

3. Combine flour, margarine, and brandy in a large mixing bowl and blend together to make dough.

4. On a lightly floured surface, roll the dough into ropes approximately ½" thick.

5. Cut the ropes into 5" strips.

6. Twist 2 pieces together; shape into a ring; pinch ends together to seal.

7. Repeat with remaining dough.

8. Place rings a good distance apart on prepared baking sheets. Bake rings until golden, approximately 12–15 minutes.

Chocolate Crinkles

Chocolate fans take note:
This is a Christmas treat
worth waiting for!

1. In a large mixing bowl, mix oil, melted chocolate, and granulated sugar.

2. Beat in eggs, 1 at a time, beating well after each addition.

3. Add vanilla. Beat in flour, baking powder, and salt.

4. Cover mixing bowl with plastic wrap. Chill for several hours.

5. When ready to cook, preheat oven to 350°F.

6. Grease 2 medium baking sheets.

7. Drop dough by teaspoonfuls into confectioners' sugar. Roll dough in sugar and shape into balls.

8. Bake cookies on greased baking sheets until set, 10–12 minutes.

½ cup vegetable oil
4 ounces unsweetened chocolate, melted
2 cups granulated sugar
4 large eggs
2 teaspoons vanilla
2 cups all-purpose flour
2 teaspoons baking powder
½ teaspoon salt
1 cup confectioners' sugar

Christmas Cutout Cookies

½ cup butter

½ cup granulated sugar

2 large eggs, lightly beaten

1 teaspoon vanilla extract

¼ cup sliced almonds

2 teaspoons baking powder

2¾ cups all-purpose flour

Red and green sugar crystals

Icing (commercially prepared, in tubes)

Vary the shapes for lots of kid-friendly fun.

1. Preheat oven to 400°F.

2. In a large mixing bowl, beat together butter and sugar until light and fluffy.

3. Beat in eggs, vanilla, and almonds.

4. Beat in baking powder and flour ½ cup at a time, until blended.

5. Wrap dough in plastic wrap and chill for several hours.

6. On a floured surface, roll-out dough using a floured rolling pin.

7. Using several different-shaped cookie cutters, cut out cookies.

8. Decorate with colored sugar and icing.

9. Bake cookies until just golden, approximately 6–7 minutes.

Christmas-Theme Sugar Cookies

Remember; bake large cookies with large ones and small cookies with small ones for best results. Placing cookies of unlike sizes on the same sheet will result in uneven cooking.

1. Preheat oven to 350°F; grease a cookie or baking sheet.

2. In a large mixing bowl, beat together margarine and sugar.

3. Beat in egg, extract, baking powder, and salt. Gradually add in flour.

4. Add salt and baking powder. Gradually add in flour. Mix well.

5. On a floured surface, knead dough by hand and shape into a large ball. Wrap in plastic wrap and chill up to 2 hours, until firm.

6. Roll dough out on floured surface to ¼" thickness. Cut out shapes with Christmas-theme cookie cutters. Gather trimmings; roll out and cut more cookies. Decorate with sugar crystals, jimmies, and candies.

7. Bake in batches for 10–12 minutes, or until brown.

1 cup granulated sugar
1 cup margarine
1 large egg
½ teaspoon almond or vanilla extract
1½ teaspoons baking powder
½ teaspoon salt
2½ cups all-purpose flour
Red and green sugar crystals
Colored jimmies
Small silver-ball candies

Coconut Wreath Cookies

½ cup butter or margarine, softened

½ cup granulated sugar

1 large egg

1 (3½-ounce) pack of shredded, sweetened coconut

1¾ cups all-purpose flour

Red and green candied cherries, sliced

A real sign of the season!

1. Preheat oven to 375°F.

2. Grease and flour a baking sheet.

3. In a large bowl, beat together butter and sugar.

4. Blend in egg and coconut. On low speed, add flour, ½ cup at a time, until blended.

5. Wrap dough in plastic wrap and chill for several hours.

6. On floured surface, roll ⅓ of dough at a time to ¼" thickness. Using a 2½" doughnut cutter, cut dough into rings. Gather trimmings; roll out dough; cut more cookies.

7. Remove any excess coconut from edges; edges of cookies should be smooth.

8. Place cookies on prepared baking sheet 1" apart.

9. Arrange cherry slices on cookies to resemble flower petals; press into cookies.

10. Bake cookies in batches for 10 minutes, or until brown.

Crunchy Christmas Candy

A favorite with the little ones.

1. Bring sugar, evaporated milk, and margarine to a boil, stirring frequently.

2. When sugar is dissolved, remove from heat and stir in peanut butter and vanilla.

3. Mix in oats and peanuts. Drop mixture by rounded teaspoon onto wax paper so that each morsel has a peak. (If mixture is too stiff, add a few drops of milk.)

4. Chill candy until firm.

1 cup granulated sugar
½ cup evaporated milk
¼ cup margarine
¼ cup crunchy peanut butter
½ teaspoon vanilla extract
1 cup old-fashioned dry oats
½ cup peanuts

Crunchy Christmas Nut Treats

1 cup solid vegetable shortening
¼ cup confectioners' sugar
1 teaspoon vanilla extract
2 cups all-purpose flour, sifted
½ cup chopped almonds
½ cup chopped walnuts

Leave some of these out for Santa—you'll be glad you did.

1. Preheat oven to 300°F.

2. In a large bowl, beat together shortening, confection-
    ers' sugar, and vanilla extract.

3. At low speed, beat in flour.

4. Stir in nuts.

5. Shape dough into round balls and place several inches
    apart on an ungreased baking sheet.

6. Bake in batches for 15–18 minutes. Check frequently
    near end of cooking time; do not scorch.

7. Transfer cookies to a wire rack. Roll warm cookies in
    confectioners' sugar.

8. Let stand until cool, 30 minutes.

Gingerbread from Home

Real home-style gingerbread—perfect for holiday snacks!

1. Preheat oven to 325°F.

2. Grease and flour an 8" square baking pan.

3. In a large bowl, mix together brown sugar and butter. Mix in baking soda and molasses.

4. Add flour, cinnamon, and ginger. Mix well.

5. Add in egg.

6. Add boiling water. Mix well.

7. Pour batter into prepared pan; smooth top.

8. Bake gingerbread until a toothpick inserted into the center comes out clean, approximately 40 minutes.

½ cup firmly packed light brown sugar
⅓ cup butter
½ cup light molasses
1 teaspoon baking soda
1¼ cup all-purpose flour
1 teaspoon ground cinnamon
½ teaspoon ground ginger
1 large egg
½ cup boiling water

Gingerbread Men

2¼ cups all-purpose flour
½ cup granulated sugar
½ cup solid vegetable shortening
½ cup light molasses
1½ teaspoons ground cinnamon
1 teaspoon baking powder
1 teaspoon ground ginger
1 teaspoon ground cloves
½ teaspoon baking soda
½ teaspoon salt
1 large egg
Green and red prepared
  frosting

Decorate these men with the season in mind!

1. Preheat oven to 350°F.

2. In a large mixing bowl, beat together sugar and shortening.

3. Add egg, salt, baking powder, baking soda, ginger, cinnamon, cloves, and molasses. Add flour ⅓ cup at a time, beating until dough forms.

4. Shape dough into a ball, wrap in plastic wrap, and chill for up to 2 hours or until firm.

5. On floured surface, roll dough out to ¼" thickness.

6. Using a gingerbread-man cookie cutter, cut out cookies. Place on an ungreased cookie sheet at least 1" apart.

7. Bake cookies in batches for 8–10 minutes for small men, 12–15 minutes for larger. Transfer baking sheet to a wire rack to cool.

8. Spread frosting over cookies. Decorate with candies.

Fruitcake Trio

You've all heard the jokes, but Christmas wouldn't be Christmas without fruitcake. Grease 3 9" × 5" baking pans, then line with aluminum foil, then grease again. Now you're ready to prepare the main batter first, and then follow the individualized instructions for making 3 quite different fruitcakes to suit any taste.

1. In a large bowl, cream together butter and sugars.

2. Beat in eggs at low speed, one at a time.

3. Slowly combine flour into butter mixture until it forms a light, fluffy batter.

4. In a small bowl, blend next 4 ingredients. Mix into large bowl.

5. By hand, fold chopped almonds into the batter.

6. Preheat the oven to 300°F.

At this point, divide batter into 3 different bowls to make 3 different kinds of fruitcake. (You can choose to make 3 fruitcakes all of the same kind, but remember the amounts that follow are calculated for just one of each loaf.)

continued . . ..

Main batter

1½ cups butter or margarine

1½ cups granulated sugar

1½ cups dark brown sugar, packed

9 large eggs

5 cups flour

1½ teaspoons baking powder

1½ teaspoons salt

1½ teaspoons ground cinnamon

1½ teaspoons ground nutmeg

1½ cups almonds, coarsely chopped (optional)

Dark Raisin Fruitcake

As directed above, take ⅓ of the batter formed in the Main Batter
section and add in the following until well blended:

¼ cup molasses
¼ teaspoon cloves
½ teaspoon ground allspice
2 cups each dark raisins and golden raisins
⅓ cup chopped dates

Morning Sunshine Fruitcake

As directed above, take ⅓ of the batter formed in the Main Batter section and add in the following until well blended:

¼ cup orange juice
¼ teaspoon crushed cardamom seed
½ cup each orange peel and lemon peel, chopped
1 tablespoon lime juice
1½ cups mixed candied green cherries and yellow candied pineapple,
chopped

Nut-Lovers' Fruitcake

As directed above, take ⅓ of the batter formed in the Main Batter section and add in the following until well blended:

1 cup each pecans and walnuts, chopped
½ cup hazelnuts, chopped
1½ cups candied mixed fruit, chopped

If desired, wrap fruitcake in brandy-soaked cheesecloth and then in foil. Remoisten cloth every other week. Or wrap without liquor. Store for up to 2 months; freeze for longer periods. Before giving, glaze tops with small quantity of pineapple preserves, apple, jelly, or orange marmalade. Decorate with halved nuts and candied fruits.

1. Pour each batter into 1 prepared 9" × 5" pan.

2. Place a shallow pan of water on the lower oven rack to prevent drying.

3. Place the 3 pans containing the batter next to each other, but not touching, on the top rack.

4. Cook for 1½ hours or until cake tester inserted into the center of each cake comes out clean. If the tops of the cakes start to become too brown near the end of cooking time, cover them with aluminum foil.

5. Cool in pans on cooling racks for 15 minutes. Using aluminum foil, carefully pull cakes out of pans and let cool on cooling racks.

Holiday Fudge

4½ cups granulated sugar

1 can evaporated milk

¼ cup butter

12 ounces of milk chocolate bar

12 ounces chocolate chips

1 tablespoon vanilla extract

⅛ teaspoon salt

1 pint marshmallow spread

2 cups walnuts, coarsely chopped

It's the hint of marshmallow that makes the difference in this recipe. And there's no baking!

1. Grease a 13" × 9" pan.

2. In a large saucepan, heat sugar, milk, and butter for 5 minutes, stirring constantly.

3. Dissolve chocolate bar and chocolate chips in saucepan.

4. Mix in vanilla, salt, marshmallow, and walnuts.

5. Pour fudge into prepared pan.

6. Chill overnight.

Lemon Bars

Simple to make, and always a big hit at family gatherings.

1. Preheat oven to 350°F.

2. Grease an 8" × 8" × 2" pan.

3. Mix together flour and confectioners' sugar. Using a pastry blender, cut butter into flour mixture until coarse crumbs form.

4. Pat crumb mixture into prepared pan.

5. Bake crust until golden, approximately 10–12 minutes. Set aside.

6. In a large bowl, combine beaten eggs with sugar and lemon juice. Beat until thickened.

7. Beat in flour and baking powder.

8. Pour batter over prepared crust.

9. Return pan to oven; bake lemon bars until set, approximately 20–25 minutes.

10. Transfer pan to wire rack and let cool.

11. Sift confectioners' sugar over top and let cool. Cut into 1" squares.

1 cup all-purpose flour
¼ cup confectioners' sugar
½ cup butter, softened
2 large eggs, lightly beaten
¾ cup granulated sugar
3 tablespoons fresh lemon juice
2 tablespoons all-purpose flour
½ teaspoon baking powder
Confectioners' sugar (for dusting)

Maple Bells

4 cups all-purpose flour

1 cup butter or margarine, softened

¾ cup firmly packed light brown sugar

½ cup maple syrup

2 teaspoons cream of tartar

1 teaspoon baking soda

¼ teaspoon salt

2 large eggs

One of the perennial symbols of Christmas— and a darned good cookie, too.

1. Preheat oven to 350°F.

2. Grease a baking sheet.

3. In a large mixing bowl, beat together butter and sugar at medium speed until light and fluffy.

4. Beat in eggs and maple syrup. Beat in cream of tartar, baking soda, and salt.

5. At low speed, beat in flour until dough forms.

6. Shape dough into a ball; wrap in plastic wrap and refrigerate for 1 hour.

7. On a floured surface, roll out dough to ⅛" thickness; using bell-shaped cookie cutters, cut-out cookies. Place cookies in batches on prepared baking sheet.

8. All large pieces should be baked together and all small pieces should be baked together, so that each batch will cook evenly.

9. Bake cookies until golden brown, approximately 10 minutes.

Meatless Mince Pie

A real holiday treat!

1. Preheat oven to 450°F.

2. Grease a medium-sized pie pan.

3. Mix together rice, raisins, currants, honey, orange, lemon peel, butter, cinnamon, and nutmeg.

4. Fit shell into prepared pie pan. Spoon rice mixture into shell. Cover with remaining dough and press edges together to seal. Brush pie with beaten egg white. Sprinkle with sugar.

5. Bake pie until crust is golden, approximately 10 minutes. Reduce temperature to 350°F; bake about 30 minutes more. Check frequently; do not scorch or overcook!

6. Transfer pan to a wire rack to cool.

½ cup cooked rice
½ cup seedless raisins
½ cup currants
½ cup honey
2 tablespoons chopped orange sections
1 tablespoon grated lemon peel
1 tablespoon butter
⅛ teaspoon cinnamon
⅛ teaspoon nutmeg
Sprinkling of granulated sugar
1 large egg white, lightly beaten
Prepared, uncooked double-layer pastry shell

Old-Fashioned Christmas Tea Cakes

1 cup margarine
1 cup granulated sugar
3 large eggs
1 teaspoon nutmeg
3½ cups all-purpose flour

Sometimes the old recipes are the best.

1. Preheat oven to 350°F.

2. Grease a baking sheet.

3. In a large bowl, beat together sugar and margarine until light and fluffy.

4. Beat in eggs and nutmeg. Beat in flour ½ cup at a time, beating until blended and smooth.

5. Drop batter by rounded tablespoonfuls onto floured surface. Roll cakes out to ¼" thickness.

6. Place cakes 1" apart on prepared baking sheet.

7. Bake cakes in batches until golden and set, approximately 10 minutes.

8. Transfer baking sheet to a wire rack to cool.

Pecan Pie

Irresistible at any time of the year, but a special favorite during the holidays! The pecans will float to the top, forming a firm crust that will brown nicely.

1. Preheat oven to 350°F.

2. Place pie crust in greased pie pan (or, if crust comes in aluminum pie pan, use that); put in oven and brown slightly, 5–10 minutes. Remove.

3. In a large bowl, beat eggs until foamy. Add sugar, pecans, vanilla, corn syrup, and salt. Mix well.

4. Pour filling into prepared crust.

5. Bake pie until top is set, approximately 40–45 minutes.

6. Transfer pan to a wire rack to cool.

Prepared, uncooked pie crust to fit standard pie pan
1 cup dark corn syrup
1 cup coarsely chopped pecan pieces, toasted
½ cup granulated sugar
3 large eggs
1 teaspoon vanilla extract
½ teaspoon salt

Peppermint-Flavored Candy-Cane Cookies

Cool and refreshing.

1¼ cups margarine

1 cup confectioners' sugar

1 teaspoon vanilla extract

¼ teaspoon salt

1 large egg

3¼ cups all-purpose flour

¼ teaspoon peppermint
   extract

Pinch of red food coloring

1.   Preheat oven to 350°F.

2.   Grease a baking sheet.

3.   Beat together margarine and sugar on medium speed until light and fluffy.

4.   Mix in vanilla, salt, and egg. On low speed, beat in flour ½ cup at a time, until dough forms.

5.   Shape dough into a ball and divide in half.

6.   In a small bowl, mix red food coloring and peppermint extract.

7.   Knead food coloring mixture into one half of dough.

8.   With lightly floured hands, roll 1 teaspoon of plain dough into a 4" rope.

9.   Repeat rolling process with red dough. Braid ropes together and shape as a candy cane. Pinch ends together to seal.

10. Repeat with remaining dough.

11. Place cookies at least 1" apart on prepared baking sheet. Bake in batches for 10 minutes, or until golden brown.

12. Transfer baking sheet to a wire rack to cool. Let stand until cool (about 20 minutes).

Peppermint-Twist Brownies

Brownies with a special twist—peppermint!
Package them for gift giving in a round tin with
red bakers' waxed paper between layers.

1. Preheat oven to 350°F.

2. Grease bottom and sides of 8" × 8" pan and then sprinkle with a little extra cocoa (instead of flour).

3. In a large bowl, stir together flour, cocoa, salt, peppermint extract, and baking powder.

4. In a smaller bowl, cream together butter and sugar, then add eggs one at a time. Slowly add mixture into dry ingredients. Mix well.

5. Place half the batter into the pan, spreading to cover the bottom. Sprinkle crushed peppermint candies evenly over the batter. Place the remaining batter on top to cover the candies.

6. Bake for 30 minutes, or until a cake tester inserted into the middle comes out clean.

7. Makes 9 large or 12 small brownies.

1 cup flour
⅓ cup unsweetened cocoa
    powder
¼ teaspoon salt
½ teaspoon baking powder
1 cup butter or margarine
1 cup sugar
1 teaspoon peppermint extract
3 large eggs, room temperature
½ cup peppermint candies,
    broken into pieces

Pfeffernusse/Peppernuts

3 large eggs

½ cup dark brown sugar, packed

½ cup granulated sugar

3 cups all-purpose flour

½ teaspoon baking powder

½ teaspoon freshly ground pepper

½ teaspoon ground cloves

½ teaspoon ground cardamom seeds

¼ cup finely ground almonds

¼ teaspoon salt

2 tablespoons lemon juice

Zest of one lemon

Confectioners' sugar, approximately 1 cup

Offer this updated version of the traditional peppery German treat to the person on your Christmas list who just can't get enough heat—but start early, because they take three weeks to gain full flavor. Don't forget the apple slice that the recipe includes, or cookies will become quite hard!

1. Preheat oven to 350°F.

2. Break eggs in large bowl and beat with a fork until frothy.

3. Add sugars and beat until well mixed.

4. In a small bowl, mix together the flour with the rest of the dry ingredients, except the confectioners' sugar.

5. Slowly combine dry mixture with egg mixture.

6. Blend in lemon juice and zest.

7. Cover bowl with plastic wrap and place in refrigerator for 1 hour.

8. With floured palms, roll the dough into 1" balls.

9. Bake for 10–15 minutes on greased or nonstick cookie sheets, or until bottoms are just beginning to brown.

10. As each batch comes out of the oven, roll immediately in powdered sugar and cool on a wire rack.

11. As soon as cookies are cool, place in an airtight container with 1 apple slice. Change apple slice every few days. After 3 weeks, flavors will have had a chance to blend, and cookies are ready for giving. Makes 3½ dozen.

"Perfect Every Time" Chocolate Chip Cookies

Make a lot—they disappear quickly!

1. Preheat oven to 375°F.

2. Grease a large baking sheet.

3. Mix together flour, baking soda, and salt.

4. In a large mixing bowl, beat together shortening, sugar, and butter at medium speed, until light and fluffy.

5. Beat in vanilla and eggs.

6. Using low speed, beat in flour ½ cup at a time, beating until dough forms.

7. Stir in chocolate chips and nuts.

8. Bake cookies in batches until golden, approximately 10–12 minutes.

9. Let stand until cool.

2 cups firmly packed dark brown sugar
1 cup granulated sugar
¾ cup butter
1¼ cups solid vegetable shortening
4 large eggs, lightly beaten
6 cups all-purpose flour
2 teaspoons baking soda
1 teaspoon salt
4 teaspoons vanilla extract
1 large bag chocolate chips
2 cups coarsely chopped pecans (optional)

Red Velvet Cake

Cake:

½ cup solid vegetable shortening
1½ cups granulated sugar
1 teaspoon vanilla extract
2 large eggs
2 ounces red food coloring
2½ cups all-purpose flour
2 tablespoons cocoa powder
1 teaspoon baking soda
1 teaspoon salt
1 cup buttermilk
1 tablespoon white vinegar

Icing:

1 cup milk
5 tablespoons flour
1 cup sugar
1 cup butter, softened
1 teaspoon vanilla extract

Delightful and delicious!
And the color couldn't be more Christmas appropriate!

1. Preheat oven to 350°F.

2. Grease two 8" cake pans.

3. In a large bowl, beat together shortening, sugar, and vanilla until light and fluffy.

4. Add eggs to the mixture one at a time, beating well after each addition.

5. Mix in food coloring.

6. Mix together flour, cocoa powder, baking soda, and salt in a separate bowl.

7. Pour batter into prepared pans; smooth tops.

8. Bake cakes until a toothpick inserted into the center comes out clean, approximately 30 minutes.

9. Transfer pans to wire racks to cool. After 20 minutes, carefully use a spatula to turn cakes out onto rack to cool completely.

10. Slice each layer in half horizontally.

11. In top of double boiler, cook milk and flour over medium heat until thick, stirring constantly. Let cool.

12. In a medium bowl, beat sugar, butter, and vanilla until light and fluffy. Add milk mixture. Mix until combined.

13. Cool icing completely before using. Spread icing evenly on top and sides of cake.

Snowball Cake

A winter wonderland for the senses!

1. Preheat oven to 350°F.

2. Grease and flour a medium-sized Bundt pan.

3. In a large bowl, combine cake mix, eggs, oil, water, and almond extract.

4. Mix for 2–3 minutes until mixture attains a uniform consistency; fold in ginger and almonds.

5. Pour batter into prepared pan.

6. Bake cake until a toothpick inserted into center comes out clean, approximately 50 minutes. Cool in pan 25 minutes. Remove and cool on rack for an additional 2 hours.

7. Put in freezer until hard enough to cut. Using either a cake divider or a very long serrated knife, slice cake horizontally into 2 layers. Remove and set aside the top. Hollow out bottom half, leaving ½"–¾" on the sides and bottom.

8. Beat cream cheese, sour cream, confectioners' sugar, and vanilla extract in large bowl until smooth.

9. Spoon filling into hollow of cake. Replace top.

10. Spread prepared white frosting over top and sides of cake.

1 package yellow cake mix
3 large eggs
⅓ cup vegetable oil
1¼ cups water
1 teaspoon almond extract
½ cup coarsely chopped crystallized ginger
¾ cup coarsely chopped almonds, toasted
1 (12-ounce) can prepared white creamy frosting
Shredded, sweetened coconut

Filling:

1 (8-ounce) package cream cheese, softened
½ cup sour cream
3 tablespoons confectioners' sugar
½ teaspoon vanilla extract

Special Christmas Oatmeal Cookies

1 stick butter or margarine

4 tablespoons solid vegetable
   shortening

1 cup firmly packed light
   brown sugar

½ cup granulated sugar

1 large egg

¼ cup water (4 tablespoons)

1 teaspoon vanilla extract

3 cups old-fashioned rolled
   oats

1 cup all-purpose flour

1 teaspoon salt

½ teaspoon baking soda

1 teaspoon ground cinnamon

½ cup chocolate morsels

Macadamia nuts, walnuts,
   and raisins in desired
   amounts

A classic, but with extra goodies for a special time of year. The more extra goodies you add to these cookies, the better they are!

1. Preheat oven to 350°F.

2. Grease a large baking sheet.

3. Beat butter and shortening together until mixture is smooth.

4. Beat in sugar, egg, water, and vanilla until light and fluffy.

5. Add remaining ingredients. Mix well.

6. Drop mixture by rounded teaspoonfuls onto prepared baking sheet.

7. Bake cookies in batches until golden, approximately 12–15 minutes.

8. Transfer cookies to a wire rack to cool.

Springerle

A great present for coffee lovers—you can't find a better cookie to have with coffee! For gift giving, wrap springerle in a basket with a bag of gourmet coffee beans.

3 large eggs
3 cups granulated sugar
3 cups flour
1½ teaspoons baking powder
2 tablespoons ground aniseed

1. Preheat oven to 350°F.

2. Beat eggs and blend in sugar.

3. Add flour, baking powder, and aniseed and mix to form a dry dough.

4. Place dough in a large zipper-style plastic bag, pressing out as much air as you can before sealing. Press the dough together into a large ball and chill in the refrigerator in the bag.

5. After 1 hour, remove dough from refrigerator and form into 1" balls. These can be baked as is, or carefully flattened with a 2¼" cookie press after being dusted with confectioners' sugar.

6. Bake on greased cookie sheets for approximately 12 minutes, or until bottoms are beginning to brown. Makes 4½ dozen cookies.

7. Let cookies cool on a wire rack, then store in airtight container.

Trifle

A holiday treat that's likely to become a tradition at your house after the first time you serve it. There are countless variations on this recipe, so don't be afraid to experiment with some of your own.

1½ dozen ladyfingers, split in half
¼ cup sherry
1 dozen almond macaroon cookies, broken in pieces
¼ cup toasted almond slices
¾ cup fresh strawberries, sliced
¾ cup fresh blueberries, sliced
¾ cup fresh peaches, sliced
1 cup custard (see separate recipe below)
1 pint whipped cream

Custard:

3 large eggs
¼ teaspoon salt
½ stick butter
1¼ cups granulated sugar
1 teaspoon vanilla extract
⅓ cup all-purpose flour
3 cups milk

1. In a trifle bowl, arrange ladyfingers.

2. Sprinkle sherry over ladyfingers.

3. Add one layer of macaroon cookie pieces and half of the toasted almond slices.

4. Add one layer of strawberries, peaches, and blueberries. Top with custard and whipped cream. Garnish with more almond slices.

Custard:

5. Scald milk in top of large double boiler.

6. In a mixing bowl, beat eggs, sugar, flour, and salt at medium speed until light and fluffy.

7. Add egg mixture to scalded milk; cook over medium heat, stirring constantly, until thickened.

8. Add vanilla and butter.

9. Place a piece of wax paper directly over top of surface. Cool for 30 minutes.

The Everything Family Christmas Book

Wish Cookies

You'll wish you'd made more!

1. Preheat oven to 350°F.

2. In a large mixing bowl, combine melted butter with graham crackers. Mix well.

3. Press crumb mixture into bottom of a 13" × 9" pan.

4. Sprinkle nuts, then chocolate chips, and coconut (in that order) over cracker crumbs.

5. Gently pour condensed milk over top.

6. Bake for 15–20 minutes, or until golden brown.

7. Let cool before cutting.

10 graham crackers, crushed
½ cup butter or margarine, melted
½ cup chopped almonds
6 ounces chocolate chips
½ cup sweetened, shredded coconut
1 can condensed milk

Brandy Cocoa

2 tablespoons unsweetened
   cocoa powder
⅓ cup granulated sugar
1½ cups boiling water
4 cups whole milk
3 teaspoons brandy

A mellow and delicious drink for the holidays.

1. In a saucepan, scald milk.

2. In another saucepan, mix cocoa, sugar, and enough boiling water to make a smooth paste.

3. Add remaining water and boil 1 minute, then add to milk.

4. Mix well; add brandy, then beat mixture with egg beater for 2 minutes.

5. Serve in large mugs.

Cranberry Glogg

*A New England favorite. It's funny to say, great to drink.
This is a warmhearted cup of holiday cheer guaranteed
to start even the coldest evening off right.*

1. Combine juice, cloves, and cinnamon in a large saucepan.

2. Warm over medium heat for 15 minutes. Reduce heat and let sit for 5 minutes.

3. Remove cinnamon sticks and cloves.

4. Pour into mugs.

5. Add schnapps as desired, depending on the amount of warmth you have in mind.

6 cups cranberry juice cocktail
6 whole cloves
2 cinnamon sticks
Cinnamon schnapps to taste

Homemade Coffee Liqueur for Christmas, Begun in November

4 cups granulated sugar

2 ounces instant coffee crystals

2 cups water

3 cups vodka

1 vanilla bean, split in half
  lengthwise

The stuff you buy in the store is pretty good, but our guess is you'll get more of a kick out of putting this variation together yourself. Try it: It takes some time, but it's worth it. You may never go back to the labeled version again.

1. Mix sugar and coffee in the bottom of a large pitcher.

2. Add water.

3. Chill for 90 minutes, then add vodka. Mix well.

4. Drop the vanilla bean into an empty half-gallon bottle with a screw top.

5. Pour the coffee mixture into the bottle, seal, and store for 30 days in a dark place.

Hot Candy Cane in a Holiday Mug

An inspired twist on a peppermint theme.
(Note: Cocoa made from scratch is best, but prepared
mixes to which you add boiling water will serve, too.)

2 cups hot cocoa
Peppermint liqueur
Whipped cream
2 red maraschino cherries,
  halved
2 green maraschino cherries,
  halved

1. Pour hot cocoa into 2 large mugs.

2. Add peppermint liqueur to taste.

3. Top with whipped cream and red and green maraschino cherries.

Hot Cinnamon Stocking

2 cups hot cocoa
Cinnamon-flavored liqueur
Whipped cream
2 red maraschino cherries,
*   halved*
2 green maraschino cherries,
*   halved*

The perfect drink for Christmas Eve.

1. Pour hot cocoa into 2 large mugs.

2. Add cinnamon-flavored liqueur to taste.

3. Top with whipped cream and red and green maraschino cherries.

Perfect Egg Nog

Forget the store-bought stuff; the real thing is easy to make and much, much better.

1. Place egg yolks in a large bowl.

2. Add sugar to the yolks, beating at medium speed.

3. After the yolks have been beaten very stiff, mix the egg whites with the yolk mixture.

4. Stir in cream and milk.

5. Add whiskey and rum. Stir thoroughly.

6. Chill for 2 hours. Serve with grated nutmeg on top.

6 large eggs, separated
½ cup granulated sugar
1 pint heavy cream
1 pint milk
1 pint whiskey
2 ounces rum

Merry Mocha Coffee Mix

16 ounces instant coffee

2 cups cocoa powder

4 teaspoons ground cinnamon

2 teaspoons ground nutmeg

Water (amount will vary depending on number of cups you are preparing)

Coffee lovers take note: This is a delicious holiday treat you will not soon forget!

1. In a mixing bowl, stir together dry ingredients.

2. Boil required amount of water in a kettle, then pour into medium-sized mugs.

3. Add one spoonful of mixture to each mug—or more or less, according to taste.

Unforgettable Christmas Irish Cream

Here's something to lift your spirits on a cold holiday night!

1. Mix all ingredients together in a blender.
2. Chill for 1 hour and serve.

1 (12-ounce) can condensed milk
8 ounces Irish whiskey
4 large eggs
1 tablespoon chocolate syrup
1 teaspoon vanilla extract
1 teaspoon coconut extract

Wassail

*The classic recipe. This drink has warmed many
a holiday heart, and will likely be popular for years to come.
(Note: A teaspoon of honey may be substituted for the cloves.)*

2 quarts apple cider
2 cups orange juice
1 cup fresh lemon juice
1 teaspoon cloves
Cinnamon sticks

1. Put apple cider, orange juice, and lemon juice into a large saucepan. Add the cloves and two cinnamon sticks; warm over medium heat for 20 minutes.

2. When ready to serve, strain off cloves and cinnamon sticks and pour liquid into mugs.

3. Place a new cinnamon stick in each mug and serve.

Appendix A

Christmas Festivals Across North America

Most towns and cities across North America schedule annual holiday festivities of one kind or another. What follows is a sampling of festivals: some big-city events; some historically important celebrations; and some smaller gatherings that seemed too interesting to omit. This chapter is not an exhaustive list of all festivals; if you would like more information on seasonal celebrations, try calling the local chamber of commerce or visitor's bureau for detailed information about holiday events. Your state or province's tourism office will also be helpful.

Alexandria, Virginia

Alexandria Community Scottish Christmas Walk
Alexandria's Scottish heritage is saluted with a parade through historic Old Town. Special activities include bagpipes, highland dancers, tours of old homes, and children's events. Early December. Information: 703-838-5005; *www.campagnacenter.org.*

Annual Woodlawn Plantation Christmas
Carolers, musicians, and costumed actors portraying a family from the 1820s welcome you to a Christmas party. Wagon rides, a burning Yule log, and refreshments provide a taste of the old Virginia Christmas. Early December. Information: 703-780-4000; *www.woodlawn1805.org.*

Civil War Christmas Open House
At the Fort Ward Museum and Historic Site. Mid-December. Information: 703-838-4848; *http://oha.alexandriava.gov/fortward/.*

Aspen, Colorado

Tree Lighting
The annual lighting of Aspen's tree, at the Sardy House. Early December. Information: 888-290-1324; *www.aspenchamber.org.*

Auburn, California

Auburn Christmas Crafts and Music Festival
Beat the Christmas rush—and still enjoy the carols. Veteran's Day weekend. Information: 209-533-3473; *www.fireonthemountain.com.*

Boothbay Harbor, Maine

Harbor Lights Festival
A seafaring holiday celebration. First Saturday in December. Information: 207-633-2353; *www.boothbayharbor.com.*

Charlottesville, Virginia

Sounds of the Season: A Holiday Concert and Tour
Music and celebration at Ash Lawn-Highland. Late December. Information: 434-293-9539; *www.ashlawnhighland.org.*

Chicago, Illinois

Millennium Park Ice Skating Rink
Ice-skating fun for the whole family at the McCormic Tribune Plaza and Ice Rink. Beginning in November. Information: 312-742-1168; *www.millenniumpark.org.*

Magnificent Mile Lights Festival
A sparkling local tradition. On Michigan Avenue from the Chicago River to Oak Street. Mid-November to December 31. Information: 312-642-3570; *www .themagnificentmile.com.*

City of Chicago Christmas Tree Lighting
The official beginning of the Christmas season in Chicago takes place in Daley Plaza. Late November. Information: 877-244-2246; *www.choosechicago.com.*

Zoolights
Lighting up the night at the Lincoln Park Zoo. Late November/early December. Information: 312-742-2000; *www.lpzoo.org.*

Festival of Lights
A memorable evening at the Swedish American Museum Center. Mid-December. Information: 773-728.8111; *www.samac.org.*

Clermont, New York

Christmas at Clermont Open House
The Livingston family home, a state historic site, is decorated for the holidays and offers music for the season. Early December. Information: 518-537-4240; *http://nysparks.state.ny.us.*

Corona del Mar, California

The Christmas Walk
A street fair with merchants offering lots of free edibles and entertainment. First Sunday in December. Information: 949-673-4050; *www.cdmchamber.com*.

Croton-on-Hudson, New York

Candlelight Tour
A celebration of the early eighteenth-century English Christmas, complete with carolers, musicians, and a bonfire. At Van Cortlandt Manor. In December; dates vary. Information: 914-631-8200; *www.hudsonvalley.org*.

Dallas, Texas

Christmas at the Arboretum
The stately DeGolyer mansion is decorated for the season. Early December. Information: 214-515-6500; *www.dallasarboretum.org*.

The Neiman Marcus Adolphus Children's Parade
A seasonal parade for all ages. Early December. Information: 214-742-8200; *www.childrensparade.com*.

Candlelight Tour
A candlelight holiday festival set among the Victorian and pioneer homes of Old City Park. Mid-December. Information: 800-232-5527; *www.dallascvb.com*.

Des Moines, Washington

Sounds of the Season
Live holiday music in the tropical setting of the Des Moines Botanical Center. Information: 515-323-6291; *www.botanicalcenter.com*.

East Haddam, Connecticut

Victorian Christmas at Gillette Castle
Music and revelry of the era. First weekend after Thanksgiving to the weekend before Christmas. Information: 860-526-2336; *www.ct.gov.*

Franklin, Tennessee

Dickens of a Christmas
Christmas carolers in Victorian garb serve up good things to eat and drink and lots of entertainment in a two-day festival. Mid-December. Information: 615-591-8500; *www.historicfranklin.com.*

Galveston, Texas

Dickens on the Strand
The author who did more than any other to develop the modern notion of Christmas is celebrated in this two-day event. First weekend in December, beginning Friday. Information: 888-425-4753; *www.galveston.com.*

Gloucester, Massachusetts

The Victorian Christmas Festival Weekend
A celebration of the Victorian Christmas, complete with costumed participants, at Hammond Castle. Mid-December. Information: 978-283-2080; *www.hammondcastle.org.*

Hollywood, California

Hollywood Christmas Parade
Hollywood Boulevard becomes Santa Claus Lane for the season; the parade is held the first Sunday after Thanksgiving. Information: 323-469-8311; *www .hollywoodchamber.net.*

Hot Springs, Arkansas

Holiday Highlights
More than a million lights transform the Garvan gardens into a winter wonderland. Mid-November through December. Information: 501-262-9300; *www.garvangardens.org*.

Houston, Texas

Christmas Boat Lane Parade
Some 200 lighted boats sail around Clear Lake and through the channel to Galveston Bay. Mid-December. Information: 281-488-7676; *www.clearlakearea.com*.

Hyde Park, New York

A Historic Hyde Park Christmas
Springwood is decorated as it was in 1944, the last holiday season President Roosevelt spent there. December; dates vary. Information: 800-FDR-VISIT; *www .nps.gov*.

Kingsburg, California

Julgransfest Christmas Tree Lighting Ceremony
An enchanting celebration of Swedish Christmas traditions. Day after Thanksgiving. Information: 559-897-1111; *www.kingsburgchamberofcommerce.com*.

Santa Lucia Festival Christmas Village Celebration
Arts and crafts, parades, and other enjoyable aspects of the season. Early December. Information: 559-897-1111; *www.kingsburgchamberofcommerce.com*.

Leavenworth, Washington

Christmas Lighting Festival
Rides on sleighs, choir performances, and dazzling lights are the highlights of this Cascade Mountain celebration. Information: 509-548-5807; *www.leavenworth.org.*

Los Angeles, California

Las Posadas
Olvera Street provides the most prominent Southern California venue of the parade re-enacting Mary and Joseph's search for shelter for the Christ Child; from mid-December to Christmas Eve. Information: 213-625-5045; *www.olvera-street.com.*

Lynchburg, Virginia

Christmas at the Market Craft Show
Lots of distinctive holiday crafts and other offerings. At Lynchburg Community Market, Late November/early December. Information: 434-847-1499; *www .discoverlynchburg.org.*

Lynden, Washington

Dutch Sinterklaas Celebration
For a taste of the colorful (and enormously influential) Dutch tradition of observing the yearly appearance of St. Nicholas, check out this delightful festival. First Saturday in December. Information: 360-354-5995; *www.lynden.org.*

Miami, Florida

Santa's Enchanted Forest
In the Tropical Park, west of Coral Gables. Mid-November to late January. Information: 305-559-9689; *www.santasenchantedforest.com.*

Minneapolis, Minnesota, and Environs

Holiday Music Festival at the Mall of America
The season is observed in high style at this mall, one of the world's largest (also one of the nation's largest tourist destinations). Mid-November through December. Information: 952-883-8800; *www.MallofAmerica.com*.

Festival of Trees
More Christmas trees than you can shake a sugarplum at. Early December to early January at the Minnesota Landscape Arboretum. Information: 952-443-1400; *www.arboretum.umn.edu*.

Folkways of Christmas
Lovely music and seasonal celebrations. Weekends in early December at Historic Murphy's Landing. Information: 763-694-7784; *www.threeriversparkdistrict.org*.

Mount Vernon, Virginia

Holidays at Mount Vernon
Historic Mount Vernon Estate is the site for a recreation of an authentic eighteenth-century holiday season. Early December to early January. Information: 703-780-2000; *www.mountvernon.org*.

Nantucket, Massachusetts

Nantucket Noël and Christmas Stroll
Local merchants put out festive decorations during this lively festival. Late November through December. Information: 508-228-1700; *www.nantucketchamber.org*.

Nashville, Tennessee

A Country Christmas at Gaylord's Opryland
The event, which features lights, decorations, food, and special entertainment, is held from late November through December. Information: 866-972-6779; *www.gaylordhotels.com*.

New York, New York

Christmas Tree Lighting at Rockefeller Center
The big one—especially if you're a New Yorker. Late November. Information: 212-632-3975; *www.rockefellercenter.com.*

Newport News, Virginia

Celebration in Lights
Drive-through holiday light display at Newport News Park. Mid-November through December. Information: 757-926-1400; *www.nngov.com.*

Nogales, Arizona

Christmas Parade & Annual Christmas Tree Lighting
The festival includes Santa Claus and his reindeer, a children's parade, and the lighting of a 30' Christmas tree. December. Information: 520-287-3685; *www.thenogaleschamber.com.*

Norfolk, Virginia

Holidays in the City
The major downtown event of the season. December. Information: 800-368-3097; *www.norfolkcvb.com.*

Northeast Harbor, Maine

A Northeast Harbor Christmas
Crafts, pageants, music, and more. First weekend in December. Information: 207-276-5040; *www.mountdesertchamber.org.*

Old Westbury, New York

Holiday Celebration
Annual festive event at Old Westbury Gardens with decorations, Santa, and more. December. Information: 516-333-0048; *www.oldwestburygardens.org.*

Oroville, California

A Frontier Christmas
Features costumed characters and an emphasis on Gold Rush history. First weekend in December. Information: 888-OROVILLE; *www.orovillechamber.net.*

Oxnard, California

Parade of Lights
At the Channel Islands Harbor. Second Saturday in December. Information: 800-269-6273; *www.visitoxnard.com.*

Philadelphia, Pennsylvania

Fairmount Park House Christmas Tours
Seven historic houses located throughout the park are decorated for the holidays in themes reminiscent of an old-fashioned Christmas. Early December. Information: 215-683-0200; *www.fairmountpark.org.*

Phoenix, Arizona

Santa's—A Christmas Theme Park
Santa hits the Firebird Raceway from late November to early January. Information: 888-PHX-SANTAS; *www.visitsantas.com.*

Heritage Square Holiday
Crafts, foods, historic celebrations, and Santa. Early December. Information: 602-262-5071; *http://phoenix.gov.*

Portland, Oregon

Festival of Lights
At the Grotto; late November through December. Information: 503-261-2400; *www.thegrotto.org.*

Providence Festival of Trees
At the Oregon Convention Center. Late November/early December. Information: 503-215-6070; *www.providence.org.*

Zoolights
At the Portland Zoo. Late November through December. Information: 503-226-1561; *www.oregonzoo.org.*

Poulsbo, Washington

Yule Fest
A festive Scandinavian celebration that features costumed Vikings, authentic food, and torchlight parade. Early December. Also of interest: the Holiday Heritage House. Information: 360-779-4848; *www.poulsbochamber.com.*

Provincetown, Massachusetts

Lighting of the Pilgrim Monument
The Pilgrim Monument, tallest granite structure in America, is strung with countless lights on Thanksgiving Eve; continues through New Year's Day. Information: 508-487-1310; *www.pilgrim-monument.org.*

Richmond, Virginia

Joy from the World
At the Science Museum of Virginia. Late December to early January. Information: 800-659-1727; *www.smv.org.*

Roseburg, Oregon

Umpqua Valley Festival of Lights
Art, crafts, wine, lights, holiday village, and other festive elements mark this popular festival. Late November through December. Information: 800-444-9584; *www.visitroseburg.com*.

St. Croix, Virgin Islands

Crucian Christmas Festival
Steel bands, cool drinks, and tropical winds make for a very different kind of Christmas celebration. Generally late December and early January. Information: 800-372-USVI; *www.usvitourism.vi*.

San Francisco, California

The Nutcracker
The San Francisco Ballet mounts a much-loved annual production of the seasonal ballet. Information: 415-865-2000; *www.sfballet.org*.

Sanger, California

Trek to the Nation's Christmas Tree
Since 1926 people have celebrated the holiday beneath the huge General Grant tree in Kings Canyon National Park. Second Sunday in December. Information: 209-875-4575; *www.sanger.org*.

Schenectady, New York

Annual Christmas Parade
Bands, lighted floats, over 100 costumed characters, and, of course, Santa. Late November. Information: 800-962-8007; *www.schenectadychamber.org*.

Seattle, Washington

Winterfest
Downtown Seattle's annual festival. Late November through December; dates vary. Information: 206-684-7200; *www.seattlecenter.com*.

Silver City, New Mexico

Festival of Trees
The annual celebration of seasonally decorated trees. First week in December. Information: 505-538-3785; *www.silvercity.org*.

Sonora, California

Sonora Christmas Crafts and Music Festival
More music and handcrafted goodies. Weekend immediately following Thanksgiving. Information: 209-533-3473; *www.fireonthemountain.com*.

Stevenson, Washington

Christmas in the Gorge
A celebration that lights up the Columbia Gorge and all the towns nestled along it. Carols and a visit from Santa, too. Late November/early December. Information: 509-427-8911; *www.skamania.org*.

Sturbridge, Massachusetts

Christmas by Candlelight
Old Sturbridge Village celebrates a festive and historical Christmas. Early December. Information: 508-347-3362; *www.osv.org*.

Taos, New Mexico

Yuletide in Taos
Local artists and craftspeople—of which there are many in Taos—help make this a colorful and unforgettable festival. Early December. Information: 800-732-TAOS; *www.taoschamber.com*.

Tortugas, New Mexico

Fiesta of Our Lady of Guadalupe
Inspiring festival with strong Catholic and Native American emphasis. Early December. Information: 505-526-8171; *http://lascrucescvb.org*.

Tucson, Arizona

Las Posadas
Schoolchildren take part in the parade commemorating Mary and Joseph's quest for shelter for the Christ Child. Early December. Information: 800-638-8350; *www.visittucson.org*.

Virginia Beach, Virginia

Medieval Yule Celebration
The traditional Yule log celebration at the Adam Thoroughgood House. Early December. Information: 757-460-7588; *http://vbgov.com*.

Warsaw, Virginia

Tree of Love Illumination
Caroling, memorial lights, and decorations at the Richmond County Museum. Early December. Information: 804-333-3607; *www.co.richmond.va.us*.

Washington, D.C.

A Christmas Carol *at Ford's Theatre*
The historic site is always bustling at this time of year, thanks to the annual stage adaptation of the Dickens holiday classic. Late November to late December. Information: 202-347-4833; *www.fordstheatre.org*.

Christmas Pageant of Peace and People's Christmas Tree Lighting
Annual since 1954, the pageant is usually initiated by a member of the First Family lighting the National Christmas Tree, the magnificent Christmas tree on the west side of the U.S. Capitol. Military bands perform in concert. Early December. Information: 202-208-1631; *www.nps.gov*.

Wickenburg, Arizona

Cowboy Poetry Gathering
Poems, songs, and ideas with a western theme. Early December. Information: 928-684-5479; *www.wickenburgchamber.com*.

Wickford, Rhode Island

Festival of Lights
This historic town, founded in 1662, is the site of a delightful celebration of colonial times during the holiday season. Early December. Information: 877-295-7200; *www.wickfordvillage.org*.

Willcox, Arizona

Christmas Apple Festival
Country-crafts fair held the first weekend in December (dates vary). Information: 520-384-2272; *www.willcoxchamber.com*.

Williamsburg, Virginia

A Colonial Christmas
At the Jamestown Settlement and Yorktown Victory Center; a rich examination of past traditions. Late December. Information: 888-593-4682; *www.historyisfun.org*.

Woodstock, Vermont

Winter Wassail Weekend
Three-day festival offering a parade, historic house tours, Christmas musical, and more. Second weekend in December. Information: 888-496-6378; *www .woodstockvt.com*.

Across Canada

Santa Claus Parade; Toronto, Ontario
A Canadian tradition for more than 100 years, the parade is one of North America's biggest. Mid-November. Information: 800-499-2514; *www.thesantaclausparade.com*.

Old-Fashioned Christmas; Sherbrooke, Nova Scotia
The restored Sherbrooke Village historical site celebrates an old-fashioned Christmas each year. Late November. Information: 888-743-7845; *www.sherbrookevillage.ca*.

Zoolights; Calgary, Alberta
The Calgary Zoo brightens the night with more than 1.5 million lights. Between late November and early January. Information: 800-588-9993; *www.calgaryzoo.org*.

Festival of Trees; Saskatoon, Saskatchewan
More than 100 decorated trees, wreaths, and designer stockings are sold to raise funds for the Saskatoon City Hospital. The last week of November. Information: 306-384-9277; *www.festival-of-trees.com*.

Christmas at the Manitoba Children's Museum; Winnipeg, Manitoba
The Children's Museum at the historic Forks district showcases the original Eaton's Santa's village. From early December to mid-January. Information: 204-924-4000; *www.childrensmuseum.com*.

Carol Ships Parade of Lights; Vancouver, British Columbia

More than 80 decorated boats parade through the harbor nightly during the first three weeks of December, offering music both onboard and onshore. Information: 866-652-4422; *www.carolships.org*.

St. Andrews by-the-Sea Winter Festival; St. Andrews, New Brunswick

A December-long festival that includes a candlelight parade, holiday music, mulled cider, the decorated Ross Memorial Museum, and more. Information: 506-529-3555; *www.standrewsby-the-sea.ca*.

Nutcracker*; Montreal, Québec*

The magical story of little Clara in the Land of Snow, presented by Les Grands Ballet Canadiens de Montreal, has long been a holiday favorite. Mid- to late December. Information: 514-849-8681; *www.grandsballets.com*.

A Green Gables Christmas; Cavendish, Prince Edward Island

A nineteenth-century Christmas afternoon at Green Gables, home to the fictional Anne of Green Gables. December. Information: 902-963-7874; *www.pc.gc.ca*.

The Downtown Christmas Parade; St. John's, Newfoundland and Labrador

More than 100 entries, plus zany clowns, marching bands, colorful cheerleaders, and a food drive. End November or early December. Information: 709-579-4139; *www.downtownstjohns.com*.

Appendix B

Looking for something good to watch? The vast majority of these DVDs—special Christmas movies and those that have become holiday-viewing traditions—are suitable for viewing by all members of the family. The most notable exceptions may be found in the *Home Alone* films, which some parents may consider too violent for small children.

How many of the following have you seen?:

☐ *All I Want for Christmas*
☐ *Alvin and the Chipmunks—A Chipmunk Christmas*
☐ *Avonlea Christmas*
☐ *Babes in Toyland*
☐ *Barney's Christmas*
☐ *Barney's Night Before Christmas*
☐ *Beauty and the Beast—The Enchanted Christmas*
☐ *Ben-Hur*
☐ *Benji's Very Own Christmas Story*
☐ *The Berenstain Bears' Christmas Tree*
☐ *The Best of Andy Williams Christmas Shows*
☐ *A Charlie Brown Christmas*
☐ *A Child's Christmas in Wales*
☐ *A Christmas Carol* (1938 and 1951 versions)
☐ *Christmas Eve on Sesame Street*
☐ *Christmas in Connecticut*
☐ *Christmas Lilies of the Field*
☐ *A Christmas Story*
☐ *A Christmas to Remember*
☐ *Christmas Unwrapped—The History of Christmas* (The History Channel)
☐ *A Disney Christmas Gift*
☐ *Dora's Christmas*
☐ *Dr. Seuss's How the Grinch Stole Christmas*
☐ *Elf*
☐ *Elmo Saves Christmas*
☐ *Ernest Saves Christmas*
☐ *A Flintstone's Christmas Carol*
☐ *Franklin's Magic Christmas*
☐ *Frosty the Snowman*
☐ *The Greatest Story Ever Told*
☐ *Hans Brinker*
☐ *The Happy Elf*
☐ *The Holiday*

- [ ] *Holiday Affair*
- [ ] *Holiday Inn*
- [ ] *Home Alone*
- [ ] *Home Alone II*
- [ ] *Home Alone III*
- [ ] *I Want a Dog for Christmas, Charlie Brown*
- [ ] *It Came upon a Midnight Clear*
- [ ] *It's a Very Merry Muppet Christmas Movie*
- [ ] *It's a Wonderful Life*
- [ ] *Jack Frost*
- [ ] *Jesus of Nazareth*
- [ ] *Jiminy Cricket's Christmas*
- [ ] *The Kid Who Loved Christmas*
- [ ] *King of Kings*
- [ ] *The Little Drummer Boy*
- [ ] *Little House on the Prairie: Christmas at Plum Creek*
- [ ] *Little Women* (1933, 1949, and 1994 versions)
- [ ] *The Man in the Santa Claus Suit*
- [ ] *March of the Wooden Soldiers*
- [ ] *Mickey's Magical Christmas—Snowed In at the House of Mouse*
- [ ] *Mickey's Once Upon a Christmas*
- [ ] *Mickey's Twice Upon a Christmas*
- [ ] *Miracle Down Under*
- [ ] *Miracle on 34th Street* (1947 and 1994 versions)
- [ ] *Mister Magoo's Christmas Carol*
- [ ] *The Muppet Christmas Carol*
- [ ] *A Muppet Family Christmas*
- [ ] *National Lampoon's Christmas Vacation*
- [ ] *The Night They Saved Christmas*
- [ ] *The Nutcracker*
- [ ] *The Nutcracker Prince*
- [ ] *One Christmas*
- [ ] *One Magic Christmas*
- [ ] *The Original Television Christmas Classics* (1969)
- [ ] *Pinocchio's Christmas*

- [ ] *The Polar Express*
- [ ] *Prancer*
- [ ] *The Santa Clause*
- [ ] *Scrooge*
- [ ] *Scrooged*
- [ ] *The Sound of Music*
- [ ] *The Ten Commandments*
- [ ] *Thomas the Tank Engine & Friends—Thomas's Christmas Wonderland*
- [ ] *The 12 Dogs of Christmas*
- [ ] *White Christmas*
- [ ] *Winnie the Pooh and Christmas Too*
- [ ] *The Wizard of Oz*
- [ ] *The Year without a Santa Claus*
- [ ] *Yogi's First Christmas*

The Everything Family Christmas Book

Index

Christmas Wish List